PULLING A RABBIT OUT OF A HAT

The Making of Roger Rabbit

PULLING A RABBIT OUT OF A HAT

ROSS ANDERSON

University Press of Mississippi • Jackson

The University Press of Mississippi is the scholarly publishing agency of the Mississippi Institutions of Higher Learning: Alcorn State University, Delta State University, Jackson State University, Mississippi State University, Mississippi University for Women, Mississippi Valley State University, University of Mississippi, and University of Southern Mississippi.

www.upress.state.ms.us

Designed by Peter D. Halverson

This book makes reference to various DISNEY copyrighted characters, trademarks, marks, and registered marks owned by the Walt Disney Company and Disney Enterprises, Inc.

The University Press of Mississippi is a member of the Association of University Presses.

First printing 2019
∞

Library of Congress Cataloging-in-Publication Data

Names: Anderson, Ross, 1955– author.
Title: Pulling a rabbit out of a hat; the making of Roger Rabbit / Russ Anderson.
Description: Jackson: University Press of Mississippi Jackson, [2019] | "First printing 2019." | Includes bibliographical references and index. |
Identifiers: LCCN 2018058221 (print) | LCCN 2019000206 (ebook) | ISBN 9781496822307 (epub single) | ISBN 9781496822291 (epub institutional) | ISBN 9781496822321 (pdf single) | ISBN 9781496822314 (pdf institutional) | ISBN 9781496822284 (cloth) | ISBN 9781496822338 (pbk.)
Subjects: LCSH: Animated films—United States—History and criticism.
Classification: LCC NC1766.U5 (ebook) | LCC NC1766.U5 A475 2019 (print) | DDC 791.43/340973—dc23
LC record available at https://lccn.loc.gov/2018058221

British Library Cataloging-in-Publication Data available

Dedicated to Bob Hoskins and Annie Elvin and the others who brought us Roger Rabbit *and are not here to enjoy its continuing legacy and the enjoyment it gives to new generations of moviegoers.*

CONTENTS

FOREWORD

"Be sure and use the post 1945 Dick Lundy Woodys,
and not the early 40s Shamus Culhane Woodys . . ."

—GRACIE LANTZ TELEFAX TO ME REGARDING THE DESIGN OF WOODY WOODPECKER IN HIS CAMEO SHOT

Many of my generation born after World War II, called the Baby Boomers, spent their formative years in front of a new device called a television. Since the early 1950s, Hollywood studios had dumped box loads of their old theatrical short films on local metromedia television stations like a restaurant kitchen dumps out piles of stale bread for the pigeons. These old films helped fill out the lack of original content that the nascent TV animation studios were only beginning to fill. Every Saturday morning, kids like me, our chins dribbling with pre-sweetened cereal, delighted to short films from the Golden Age of Hollywood: Buster Crabbe as Flash Gordon, Laurel and Hardy, Abbott and Costello, and most importantly, the Looney Tunes, Bugs Bunny, Betty Boop, Popeye, Tom and Jerry, and Woody Woodpecker.

When Baby Boomers became adult consumers, we wished to look back upon the things that formed us as children. So George Lucas's 1977 film *Star Wars* was originally conceived as an homage to the *Flash Gordon* serials, Steven Spielberg's 1981 *Raiders of the Lost Ark* recalled the two-reel serial cliffhangers like *Captain Marvel*, and 1988's *Who Framed Roger Rabbit* harkened back to our love for the high quality cartoons of Warner Bros., Max Fleischer, and MGM.

I first learned of *Who Framed Roger Rabbit* in 1982, when I was an animator at the Richard Williams West Studio in Los Angeles, working on *Ziggy's Gift*. A friend in the Walt Disney Animation Training Program told me that young animator Darrell Van Citters was developing it. It seemed intriguing, but few of us had any allusions that the very staid Disney management would ever greenlight such an unusual project. Little did I know then that both Dick and I would one day be a part of that project and that *Who Framed Roger Rabbit* would become one of the landmark films of my career, and help jump-start the great Animation Renaissance of the 1990s. It was the highest earning film of 1988, and the winner of three Oscars. That kind of success for an animated film had not been seen since the days of *Jungle Book* (1967). Pixar then was a little software house, trying to convince its chief financier Steve Jobs to let them make a theatrical film. The kind of monster box-office receipts that a *Despicable Me* or a *Frozen* earn today was still years in the future. Before *Roger*, if an animated feature just made its money back, it was considered a success. The studio's real profits would come in ancillary sales to TV and videocassettes. The conventional wisdom of the time was quality theatrical animation was too expensive and too time-consuming to ever be profitable. *Roger Rabbit* changed all that.

Who Framed Roger Rabbit was a game-changing film in my career, as it was for many others. Those of us who burned to make the kind of quality character animation we enjoyed as children, moved from city to city looking for worthy projects to ply our talents. Even country to country. We called ourselves the Animation Gypsies. Much of the animation scene in the 1980s was moribund with safe, politically correct, children's low-budget TV. Except for the lucky ones working at Walt Disney, Don Bluth, or Ralph Bakshi, the rest of us scrambled to find decent projects. *Roger Rabbit* came as a godsend for many of us. We were going to get to animate Bugs Bunny and Mickey Mouse! And Donald Duck facing Daffy! Being voiced by legendary voice artists like Mel Blanc and June Foray. We would be using the characters original 1940s designs, not the modern, more angular, limited styles. When you get to animate one of those classic designs, it's like being a valet getting to park an elegant Porsche or Ferrari. They just handle better than the cheap stuff.

Small wonder the animation unit Dick Williams assembled in Camden Town looked like a mini United Nations. Animators from England, France, Italy, Germany, Canada, Holland, Hong Kong, Zimbabwe, and Brooklyn (me). All of us there with a common goal: to at last be able to attempt to draw character animation as good as anything done by the Hollywood masters of the 1940s and '50s. Director Robert Zemeckis told us, "I don't really know how you do what you do. I see the pencils being sharpened and the paper being flipped, and soon I see moving tests. I, as a director, know how to tell actors where to stand, and where to move. So to me, you are all actors with pencils. I will tell you where to make the toons stand, and where to move them." Which is all we animators have always wanted: to be considered actors with pencils.

In my forty-plus years as a professional animator, I look back on my favorite film projects much like an old soldier looks back on his old campaigns—because a production crew lives and works together much like a regiment. We spend long hours, collaborating, arguing, and creating, all so the final result looks effortless. Robert Zemeckis observed at the premiere, "You animation people are amazing. I'm used to using my same gang. We'd get together, get some lights, and go shoot a few setups. But you guys come together and live like a family for years! You marry each other, have each other's kids, bury each other's grandfathers. And when the film is done . . . Phfft! You all scatter to the four winds . . ."

Ross Anderson has written a meticulously detailed account of the making of this landmark movie. He spent years interviewing many of its principal creators. His narrative lays out all the back room discussions and negotiations that made this project possible, including Gary Wolf's original novel, its aftermath, and why there were never any sequels. He shows how for this one brief shining moment, the Walt Disney Studios, Warner Bros, ILM, and Amblin all joined forces to make something unique.

So let's hop the next Red Car to Toontown, and see how the amazing world of *Who Framed Roger Rabbit* came to be.

—Tom Sito,
Professor of Animation, University of Southern California, 2017

PREFACE

I was born just after the opening of Disneyland, so although I may be vague in my memory of the latter original broadcasts of *The Mickey Mouse Club*, I certainly remember the syndicated reruns and was hooked on Disney. It was a special day at school if it included a 16mm Disney educational film, and it was a wonderful treat to see a rerelease of one of the classic Disney animated films. Sunday evenings were a special family time—all crowded around the television set to see Walt Disney introduce *Walt Disney's Wonderful World of Color*, even though it would be a few years before we actually saw the show in color. The best shows were those in which Walt "pulled back the curtain" to show us what happened behind the scenes. It did not diminish the magic of the film experience; for me, learning how the films were made enhanced my interest—and the process was still magical.

In the course of researching this book and interviewing many people involved in the making of *Who Framed Roger Rabbit*, I found that the majority of those individuals I spoke with shared exactly that same family experience and same feeling about animation, especially Disney animation. In fact, there were more than a few times when I felt that we were twin sons of different mothers. The Disney animators who came of age in the 1970s were unapologetic animation fans, and often serious animation historians. At the same time, that they were involved in creating films that are today judged as "classics," they were also geeking out at sharing spaces once occupied by their heroes. The luckiest of those fledgling animators were fortunate enough to have those "heroes" also become their mentors.

Being unapologetic about their interest in animation set them apart from many of their friends. There was always something wonderful to be found in a Disney animated feature film, even those released in the 1970s—but it was not *cool* to go to a Disney film . . . of any sort.

Fast-forward to 1988, and *Who Framed Roger Rabbit* appears in movie theaters to grand acclaim. It was suddenly okay to talk about cartoons without being disparaging. It was almost *cool* to be an animation geek.

Who Framed Roger Rabbit was made, with love, by those geeks. It was a film about which you could have an adult conversation. It was a film that worked on so many levels and it developed a wide general audience. It also made a lot of money—$329,803,958 in its initial release, second only to *Rain Man* as the highest grossing film of 1988. It, along with *The Little Mermaid*, consolidated a growing self-awareness at Disney and shepherded in the "silver age" of animation.

But it almost didn't happen! *Who Framed Roger Rabbit* had a long and difficult gestation and required input and influence from outside the Disney organization of the 1970s. The story of how *Who Framed Roger Rabbit* came to be is the story of an historically important confluence of people and circumstances. The involvement of people in *Who Framed Roger Rabbit* established and consolidated reputations that have allowed many individuals greater contributions to the film industry and popular culture.

The film had the grand conceit of cartoons living in the real world, but the attention to detail in the filmmaking caused us to accept that premise—and the magnitude of the number and complexity of special effects required to provide the subliminal criteria of acceptance could easily go unnoticed. It seemed "normal" that a cartoon rabbit should be Bob Hoskins's sidekick. In the same way, as it was fascinating to have Walt Disney pull back the curtain in his Sunday evening television show—the more I found out about the making of *Who Framed Roger Rabbit*, the more fascinating it became. *Who Framed Roger Rabbit* extended beyond the influence of Disney themes and history. It is imbued with the affection the filmmakers had for the other major cartoon studios and animation titans.

The filmmakers faced a formidable task, but they tapped into something magical, and that something special found its way on to the screen. This book chronicles the circumstances at Disney in the late 1970s and early '80s in order to put into context the subsequent directions and decisions that got this film to the screen. The film industry is not so large that coincidences should be unlikely, but *Who Framed Roger Rabbit* sat at a nexus of people and circumstances that is historically significant. At the time of the film's release, the Disney marketing program and the articles in newspapers, popular magazines, fan magazines, and trade journals might have the reader believe that *Who Framed Roger Rabbit* was made solely by Bob Zemeckis, Dick Williams, and ILM. While it couldn't have been made without them, it was also made with the love and talent of many, many other artists. This story is my gift to them. For those involved, it remains a very special time. They were creating something magical . . . they were *pulling a rabbit out of a hat!*

The film rights for the book Who Censored Roger Rabbit? *were purchased by Walt Disney Productions ("Disney") in 1981, and a significant amount of effort was put into developing it as a film. Nevertheless, it took the involvement of parties outside of Disney to bring the book to the big screen. There was a "changing of the guard" at Disney in the late 1970s and early '80s, which influenced the quality of its animation products and provided opportunities for animation outside of the Disney environment. Some people who were involved in the initial development of* Roger Rabbit *at the Disney Studios stayed at Disney and had long and distinguished careers there, but many more people passed through the Disney Studios and found outlets for their creativity elsewhere. Some of those people were able to reconnect with the Roger Rabbit project after it left Disney, and many achieved phenomenal success in animation ventures following their early time at Disney.*

To fully appreciate the Roger Rabbit *story, especially how Disney came to bobble its early handling of the* Roger Rabbit *property and the context of why certain decisions were made in later development of the property, it is important to have some background information on the studio dynamics and people. A short history of the Disney Studios—from the death of Walt Disney, in 1966, until 1984, when Michael Eisner, Frank Wells, and Jeffrey Katzenberg came on board—is provided in the appendix. The appendix also contains short biographies of some of the key people in this period of Disney Studios history and throughout the period of the* Roger Rabbit *story.*

The reader should note that the Walt Disney Company denied permission for use of any Disney copyrighted images in this book, including photographs related to Roger Rabbit *from its theme parks. There are many images on the internet from most aspects of the* Roger Rabbit *story. A simple internet search will provide many images related to the subject matter of this book.*

PULLING A RABBIT OUT OF A HAT

Chapter One

EARLY DAYS AT DISNEY

Who Censored Roger Rabbit?—The Novel

"Look at this, children. Look at this silly picture. Everybody knows cows are black, brown, or white. Never, ever are cows blue." These are the words of Gary K. Wolf's first-grade teacher when she criticized him in front of his classmates after handing in a coloring assignment showing a brightly colored blue cow. Wolf says, "I had heard my mother say that when people were sad, they were blue. The cow looked so lonely out there all alone in the field. I figured she must be blue, too." His mother went to the school, where the teacher told her to not let little Gary do that anymore. It was advice she ignored. "The gift that my parents gave to me is that they encouraged me to keep coloring cows blue."[1]

Wolf was an avid reader, devouring all the comic books he could lay his hands on before moving on to noir mysteries and science fiction as he got older. He spent a lot of time in the library, getting a library card at age seven. The librarian often reproached him for selecting books with themes that she considered too adult. His parents encouraged him to read, and chose to not limit the scope of his interests or imagination. His mother made sure that the librarian would not restrict his book choices.[2]

He followed his interest in science fiction and had three novels in the genre published by Doubleday Books in the 1970s: *Killerbowl* in 1975, *A Generation Removed* in 1977, and *The Resurrectionist* in 1979. *Who Censored Roger Rabbit?* was Wolf's fourth published novel.

When Wolf started working on *Who Censored Roger Rabbit?* he was looking for a way to combine his main interests—comics and mysteries. He went back to reading his comics, studying them for subject material rather than reading them just for entertainment. He also started watching Saturday morning children's cartoon shows. What intrigued him the most were the commercials. In the commercials, the animated brand representatives routinely interacted with the real world and it seemed the most natural thing in the world. Cap'n Crunch, Count Chocula and Frankenberry, the Trix Rabbit, Frosted Flakes' Tony the Tiger, Rice Krispies' Snap, Crackle, and Pop, and Lucky Charms' Lucky the Leprechaun are amongst the advertising cartoon characters that interacted with live-action children. Wolf began to think, "Suppose you entered a world where cartoon characters were real, where would that world be?" He spent years developing a set of internally consistent rules for such a world. He researched what made cartoon characters "cartoony" and studied the conventions of comic strips and cartoons in order to define the parameters of a self-consistent toon/human world.[3]

In Wolf's world, the cartoon characters were called "toons." The toons in the entertainment business were comic strip characters, with comic strips being produced by photographing the toons. Toons spoke in word balloons, although some were capable of verbal speech. The word balloons could sometimes be used as tools or for some "effect," not unlike how Felix the Cat used his tail. Toons were also able to create doppelgängers. A doppelgänger is a paranormal "double," or a "shadow self," although the term is often used to describe people who very closely resemble each other physically. In Wolf's world, a toon could create another incarnation of itself, which usually crumbled to dust within a few minutes. It would allow them to be in two places at once and also have the doppelgänger serve as a stand-in double for dangerous stunts.

Roger Rabbit is a second banana who hires a private detective, Eddie Valiant, to find out why his employers, the DeGreasy brothers, have reneged on a promise to have him star in his own comic strip. Roger Rabbit is soon found murdered in his home and his final word balloon, found at the scene of the crime, indicates that his murder was a way of "censoring" him. Before he is shot, Roger creates a doppelgänger that lasts for a couple of days and works with Eddie Valiant to solve his murder. Roger had made the doppelgänger for the purpose of going out to buy some new red suspenders.

Wolf's Roger Rabbit is an amalgam of Bugs Bunny and Mickey Mouse. He wanted Roger Rabbit to be a very moral character. He was to have an innocence without being quite as "nice" as a typical Disney character. Roger was named after Wolf's first cousin.[4] Jessica Rabbit comes from Tex Avery's world and is an amalgam of Red Hot Riding Hood with a bit of grown-up Tinkerbell and a dose of Marilyn Monroe. Over the course of the writing of the novel, Baby Herman evolved to be "Danny DeVito in diapers."[5] Eddie Valiant is based on author Mickey Spillane's detective, Mike Hammer, with lots of Dashiell Hammett's Sam Spade and Raymond Chandler's Philip Marlowe mixed in.[6] The cartoon star cameos in the book tend to be comic strip stars, such as Dagwood Bumstead (from the *Blondie* strip) and *Beetle Bailey*.

Although Wolf started to think about what would become *Who Censored Roger Rabbit?* as early as 1971, the novel was not completed until 1980. Wolf had a four-book contract with Doubleday and submitted *Who Censored Roger Rabbit?* as the fourth book in the contract. Doubleday rejected it. They said that it was "not categorizable" and that there was no "place" for it on bookstore shelves. Wolf asked, "What would you do if somebody brought you *The Wizard of Oz, Gulliver's Travels*, or *Alice in Wonderland*?"— and they answered, "Well, we couldn't sell those either." Wolf eventually received 110 rejections in his attempt to find a publisher for the novel.[7]

Luckily for Wolf, Rebecca Martin, an editor at St. Martin's Press, had just handled a bestseller and was given the opportunity for a "vanity project" just as his manuscript for *Who Censored Roger Rabbit?* came across her desk. Rebecca wanted to publish it but was told that she could not. She held her ground and went to bat for the book until the publisher relented. *Who Censored Roger Rabbit?* was published by St. Martin's Press in 1981; the initial hardback cover print run was quite small.[8] For the cover, Wolf had a stuffed rabbit made by a Los Angeles toy company and a photo was taken of the toy rabbit, cloaked in a trench coat, from the back, with Wolf himself in a trench coat and fedora, facing the camera. The cover was changed when the novel was published as a paperback. Wolf jokes, "As soon as they took me off the cover, the sales immediately went up." The cover art shows a square-jawed Eddie Valiant, in trench coat and fedora, and Roger Rabbit posed in front of the Los Angeles City Hall. Roger's word balloon says, "Help! I'm stuck in a mystery of double-crosses, steamy broads, and killer cream pies." Roger is drawn as an anthropomorphic rabbit, but more realistic than the cartoony version from the film. He wears yellow pants, with green stylized flower patterns, red suspenders, and a blue bow tie. The paperback was reprinted three or four times, in different editions. The Ballantine Books edition, third printing (July 1988), proclaims, "A Cult Classic!" on the cover. A fifty-thousand-copy print run of a hardcover book club edition was later published.[9]

Disney's technical excellence with animation and its history with live-action/animation techniques made it seem like an obvious fit for producing a film based on the novel. But . . . many felt that *Star Wars* was a film Disney should have made. It didn't! It made *The Black Hole* as a response to *Star Wars*. Yet, it also made *Tron*, which, although it didn't capture everybody's imagination, was an adult departure from what it had done in the past and full of technical innovation. Wolf's novel was edgy and dark. It was a cartoon world, but with adult themes. Walt Disney was unafraid of producing films covering the entire range of human emotions. He was constantly challenging his artists . . . and each film was different from the last. Walt Disney was long deceased in 1981, yet people were still asking, "What would Walt do?" The daring had stopped, and Disney was stuck in the groove of Walt's last presence. Progressive elements within the Disney organization saw the potential of the Gary K. Wolf novel and acted on it. Disney acquired the film rights to *Who Censored Roger Rabbit?* It is important to understand the situation at the Disney Studios in 1981 to understand the difficult path for development of the *Roger Rabbit* film.

Disney Studios—1981

Walt Disney died on December 15, 1966. He left a legacy, but he did not leave a creative successor. His brother and partner, Roy O. Disney, always had Walt's back and postponed his retirement to see the first iteration of Walt's dream of something bigger than a theme park through to completion. Walt Disney World was opened in 1971. The first major expansion, EPCOT, opened in 1981, with Tokyo Disneyland to follow in 1982. The theme parks were big business and were the focus of much of the Disney executive management attention. At the Disney Studios there was no real leader. In 1981, they were still asking, "What would Walt do?" They were not Walt Disney; and with each effort of challenging themselves, they regressed to their comfort zone. As the legacy Animation leadership retired, leadership fell to the legacy "followers." It had a real impact when truly exciting properties came into their reach. The acquisition of *Who Censored Roger Rabbit?* is a case study on inadequate succession planning.

Ron Miller was Walt Disney's son-in-law. He met Walt's eldest daughter, Diane, on a blind date while at the University of Southern California. They married in 1954. Miller had played a season in the NFL as a tight end with the Los Angeles Rams. Walt eventually convinced Miller to work for him at the Disney Studios. Miller rose through the producer ranks and became president of Walt Disney Productions in 1978.

Ed Hansen started at the studio in 1952 as an effects artist on *Peter Pan*. He moved into management in 1972 and took on administrative responsibility for the Animation Department in 1975. The Animation Department was largely left to do what it had been doing, without a great deal of over-sight. The expectations were not high, and neither was the motivation. The "Nine Old Men," who with a few others comprised the Animation Board, had all retired by 1981. The filmmaking was left in the hands of a group of lesser artists who had been waiting in the wings for decades. They were insecure about their standing and they had not been trained as leaders. Their response was to circle the wagons.

The Animation Department had hired only twenty-one people in the previous decade. The studio had established a Training Program in 1972, under the tutelage of Eric Larson, one of the "Nine Old Men." Walt Dis-ney had championed the establishment of California Institute of the Arts (CalArts), which was formed in 1961 in the merger of the Chouinard Art Institute and the Los Angeles Conservatory of Music. By the late 1970s, the studio started hiring students and graduates from the CalArts Animation Program, among them Brad Bird, Chris Buck, Tim Burton, Mike Cedeno, Mike Giaimo, Mark Henn, Glen Keane, John Lasseter, Brian McEntee, John Musker, Patty Paulick, Mike Peraza, Joe Ranft, Jerry Rees, Henry Selick, and Darrell Van Citters. John Musker started at the Disney Studios in May 1977, in the week that *Star Wars* opened—a film matching the sen-sibilities of the younger animators. The early CalArts hires were frustrated with the situation at the studio. Brad Bird described it as "a dark period at Disney—an awful period when these mediocre guys, who had been at the studio for maybe twenty years but had never been good enough to rise to the top when the old guys were there, were kind of put in charge, and they were looking after their own turf. It was the Peter Principle . . . these guys were really good at their jobs, but they were taken out of their jobs and made directors—and they were not 'directors.'"[10] There is no doubt that the CalArts guys were cocky. They were continuing as they had at CalArts, anxious to animate and make films . . . and happy to set their own agenda. They were also a very talented group.

Disney had planned for a science fiction adventure as early at 1974, but had not followed through with it. After the success of *Star Wars*, the project, now called *The Black Hole*, was put into production. It would feature major visual effects, but there was a corporate inertia that would be impossible to overcome with the people who were in place in the studio. In spite of the awe-inspiring visual effects, there was a certain clumsiness because Disney did not have motion-control camera capability at the time. The film did not have a star-laden cast, and the characters seemed shallow and a bit corny. The film was released in late 1979. Tom Wilhite had joined Disney in 1976 as the publicity director. He was put in charge of finding a way to market

The Black Hole. He was also frustrated by the isolation of Disney within the film community and the lack of resources applied to film marketing. In this case, he was also frustrated by the stark comparison between *The Black Hole* and *Star Wars.* He focused the marketing campaign on the film's visual effects. The film was only a modest success, but it did move Disney away from the staid period films and corny family comedies that had been the staple for decades. Miller promoted Wilhite to be vice president in charge of development and head of live-action production. Wilhite and Hansen would have a strained and uneasy working relationship.

Wilhite brought *Tron* into Disney after persuading Miller to buy the script and contract Steven Lisberger's organization to set up at the Disney Studios. Bill Kroyer had started at Disney in 1977 but had been recruited by Lisberger to work on his developing projects. Kroyer was now back on the Disney lot. Future Disney animators Roger Allers, Barry Cook, and Dave Stephan also came on to the Disney lot with the *Tron* group.

In 1981, Tom Wilhite was twenty-eight years old, whereas Ed Hansen was fifty-five years old. Wilhite had a wonderful ability for recognizing and cultivating young creative talent. He could "spot" people who were a bit left of center and nurtured their strengths.[11] He was very aware of the frustration young animators were feeling in the Animation Department due to his empathy and the similarities in their ages. Many animators, such as John Lasseter, confided in him. Jerry Rees was dissatisfied with the limitations being put on him during production of *The Fox and the Hound* by directors he felt were unimaginative and derivative. He was curious about the new group setting up offices in the third floor of the Animation Building and asked Wilhite if he could look around. Wilhite listened to Rees's appeal to be part of the *Tron* production rather than being unproductive on *The Fox and the Hound*, and Rees was hired into the new group to do storyboards for *Tron* with Kroyer.[12]

Wilhite advocated to have John Musker made a co-director on *The Black Cauldron* in order to ensure the production had the input of a youthful perspective, and it was Musker who advocated for Tim Burton's outside-of-the-box concept drawings for the film. As the dysfunctional leadership of *The Black Cauldron* became more apparent and frustration mounted, several animators left Disney and many artists were receptive to other projects. Musker joined Burny Mattinson and Ron Clements on Story for *Basil of Baker Street* (later renamed *The Great Mouse Detective*).

When the debate about the direction of *The Black Cauldron* came to a head, the producer, Joe Hale, made a proclamation: "We are going to do a traditional Disney movie! That is what we are making!" The proclamation was disturbing to many of the young animators. They interpreted it as saying, "Don't get any big ideas in your head!"—further evidence that Disney was trying the imitate the past with formulaic productions.

Mike Giaimo worked on *The Black Cauldron* in the Story Department for eight months. His story work was a bit zany, and co-director Rick Rich did not care for it. One time when Giaimo pitched his storyboards, Rich sniped, "Are we working on the same picture?"[13] Rich could be very manipulative, which made for difficult team dynamics.

Darrell Van Citters said of the late 1970s and early 1980s at Disney: "There were lots of high spirits and not much outlet in the work."[14] But creativity cannot be bottled up for long, and its pressure will find some relief. The outlets included the after-hours film projects, *Doctor of Doom* and *Luau* (co-directed by Tim Burton and Jerry Rees), and events, such as the "Eddie Fisher Show" and the 1980 producer-animator volleyball challenge (led by Van Citters). Van Citters complained bitterly during his time on *The Fox and the Hound* and was taken off the production after a disagreement with co-director Ted Berman, who punished Van Citters by putting him back in Clean-Up.

Ted Berman was a co-director of *The Black Cauldron*, along with Rick Rich and Art Stevens. In earlier days, Stevens had been part of the Ward Kimball unit, but his later work showed none of the quirky zaniness one might have expected from somebody who had fit in and worked well with Kimball. He had grown conservative and paranoid. He had responsibility for the "fairfolk" sequence, but he did not want anybody to see it until he was really ready. He locked the door to his hallway and would not let anybody in except the members of his team—for a year! It was finally demanded that the sequence be shown . . . and it was judged as horrible and unusable.[15] While the animators were playing volleyball during lunch, they had often noticed Stevens standing and scowling at them. When they asked Don Hahn, who was entering the producer ranks and had been able to negotiate successfully the gulf between the various factions, whether Art Stevens disliked them as much as it seemed, all he could say was, "Yeah, you're right. He really doesn't like seeing young people have fun."[16]

John Musker said that when Wilhite was moved from Disney Public Relations into the production side of the studio, he was viewed as "the Irving Thalberg of Disney," "the Boy Wonder," and "the young guy."[17] He had the ear of Ron Miller. Ed Hansen was the Animation Department manager and did not want Wilhite involved at all. Wilhite saw the waste of young talent and did what he could to satisfy their creativity and retain them at the studio. He was the head of Live-Action and Television and greenlit projects that showcased the talents of young Animation Department artists. Hansen felt ignored and trampled on. Musker characterized him as "an old-school middle manager"; Wilhite characterized him as "running his department like a principal at a high school, in which he treated his artists like they were students who had to be tolerated."[18] Randy Cartwright made a "home movie" tour of the Animation Department in 1983, with John Lasseter and Joe Ranft sharing duty as cameramen. They bumped into Hansen as they roamed the halls; in fact, they treated Hansen almost like the high school principal in the film *Ferris Bueller's Day Off*.[19]

Wilhite brought Tim Burton and Rick Heinrichs into the Live-Action Department, where they made the stop-motion short *Vincent* and the live-action short *Frankenweenie*. They also made a television special for the Disney Channel, entitled *Hansel and Gretel*, and worked on several other projects that were never produced. It was Wilhite who managed to get Vincent Price as the narrator for *Vincent*.

One of the first computer-generated imagery (CGI) scenes in *Tron* to be rendered and shown on a rented VistaVision projector was a Light Cycle sequence. John Lasseter was curious about what his friends were up to and was one of the first people to see these images. He became intrigued with computer animation. Lasseter brought Thomas Disch's 1980 novel, *The Brave Little Toaster: A Bedtime Story for Small Appliances* to Wilhite's attention as a story that would be especially suitable for computer animation. It was to be the world's first CGI animated feature film. *The Brave Little Toaster* team included Lasseter, Joe Ranft, and Brian McEntee. It was to be done in a Grant Wood-esque painterly style. The animation would be more geometric to fit with a 3D computer graphic background. A test-of-concept was done, a piece using Maurice Sendak's book *Where the Wild Things Are*. Glen Keane did the character animation and Lasseter coordinated the computer work with Mathematical Applications Group, Inc. (MAGI). It was planned to use the COPS computer animation concept that Jerry Rees had developed during the production of *Tron*. The *Where the Wild Things Are* test was fluid and entertaining. It was amazing how far things had come during the short time since the production of *Tron*. Lasseter had been part of a Disney animation group that toured Pixar (at Lucasfilm in San Rafael) in February 1983. He was blown away by the new CG rendering developments and wanted to know whether he could work with Pixar to fit his hand-drawn characters into CG backgrounds.[20] Shortly after, the *Where the Wild Things Are* test and storyboards were pitched to Ron Miller. The cost of *The Brave Little Toaster* was estimated to be $13 to $17 million, which was a little less than a typical animated feature film at the time. *The Brave Little Toaster* was being developed under the auspices of Wilhite's Live-Action Department, which was very threatening to the Animation Department management. Miller felt compelled to support Hansen, and soon thereafter, Hansen fired Lasseter.[21] John Musker, famous for his caricatures of studio denizens and events, did a drawing with caricatures of Wilhite and Hansen as gunfighters facing off and shooting at each other—only to look down after the shooting had stopped and find Lasseter lying in a pool of blood . . . holding his toaster.[22]

Tad Stones was developing television projects for EPCOT at Walt Disney World in Florida, which was to open in October 1981. There were to be four one-hour television specials for broadcast on the Sunday evening Disney/NBC show. Stones rescued Van Citters from Clean-Up and paired him with Joe Ranft, who had recently left CalArts to work for Disney. They had a Ward Kimball model in mind, similar to his series of space-themed television shows and his special featurettes, *It's Tough To Be a Bird* (1969) and *Dad, Can I Borrow the Car?* (1970). Disney eventually pulled the plug on the EPCOT television specials. Van Citters did not want to go back to the main Animation Department and have to work on *The Black Cauldron* so, like so many others, he went to speak with Wilhite. Ed Gombert, a young story man, had the idea to salvage some of the zany (some might say, bizarre) work they had done for the EPCOT specials by using an audio-animatronic mechanical head—a spare, skinless Lincoln head—to host a show linking the disparate elements. Wilhite gave the greenlight to proceeding on *Fun with Mr. Future.* Van Citters enlisted Mike Giaimo to do character and story design,[23] and rounded off the team with Chris Buck. *Fun with Mr. Future* is an obscure Disney animated short that has a much diminished scope than what was intended for the television specials, but at least it was completed. It eventually got limited release, starting on October 27, 1982, in some Los Angeles movie theaters in order to qualify for Oscar consideration.[24]

While he was still in Miller's good graces, Wilhite filled the pipeline with *Something Wicked This Way Comes*, based on Ray Bradbury's book, *Never Cry Wolf*, and *Return to Oz*. He also acquired a script for a romantic fantasy film called *Splash*, as well as the film rights for an as-yet-unpublished novel entitled *Who Censored Roger Rabbit?*[25]

Roger Rabbit Development Unit

The Disney Studios Story Department would receive scripts and books from literary agents. Some scripts and books were sent directly to Ron

Miller, who was made president and chief operating Officer of Walt Disney Productions on June 3, 1980. Earlier in his career, he was sent the book *Car, Boy, Girl* directly from its author, Gordon Buford.[26] The story was later made into the film *The Love Bug.* The Story Department would also assess published short stories and books for material on which to base film projects. Willard Carroll graduated from the University of Southern California (USC) School of Cinema and began his career in the story departments of ABC Motion Pictures, Orion Pictures, and Zoetrope Studios before becoming a development executive at Walt Disney Productions. As a senior story editor, he headed a team of story analysts who would summarize and assess source material.[27] The story analyst reports would be circulated amongst the studio's seven or eight staff producers. If a property was felt to have promise as a Disney project, a producer would be attached and a development team would be established.

The Disney Studios received a galley manuscript of *Who Censored Roger Rabbit?* in 1980, ahead of its publication.[28] It was later determined that an employee at St. Martin's Press had photocopied the manuscript and sent it to Disney without permission and without the knowledge of Gary K. Wolf's agent. An analysis of the book was made and circulated to the producers; staff producer Marc Stirdivant was excited by the possibilities and championed the acquisition of the film rights to the book. Ron Miller had recently promoted Tom Wilhite from Publicity to lead the Development and Live-Action Production. Wilhite convinced Miller to purchase the film rights, which he did—for $25,000—over the objections of CEO Card Walker. Gary K. Wolf remembers that it was Roy E. Disney who first contacted him to buy the film rights to his book.

Stirdivant was part of the Live-Action side of the studio, responding to Wilhite. Since the story was so clearly appropriate as an animation/ live-action combination project, Wilhite suggested that Stirdivant discuss the possibilities with Van Citters, who was just finishing *Fun with Mr. Future.*[29] With the blessing of Wilhite, the *Roger Rabbit* project proceeded into development in 1981. Darrell Van Citters was assigned as the director of the unit.

The *Fun with Mr. Future* team made the transition to the *Roger Rabbit* development unit. It was quickly decided that, for the film, "toons" would be involved in the production of cartoon films rather than comic strips. Darrell Van Citters and Mike Giaimo set the tone. Giaimo did the initial production design and developed many character designs during two years of work from 1981 through 1982.[30] Chris Buck came into the unit a bit after Giaimo to work mostly on visuals.[31] Van Citters was attracted by the unique character relationships, seeing it as "a buddy film, with a twist."[32] He saw it as a live-action film and, indeed, the development unit was working under the auspices of the Live-Action Department. Roger Rabbit was designed to "look like a goon,"[33] affixed with the big nose of an archetypal cartoon look. The clownish look was intended to belie an inner core of emotional depth and heart. Van Citters and Giaimo explored many different looks for Jessica; ultimately, they settled on a design reminiscent of a young Katharine Hepburn. Baby Herman has an the look of an infant when he is performing, but the look is modified to fit his attitude and behavior in his "real" toon life. In the earliest versions, he resembled the "Danny DeVito in diapers" that Gary K. Wolf had described. Captain Cleaver is an enormous block of a toon that seems to be nothing but chin and bluster. They had animator Mike Gabriel pose in the Disney backlot and created a number of drawn/live-action combination images to evaluate the concept. It is a drawn element from one of these combination images that was used in the 1981 Walt Disney Productions Annual Report (prepared for the January 28, 1982, annual meeting of stockholders).

The "Motion Pictures and Television" section of the 1981 Disney annual report mentions the release of *Fantasia*, with a new soundtrack, and the reissue of *Bambi*, *Cinderella*, and *Robin Hood*. It identifies *Never Cry Wolf*, *Night Crossing*, *Something Wicked This Way Comes*, *Tex*, and *Tron* as productions intended for release in 1982, and describes the animated films in various stages of production. On page twenty-two, the annual report describes the early footage of *The Black Cauldron* as providing "dramatic evidence that this may take a place beside the great animated features." *Basil of Baker Street* is mentioned as being in story development and *Mickey's Christmas Carol* is announced for Christmas 1982 release. On page twenty-six of the annual report is the first public mention of *Roger Rabbit*. The image shows the earliest character design for Roger Rabbit and the caption reads,

> *Who Censored Roger Rabbit?* uncovers the crime of the century when Roger, Hollywood's top animated star, becomes the principal subject in the murder of a real-life film producer. This totally original, inventive comedy-mystery, scheduled for 1983 release, assumes that animated characters are real and co-exist with their human counterparts. Marc Stirdivant is producing with Disney artist Darrell Van Citters directing the animation sequences. (26)

The image below that caption announces *Trenchcoat*, a comedy-mystery starring Robert Hays and Margot Kidder, a Walt Disney Productions film that would ultimately not be released under the Disney name due to more adult themes—presaging the establishment of Touchstone Pictures.

The Animation Department was working away at *The Black Cauldron* at this time. Lisberger's *Tron* unit was winding down, so the novelty of groups doing animation outside of the direct management of the Animation Department had worn off. The *Roger Rabbit* development unit was not a secret group, but it was under the radar for many people at the studio at its inception.[34] Van Citters was happy to show people, usually friends from CalArts days, what the development unit was doing on *Roger Rabbit*.[35] He initially intended to have the film set in the television world. They settled ultimately for the film to be set in the 1940s, with a film noir tone similar to Wolf's novel.[36]

The young writing team of Peter Seaman and Jeffrey Price was on the Disney lot, having just completed a screenplay entitled *Malta Wants Me Dead*, which was eventually renamed *Trenchcoat*. Wilhite suggested that Seaman and Price should work with the *Roger Rabbit* unit to develop a screenplay. It was clear that the budget for an ambitious animation/live-action combination film would be much higher than for typical Disney animated productions at the time. Although it was not uncommon for animated feature films to have a screenplay, of sorts, story development in Animation was more typically done in the Story Department by means of storyboards. It was more typical in Live-Action to work from a screenplay. The displaced *Roger Rabbit* animation group had been developing story scenarios and storyboards in their Disney Animation fashion, so the intrusion of live-action customs came as an unpleasant surprise.

At this stage, the *Roger Rabbit* unit comprised of Van Citters, Giaimo, and Joe Ranft. Chris Buck came in later and did not work with Seaman and Price.[37] At first, the relationship between Van Citters and Seaman and Price was collaborative, but it soured over time.[38] Seaman and Price ordered up old Tex Avery cartoons and cataloged "bits of business."[39] Van Citters's complaint was that the script did not come from a place of *knowing* and *understanding* animation, but rather of *observing* and *copying* animation.[40] Conversely, Van Citters may not have fully understood the language and needs of live-action film production. It became a less collaborative process as time went on. As Van Citters describes it, "Seaman and Price would go away and write their stuff, then present it." He did not like the Seaman and Price treatment. He says, "I probably created a lot more antagonism than I needed to, because . . . I really hated it! And I said so! Now, I would be a little more discrete about my criticism, but I really didn't like it. They went off and wrote a second draft that, to me, still didn't resolve the problems."[41]

Indeed, Van Citters's copy of the second draft is peppered with comments that reflect his displeasure. Many of the comments are cynical and not especially helpful, which is indicative of a breakdown in communication between the parties. Jeffrey Price has said that too much was made of the director and screenwriters not getting along.[42]

The second draft of Seaman and Price's screenplay is dated July 26, 1982.[43] Roger Rabbit is described as a six-foot-high bunny. The screenplay begins with a cartoon short, very similar to that in the final film, and makes the transition to live-action very similarly to the final film . . .

Roger Rabbit hires Eddie Valiant for a stakeout to find out who steals (and returns) his wife's car every night. Eddie finds out that it is Roger's wife, Jessica, who is taking her own car. He follows her to the Cartoon Equity Home for the Aged, where he finds that she reads for the old toons. We are introduced to Lt. Santino and Capt. Cleaver [a character Gary K. Wolf created in the novel]. *Perry Passou, a producer at the DeGreasey Cartoon Studio in Hollywood, is murdered and Roger is suspected. Roger and Jessica are in Passou's new film,* Rabbit on the Lam. *It turns out that Jessica was having an affair with Passou so that she could get a part in the film. Eddie and Roger confront Passou's gofer, a gopher named Norman Burrows. They find out that Passou was "blackmailing" Rocco DeGreasey by withholding the film from release. He wouldn't let anybody see the film and had it locked in a vault at his home. They also find out that Jessica was terrible in the part and Passou had cut her part out of the film.*

DeGreasey is taking advantage of Roger being wanted for murder in promoting the film, Rabbit on the Lam, *which points to Roger as a potential murder suspect. Jessica falls for Eddie. The gopher, Norman Burrows, is killed and Eddie is framed for the murder, but the police think Roger did it. While Roger is in hiding, Jessica invites Eddie to accompany her to the premiere of* Rabbit on the Lam.

During the premiere, Eddie sees that Jessica is still in the film. He calls the police to turn Roger in, but when the police arrive to arrest Roger—Eddie uncovers the murder plot. It turns out that Jessica had killed Passou and framed Roger Rabbit. She had been "stealing" her own car every night to visit Passou. She had learned that Passou was going to cut her scene out of the film. On the night Eddie had followed her, she had gone to the Home for the Aged in order to read the old toons to sleep and give herself an alibi by slipping out the back to kill Passou while Eddie was staking out the front of the home. She had also killed the gopher because he had seen the film (with her cut out), and she had seduced Eddie to secure his silence.

In the end, Eddie and Roger become partners in a Private Investigator business.

Although Roger and Baby Herman are in a film, the screenplay is set in the television age, with cameo appearances by Fred Flintstone, Rocky and Bullwinkle, Casper, Heckle and Jeckle, Mighty Mouse, Mr. Magoo, and even Elliot from *Pete's Dragon*. There is a perplexing assortment of live-action cameo appearances, especially at Passou's funeral, including Jack Benny, Zsa Zsa Gabor, and Ringo Starr. One of the only direct lines that made it into the final film is Baby Herman saying, "My problem is I got a fifty-year-old lust and a three-year-old dinkie." It is clear from Darrell Van Citters's comments on his copy of the script that he did not envisage Toontown in the film—at all. He thought that Seaman and Price's use of the zany Tex Avery-style gags was superficial and did not add to Roger Rabbit's character development.

The opinions of the other people in the *Roger Rabbit* unit (Giaimo, Stirdivant, and later, Randy Cartwright) regarding the screenplay, and the final *Who Framed Roger Rabbit* film, are closely aligned with those of Van Citters. They felt that Roger should be more nuanced and thoughtful, under the clown exterior.[44] They all saw a chasm grow between Van Citters and the screenwriters. The screenwriters were perplexed by Van Citters's enmity. The humor suited their sensibilities, but Van Citters's disapproval with the script seemed disproportionate to the variance in their senses of humor. That the screenwriters did not "get it" fueled Van Citters' scorn. He was afraid that a live-action director might only see wild gags, fast timing, impossible situations, and enormous pliability. Van Citters said, "I was afraid that in the wrong hands, we might end up with animated equivalent of an *Animal House*."[45] Giaimo sheds some light on Van Citters's frame of mind, saying that Van Citters believed, at the time, that animation was "hanging on by a thread," especially at Disney. He says that Van Citters wanted to be taken seriously and he wanted animation to be taken seriously.[46] Van Citters reacted poorly to animation being played over the top.

Van Citters felt that the story could showcase subtlety and nuance in animation. Van Citters, and most of the others from CalArts, were passionate about animation and its potential for conveying complex stories and emotions. Their experience at the Disney studio at that time led to a belief that animation was held in relatively low regard. Van Citters even viewed the antagonistic relationship between Eddie Valiant and Roger Rabbit as a metaphor for the relationship between live-action production and animation at the Disney studio. The others were not as passionate in that aspect of their roles, but were inclined to think that Seaman and Price had a low respect for animation and tended to resort to animation stereotypes and insert Avery-style gags where they didn't belong.[47] Regardless, the direction for the film, and the development unit, did not coalesce around the screenplay and Van Citters was unable, or unwilling, to instill his vision for the film in the screenwriters.

Although Van Citters had a proprietary interest in the film, even he realized that his role would eventually be as the director of animation. He did not have the clout in Hollywood to helm a film budgeted initially at $12 million and knew that they would need a name brand director to get the project sold. Disney would need to go elsewhere for the live-action director. In 1982, Disney contacted Bob Zemeckis. Tom Wilhite says that Zemeckis campaigned for the director job on *Roger Rabbit*. His first two films, *I Wanna Hold Your Hand* and *Used Cars*, received good reviews from the critics, but did not do especially well at the box office. Steven Spielberg was his mentor and was the executive producer on those films. Zemeckis had a fallow period following *Used Cars* (1980), although he used the time to prepare a script for what would become *Back to the Future*. Zemeckis visited Disney and expressed interest in *Roger Rabbit*.[48] He said, "When I read *Roger Rabbit*, I knew it had great potential. I couldn't get it out of my mind. But in those days, the Disney Studios weren't in gear. I went off to do *Romancing the Stone*. When I came back, Disney still wasn't very serious about it."[49]

Other directors considered by Disney were:[50]

- John Landis, who had *National Lampoon's Animal House* (1978) and *The Blues Brothers* (1980) under his belt and had just directed *An American Werewolf in London* (1981).
- Joe Dante, who had directed *The Howling* (1981) and was just about to direct *Gremlins* (1984).
- Jack Fisk, who had been the art director on *Phantom of the Paradise* (1974) and *Carrie* (1976) and had just directed *Raggedy Man* (1981).
- Michael Apted, who had directed *Coal Miner's Daughter* (1980) and *Continental Divide* (1981), and was just about to direct *Gorky Park* (1983).
- Ron Howard, who directed *Grand Theft Auto* in 1977, while still acting in the television series *Happy Days* and had just finished directing *Night Shift* (1982). He would go on to direct Disney's 1984 smash hit *Splash*, the first film released under the Touchstone Pictures label. He later replaced Zemeckis as the director in *Cocoon* (1985), before *Romancing the Stone* (1984) was released and proved to be a hit—due to the anxiety of the producers about Zemeckis's poor box-office track record at that stage in his career.

Another director had been approached very early in the project, even before Seaman and Price had become involved. Disney had offered the director job to Terry Gilliam, the lone American in the *Monty Python's Flying Circus* troupe. He did the quirky animated skit interstitial elements. *Monty Python* had a five-year run on BBC Television, from 1969 to 1974. Gilliam went on to direct *Jabberwocky* (1977), *Time Bandits* (1981), *The Meaning of Life* (1983), *Brazil* (1985), *The Adventures of Baron Munchausen* (1988), and many other subsequent films. As Gilliam says, "I passed on that one, but it didn't matter because it was a stage when it was still just a book and I didn't want to get into animation. I just read the book and said, 'This is too much work.' Pure laziness on my part."

Tom Wilhite had his own issues at the time. *Tron* had opened on July 9, 1982. It had cost $19 million to produce—a large budget for the time, especially for Disney. It was not doing well at the box office. In spite of his other concerns, he saw that the *Roger Rabbit* development unit was not making the headway he had expected and that Van Citters was not leading as he had hoped. He has said that Van Citters and the screenwriters had adjoining offices with an inter-connecting door, and that he was not aware of it having been opened or that they spoke. Wilhite tried to coach both Van Citters and Stirdivant in order for the *Roger Rabbit* project to gain more traction. Stirdivant had obtained permission for use of Woody Woodpecker in the film, but that was facilitated by the fact that Walter Lantz and Walt Disney had shared a long and cordial relationship. Similar requests to other studios had not been as successful.[51] Disney did not have the weight in Hollywood, and Ron Miller did not have the relationships with other studio heads, to make things happen.[52]

On February 24, 1983, Card Walker resigned as chief executive officer, and Ron Miller was elected as the new CEO of Walt Disney Productions. On April 18, the Disney Channel, a new cable-TV network, began broadcasting. The next day it began airing a show called *Disney Studio Showcase*. In the April 1983 episode, noted Disney historian John Culhane wanders the studio halls and as he pokes his head into doors, in a way reminiscent of Robert Benchley in *The Reluctant Dragon*, he highlights various studio projects in preparation. He looks in on *Something Wicked This Way Comes* and the special effects on *Baby*. He has a short interaction with Tim Burton about his short film *Vincent*, and we even get a glimpse into Burton's *Hansel and Gretel* Disney Channel television special (which was aired only once, on Halloween night of 1983, until it surfaced again as part of the Tim Burton retrospective at MoMA, in New York, in 2009). He finally pushes his head into a room to find Darrell Van Citters, Mike Giaimo, and Marc Stirdivant. Stirdivant explains the premise of the proposed *Roger Rabbit* film, which follows the second draft of Seaman and Price's screenplay. Two rough pencil tests are shown: one features an animated Captain Cleaver confronting a live-action Eddie Valiant, and the other pencil test shows Jessica Rabbit trying to seduce Eddie Valiant. Finally, a short colored animation test is shown of Roger Rabbit, voiced by Paul Reubens (of Pee-wee Herman fame).[53]

In the test-of-concept film clips, Eddie Valiant is played by Peter Renoudet (also known as Pete Renaday). Renoudet started at Disney in 1959 in the Art Props Department. He made many of the props for *Mary Poppins*. He also often did "stand-ins" during screen tests, and occasionally had bit parts in the Disney comedies of the 1960s (including *The Love Bug* and *The Million Dollar Duck*). He continued his career with Disney and extended it into voice acting. His time on *Roger Rabbit* amounted to "one unremarkable day of filming."[54]

In Randy Cartwright's Disney studio tour home movie of 1983, he wanders the halls of the Animation Building, peering into office doorways and getting reactions from the occupants. He enters Darrell Van Citters's office . . .[55]

RANDY: What is Darrell working on?

DARRELL: Roger Rabbit!

RANDY: Explain what you mean by . . . Roger Rabbit . . . Darrell.

DARRELL: [*silence*]

RANDY: Darrell's usually good at this stuff.

DARRELL: [*silence, Darrell shakes his head, camera pans down to show character maquettes on desk*]

RANDY: At least he's working harder than he was during the last film. [*Note: unsure whether this refers to the last Studio Tour home movie in 1980 or Van Citters's time on* The Fox and the Hound]

DARRELL: [*holding Roger Rabbit maquette*]

This is Roger. Some day you might see him . . . but then again, you might not.

That's the way things go around this place [*holding Captain Cleaver maquette*].

This is Captain Cleaver, the cop [*raising a hammer off the desk*].

This is a hammer, and . . . uh . . .

RANDY: That's it?

DARRELL: That's it.

RANDY: [*to the camera*] That's . . . Roger Rabbit!

DARRELL: [*mumbling*] That's about all that you're ever going to see of
Roger Rabbit.

There was clearly something in the wind at the Disney Studios.

Richard Berger was trained as a certified public accountant, but he had
show business in his blood; his mother was a former Ziegfeld girl and his
father was a theatrical producer. Berger joined 20th Century Fox in 1973,
as vice president of programming. He spent a short stint at CBS as vice
president of programming, then joined Disney in 1983 as president of Walt
Disney Pictures. Tom Wilhite was now working for Berger, who approached
Steven Spielberg about producing *Roger Rabbit*.[56] He even arranged for Van
Citters to send Spielberg the *Roger Rabbit* character maquettes that Van
Citters had made, as well as the script and test footage—in an attempt to
pique Spielberg's interest in the project. Spielberg was intrigued, but he did
not bite.[57] Producer deals were not a part of Disney's practice at the time,
and Berger backed off when Spielberg told Berger his fee.

Wilhite suggested that Stirdivant and Van Citters get the writing team
of Lowell Ganz and Babaloo Mandel involved. They had written the screenplay for *Night Shift* and were at the Disney Studios, just finishing the script
for *Splash*—both films directed by Ron Howard. Ganz and Mandel provided
two drafts of a screenplay; the second draft is dated December 13, 1984.[58]
Van Citters felt that the script was "more respectful of cartoons."[59] The
screenplay begins with a cartoon . . .

*Music swells and a cartoon studio logo emerges from the screen . . . Swell Pictures
Presents . . . Baby Herman in* Sour Krauts. *Baby Herman, Roger Rabbit, and
new character, General Mayhem, are in a house pretending to be soldiers . . .
and chaotic hilarity ensues. When the cartoon transitions to live action, we find
that Baby Herman's off-screen personality is suave and Ronald Colman-like.*

*Roger used to be a star (in 1940), but it's now 1944 . . . and he's a has-been
second banana. He has blown his lines and Myron Swell kicks him off the picture.*

*The scene switches to Eddie Valiant, a private investigator and accordion
teacher. He is upset that D-Day has just happened and he is not there to fight.
Roger comes into Eddie's office, says that his house was broken into, and hires
Eddie to investigate. In the course of his investigation, Eddie hears from Goofy
that Myron Swell is also stealing Roger's wife, Jessica.*

*Later, Swell is shot and killed and Eddie sees Roger fleeing from Swell's office.
Another shot is taken from outside the office window, by somebody in a Nazi
uniform. Eddie gives chase, only to find that they are filming* Sour Krauts *at*

the studio and everybody seems to be wearing a Nazi uniform, including Konrad Schumtz, the lead actor.

Myron's brother, Lesley, assumes leadership of Swell Pictures. Lesley hated his brother. He finds that the Sour Krauts film is missing and it must be found before the scheduled premiere—the fate of the studio hinges on it.

Schumtz has been spying on both Eddie and Roger. Somebody tries to drown Eddie in a swimming pool and takes a parcel that Roger had given to Eddie to pass on to Jessica. Roger saves Eddie from drowning. Their vehicle is ambushed and Eddie gives chase into Griffith Park, up to the Hollywood sign. There is a gunfight and Roger is shot. The gunfight continues around the sign and a Nazi, named Otto, gets away in a helicopter. Eddie and Roger pursue the helicopter by Roger spinning his ears like chopper blades. While in pursuit, Dumbo (and Timothy) fly past. When the helicopter lands, Eddie and Roger sneak up but everybody is gone. Roger starts to sink in quicksand and soon disappears. Eddie decides to jump in after him and falls through the quicksand pit into an underground cave. The quicksand pit is a secret entrance to the Nazi's West Coast headquarters.

Eddie and Roger see Konrad and Otto as they discover that the parcel contains a necklace for Jessica rather than the film they believed Roger had taken from Myron Swell's office on the night of his murder. Konrad shoots Otto because of the mistake. It turns out that stolen jet plane designs have been "hidden" in plain sight, in the Sour Krauts film. ("Who would look for a stolen film, in a film?") The Nazis had heard that Myron Swell was going to cut Jessica out of the film and knew that he would discover the stolen film segment when he was making the cuts.

Eddie and Roger are discovered and Eddie saves Roger from Konrad. They escape from the Nazi soldiers in the helicopter. Eddie figures out that Jessica killed Myron Swell and stole the film segment because Myron threatened to burn it. Jessica's next gambit is to try seducing Eddie. Roger sees this and runs for Toontown.

The screenplay calls for Eddie to pause before entering the tunnel into Toontown, similar to the final version of Who Framed Roger Rabbit.

Toontown is similar to what is seen in Who Framed Roger Rabbit, but is darker and more sinister. Eddie goes to the Boop-boop-ba-doop Club, where there is an octopus bartender and we hear the "drink on the rocks" gag. Betty Boop is the headliner. Eddie finds Roger in a back room where Mighty Mouse, Woody Woodpecker, Casper, and Felix the Cat are playing poker. Eddie finds out that toons are not allowed in the army either.

Jessica lies to the police to make them think that Eddie and Roger are guilty of Myron Swell's murder. They are captured and thrown into jail. The jailhouse graffiti shows them that Jessica has left a lot of broken hearts. Eddie pretends to hang himself (Roger disguises himself as "the rope") as a ploy for a jailbreak. They break out just in time to go to the premiere for Sour Krauts. *The screenplay has a running gag with Donald Duck trying to crash the premiere after Daisy goes in without him.*

Konrad Schumtz steals the film and makes a run for it to Toontown, where he finds himself at the Boop-boop-ba-doop Club. Mickey and Minnie have a cameo at a table. Eddie and Roger confront Konrad, but Nazi U-boat officers intervene. The surrounding toons are not inclined to help because they have been treated as second-class citizens, but Roger gives a rousing patriotic speech and the toons end up helping Eddie and Roger recover the film from the Nazis off the U-boat.

In the end, Eddie and Roger are accepted into the army and are shown getting on to a troop transport plane.

The *Roger Rabbit* development unit storyboarded the Ganz and Mandel script. Giaimo and Van Citters worked on character designs for the new treatment. Chris Buck had done the experimental animation pencil tests that were seen on the *Disney Studio Showcase* episode, and Randy Cartwright was assigned to the unit briefly to animate the walk cycle that was used in the fully rendered animation test-of-concept film clip. Cartwright's time on *Roger Rabbit* lasted only a couple of months. He was unaware of Joe Ranft's involvement with the unit, so it seems that Ranft had moved on to different things by that time. Then, development on *Roger Rabbit* was stopped suddenly. The shutdown was in late 1983.[60]

Tom Wilhite tried hard to do the right thing, but he no longer had the support of the studio. *Tron* had not been the box-office success that the studio had hoped for and, on the heels of the disappointment of *The Black Hole*, Wilhite no longer had his previous sway with Ron Miller and seemed to be constantly at odds with Ed Hansen in the Animation Department. In fact, Miller was under pressure himself. The disappointing returns from *Tron* were a problem for pushing other novel projects.[61] The dysfunction in the Animation Department continued throughout the production of *The Black Cauldron*, but Animation management grew increasingly upset that Wilhite, and Live-Action, had been poaching its talent. Miller could not, or would not, put anybody into Animation who could *lead*. Animation's middle management was causing the antagonism.[62] There was not a strong person to wrangle the disparate groups within Animation. Miller realizes that he may not have nipped things in the bud, as he might have wanted to. He was distracted by other things happening with the Disney company.[63] The young CalArts animators were not blameless. Chris Buck says that he and the other animators often behaved like "snot-nosed brats who thought they knew everything and wanted to make their imprint."[64] He readily admits, now, that they did not know as much as they thought they did at the time. Others thought that Miller was interested enough to allow Wilhite some freedom, but that he did not have the interest to *really* move *Roger Rabbit* along.[65] He was not a "creative" and was not as passionate about the project. It was felt that he did not have "a *fire* under him" and was just trying to maintain the status quo.

On the other hand, this was very early in the careers of the young animators. They were impatient, and that impatience added to their frustration. It was their first big project—their first opportunity to guide the development of a potential feature film. They did not yet know that many projects would die on the vine during their careers. They were passionate about their designs and their choices of direction, and they felt wounded that it was being taken away.[66] Those who were involved in the early *Roger Rabbit* development unit point to the test-of-concept voiced by Paul Reubens. Reubens provided the voice for Roger while he was still with the improvisation corps, the Groundlings—long before his fame as Pee-wee Herman in *Pee-Wee's Big Adventure* (1985), directed by Tim Burton. Van Citters saw Roger as having deep pathos, not being just a clown. The Ganz and Mandel treatment allowed Roger more depth—to be more of a tragic clown, as in Leoncavallo's opera *Pagliacci* or even like Emmett Kelly. It is said that Paul Reubens's reading for Roger must be heard to more fully understand Van Citters's strong point-of-view.[67] He brought a sympathetic goofiness that was hard to define.[68]

Beyond these factors, Card Walker was extremely conservative. He may have hindered Miller's efforts to effect change at Disney. In spite of the conservatism of his superiors and predecessors, Miller was able to institute a surprising amount of change during his short tenure as president and CEO. It was during his time that Walt Disney Productions brought the Disney Channel, Buena Vista Home Entertainment, and Touchstone Pictures on stream. Also, Tokyo Disneyland was developed and built, and EPCOT was constructed, during this time. Miller (and Wilhite) acquired and put into production *Tron* and *Splash*. *Splash* showed that Disney was capable of producing witty and engaging adult comedies and, beyond its box-office success, it helped to open the doors to Hollywood creative people who would previously have avoided working at Disney. In spite of the disappointing box office, *Tron* developed a strong cult following and, eventually, a strong franchise. The other organizational changes reaped great rewards for the company in the years to come; rewards for which successors took credit. Richard Berger arrived at the studio in 1983, and Wilhite no longer had the clout that he had once enjoyed. Berger and Wilhite weren't getting along. By April 1984, Wilhite had left Disney.

Nevertheless, and for a multitude of reasons, not the least of which was Disney's reluctance to invest over $12 million in the production, *Roger Rabbit* failed to gain the necessary traction within the studio and within Hollywood . . . and the development unit was shut down in late 1983. Chris Buck was assigned to *The Black Cauldron*. He lasted only one week before he left Disney (in early 1984). He departed before Michael Eisner, Frank Wells, and Jeffrey Katzenberg came on board. He found work storyboarding on Tim Burton's live-action special film *Frankenweenie* (1984). An earlier stop-motion project, *Trick or Treat*, had been aborted. *Frankenweenie* was another of Tom Wilhite's efforts to keep the highly creative Burton at Disney. The production was done off-the-lot in a nondescript building in north Burbank.[69]

Following the cessation of further development on *Roger Rabbit*, a Special Projects Unit was established, with Van Citters as its director. This unit was also set up off the main Disney lot in an office building, which formerly housed a bank, on Glen Oaks Boulevard in northern Burbank. Van Citters engaged in what he called "guerrilla practices." The unit used standard animation paper, and registration holes, none of which were the Disney Standard.[70] He was quite happy with the autonomy of being off the main Disney lot. They eventually began work on a "Sport Goofy" project. The special featurette, *Sport Goofy in Soccermania*, was intended to be the link pin for a Disney marketing initiative to refresh and renew the library of Goofy sports-related *How To . . .* shorts. It was never intended to have production values similar to the feature films. Disney marketing saw an opportunity, likely associated with the upcoming 1984 Summer Olympic Games in Los Angeles, to emblazon sports merchandise with a Disney brand. Disney had a library of Goofy shorts in which the Goof got into comic situations as a consequence of his ineptitude. The shorts could be repackaged in any number of formats for a new, young audience. When it was finally released in 1987, it was preceded by a mockumentary showing a compilation of clips from older shorts, with Goofy getting everything wrong. The show segued into the new cartoon featurette, in which Goofy is shown to be competent, athletic, and heroic.[71] The Sport Goofy initiative yielded a wide variety of branded merchandise, not always sports-related.

The campaign was not very prominent in North America, but it took root in Europe. By the mid-1980s, "funny animal" comic books had almost disappeared, to be replaced by dark versions of superhero comic characters and graphic novels. But in Europe there was, and continues to be, a strong market for the Disney characters in comic books. Belgium, Denmark, France, Germany, Italy, the Netherlands, Norway, Poland, Spain, Sweden, and the United Kingdom have regular publication of Disney comic book titles. Donald Duck, in particular, was, and remains, extremely popular and is often published under several distinct titles in each country. Carl Barks is revered, but Europe has produced its own talented Disney comic book artists: Giovan Battista Carpi, Giorgio Cavazzano, Daan Jippes, Claude Marin, Jukka Murtossari, Pierre Nicolas, Romano Scarpa, and Vicar. Finland, in particular, is crazy about Donald Duck (Aku Ankka, in Finnish) and publishes Donald Duck titles in Finnish—sometimes, even in regional Finnish dialects. In 2001, the Finnish Post Office issued a stamp commemorating the fiftieth anniversary of Donald Duck comics in Finland.

This was a fertile environment for the Sport Goofy initiative. Although the featurette and initiative was named for the Goof, it features Huey, Dewey, and Louie and characters of Carl Barks creation, Uncle Scrooge, and the Beagle Boys. Disney assembled a television series, *Quack Attack*, which linked vintage Donald Duck shorts, as early programming for the Disney Channel. That satisfied the North American demand, but the Disney Channel was not available in Europe. The Goofy shorts were mostly mime-action and had little dialogue except for his yelps and chuckles.

They were perfect for compilation and repackaging for a burgeoning European videocassette market. The *Sport Goofy in Soccermania* vehicle fed right into the insatiable European demand for Donald Duck comics. *Sport Goofy in Soccermania*, on videocassette and DVD, is impossible to find in English in North America, except on the internet,[72] but it is easy to find copies of the featurette in many other languages. The Sport Goofy brand is still used to sponsor the Spanish National Youth Tennis Championship tournament. The featurette was also the first new animation to feature the Donald Duck gang and was a prelude to the *DuckTales* television series in 1987. Tad Stones had worked briefly with WED Enterprises (later Walt Disney Imagineering) on projects related to the World in Motion and Imagination pavilions at EPCOT. It was Stones who commissioned the early work that resulted in *Fun with Mr. Future* and the core of the *Roger Rabbit* development unit. Stones was a writer on *Sport Goofy in Soccermania* and would later go on to be the creative force behind *DuckTales* and many other Disney Television animated series.

But, that was . . . 1987 and later. In 1984, the environment was not as urgent as it maybe should have been with the Olympics almost upon them. In addition to Tad Stones, Joe Ranft, and Mike Giaimo received writing credits. There was no producer credited on the featurette, although Clive Reinhard may be said to have served that function. Most of his career credits are as a production accountant.[73] It wasn't a "holiday" for the Special Projects unit in north Burbank, but they had fun and engaged in a little subversion. Roger Rabbit, the clownish incarnation of that time, appears in a crowd scene—wildly clapping along with other "funny animal" spectators at the soccer game.

Chris Buck came back to Disney in late 1984 to work in the Sport Goofy unit, and again complete the team. The Special Projects unit was still located off the main Disney lot when Eisner and Wells arrived at Disney in late September 1984. Jeffrey Katzenberg was hired from Paramount soon afterward. Things changed quickly on the main lot, with many long-service Disney employees suddenly gone and many new executives suddenly appearing. The studios at Disney were no longer to be the backwater of Hollywood. Eisner and Wells hit the ground running and reviewed all of the current productions. The feedback to Van Citters was that they were satisfied with the way that *Sport Goofy in Soccermania* was proceeding. Not long afterward, there was a change of heart and *Sport Goofy in Soccermania* was deemed "unreleasable." Van Citters's style had much snappier timing than typical Disney fare. The Sport Goofy project came in slightly under budget and Van Citters asked Katzenberg whether some of the leftover monies could be distributed to the crew as a bonus. The request seemed reasonable, but was pushing the norms for the studio at that time. Katzenberg's opinion was that providing that sort of incentive on projects opened a potential for abuse. Whether the request contributed to a change in perception about Van Citters or not—something had changed.

Gary Krisel had been the president of the Disney subsidiary, Disneyland/Vista Records, but in November 1984—when Walt Disney Productions was reincorporated as the Walt Disney Company—a new subsidiary, the Walt Disney Pictures Television Animation Group, was formed and Krisel was named as its first president. The Special Projects unit was doing work that would have now fallen under the jurisdiction of the Television Animation Group, and Van Citters was convinced that Krisel had played studio politics to change Eisner's opinion on the state of *Sport Goofy*. Van Citters felt that he had been "stabbed in the back."[74] Van Citters's and Giaimo's take on *Sport Goofy* was, admittedly, zany/quirky. Ward Kimball was brought in, as a consultant, to fix it. Even Kimball thought that it was "bizarre." Eventually, Matt O'Callaghan was brought in as director.[75] It was a difficult time for Van Citters (and O'Callaghan). Van Citters had lost control of *Sport Goofy in Soccermania*, but *Roger Rabbit* was not completely dead. Marc Stirdivant was continuing to try to make things happen.

Soon after Katzenberg arrived at Disney, he came to Eisner wanting to move the Animation group off the main Disney lot so that their offices in the Animation Building could be used for the producers, directors, and writers that Disney was beginning to sign to long-term contracts.[76] There was palpable and credible fear in the Animation Department that Disney Animation would be shut down altogether. Disney already had a presence in an industrial/warehousing neighborhood, surrounding the former Glendale municipal airport terminal, in nearby Glendale. WED Enterprises, soon to become known as Walt Disney Imagineering (WDI), had long been located at 1401 Flower Street. A converted one-story office/warehouse building at 1420 Flower Street was taken over by Disney to house some growing units for which there was no space on the main Burbank lot. Individuals began drifting over to Glendale to set up their workspaces at the converted Flower Street building in late 1985. The growing computer graphics (CG) group moved there from the main lot in early 1986,[77] and the balance of the Animation group followed in early 1986. *The Little Mermaid* was the first project to be produced in its entirety in Glendale.

In the "live-action film world"—everywhere, except at Disney—a studio would seek a producer for interesting projects. The studio is essentially the banker—with some level of creative control. That is the world Katzenberg came from, so he did not think anything of discussing *Roger Rabbit* with Steven Spielberg. It wasn't a big decision, and his seeking an outside producer was not an indictment against Disney. It was simply an acknowledgment that Disney had been working on *Roger Rabbit* for more than three years and still had neither the resources nor the corporate energy for producing it. Nevertheless, it was a shock for those inside Disney for *Roger Rabbit* to slip away from them.[78]

There have been several corporate myths perpetrated to burnish the already sterling reputations of Eisner and Katzenberg. A number of the myths are related to *Roger Rabbit*. The myth is that they went "mining for gold" in the Disney morgue and found the *Roger Rabbit* screenplays, lost and languishing (and unloved). The truth is that the *Roger Rabbit* development unit had been very active only nine months prior to the arrival of Eisner and Katzenberg, and Marc Stirdivant had continued trying to make things happen while Van Citters and his crew were biding their time, in anticipation of the opportunity for further development in order to greenlight the production. The myth is that Eisner and Katzenberg found a dozen—well, at least . . . ten—*Roger Rabbit* screenplays. The truth is that there were four screenplays: two drafts from Seaman and Price and two drafts from Ganz and Mandel. The myth is that Eisner and Katzenberg performed some kind of magic to get Spielberg on board, with some of the magic based on favors granted and owed for helping to get the *Indiana Jones* franchise off the ground while Eisner and Katzenberg were at Paramount. The truth is that Disney already had Spielberg and Zemeckis sold on *Roger Rabbit* before Eisner and Katzenberg arrived. Both Spielberg and Zemeckis were intrigued by *Roger Rabbit* but neither of them thought that the "old" Disney had the corporate will to mount the production. Whether Spielberg or Katzenberg first brought up the topic of *Roger Rabbit* is unclear and not especially relevant. *Roger Rabbit* was not a "lost property," and the topic was going to be raised one way or the other. What Eisner and Katzenberg did was give a significant percentage of the profits to Spielberg and Zemeckis—and Disney gave them creative control of the production. Disney kept all merchandising rights.[79] Katzenberg negotiated the production deal with Amblin Entertainment (i.e., Spielberg) and Spielberg selected Zemeckis as his director. Then, Zemeckis (and Amblin) assembled the production team.[80]

Peter Schneider came from a theater background. He was the associate director of the 1984 Los Angeles Olympic Arts Festival before being hired by Disney as the first president of Disney Feature Animation. He started at Disney on Monday, October 14, 1985, and was told by Katzenberg to go to a meeting with Steven Spielberg, Bob Zemeckis, Frank Marshall, and Kathleen Kennedy to discuss *Roger Rabbit* at the Amblin compound on the Universal lot on Friday, October 18. He admits to knowing nothing about animation at that time and took Van Citters and Giaimo along with him. It became clear to Schneider very early in the meeting that Spielberg was not at all impressed with Disney over the past twenty years. Worse than that, Spielberg said that he saw nothing to indicate that Disney could do any better.[81] At some point after Michael Eisner had come to Disney and things *had* started to turn around, Ron Clements shared with him that in the dark days, when Joe Hale had made the proclamation, "We are going to do a traditional Disney movie!" the unofficial Disney motto amongst the animators had become, "We may bore you, but we will never shock you." That quote has been ascribed to Card Walker.

Unfortunately for Van Citters, they had brought along *Sport Goofy in Soccermania* and showed it to Spielberg. The featurette was a bit of fluff and was never intended to be the stuff for a showreel. Spielberg was not impressed.[82] Schneider felt that Van Citters must have been worn down by recent circumstances or the dysfunctional environment at the studio. Schneider was brand new at Disney Animation and he felt that he was doing more during the meeting to assuage Spielberg's concerns about Disney than Van Citters.[83] Zemeckis was looking for "the extraordinary," and Schneider had to admit that Disney people at the time "didn't have the spark of extraordinary." They found that spark later.[84] After that first meeting, Peter Schneider said to Mike Giaimo, "You know who Roger Rabbit is? It's him!" (pointing to Zemeckis).

It was too easy for Amblin to say "Disney was not good enough," but Zemeckis was interested in whoever would be the best animation director. Whether it was a matter of taste or trust or "the spark of extraordinary," it seemed clear from the outset that Zemeckis's choice for animation director was not going to be Darrell Van Citters.[85] Van Citters was outspoken and antagonistic during the meeting and Zemeckis was uncomfortable with him.[86] Their visions were very different. John Musker and Glen Keane, and maybe others from Disney, were asked to go over to Amblin to be interviewed. Musker had a sense that Zemeckis was just going through the motions, but that may be because he soon realized that he had not really prepared for the interview adequately.[87] At the time, he had only been the co-director on The Great Mouse Detective. Zemeckis was very analytical in his selection of camera angles and camera movement. It was the kind of intensity and cinematographic analysis that Musker had seen in Brad Bird. When Zemeckis asked about why Musker had chosen certain approaches in The Great Mouse Detective, Musker was embarrassed to realize that he could not answer the questions—and more embarrassed to realize that he had not ever considered the options that Zemeckis identified.[88] It was a wake-up call that ultimately contributed to Musker becoming a better director. Other people who were considered for animation director included Chuck Jones, Don Bluth, Dale Baer, Eric Goldberg, and Richard Williams.[89]

Schneider's view was that the Special Projects unit was extraordinarily uncollaborative. It (i.e., Van Citters) fought hard against "establishment."[90] He had always been a bit subversive and a bit cynical—the producer volleyball challenge and the Eddie Fisher Show are examples. He enjoyed the role of renegade—later, even naming his own studio . . . Renegade Animation. That attitude can be seen in Van Citters's delight in the "guerrilla tactics" he adopted when the unit moved off the main Disney lot. Tom Wilhite had tried to be a mentor for Van Citters and had counseled him to "play the game!" and "not be so belligerent!"[91] Now, Van Citters wanted to be more independent and Schneider felt that he had to be harnessed. Schneider was new at the job, and the pressure was enormous. He tended to be volatile in these early days at Disney and, truth be told, the place needed to be shaken up. He had the Special Projects unit moved closer to the main lot—to 1420 Flower Street in Glendale. There was an increasing frequency and intensity to the altercations between Van Citters and Schneider. Mike Giaimo had a work station that shared a wall with Schneider's office and he was witness to colorful confrontations.

Van Citters regretted that they had ever "teased" Spielberg with *Roger Rabbit*. He felt very protective of *Roger Rabbit* and now he had been pulled off of it. Tom Wilhite had left Disney in April 1985 and now Van Citters felt that he had "no protector within the Company"—that "nobody had his back."[92] There is no denying that Van Citters exhibited prickly and refractory behavior, and did not do himself any favors in that regard. He had been coached on playing nice, but he was not able to temper his interactions with people he did not respect. The attitude was borne out of a deep love of the medium of animation and his craft, and it is unfortunate that Disney Animation management in the 1970s and 1980s was not more progressive and that the institutional artistic vision was limited to trying to mimic past glory—because he may then have not felt the need to challenge their thinking in a way that was perceived as being negative. He had graduated from CalArts and had become an employee in a *business*, with a business hierarchy, and there was a certain confusion and naïveté on the part of many of the CalArts graduates about their role in the organization. Many of them became disillusioned and left Disney. Van Citters grew more bitter at his situation and finally left Disney on March 5, 1986.

Mike Giaimo continued on for a bit. He did some new character designs for Roger Rabbit based on Zemeckis's wishes. Zemeckis had finished *Back to the Future* and was already working on a sequel. He had an attachment to Michael J. Fox and the new design for Roger looked and behaved like Fox.[93] Giaimo left Disney in April 1986 and went on to do some freelance work on *The Brave Little Toaster* for Hyperion Pictures. When Wilhite left Disney, he negotiated with Richard Berger to take *The Brave Little Toaster* with him. He and Willard Carroll formed Hyperion Pictures. When Brad Bird's and Jerry Rees's efforts to get backing for *The Spirit* failed, Rees became attached to *The Brave Little Toaster* as director. He had to completely retune the story. The actual production was done in Taiwan. Joe Ranft went to Taiwan with Jerry and Rebecca Rees to work on it. A further coincidence is that another member of the Groundlings improvisation troop, Deanna Oliver, was selected to provide the voice for the Toaster. She later became the writing partner of Sherri Stoner and they wrote a screenplay for a *Roger Rabbit* prequel in the mid-1990s.

There is a question about whether Darrell Van Citters was removed from his film solely because of the frankness of his opinion regarding the tone of the proposed production and its variance from that of Zemeckis, or whether part of it was due to his honesty about the proposed budget. It was a surprise to the early animators starting on the film in London that it was to be done on "ones" (one drawing for every frame—i.e., twenty-four drawings for every second of screen time) and that the camera was to be moving.[94] In hindsight, it seems clear that the film was never going to be completed on the schedule and budget that had been proposed.

Chapter Two

ENTER AMBLIN

Bob Zemeckis had been sent the Seaman and Price script in 1982 and had been very interested in the *Roger Rabbit* concept: an opening cartoon that is interrupted by a human director shouting, "Cut, cut, cut!" as he walks onto the animated stage. "The ultimate concept shot," mused Zemeckis in 1982, when he read the early script.[1] But, he did not believe that Disney had the corporate will at that time to execute the project in the way he felt it should be done. The discussions lingered, and the project did not gain the necessary traction within Disney. Zemeckis moved on to direct *Romancing the Stone.*[2]

Richard Berger sent the script and a set of maquettes of the animated characters to Steven Spielberg in 1983. Spielberg, also, was very interested in the concept, but Berger (i.e., Disney) backed off when Spielberg gave his fee for involvement in the project.

Spielberg was an animation fan and had been the executive producer of *An American Tail* (Universal, 1986), directed by Don Bluth and produced through Amblin Entertainment and Sullivan Bluth Productions. Disney's reluctance to proceed did not stop Spielberg's continued interest in the *Roger Rabbit* project. Amblin had produced *Gremlins* for Warner Bros., released in June 1984. Joe Dante was the director and Spielberg was the executive producer. After *Gremlins* wrapped, Spielberg and Dante explored the *Roger Rabbit* concept further to better understand what would be required to bring the project to the screen. Spielberg knew animation sufficiently to make a reasonable estimate of the cost of production. By the time the topic of *Roger Rabbit* came up again with Disney in 1985, Spielberg had a much better handle on *Roger Rabbit* than Disney management.

Roy E. Disney initiated the episode of corporate raiding on Walt Disney Productions when he resigned from the Disney board of directors on March 9, 1984. On that day, he purchased more shares of Disney, bringing his stake in the company to 4.7 percent. On March 12, Saul Steinberg began to purchase shares of Walt Disney Productions, and by April 11, he had acquired 9.3 percent of the company's outstanding shares. On April 25, he made a filing with the SEC that he intended to acquire 25 percent of the company. On June 10, Disney negotiated the buyback of Steinberg's shares at a premium ("greenmail"), plus $28 million for Steinberg's expenses. That was not the end of Disney's problems though; Irwin Jacobs began another raid and arbitrageurs Michael Milken and Ivan Boesky got into the mix. Ultimately, Roy E. Disney and his cohort, Stanley Gold, convinced Sid Bass (and his brothers) to buy up Disney shares and stabilize the company. The Bass brothers ended up with over 24 percent of the outstanding shares.[3] Roy E. Disney and Gold proposed the management team of Michael Eisner (an executive from Paramount) and Frank Wells (an entertainment lawyer who had been at Warner Bros.), and on September 24, Eisner and Wells began their first official day of work at Disney. Jeffrey Katzenberg soon followed from Paramount. Roy E. Disney was named the head of Animation.

On September 23, Eisner and Wells took a tour of the Disney Studios, where they were introduced to the staff in a gathering in the residential street square in the Disney backlot. Eisner announced how happy he was to be at Disney and explained that he grew up loving all of the wonderful Disney characters. He said, "After all, who could ever forget Heckle and Jeckle and Mighty Mouse?" Of course, neither Mighty Mouse nor Heckle and Jeckle are Disney characters . . . the backlot went silent and the animators were aghast.[4] When *The Black Cauldron* was screened for the new management, Katzenberg asked for "cover shots," not realizing that drawings from different camera angles were not a typical part of the animation process. Many new executives showed up on the Disney lot soon afterward. It may be unfair to characterize the new management by unfortunate misspeaks, but it was clear to Disney staff that they did not know animation. It also became clear that the new management had every intention of shutting down Disney animation. It was Roy E. Disney who convinced them otherwise. Katzenberg had responsibility for the Film Division, which included Animation. Eisner said to Katzenberg, "That's your problem now."[5]

The new management team *did* know the film business, though. Walt Disney Productions in early 1984 was a boutique operation, with only three or four films per year. It had no ties to hot directors such as Steven Spielberg, Ivan Reitman, or John Hughes, and box-office superstars would not be caught dead on the Disney lot. In 1976, Disney had $54 million in profit from its film division. In 1982, the earnings had slid to $19.6 million, with most of that coming from rereleases. In 1983, Disney took write-offs on *Something Wicked This Way Comes* and *Trenchcoat* for a $5 million loss; plus, it had to absorb a startup cost for the Disney Channel of $29 million. Eisner and Katzenberg knew how to make hit films and they could draw top flight talent.[6]

Eisner's story about Katzenberg coming to him with plans for moving the Animation Department off the Disney main lot must be seen through the lens of somebody who was embroiled in a lawsuit with Katzenberg at the time of its telling. It was Eisner who ordered Imagineering to draw up plans for bulldozing the Disney backlot in order to put up bungalows for producers. Eventually, though, $500,000 was invested to renovate the Animation Building for producer suites and the Animation Department was moved off the lot.

Two weeks after arriving at Disney, Eisner, Katzenberg, and Wells sorted through scripts and the films currently in production. At some point in the following year the topic of *Roger Rabbit* was raised with Spielberg, although it may have been Spielberg who raised it with Disney. Spielberg had done some homework and his initial budget estimate for *Roger Rabbit* was $25 million. That estimate was based on Amblin's experience with conventional feature animation.

Roy E. Disney, while not just a figurehead, was little interested in running the operational aspects of Disney Animation. He took the title of Chairman of Disney Animation, and Peter Schneider was hired to be president of Disney Feature Animation in October 1985. One week after starting at Disney he found himself in a meeting about *Roger Rabbit* with Spielberg, Zemeckis, Frank Marshall, and Kathleen Kennedy at Amblin's offices.

Amblin Entertainment was founded in 1981 by Spielberg, Marshall, and Kennedy. It was named after Spielberg's first commercially released film, *Amblin'*, which was made when he was an unpaid intern at Universal Studios in 1968. After seeing it, Sidney Sheinberg made Spielberg the youngest director ever signed to a long-term deal by a major Hollywood studio.[7] Amblin operated out of a Mexican-style hacienda complex located on the Universal lot; it was jokingly called "Taco Bell," while others called it "the Alamo."

Zemeckis was coming off the success of *Romancing the Stone* and *Back to the Future*. He says, "I think that Joe Dante fooled around with it [*Roger Rabbit*] for a while. One day, after *Back to the Future*, I was in Steven's office and saw a copy of *Roger Rabbit* [the 1982 Seaman and Price script] on his table. He asked what I thought about it. I said, 'Oh God, I know about that project. I've known about it for years. It's one of those great concepts that *really* should be done,' and Steven said, 'Why don't we think about doing it?'"[8]

Schneider had taken Darrell Van Citters and Mike Giaimo with him to the October 18 meeting at Amblin. By this time, Zemeckis had very definite opinions about the *Roger Rabbit* project and the tone he would like to see in the film. Van Citters did not share Zemeckis's vision, and said so. He also disagreed with Amblin's estimate for the budget and schedule, which was the rule of thumb that one minute of animated feature film cost approximately $100,000 to produce—the cost of twenty animators working for about one week. Schneider had not been at Disney long enough to have an opinion. Soon after, Van Citters was off the *Roger Rabbit* project.

Tense negotiations went on between Disney and Amblin for several weeks for a joint animation unit to be run by Amblin. Disney convinced Spielberg that it had the will and the bank account to do it right.[9] Spielberg would have autonomy to hire a director of animation. Spielberg would also have a healthy percentage of the profits and a share of the merchandising rights.[10] Meanwhile, Spielberg proceeded to work his magic by getting the rights to a number of cartoon characters from other studios, including Bugs Bunny, Porky Pig, Daffy Duck, and others from Warner Bros., Woody Woodpecker from Universal, and Droopy from MGM/UA, at the cost of $5,000 per character. Warner Bros.' condition was that Bugs Bunny could appear only alongside Mickey Mouse—and only if they each had the same number of spoken words. Warner Bros. would also have the right to preview and approve the look and lines given to its characters. Zemeckis proceeded to assemble his production team.

Zemeckis selected key production supervisors with whom he was comfortable and with whom visions were aligned. He had worked with most of them previously. His most recent production was *Back to the Future* (1985), and a scan of the credits shows the core of his *Roger Rabbit* team: Alan Silvestri (composer), Dean Cundey (cinematographer), Arthur Schmidt (editor), Ken Chase (make-up), David McGiffert (first assistant director), Frank Marshall (second-unit director), Charles Campbell (supervising sound editor), Larry Singer (supervising ADR editor), Greg Orloff (Foley mixer), Howard Stein (supervising visual effects editor), and Bonne Radford (production controller). Of course, the team included the Amblin executive management: executive producers Steven Spielberg, Kathleen Kennedy, and her husband, Frank Marshall. Kennedy and Marshall tended to Spielberg's day-to-day affairs, and at Amblin, they were called "the Parents." It gave Amblin Entertainment a family quality.[11]

An early call was to Arthur Schmidt, whose father had been a film editor at Paramount. He had worked on many classic films, including Billy
Wilder's *Sunset Boulevard* (1950) and *Some Like It Hot* (1959). Even though
Arthur initially followed a different path, he eventually found his way back
to Hollywood, and after a long apprenticeship became a much sought-after
editor in his own right.[12] After working with Zemeckis on *Back to the Future*,
they formed a bond of trust. The editing of a film is a key element for ex-
pressing the story, so the director and editor must be in sync. Schmidt and
Zemeckis were in lockstep, but more than with most live-action films . . . in
Who Framed Roger Rabbit the film would have to be edited with many of the
actors (the animated ones) missing from the scene. It required a degree of
understanding and anticipation that is rare between two creative people,
so Schmidt had a key responsibility for the success of the film.

Chief amongst Zemeckis's associates was Ken Ralston, the supervisor
of visual effects and a key element of the ascendancy of ILM in the special/
visual effects field. Ralston had worked with Zemeckis on *Back to the Future*.
His credits included *Star Wars: Episode IV—A New Hope* (1977), *Star Wars:
Episode V—The Empire Strikes Back* 1980), *Dragonslayer* (1981), *Star Trek II:
The Wrath of Khan* (1982), *Star Wars: Episode VI—Return of the Jedi* (1983),
Star Trek III: The Search for Spock (1984), *Cocoon* (1985), *Back to the Future*
(1985), *Star Trek IV: The Voyage Home* (1986), and *The Golden Child* (1986).
Therefore, one of the first calls Zemeckis made was to Ralston to get him
interested in the project. Ralston brought with him ILM's resources, visual
effects wizardry, and twenty-seven ILM wizards who had worked on *Back
to the Future*. Zemeckis knew that one of the major elements in selling the
conceit of toons interacting in the real world would be the optical compositing expertise at ILM. They would end up using the same techniques as for
compositing models into the *Star Wars* films.[13]

Ralston grew up shooting 8mm effects films with his buddies, as had
Zemeckis (and Spielberg before him). At seventeen years old, he was hired
for the summer at Cascade Studios, one of the pioneer producers of animated ads for television, to do stop-motion animation. Ralston stayed at
Cascade and received a thorough apprenticeship in most aspects of film
production, along with other people, such as Tom St. Amand, who would
later become part of the *Roger Rabbit* story. Cascade created the Pillsbury
Doughboy and Green Giant interactive animation/live-action commercials.
Another coincidence, which made Ralston one of the few direct links to
the artist to whom so much homage was directed in the animation of *Who
Framed Roger Rabbit*, was that Tex Avery was a freelance director at Cascade
Studios at the time, and Ralston got to know him well.[14]

Zemeckis sent Ralston an early script, but it would go through many changes. In Ralston's first meeting regarding *Roger Rabbit* at the Amblin offices, the *Roger Rabbit* character maquettes—the ones made by Darrell Van Citters and sent to Steven Spielberg in 1983—were on the conference table. Ralston became involved in the project very early in 1986 due to the lead time that would be required to build cameras and sets. He was also involved in the process of selecting an animation director.[15]

After Van Citters was released from the *Roger Rabbit* project, an immediate priority was to find the right director of animation. Lucasfilm's ILM said that it could do the animation. Its Pixar division had just completed a short computer graphics animated film, *Luxo Jr.* (directed by John Lasseter), which would soon be causing a stir at the 1986 SIGGRAPH conference—but it didn't have the experience or depth to undertake the animation on the *Roger Rabbit* project at that time. Not only did the candidate need to have that "spark of extraordinary," but his personality and vision also had to mesh with that of Zemeckis. A number of potential candidates were interviewed by Zemeckis, Ralston, and Steve Starkey; the candidates included Chuck Jones and Don Bluth.[16]

Eric Goldberg had majored in illustration at the Pratt Institute in Brooklyn before joining the crew of *Raggedy Ann & Andy: A Musical Adventure* (1977), directed by Richard Williams. He went to London with Williams, after the film was completed, to join him at Richard Williams Animation as a director-animator on commercials and film titles. Goldberg eventually left the studio, but Williams got him back to work on *Ziggy's Gift* in Los Angeles. Goldberg moved to Los Angeles to work on the 1982 Emmy Award-winning television Christmas special. Williams was the nominal director and Goldberg was credited with art direction, but Goldberg functioned ostensibly as the director on the production. He was twenty-years old at the time. Russell Hall, a senior animator-director at Richard Williams Animation (RWA), recalls that there was a falling out between Goldberg and Williams.[17] Goldberg returned to London after completing *Ziggy's Gift* and co-founded Pizazz Pictures, developing a worldwide clientele with smart commercials done using a variety of techniques.

Amblin/Disney put an ad in *Variety*: "Looking for Animation Director for new project . . . free to apply at Department RR." Eric Goldberg applied and was contacted by Amblin with an expression of interest.[18] Indeed, Amblin was very interested in Goldberg.[19] He had included material in his showreel that had the '40s ethos,[20] and his reel included many examples of animation executed using a variety of techniques. He also had a wicked sense of humor and an animation sensibility that tended more to the Warner Bros.

Termite Terrace style. Amblin had interviewed a number of people from
the Disney Studios, including John Musker.[21] The prevailing feeling within
Amblin was that anybody at Disney, who predated Eisner, was "asleep at
the wheel" and that their opinion was not worth hearing.[22] It is unfortunate
that the first "creative executive" they dealt with (Peter Schneider) had
been with Disney for less than a week before the initial meeting and, by
his own admission, did not know animation at all at that time. Zemeckis
found Van Citters to be intractable and intent on the character-focused,
"touchy-feely" animation that left him cold. Also, by his own admission,
Musker did not feel that he presented himself adequately.[23]

Robert Watts is a British film producer who is best known for his involvement with George Lucas and Steven Spielberg in the *Star Wars* and
Indiana Jones film series. He had also been a production manager on the
James Bond film *You Only Live Twice* (1967) and Stanley Kubrick's *2001: A
Space Odyssey* (1968). In 1985, Watts was the vice president of European
production for Lucasfilm. He was asked to visit Richard Williams at his
small animation studio at 13 Soho Square in London. Williams had contacted Lucasfilm to say that he had an amazing film he would like George
Lucas to see. It was a ten-minute reel of finished film for *The Thief and
the Cobbler.* Williams showed the clip to Watts and asked if George Lucas
might be interested. Watts told Williams that Lucas rarely took on outside
projects, but he offered to take the reel to California to show it at ILM.[24]
In an unpublished 1996 interview, Williams was adamant that his only
intention in sending the clip to ILM was for use of ILM's special projector
to show the clip to his idol, Milt Kahl, who had retired from the Disney
Studios and was living in Sausalito and was extremely ill at the time.[25] Lucas
was not interested in backing the film, but Watts was working on *Indiana
Jones and the Temple of Doom*, with both Lucas and Steven Spielberg, at the
time, so he decided to take the reel down to Amblin to show it to Spielberg.
Spielberg was "blown away." It was at that time that he told Watts about
Roger Rabbit and asked whether Watts would like to be the producer. Watts
met Zemeckis and agreed to be part of the team.[26] It turns out that Williams was upset that *The Thief* clip had been shown to Spielberg without
his permission.[27] Watts's first task was to get Richard Williams to agree to
be the director of animation.[28]

Richard Williams was born on March 19, 1933, in Toronto, Canada. At
fourteen years of age, he traveled on his own to Los Angeles to visit the
Disney Studios and was befriended by master animator Milt Kahl. Williams resisted the lure of working for Disney and he emigrated to Ibiza, an
island in the Mediterranean Sea off the eastern coast of Spain in 1953 to

develop as a fine artist. He moved to London in 1955 to work on his short subject film, *The Little Island* (1958). He established his own studio, Richard Williams Animation, which did a magnificent variety of commercials and film titles and became the standard-bearer for the British commercial animation industry. He created the title sequences for *What's New Pussycat?* (1965), *A Funny Thing Happened on the Way to the Forum* (1966), *Casino Royale* (1967), *The Charge of the Light Brigade* (1968), *The Return of the Pink Panther* (1975), and *The Pink Panther Strikes Again* (1976). He won an Oscar for his direction of *A Christmas Carol* (1971), a co-production with Chuck Jones. He directed *Raggedy Ann & Andy: A Musical Adventure* in 1977 and *Ziggy's Gift* in 1982. Eric Goldberg worked with Williams on both films, as did another young New York animator, Tom Sito. Williams also did his own projects, often funding them himself out of the proceeds from his successful commercial enterprises. A short animated film, *Love Me, Love Me, Love Me*, was released in 1962. Then follows the long saga associated with the making of the film *The Thief and the Cobbler*. It is the subject of a number of documentary films, including *Persistence of Vision* (Kevin Schreck, 2012). *The Thief and the Cobbler* was worked on, off-and-on, for over twenty years. In the course of making the film, Williams brought such veteran animation greats as Grim Natwick, Ken Harris, and Art Babbitt over to his studio in London to work on the film and to give seminars for the improvement of the skills of his animators. Williams was on a quest for his own mastery of the medium, and in spite of his stellar reputation as an animator, he was the most attentive pupil in the seminars. Williams worked away on *The Thief* between projects, and many of his employees would be given scenes during the occasional downtime. Roy Naisbitt, a master of complex layout, worked at Richard Williams Animation and designed inspired and spectacular sequences for the film.

In spite of the level of recognition Williams was receiving in Europe, he was not on the radar in the live-action film community in Hollywood—but, two coincidences would conspire to change that. Watts had known of Spielberg's interest in animation and brought a reel of *The Thief* to Spielberg at Amblin.[29] Frank Marshall had been in London with the Amblin production *Empire of the Sun* and saw Richard Williams's television commercial for Foster's Long Life Beer. It featured a character called the Long Life Cat, who used up its nine lives in a series of attempts to get a taste of Foster's Long Life beer reminiscent of Sylvester the Cat's attempts to get Tweety in the Warner Bros. cartoons. But, the gags were zanier—like in Tex Avery's *King-Size Canary* (MGM, 1947). It was done in exactly the style that had been discussed at Amblin and Marshall came back to Los Angeles to report his finding. Both Marshall and Watts showed up at Amblin simultaneously and it all fell together that same day. As Marshall said, "It was very weird."[30] In later years, after Williams had lost control of *The Thief and the Cobbler* to a completion bond company, he would say, "People see my good work and see it's too far out, but they see my junk and want big money projects. It was more the commercials—the well-done trash."[31]

Zemeckis flew to London to meet Williams in March 1986. They met at St. James's Club, a *pied-à-terre* for celebrities visiting London, and Zemeckis presented the *Roger Rabbit* project. Williams initially turned up his nose at the prospect: "I hate animation with live-action," he said. Zemeckis agreed with him, and they thought about how it could be done in a way that would be satisfying to each of them. Zemeckis said, "This is the guy." Spielberg, also in London on *Empire of the Sun*, joined Zemeckis and Williams later in the day for a brainstorming session. They had found their man and Amblin did not pursue the search process any further.[32] Goldberg was not interviewed during the trip to London.[33]

Watts said, "Dick was the guy they wanted from the time they saw the film [the ten-minute finished reel from *The Thief*]—it was going to be Richard or nothing." Nevertheless, Williams was not yet solidly on board. He visited Hans Bacher in Dussëldorf shortly after and said, "You know, it's a funny thing—these guys from Los Angeles called me and they want me to work on this feature film, but it sounds really weird. It's a crazy story and I have no idea whether I should do it . . . it sounds too crazy. It's a story between a big-boobed blonde and a rabbit."[34] He asked Bacher what he should do, and Bacher told him, "It might help you to finish your own film." They did some doodles and sketches of Jessica.[35]

Andrew Ruhemann, production manager at RWA at the time, remembers that the Foster's Long Life Beer commercial, with its Long Life Cat, got the folks at Amblin very excited. He recalls Williams being "courted," and that the initial contact was made by Spielberg and Watts while Williams was visiting family in Canada. Williams was not excited about the prospect at the start and had to be convinced. In fact, the discussions between Williams and Ruhemann were very animated—as interactions with Williams could sometimes become. Ruhemann convinced Williams that they would be in a better position to make *The Thief* after making a Hollywood picture with Spielberg, and that it may even be made a part of the deal with Amblin/Disney.[36]

Chuck Jones called Williams from California and said, "Take the job. Spielberg is marvelous with his people. You'll get your own movie made. You stupid bastard, take the job!"[37] It was good advice, but others remember

Jones being incensed at not being chosen as the animation director and complaining about it to Spielberg. Jones said, "I'm the one . . . I'm the personality behind the rabbit and all of those characters. I should be directing that film." Of course, the "rabbit" he was talking about was Bugs Bunny, who had only a cameo part in the film; it was consistent with an unfortunate tendency for Jones to coopt and revise animation history, with himself as the central figure. He was asked to consult on the dueling piano sequence, but that did not last long.

Robert Watts spent a lot of time talking to Williams. According to Watts, "the biggest hurdle seemed to be that the involvement of Disney was like 'a swear word' to Dick." Watts promised Williams three things if he did *Roger Rabbit* . . . "You will get *The Thief* made, you will be more famous than you've ever been, and you will win an Academy award." Williams eventually said yes, but Watts was not absolutely correct with one of his promises . . . Williams ended up winning a pair of Academy Awards with *Roger Rabbit*.[38]

Hans Bacher was in the same class at Folkwang School in Essen, Germany, as Andreas Deja. They made commercials in their spare time. While students, Bacher accompanied Deja on a road trip to meet Eric Larson at the Hamburg port-of-call on his North Atlantic vacation cruise. Some time later, they went to London to meet Richard "Dick" Williams—who was the preeminent animator in Europe. He was at his commercial branch-studio in Los Angeles at the time. Later still, they were in Los Angeles and went to see Williams at the studio—only to find that he was at the studio on Soho Square in London. Bacher said to Deja, "I think the guy doesn't exist."[39]

Bacher did not have business cards at the time, so he left a business "poster," with cartoon characters he had created, at each RWA studio location. By 1985, Bacher was working in Dussëldorf at the commercial studio (MadTParty) he had started with Harald Siepermann and Uli Meyer. He had designed a storyboard and character designs for a dog food commercial and was asked who should do the animation. He told the client that nobody could do it as well as Dick Williams. The client called Williams at RWA and, even though Williams had never actually met Bacher, he said, "If Hans is doing the designs, then I'll take the job and I'll come over." The next day, he flew to Dussëldorf and came across the room at the MadTParty offices with an outstretched hand saying, "Hey Hans, finally, great to see you! It's like we've known each other for years."[40] Both of them had major collections of Disney animation art and lots to talk about.

In the early spring of 1986, Bacher traveled to London. He would usually drop by the RWA studio to say hello to Dick and see what he was up to. Bacher went straight from the airport to the thin, green three-story house/

studio at 13 Soho Square. He saw a string of black Bentley limousines, each with a burly chauffeur and many parking tickets, standing by the curb. The secretary told him that Dick would be tied up for a couple of more hours in a meeting with some very important people and that he should maybe walk about in the city. Bacher had nothing special to do and lots to read, so he waited at the studio. After about forty-five minutes, the conference room door opened and Dick came out. He said, "Hey, what are you doing here? You don't have to sit down there—come in, come in!"[41] (A funny thing with *anybody* relating a "Dick" story is that the story is *always* told with an animated, enthusiastic "Dick" voice impression.)

Inside, the conference room was dark, and it took a while for Bacher to see anything. They had been watching some slides or a film and, as his eyes adjusted, the first thing he saw was a lot of people spread throughout the room. A person nearby said, "Here, have a chicken sandwich." Bacher looked around and took the proffered sandwich, and only then recognized that it was Steven Spielberg, sitting on the carpet. Bacher later said, "I thought—something is very strange here. Thank God I didn't see anything when I first entered the room. I would have had a heart attack."[42] "Everybody who was anybody" in the film business was seemingly inside the conference room. Bacher recognized Spielberg, Zemeckis, Watts, Kennedy, and Marshall. Andrew Ruhemann was also in that meeting.[43] They had been discussing the *Roger Rabbit* project and how to go about doing it. It was a "pre-presentation" of the steps that would be required to make the production. Bacher says that being part of that meeting was a stunning experience. He sat on the carpet beside Spielberg, finding him to be very approachable and down-to-earth. They determined quickly that they were both animation art collectors, and Bacher even showed Spielberg the *Alfred J. Kwak* comic strip that he and Siepermann had been developing. Spielberg thought that the "camera angles" they were using were wonderful.[44]

Williams invited Bacher to stay over at his house in Hampstead, in the borough of Camden in inner London, and said that he wanted Bacher to become his assistant for the *Roger Rabbit* project. Bacher was trained as an illustrator and designer, not as an animator. Williams said, "Don't worry, I'll teach you everything I know and you'll be good enough. It doesn't matter—I just want to work with you." He gave Bacher some of his rough drawings and told him to do some clean-ups with nice, precise lines. Mo Sutton, whom Williams would later marry, sat there, and Williams practiced playing his coronet, while Bacher did some clean-up drawings. Williams looked at them and said, "Great—you're hired!"[45] It was not until about a year later that Bacher actually became involved, again, with *Roger*

Rabbit. There was still a lot to do at Amblin to get the film ready for production. One of the first orders of business was to prove that they could
actually suspend disbelief with the interaction of toons in the real world.

There were several sessions similar to the one Hans Bacher walked in
on at 13 Soho Square. The sessions, held at both 13 Soho Square and at
Amblin, were where the story and techniques were hammered out—at
least sufficiently to develop budgets. For live-action films, the script dic-
tates the budget. Peter Seaman and Jeffrey Price had researched Tex Avery
cartoons and cataloged Tex Avery gags when developing the early *Roger
Rabbit* script in 1982. Although that style did not match the sensibility of
Darrell Van Citters and the others in the early Disney development unit,
it was how Zemeckis connected with the material. Amblin hired Seaman
and Price to develop a new script that would better play to the need for
interactivity between the toon world and the human world. In the early
versions, Jessica Rabbit was the villain who framed Roger Rabbit. A new
villain, Judge Doom, was created, providing more comic possibilities and
ultimately enabling the storybook ending. Nevertheless, they did not start
off with a blank page. They utilized the introductory cartoon, which is
critical to demonstrating the toon vocation of acting in animated films and
establishing the central conceit of toons interacting in the human world.
Toontown figured in the screenplays of both Seaman and Price and Ganz
and Mandel. Certain elements, such as the tunnel entrance to Toontown
and the nightclub, with its octopus waiter, were borrowed from the Ganz
and Mandel script. The premise for how toons would interact in the human
world was well understood, but Toontown and the way in which humans
would interact in the toon world had not yet been well-defined.

Mike Peraza had been in the second character animation class at CalArts, with Tim Burton, Chris Buck, and Mike Giaimo. He spent two years
at CalArts and was then hired by Disney. Ken O'Connor, a longtime Disney
layout artist, was an instructor at CalArts. Don Griffith, at Disney, wanted
Peraza in Layout, and Vance Gerry wanted him in Story. Peraza was an
excellent and flexible draughtsman, and his career at Disney included stints
in Story, Layout, Art Design, and being brought in on a freelance basis for
his cross-disciplinary talents.[46]

Darrell Van Citters had shown Peraza what the *Roger Rabbit* development unit was up to in the early days. Peraza was working with the nascent Disney Television Animation division on the *DuckTales* concept and
development when he was called by Don Hahn to work at Amblin on *Roger
Rabbit* with Bob Zemeckis. He would work as an Amblin employee from 9
a.m. to noon, then he would go the Disney Television Animation offices on

Cahuenga Boulevard in the Toluca Lake area of North Hollywood, to work on *DuckTales* from 1 until 5 p.m. At night, he was beginning the early stages of art direction for *The Little Mermaid*. He worked in this way for a couple of weeks, until Peter Schneider told him that he was needed full-time on *The Little Mermaid*. During his time at Amblin, he did concept sketches for Toontown, with the guidance from Zemeckis being to develop as many gags as possible. This was late 1985—probably, December.[47]

Joe Ranft and Mark Kausler were already at Amblin.[48] Ranft had arrived at Amblin first, Hahn having offered a return to the Disney fold after Ranft had taken a break to work on *The Brave Little Toaster* with Jerry Rees in Taiwan. Ranft and Kausler were hired by Amblin and worked in a trailer located just outside Zemeckis's office window in the Amblin complex on the Universal lot. The live-action storyboard crew (David Russell and Marty Kline) were housed in an adjacent trailer. The task Zemeckis gave to Ranft and Kausler was to develop storyboards and gags for the Toontown sequence. Zemeckis wanted a faster, almost frantic, pace—the opposite of the more sophisticated tone that Van Citters had preferred. Ranft had a longstanding friendship and working relationship with Van Citters, but it became estranged when Ranft chose to continue on the *Roger Rabbit* project under the new leadership at Amblin.[49]

Ranft said, "We were doing stuff that was character-oriented and kind of tame—'Oh, what's Roger thinking and feeling?' Zemeckis looked at it, laughed, but said, 'Now fuck the rabbit up! Keep him in the air. You want to beat him up and. . . . ' It was like . . . 'Yessss! And we just went crazy! Violence for its own sake!'"[50] Live-action storyboarding involves solving logistical problems for the director—like, determining how many camera setups are needed and can be budgeted for. Animation storyboards reveal the characters and the opportunities for gags. As Vance Gerry, the noted Disney story man said, "We're looking for gold." Another objective was to work out the preproduction details for the "practical" props for which mechanical effects would have to be devised.[51]

Ranft and Kausler boarded the dueling pianos scene for the Ink and Paint Club sequence. They had a lot of interaction with Zemeckis. Zemeckis had hired Chuck Jones for consultation on the scene, but then fired him because Jones was making the scene so slow and labored. He wanted Ranft and Kausler to speed the scene up.[52]

Seaman and Price did not appreciate others encroaching on their "story territory," since Ranft and Kausler were adding gags and new lines. They complained to Zemeckis. Zemeckis came into Ranft and Kausler's trailer, had a look at the storyboards, laughed, and told them to continue as they were. Ranft and Kausler came up with the booby trap gag.[53]

The script was in a constant state of revision. Almost every day there would be notes from Spielberg and new cameos to be written in as permissions came in for the use of new characters from different studios. But, Zemeckis had little patience for anything that did not directly advance the story. The happenings in Toontown got confused and chaotic. Ranft and Kausler had to do some writing and reorganization to make sense of it and add clarity to what was happening in order to board the Toontown sequence. Some of their material was used.[54] This searching for the story is part of a normal story development process. Ed Catmull, president of Pixar and president of Disney Animation, describes in his book, *Creativity, Inc.*, that, typically ten times the number of storyboard drawings are made than what will eventually describe the film in its final form.[55] Many inspired sequences were (story)boarded but left out of the final script because they did not maintain the pace that Zemeckis was looking for. One of the casualties was the Marvin Acme funeral sequence, boarded by Marty Kline.

The animation budget came out of Disney—through Don Hahn. Don Hahn had started at Disney as age twenty, working in the morgue, now called the Animation Research Library, in the summer while he attended Cal State-Northridge. After graduating and starting full time at Disney, he progressed through the assignments of clean-up artist and rough in-between artist, and he even did a little animation on *Mickey's Christmas Carol* (1983). He followed a career path into production management, becoming an assistant to Woolie Reitherman and then assistant director to Don Bluth in the production of *Pete's Dragon*.[56] In *Mary Poppins*, the Disney Studios had inserted humans into the cartoon world inside of a London sidewalk chalk drawing, but in *Pete's Dragon* an animated dragon, Elliott, interacted with humans in the real world. Hahn worked many ninety-hour work weeks during that production.[57] Peter Schneider had to get up to speed quickly for his discussions and negotiations with Amblin, so he asked, "Okay, who knows about live-action/animation combination movies? Hahn answered, "Well, y'know, I do," so Schneider told Hahn to accompany him. Three weeks later, Hahn was on his way to London to meet Williams and Zemeckis . . . and to start coordinating the animation end of the proof-of-concept test for *Roger Rabbit*.[58] While most of the production managers at the Disney Studios from the pre-Eisner days were quietly shown the door, Hahn found ways to demonstrate his value to the organization—and stay. He was affable, intelligent, creative, unflappable, and tough—but humane. He had an easy rapport with people, and was able to negotiate his way through trying times to what became a long and very successful career as a producer at Disney, including *Beauty and the Beast* (1991), *The Nightmare Before Christmas* (1993), *The Lion King* (1994), *The Hunchback of Notre Dame* (1996), *The Emperor's New Groove* (2000), *Frankenweenie* (2012), and *Maleficent* (2014).

In order for the project to proceed there would need to be a test to demonstrate that toons and humans could interact convincingly in a live-action environment. Such animation had been done, but *Roger Rabbit* would require a level of interaction that had not hitherto been approached. In the earliest proof-of-concept test, Ken Ralston was filmed sitting at a table and arguing—"with an imaginary rabbit." It included little interactive tricks, such as props moving and camera drift.[59] It was judged to be too simple, so Zemeckis decided to really push things. For the next version the live-action filming was done at ILM. It included neon lights, swinging lights, automobile headlights, reflections in glass panes, and reflections in water puddles. The actor in the test film was Joe Pantoliano, who was starring in *The Goonies* and an episode of *Amazing Stories* for Amblin at the time. He would later appear in *Empire of the Sun* (1987), *Midnight Run* (1988), *The Fugitive* (1993) and *U.S. Marshals* (1998), *The Matrix* (1999), *Cats & Dogs* (2001), and *The Sopranos* television series (2001–2004). Roger Rabbit's voice, for the proof-of-concept test, is believed to have been supplied by a longtime friend of Richard Williams who frequently did voice work for the commercials, although a temporary voice for Roger was done at ILM. It is a detail that seems to have faded from the memory of most people involved with the project. The film and field chart were sent to RWA in London.[60]

Chris Knott was an effects animator at the Richard Williams Animation studio. He directed a Kellogg's Tony the Tiger commercial, but found his niche when he started to specialize in visual effects (VFX) work. In 1984, RWA produced several commercial spots for Fanta using Disney characters. In previous live-action/animation combination spots, such as the Kellogg's commercials, the combination was done using an aerial image technique, whereby the live-action film was back-projected as an inter-negative and the animation was shot on top. The final image would be first-generation animation layered onto second-generation live-action. The rostrum camera had to be located in a sterile environment because any dust would show up in the final image. In addition to the loss of image quality, the combination looked false.[61]

Knott had an epiphany: the compositing process could be split to yield a more pleasing result. First, the live-action would be shot with the animation, but with no toplights—to generate a silhouette or black holdout matte. The camera operator would rewind the film and shoot it again, with the animation toplit and with no backlight—to fill in the black holdout with animation. This stage could include percentage exposure runs for shadows. In this refinement, "shadow" mattes would be prepared. As an example, a shadow matte would be included over the live-action frame and shot at 50 percent exposure, then the matte would be removed and the live-action frame shot again at 50 percent exposure. The result would be a fully exposed live-action frame with a semi-transparent "manufactured" shadow. Sculptural "tone" mattes could be used on top of the character animation to achieve a similar effect, resulting in a 3D type of "roundness."[62]

The next step in the evolution of the technique was to use a very fine ground glass filter ("fog filter") to degrade the animation image slightly so that it melded into the live-action in a more pleasing and realistic way. A further step in the evolution was to introduce highlight (or rimlight) mattes.

Exposure tests, called wedge tests, were done for each shot. The camera operator would vary the exposures, densities, and glass qualities and the best settings would be selected for the shot. The Fanta ("Disney character") commercials were done using the new technique and the results were groundbreaking. In another of many coincidences, Steven Spielberg contacted Disney in late 1984 (or early 1985) to be put in touch with RWA so that he could find out how they had achieved the combination effect. In the spring of 1986, Chris Knott was in the same meeting with Spielberg et al into which Hans Bacher had happened. ILM had optical compositing equipment, but had no previous experience with live-action/animation combination effects. Knott would be a key figure in executing the proof-of-concept test.[63]

RWA was extremely busy with commercials at the time that the proof-of-concept test was done. Shelley Page was part of the small RWA team to be involved in the test. They always knew that to make the film being described by Bob Zemeckis, as interpreted by Richard Williams, would be a complex undertaking.[64] The level of complexity that would be involved by not locking down the camera was certainly understood by Richard Williams, but it is uncertain whether Amblin really grasped the complexity for animation or the associated impact on cost and time, and it seems clear that the impact was not realized by those at Disney.

Williams provided the animation for a fifty-second-long scene in which Roger Rabbit follows Eddie Valiant down a flight of stairs into an alleyway. Roger trips and falls into a pile of boxes. He trails Eddie through a water puddle, past a Budweiser neon sign, and behind a window pane—all the while being as nervous and annoying as he could be. Eddie picks Roger up by the neck and places him on top of a trash can; then, headlights turn into the alley, Roger does a wild "Tex Avery" take, and he vanishes stage right. The combination was done using traveling mattes. Shelley Page did the airbrush shadows and three-way paint split on the animated character (Roger) to mimic the tone mattes that would be used in the film.[65] There were thirty colors used on each cel. Another, shorter-length extension of the test was done with Jessica, using the technique of tonal and shadow mattes that was developed by Knott. Wedge tests were shot at the Peerless Camera Co., an effects house, in London. The artwork, film elements, wedge tests, and exposure sheets were sent to ILM for compositing.[66] RWA also supplied the foley (sounds, such as footsteps) for the test. There was a question about what real-life toons would sound like. Ruhemann was surprised one day to see Nick Fletcher, the RWA editor, on the Soho Square studio stairway, slapping a giant sea bass on the steps.[67] Maybe it was a nod to the Monty Python fish-slapping sketch, but who knew that "fish-slapping" would be the sound of a cartoon rabbit going down a stairway? The test was completed in September 1986, so a lot was riding on its success.

The proof-of-concept test cost $100,000 to make, but when it came back Amblin knew that it had a film to make. Spielberg spoke of seeing the test for the first time as being one of his very few "epiphany" moments.[68]

Zemeckis had seen Charles Fleischer doing a stand-up comedy routine at the Comedy Store in Los Angeles in the early 1980s and had asked him to come in to audition for a part in *Romancing the Stone*.[69] Zemeckis remembered him and Fleischer got a call in early 1986 to voice Roger Rabbit in the screen tests for the part of Eddie Valiant.[70] The cartoon characters that Zemeckis liked the best had speech impediments, so he instructed Fleischer to come up with a speech impediment for Roger Rabbit. ILM had tried to insert a little whistle in Roger's delivery in the postproduction of the proof-of-concept test, but it was not what Zemeckis had in mind. Fleischer came up with the signature stutter . . ."p-p-p-puhleeze."[71] It was also Zemeckis's opinion that toons should talk quickly. He said, "Toons talk fast," and coached Fleischer in keeping up the "velocity" in his voice, as *People* magazine reported in 1988. He was also told to keep a toony quality to the delivery, which is displayed well in the plaintive delivery of Roger's line to Eddie: "*All* the times you pulled my ears."

Fleischer would also provide the voices for Benny the Cab and two of the weasels. There was a very collaborative effort, with Dick Williams, in matching the voice for each weasel with the design. Psycho was a combination of Mickey Mouse and Jack Nicholson, and Greasy was a combination of Peter Lorre and Al Pacino in *Scarface*.[72]

There had been early interest in having Harrison Ford, Paul Newman, Bill Murray, or Jack Nicholson play the part of Eddie Valiant. Fleischer was also involved in the auditions of Ed Harris and James Woods for the part.[73] Many of the actors were unable to convincingly pull off the illusion of connecting with an "Invisible Man" rabbit in the auditions. Bob Hoskins had just completed *Mona Lisa* (1986), for which he received BAFTA and Golden Globe Awards and an Oscar nomination for Best Actor. He had also demonstrated his comedy chops in Terry Gilliam's *Brazil* (1985). He was absolutely convincing in the screen test, and he nailed the tough-guy American accent.[74]

Hoskins's agent warned him not to take the part, saying, "It's a kid's film." Hoskins said, "Other people talk about being on stage with Laurence Olivier; I was going to be on a film with Bugs Bunny, Donald Duck, Mickey Mouse . . . everybody—the Big Boys. I loved it."[75] Hoskins was born in Bury St. Edmunds, in Suffolk, where his mother was living for safety from the London Blitz of World War II, but he was raised in London. He had an interesting coming-of-age, which included a job as a fire-eater in a circus. He spent two years in Syria, living amongst Bedouin tribes, and he spent six months on a kibbutz in Israel. As an actor, he often played an archetypal "Cockney bully hiding a heart of shining gold." He played a sleazy rock 'n' roll artist's agent in the film based on Pink Floyd's album, *The Wall*. In 1987, he signed a "play-or-pay" contract as a last-minute replacement to play Al Capone in *The Untouchables*. Robert De Niro came back on to the project—and Hoskins was sent a check for $200,000 to *not* play Al Capone. Hoskins called Brian De Palma to ask whether there were any other movies that De Palma *did not* want him to be in.[76] Hoskins directed *The Raggedy Rawney*, a World War II gypsy drama that was released in 1988. He was writing the screenplay while he was in San Francisco filming bluescreen Toontown scenes for *Roger Rabbit* at ILM. He has also written plays under the name Robert Williams.[77] He has said of *Roger Rabbit*, "It's the toughest film I've ever done." Nevertheless, he loved making it. He said, "I'm a cartoon nut! I love cartoons. I think they came to the conclusion that I was the most cartoonish person they could think of."

Zemeckis had seen Joanna Cassidy in her role as the lethal snake dancer, Zorah, in Ridley Scott's *Blade Runner* (1982).[78] Cassidy was forty-two at the time of *Who Framed Roger Rabbit*. She had a classic 1940s-style face and sought out the role of Dolores. She was invited to a meeting at the Amblin offices on the Universal lot to read for the part, but did not go through a traditional casting/auditioning process.[79] She was cast as Dolores; Hoskins had already signed on to play Eddie Valiant. She immersed herself in '40s things—right down to using a heavy-duty girdle, typical of that time. She could not keep her normal red hair, which would have competed with Jessica's red hair, so she became a brunette for the part. She did her own make-up, which she patterned after Joan Crawford.[80]

Cassidy was a prankster. She enjoyed playing practical jokes on Christopher Lloyd, who was shy and quiet on the set. He had just finished playing Dr. Emmett Brown in *Back to the Future*. Tim Curry auditioned for the role of Judge Doom, but Eisner, Katzenberg, and Spielberg thought that he would be too scary in the part. Zemeckis wanted villainy and a certain amount of evil, but a cartoony sort of evil; he needed to look no further than Lloyd to play Judge Doom. He had complicated make-up, so he needed to arrive at 4:30–5 a.m. each morning of filming. A mime coach was brought in prior to filming to help the actors deliver the subtle cues for "selling" the interaction with animated characters that were not present on the set.[81]

Now that the cast was assembled, the filmmakers refocused on the preproduction work. Alan Silvestri had provided the music for *Back to the Future* and Zemeckis called on him again, for Roger Rabbit. Silvestri was contacted in October 1986 to pre-score source music cues heard from the band, pianos, and other instruments that are seen on-screen, particularly in the Ink and Paint Club scene. Contrary to the typical situation of writing the film score at the conclusion of the production, the music had to be composed and orchestrated beforehand so that the special mechanical effects could be coordinated with the music during filming. Silvestri worked on *Roger Rabbit* off-and-on for a year and then worked on it full-time in postproduction starting in December 1987, when the rough edit was finished sufficiently for him to begin timing, composing, and recording the original score. He ended up completing his work in early June 1988, just two weeks before the opening date.[82]

It was decided that the film would be shot in 70mm VistaVision in order to minimize image loss, an important consideration with the anticipated multiple levels of optical compositing, and to provide suitable background Kodaliths for the animation that would follow. Ralston, Cundey, and ILM needed to specially modify the bulky VistaVision cameras for the film.[83]

Robert Watts spent the six months prior to shooting traveling back and forth between Los Angeles and London—two weeks in London and two weeks in LA. The plan was to start shooting exteriors in Los Angeles and then finish the shoot at Elstree Studio near London, and preparations were required for both locations. The time frame in LA went from Monday,

December 1, 1986, to December 23, the day before Christmas Eve. The production would then move to London to start filming on Monday, January 5, 1987. There was absolutely no leeway in the schedule. The LA filming was sandwiched tightly between American Thanksgiving and Christmas. Any slippage would mean significant overtime and cost overruns. The budget was already more than Disney cared to tolerate, and Watts knew that early overruns would result in Disney abandoning the picture.[84]

In November 1986, about two weeks before shooting, Zemeckis called his editor, Arthur Schmidt, to say that they were going to Todd-AO to record the voices for the *Somethin's Cookin'* Maroon cartoon that starts the film. Schmidt was present at the recording, and then had to edit the recorded voices for the cartoon equipped only with the script. There was no animatic or storyboard yet, for charting the timing. He called the sound effects editor, Charles Campbell, to supply specific sound effects from his library. Schmidt would be back editing the cartoon in about a year, when they had the final director's cut.[85]

Michael Lantieri had done live-action effects on many films with the Amblin group. Exterior filming was completed in a period of three weeks in December of 1986 in Los Angeles. Most of the exterior street scenes were filmed on Hope Street, in downtown Los Angeles, in the block between Eleventh and Twelfth streets. Many of the buildings were demolished in 2004, but the building used as the exterior for Eddie Valiant's office (1130 Hope Street) still stands as of this writing. The Maroon Cartoon Studio was represented by the former Desilu Studios, at 846 N. Cahuenga Boulevard, in Hollywood. It was built in 1915 on the Metro Pictures backlot. It was purchased by Lucille Ball and Desi Arnaz in 1953 for filming *I Love Lucy* and many other television shows. It has a main gate that seems just right for a fictitious cartoon studio of the 1940s. Other scenes were filmed at the Glendale Viaduct and the North Vermont Canyon Road tunnel entrance in Griffith Park, near the Griffith Park Observatory. Lantieri and his team dressed the building exteriors for the 1940s. They also dressed up buses as Red Car Trolleys and the streets were disguised for streetcar service. Some of these vehicles can still be seen on the backlot tour at Disney's Hollywood Studios theme park in the Walt Disney World Resort in central Florida.

The Benny the Car/weasel chase was done with Hoskins riding on a tricked out all-terrain vehicle. The stunt driver was in a "blind" located behind and under Hoskins's seat. The seat was rigged to move on a track, with a slight delay, when the vehicle stopped and started. The vehicle was capable of driving at forty miles per hour and could turn on a dime. It would be covered, later, by the Benny the Cab animation, but the mechanical sliding effect added to the illusion of a "squash-and-stretch" animated vehicle in the real world. Bob Spurlock worked on the stunt vehicle and the exterior effects as part of Lantieri's team. His work would touch a later aspect of the *Roger Rabbit* story, when his own visual effects company, Stetson Visual Services, made a "miniature" for the animation/live-action transitional element ending of the *Roger Rabbit* short *Trail Mix-Up*, released in 1993.[86]

The first photography involved some random shots in Los Angeles, to be used as props and set dressing during the principal photography. As an example, there was a photo shoot for the Catalina photographs that would later come out of Dolores's camera after Eddie uses it to catch Jessica and Marvin Acme playing pat-a-cake.[87] Principal photography began on December 1, 1986. The first day of shooting was at Desilu for the sequence of Bob Hoskins walking out of the studio after a meeting in R. K. Maroon's office. The first shot showed Hoskins exiting a door and down some steps, where he passed an ostrich and a frog. It was also the first shot on the film to be composited with animation. The second shot to be filmed included *Fantasia* brooms, a pelican on a bicycle, a brush with a hippo, and a "cattle call" of cows. Five thousand feet of effects elements were done in the one shot, and it was one of the last composite shots to be finished on the film. Further filming was done in the Chavez Ravine, where Benny the Cab—after eluding the weasels in an alley—careens on its accordion suspension and makes its getaway on the Glendale Viaduct.

A second unit was on Hope Street and in Griffith Park in Los Angeles. The production took over all of the businesses on the block of Hope Street between Eleventh and Twelfth streets. Watts used a shoe shop as his production office. Halfway through the first day of shooting, Zemeckis turned to Watts and said, "Robert, we're dying on the vine." At the rate they were filming, they were never going to achieve the tight timing required to meet the production budget. Watts could not see a way out—and there was no way to pick up time. As they began to fall behind schedule, Watts knew that they would not complete shooting by Christmas Eve. Even at the beginning of the first day of principal photography, they were $1 million over budget. He knew in his heart that Disney would abandon the film.[88]

And then, as if by divine intervention, Watts got a report back from the Technicolor lab that there was a scratch on a negative from the previous day's shoot. He leapt for joy, knowing that he could get an insurance claim out of the situation. The grounds for the claim would be that they would have to reshoot a day of filming due to the scratch, but would not be able to because of the hard deadline of Christmas. The production plan called for a three-day shooting sequence on Marvin Acme's funeral. Watts's plan was to push that shoot to the back end of the production when Bob Hoskins would be back in San Rafael at ILM to do the Toontown sequences. They would find a suitable graveyard in San Francisco and shoot the Marvin Acme funeral sequence then.[89]

The first person he told was Jeffrey Katzenberg, who said that the funeral scene could just be cut out of the film. Watts then told Zemeckis, who was worried that Disney would just cut out the funeral scene. Watts assured him that it was Spielberg's favorite scene. In the end, the Marvin Acme funeral scene was indeed cut. It was decided that it did not advance the story. It would certainly have been fun! They would have had look-alikes for Hollywood stars such as Clark Gable mixed with toons of the period. Watts says, "It was a bit of frippery. It was natural that it would be cut, especially in light of decisions made later in the production to cut scenes that had already been animated, such as the Pig-Head Scene."[90]

The Acme Funeral (scenes 79 through 91): R. K. Maroon is under surveillance by Eddie Valiant at the Inglewood cemetery during the funeral of Marvin Acme. Acme's casket is carried by Popeye, Bluto, Elmer Fudd, Yosemite Sam, Goofy, Felix the Cat, and Herman, but they all soon become embroiled in a cartoon fight. Yosemite Sam pulls out his guns to stop the fight and hurls the casket into the gravehole, then exhorts Foghorn Leghorn at gunpoint to start the eulogy. The royalty of Hollywood toons and actors would be caught in a variety of crying gags. Humphrey Bogart, Bugs Bunny, Mickey Mouse, and Clark Gable pull up in a roadster with golf clubs in the back. Bugs says, "What's up Doc?" before they drive off. Valiant sees Maroon looking at a photo, then going to confront Jessica. Valiant has a sidekick, Augie, who is to lip-read the argument, but Bugs Bunny and Mickey Mouse have found a spot that unfortunately blocks his view. Jessica concludes the argument with a knee to Maroon's groin, and as Maroon lies crumpled on the ground there is a chorus shriek of, "A GHOST!" as Casper the Friendly Ghost asks, "Will you be my friend?" The crowd instantly vanishes, trampling Maroon on the way out. The final shot would be Valiant saying, "When it comes to funerals, Toons are worse than the Irish!"

The postponement of the Acme Funeral scene gave them three days. Filming in Los Angeles would go on for three weeks, and everybody would be home for Christmas, but then London would be calling . . .

Chapter Three

LONDON CALLING

Live-action filming moved to England in January 1987. This may seem like a curious decision for filming what was a prototypical Los Angeles story, but London was the location of Elstree Studios, a favorite shooting location for both George Lucas and Steven Spielberg. Elstree Studios was established in the late 1920s and had become the leading film and television studio complex in the London area. It is located in Borehamwood, almost twelve miles northwest of Camden Town and only twenty minutes by rail from St. Pancras Station. It included all the shops, specialty services, and amenities for modern and technical film production. It is known as the birthplace of *Star Wars*; it is where the trilogies for both *Star Wars* and *Indiana Jones* were filmed. Producer Robert Watts had cut his teeth in Stanley Kubrick's *2001: A Space Odyssey*, which was filmed mostly at the Shepperton Studios, but he was very familiar with Elstree from working on both the *Star Wars* and *Indiana Jones* series. The stages have been transformed into distant planets, fantasy environments (for *Willow* and *Labyrinth*), post-apocalyptic environments (for *The World's End* and *World War Z*), Metropolis (for *Superman*), and a remote hotel in the American wilderness (for *The Shining*). A transformation for a period piece representing Los Angeles was easy. Or, was it?

In order to sell the conceit of toons interacting with humans in a real world, the filmmakers had planned for as many interactions of toons and real props as possible. This included rabbit-foot depressions on the bed mattress when Roger Rabbit is in Eddie Valiant's office/bedroom, as well as real trays for the penguin waiters at the Ink and Paint Club. In most cases, the props were manipulated by puppeteers through the use of wires from above or articulated rods from below. For that reason, the largest set—the Ink and Paint Club—was built six feet above the floor of Stage 3. The engineering aspects of the set were designed by George Gibbs, the in-camera effects supervisor, so that Dave Barclay, chief puppeteer, and his crew could work underneath. Gibbs, Barclay, and Bob Zemeckis would faithfully tell journalists the height of the set above the stage floor during interviews associated with the release of the film in 1988.[1] Invariably, as with a fishing tale, the height grew with the retelling; numerous stories tell of it being elevated by eight feet, the *Newsweek* cover story tells of it being elevated by ten feet,[2] and some stories had it elevated to as much as twelve feet.

The Ink and Paint Club scene was filmed in a single master shot. In order to pull off the shot, seventeen puppeteers performed a highly rehearsed and intricately choreographed *tour de force*. The puppeteers under the set manipulated aluminum rods on the top of which were gimbal mechanisms for controlling the tilt of the trays (which would be carried by penguin waiters when the animation was later added). Slots were cut in the floor of the set and disguised with overlying carpet, also cut, through which the rods would be forced. The puppeteers were coordinated through the use of radio headsets and TV monitors. The trays carried real drink glasses with real liquid. The puppeteers below got wet many times during rehearsal before they perfected the techniques. The octopus bartender was mixing drinks and pouring drinks. Rigs were developed to execute both actions realistically. The cocktail shakers were rigged with elastic above and wires below. The bottles were stabilized in midair with three wires, with which the pouring of the liquid would be controlled. It was no mean feat, since the act of pouring altered the center of gravity of the suspended bottles. The brazen puppeteers even had the temerity to suggest a gag of backing the bottle off . . . for a "long" pour . . . and they pulled it off. Barclay was controlling the rod that carried the drink tray to Hoskins. Although it was not in the script, he had the sudden, funny thought of having actual rocks in the glass. He mentioned it to Zemeckis, who loved the idea and immediately told somebody to go outside the stage building and get some rocks.[3]

Actress Betsy Brantley played the part of Jessica Rabbit, stepping through the choreography for Jessica during filming. She would be drawn over with Jessica by the animators in the next stage of production. A separate pass would be made so that ILM could split-screen the lower two-thirds of Brantley's body and allow the animators to draw the impossibly thin waist of Jessica.[4] In addition to the marionette bottles and rod-and-gimbal trays, the puppeteers manipulated the jazz band instruments in midair—with drumstick movements coordinated to Alan Silvestri's music score. Barclay was hiding behind the bass kick-drum as he manipulated the "floating" drumsticks with wires. The use of bluescreen techniques would have been easier, but the filmmakers wanted to use the real lighting of the scene, and there would have been too much light "spill" from a bluescreen effect. Cinematographer Dean Cundey was a master at lighting the scene to de-emphasize the wires and throwing off the camera focus ever so slightly to make the wires disappear. This was before digital techniques were available to eliminate unwanted intrusions in the frame. Puppeteer hands pinched Marvin Acme's (actor Stubby Kaye) cheeks and buffed his head with his handkerchief. They also manipulated Hoskins's hat and pulled on his necktie, "hand-acting" as the sensuous Jessica Rabbit. A combination of puppetry and mechanical effects was used in the dueling pianos sequence.[5]

Puppetry was used in coordination with in-camera mechanical effects in almost every shot of the film. The surprise meeting of Roger Rabbit and Eddie Valiant in the Murphy bed in Valiant's office was also done in a single master shot. The mattress had cut-outs in the shape of Roger Rabbit and his feet, in strategic locations. The mattress had a tight covering of stretchy Lycra fabric. A foam Roger Rabbit puppet was manipulated by puppeteers under the mattress to mimic Roger under the bedsheet. When Roger and Eddie discover each other and bound up in surprise, rabbit-foot-sized plywood pieces would be pulled down to make a depression in the mattress where Roger was standing.[6] Andreas Deja animated Roger Rabbit in that scene. He was directed to animate Roger, at one point in the scene, at a location slightly different than what had been planned when the live action was shot. He is still bothered to this day, whenever he watches *Who Framed Roger Rabbit*, by the presence of phantom foot depressions in the mattress.[7] The initial intent on the film had been to have one puppeteer on set for several days; instead, a core crew of seven puppeteers was on set for the whole of the three-and-a-half-month shoot, with as many as seventeen puppeteers used on the most complicated shots.

Dave Barclay was the chief puppeteer who, along with Mike Quinn, put the puppeteer crew together. They had previously auditioned for the Henson films, which were also filmed at Elstree Studios. Both of Barclay's parents were puppeteers. He was performing with puppets from the time he was four years old. Barclay had many film and television credits, including work on the *Star Wars* films and with Jim Henson. He performed in the pilot episode of *Spitting Image*, the award-winning British satirical political puppet show that featured caricature puppets of celebrities and politicians. The episode was filmed the day before the first call he received requesting his involvement in *Roger Rabbit*. George Gibbs used to jokingly introduce him on the *Roger Rabbit* set:, "This is Dave Barclay. He's getting me my next Oscar."[8]

Mike Quinn was also a precocious puppeteer. The featured puppeteers on *The Muppet Show*, which was shot at the Elstree television studio stage, would manipulate the puppets and supply the voices for multiple characters. Frank Oz performed Miss Piggy, Fozzie Bear, Sam the Eagle, Animal, and other Muppets. If two or more of those characters had to be on-stage at the same time, another puppeteer would manipulate the secondary character(s), in Oz's style, and Oz would dub in the voice later. Quinn filled in for Oz—at age sixteen. Quinn and Barclay had worked together as Audrey's lips in *The Little Shop of Horrors* (1986); Barclay operated the lower lip and Quinn operated the upper lip. In the filming of *Roger Rabbit*, when Roger Rabbit is squirming under Hoskins's trench coat at the Terminal Bar, Hoskins was equipped with air bags, cables, and other mechanisms for the long shots. For the close-ups, it was Quinn who had his arms stuck up under Hoskins's trench coat for a lower-tech but more realistic movement.[9]

George Gibbs got his start in show business in 1966, as a special effects assistant on Gerry Anderson's science fiction puppet television series *Thunderbirds*. He worked on many films, including a couple from the Pink Panther series, Monty Python's *The Meaning of Life* (1983), *Brazil* (1985), and *Labyrinth* (1986). He had won an Oscar for *Indiana Jones and the Temple of Doom* (1984), but he had also managed to be attached to the problem-plagued film *Ishtar* (1987). Compared to *Ishtar*, *Who Framed Roger Rabbit* was a dream assignment, mostly because of Zemeckis's passion for the film and the clarity with which he communicated his vision. Gibbs ended up with another Oscar.

Gibbs was a freelance special effects expert and was hired by producer Robert Watts to be the in-camera special effects supervisor. He was given a copy of the script and broke down the aspects requiring special effects. He had a crew of six technicians—designing and fabricating robotic arms, with servo motors, and other rigs and effects in anticipation of the production being greenlit. It was a period in which Disney was still hedging, and before the proof-of-concept test had demonstrated that the live-action/animation combination could be rendered appropriately. He says that Warner Bros. was "in the hunt," in case Disney had chosen not to proceed with its involvement.[10]

By the time Disney committed, the release timing was set and the film already had an aggressive production schedule. The live-action had to be shot before the animators could do their magic; therefore, day-shift and night-shift production crews worked throughout the duration of filming. Barry Wilkinson, the props master, tells of needing to fill the Acme Gag Factory with props and stunt boxes that would need a coat of shellac so that they would last through the many takes during which the set would be thrown into disarray or during which Dip would be sprayed. Each night the props and stunt boxes would be removed for drying and refurbishment, and then the set would be redressed for the next day's shooting.[11] The Acme Gag Factory scenes were shot at a former power station near the White City tube station on the central underground line. Scenic artist Ron Punter and a crew of eight or nine painters were kept busy painting props at the White City location. New props were being thought of and introduced all the time. Punter even had to paint the rubbish into which Eddie Valiant was thrown in the set of the alleyway outside of the Ink and Paint Club. Punter painted the kitchen and living room sets used for the transition element from the opening cartoon short. The fridge that fell on Roger Rabbit's head, and the kitchen, had to be painted in a flat, cartoony way to facilitate the audience's acceptance of the transition from cartoon to a real-life film set.[12]

Gibbs's special effects were interesting and varied. He and his crew made many robotic arms, with servo motors, which would manipulate real-life props and would later be painted over with the animated character that would be seen to interact with the real world. They fabricated foam models of all of the animated characters; some would be appropriately sized models with armatures or wire inside, so that they could maintain an "acting" position, or may have just been foam heads for helping the actors to mark sight lines. The scenes would be filmed during run-throughs with the foam stand-ins as guides for the animation crew—both for the lighting and tone mattes, as well as for modeling the change in perspective of the characters as they moved through the scene. There exists, somewhere, the entire *Roger Rabbit* film with the foam stand-ins. The foam stand-ins would often be manipulated by the puppeteers, and Gibbs worked very closely with the puppeteers throughout the production.[13]

Gibbs says that Zemeckis was wonderful to work with and that Zemeckis was very receptive to new ideas put forward by the expert technical staff. A typical exchange would be . . .

GEORGE GIBBS: What if we did *this*?

BOB ZEMECKIS: George, you write it down, and I'll read it and tell you what I think."

    [three or four hours later—a loudspeaker message would say, "George, Bob wants to see you on the set."]

BOB ZEMECKIS: I like your idea, George . . . but what if we do *that*?

. . . and Zemeckis would "plus" Gibbs's idea. Early in the filming, Zemeckis told Gibbs that he wanted a special effect cigar prop that Roger Rabbit would give to Eddie Valiant at the conclusion of the film, to celebrate Eddie having saved Roger and Jessica from Judge Doom. The prop was to be one of Marvin Acme's practical joke gag cigars that would blow up when lit, peeling back like a banana and blackening Hoskins's face in cartoon fashion. Zemeckis would ask, "Hey George, how's the cigar coming along?" throughout the filming, and Gibbs worked away at perfecting the special effect prop. In the end, Zemeckis chose not to use the gag, but Gibbs was surprised to receive a £20,000 bonus check from Amblin that Christmas.[14]

There was only one stunt explosion effect used in *Who Framed Roger Rabbit*; it occurred when Roger came crashing through the speakeasy backroom wall at the Terminal Bar in response to Judge Doom tapping "Shave and a Hair Cut" with his cane. An interesting and unique effect was related to the demise of Judge Doom. He was flattened by a steamroller, after which he re-inflated himself—letting us know that he was himself a toon . . . in fact, the toon who killed Eddie Valiant's brother. A curious coincidence is that later on in the same day that they filmed the steamroller gag for *Who Framed Roger Rabbit*, Gibbs got a call from John Cleese about planning for a steamroller scene in his upcoming film, *A Fish Called Wanda* (1988).[15]

Other than the stages at Elstree, the power house/factory at White City was the primary shooting location. The other film location used in England was the 1930s art deco Grays State Cinema in Grays, Essex. The 2,000-seat theater was the largest single-screen film auditorium operating in Europe in 1987. It was the cinema in which Eddie Valiant and Roger Rabbit hid out during a point in the film. It did not require much in the way of set dressing—nothing like the transformation of the White City building into the Acme Gag Factory.

Ken Ralston was on the set for the entire duration of the live-action filming. He would make sure that the live-action filming would accommodate the animation that was to be done later. He and Zemeckis would go over the shot with cinematographer Dean Cundey to ensure that the shots were framed with sufficient space for the absent toons. The use of the foam stand-ins greatly facilitated this process. One example demonstrating the value of having Ralston on the set is the "I'm not bad, I'm just drawn that way" scene. Zemeckis's original intent was to start the shot over Hoskins's shoulder, with the camera on Jessica. Ralston told Zemeckis that it would not work because Hoskins's back was so hairy that they would not be able to pull black holdout mattes off in front of Jessica for inserting her in the scene. They ended up moving Hoskins over to the side by eight-inches and solving the problem.[16] He says that the crew had a lot of fun during the filming. The *Who Framed Roger Rabbit* team would come out of the screening room each day laughing and giggling. *Willow* started filming at Elstree Studios as the live-action filming for *Roger Rabbit* was winding down. Ralston says that, by comparison, the *Willow* crew would come out of their screening room sad and grumbling.[17] New ideas were being introduced all the time on the *Roger Rabbit* set, and the technical and artistic personnel would rise to the challenge each time.

Sometimes things did not work out quite right, since the scene choreography required the coordination of actors, puppets and props, and mechanical special effects. In one case, during the scene in the Terminal Bar, in which Eddie saves Roger from the Dip and they escape Judge Doom after a dust up with the weasels, a punch was thrown too early (or the table "breakaway" came too late). There was a delay in the actions that had to be reconciled during animation. The animator made the weasel stretch, in a cartoony fashion, after being punched and then breaking the table as he retracted.[18] The prop department made "glassware" for R.K. Maroon's office award case out of toffee glass. The "glass'" shattered when Roger transformed into a steam whistle after taking a drink of whiskey. The prop department also made period beer bottles for the Terminal Bar scenes and did research on American beer bottle labels of the 1940s. They made up photos and newspaper clippings that were strewn across Eddie Valiant's desk and provided a montage that gave us Valiant's background story in a complex camera tracking shot. Nobody thought to get permission to use the masthead of the prominent Los Angeles newspaper that was made up for the scene—and when the newspaper denied permission later on, the complex scene had to be shot again.[19] The newspaper masthead then read *Los Angeles Chronicle*, and the headlines on various front pages were as follows: "Valiant and Valiant Crack Nephew Kidnapping—Donald's Huey, Louie, and Dewey, Returned" and "Goofy Cleared of Spy Charges."

Editor Arthur Schmidt was also on the set every day during filming. He had an editing room at Elstree, where he would put the scenes together immediately after filming. They never used a second camera, so there would be lots of takes, ranging from side angles to medium shots and close-ups. Zemeckis would decide on the camera angles, although Dean Cundey would also provide input. Schmidt completed the editing of a few scenes, and had them in the hands of the animators, while shooting was still going on at Elstree.[20] The editing was difficult because he and Zemeckis could not just string the best performance takes together, since they had only one side of the performance; the toons, of course, wouldn't be inserted until later.[21] The balance of the editing was completed in Los Angeles.

Joanna Cassidy reports that, for the actors, filming involved long periods of waiting in the trailers between shots due to the complicated blocking and staging and set-ups.[22]

Charles Fleischer did not just provide the voice for Roger Rabbit and other characters; unusual for a voice actor, he was present on the set for the duration of the principal photography. He projected himself into the "empty space" as he fed his lines from off-camera. He was miffed that all of the other actors on the set had costumes and did not feel right about being there in his street clothes, so he asked the costume designer, Joanna Johnston, to make him a rabbit suit for use during the filming at Elstree Studios.[23] *Superman IV: The Quest for Peace* was the latest installment in the Superman film series, as well as the last to star Christopher Reeve. Its filming was just wrapping at Elstree Studios at the time that *Roger Rabbit* started. There was a pub on site at Elstree Studios, and a *Superman IV* crew member was overheard saying, "I saw that guy playing the rabbit walking around . . . that movie is never going to work."[24] There are many other similar anecdotes about Fleischer's appearance on set.

The story behind *Roger Rabbit* is full of interesting coincidences. Warwick Davis was born in 1970 in Epsom, Surrey. When he was eleven years old, his grandmother heard a radio appeal for people under four-feet tall. Warwick's adult height is three-and-a-half feet. He was called to be an extra, as an ewok, on *Return of the Jedi* (1983). When Kenny Baker, who played R2-D2 and was set to play the lead ewok, fell ill, George Lucas selected Davis to play the role of Wicket. The part of Willow, the title role in *Willow* (1988)—produced by Lucas and directed by Ron Howard—was written specifically for Davis. It started filming at Elstree just as the live-action filming for *Who Framed Roger Rabbit* was wrapping. Prior to the start of filming for *Willow*, and immediately prior to his summer holidays from school, Davis was at Elstree, in the Traffic Department, for his school's work experience. He was assigned, as a runner, to the *Who Framed Roger Rabbit* production. He was an avid rollerskater, and he would rollerskate up and down the long second-floor corridor in the Elstree Studios office building, delivering scripts, paperwork, props, coffee . . . whatever. The part of the job that he liked least was having to photocopy scripts and stamp every page of every script with a unique number, so that they could be tracked if they ever got into the hands of a journalist or anybody outside of the studio. It convinced him that he would prefer a career in front of the camera. Davis got into the studio stages as part of his job and on

one occasion he was asked by Steven Spielberg to play the role of Roger
Rabbit for half of a day. He was the same height as the foam Roger Rabbit stand-in; he could move quickly, especially on his rollerskates; and he
could act, which made for an interesting improvement to the staging and
scene walk-throughs. There were some discussions about his taking on
that assignment, but his work experience period ended and he went on to
other things.[25] Those things have included playing the roles of both Prof.
Flitwick and Griphook in the *Harry Potter* series of films and Marvin, the
Paranoid Android, in the 2005 film version of *The Hitchhiker's Guide to the
Galaxy*. His resumé is long and interesting. He has proven to be a wonderful
comic actor, starring in a mockumentary television series, *Life's Too Short*
(2011–13), and number of projects with Ricky Gervais, including *An Idiot
Abroad*, with Karl Pilkington.

Eye contact between the actors and toons was necessary to cement the
conceit of the toon/human interaction. A mime technician was on the set
to help the actors with the difficult task of playing to an empty space. Bob
Hoskins won the role on his ability to convey this conceit during his screen
test, and he won the plaudits of his colleagues and crew throughout the
filming. His daughter was three years old at the time and he studied the
way she talked and played with her imaginary friends. Ralston says that
Hoskins was the main reason that the effects worked so well.[26] Hoskins
interacted with imaginary characters almost sixteen hours a day for over
four months and got to the point where he was hallucinating . . . and seeing
imaginary toons for real. He had to take some downtime at the conclusion
of filming to get himself back to normal. Everybody he worked with on the
crew tells of his good humor and willingness to do almost anything as part
of the team effort of filmmaking. Gibbs says that Hoskins was fabulous on
the set.[27] Barclay also says that Hoskins was fantastic. Even in a rare fit of
pique, Hoskins demonstrated his good humor. He had all kinds of cues,
and sometimes it got to be a bit much; Barclay heard him say, "Well, if you
stick a broom up my ass, I can sweep the floor at the same time you have
me doing these other things."[28] Says Hoskins, "We had to work as a team
and that's what I really liked about this picture."[29]

Zemeckis's passion for the film was contagious, and he had the ability
to make people feel good about their contributions. He also made sure
that they had fun on the set and he did not mind having a little fun with
the studio bosses. He knew that Michael Eisner had had a falling out with
director Joel Silver, so they arranged for Silver to play the cameo role of
Raoul J. Raoul, the director of the opening short, *Somethin's Cookin'*. Eisner
was not aware of it until he saw the rushes. He later admitted, "He did a

pretty good job." Robert Watts said, "Of all the films I've done, this was the most difficult. I asked myself periodically, 'If you'd known it was going to be this difficult, would you have done it?' And I always said, 'Yes, because I think in the end it is unique.'"[30]

Filming at Elstree was completed at the end of April 1987, a couple of weeks behind schedule. A few extra pickups shots were added in December 1987; a street scene was filmed in Oakland, California, at a location nearly matching the earlier shooting location on Hope Street in Los Angeles. It was the scene in which Dolores and Eddie run out of his office after Dolores catches him with Jessica. They run out to the street, where Eddie says, "I think I have a lead to wrap up this case, and when it's finished, you're going to Catalina." The film cuts to a new camera angle, with a nondescript street view in the background, and Dolores adds some more plot detail about Cloverleaf being the syndicate that is buying the Red Car trolley service. It was a plot detail that had evolved in the script, even as the live action was being filmed in London. They also filmed another scene inside an art deco theater in California, which ended up being deleted from the film.[31]

Chapter Four

ANIMATION–THE FORUM

Moving to the Forum

Richard Williams had been selected as the director of animation, and Disney assumed that the animation would be done under its management and in its facilities, but Williams had avoided the temptation of working at Disney early in his career and he would not be lured into it now. In spite of his idolization of Milt Kahl, as an animator, he did not have a high opinion of Disney animation in general—and not just because of its decades in the doldrums. Amblin thought that it might set up the animation crew at Warner Bros., or on the Universal lot, but Williams was adamant about the animation being done in London. Amblin was planning to use Elstree Studios for the live-action filming anyway, and the company was already working on *Empire of the Sun* in the United Kingdom, so it had no issues in granting Williams's wishes.

Beyond any reasons associated with artistic sensibility, production in London made terrific financial sense when viewed through the lens of a financial controller in early 1986, when Amblin took control of the project. Before 1970, the currency exchange rate was about $2.80 (US) to the British Pound Sterling (£). The exchange rate had decreased to about $2.40/£ in the early 1980s. By early 1986, the US dollar and the pound were almost at par. The production in England was budgeted at $1.34/£, so setting up a new animation production unit in London was an easy accommodation to make. It would later come back to bite them; the dollar dropped in value against the pound throughout the production, and by October 1987, the exchange rate was about $1.80/£ . . . on the way to over $2/£ before the end of the production.

Richard Williams was born in Toronto, Canada. He had an early interest and precocious skill in animation, but wanted to develop himself as a

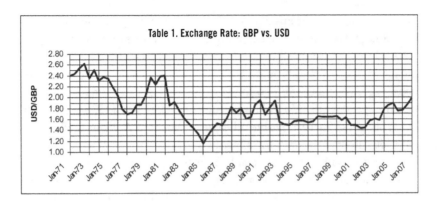

Table 1. Exchange Rate: GBP vs. USD

fine artist and emigrated to an island off the coast of Spain to pursue his dream. He moved to London in 1955 to establish his own studio, Richard Williams Animation (RWA), which produced a wide variety of commercials and film titles, becoming the standard-bearer for the British commercial animation industry. He also began the practice he was to follow his whole career: self-financing his artistic projects with the earnings from his successful commercial enterprise. He won the BAFTA Award for animated film in 1958 for his short subject film, *The Little Island*. A short animated film, *Love Me, Love Me, Love Me*, was released in 1962. He won an Oscar for his direction of *A Christmas Carol* (1971), a co-production with Chuck Jones. *The Thief and the Cobbler* was worked on, off-and-on, for over twenty years. Williams was on a quest for mastery of the medium.

RWA was located in a thin green three-story building at 13 Soho Square in the heart of London's bohemian district. The 1986 Richard Williams Animation Christmas card was painted by Errol Le Cain. It was a magnificently large fold-out card announcing that as of March 1, 1987, they were "vanishing temporarily into Walt Disney productions at 'THE FORUM' Camden Town . . ." There were usually thirty to forty people working at RWA, but forty-seven people were shown in the Christmas card as caricatures in the windows of 13 Soho Square—not including the resident Soho Square cat.

Many of those people had been with Williams for a long time. Roy Naisbitt joined RWA in 1968 after having worked on Stanley Kubrick's *2001: A Space Odyssey* with Douglas Trumbull. He worked with Williams for over twenty-five years. There is a strong sense of respect and devotion between the two men, but as Naisbitt says, "It wasn't difficult to fall out with Dick." Naisbitt's specialty was technical animation and layout. Chris Knott started at RWA in 1970 after working for a couple of years at Halas and Batchelor. He started in the Trace and Paint Department, run by Barbara McCormack,

before moving into animation and finally specializing in effects animation. Russell Hall received art training at Leeds College prior to starting at
RWA. He was apprenticed to Ken Harris, the famous retired Warner Bros.
animator who Williams brought over to London to develop the skills of the
artists at RWA and to work on *The Thief*. He was a gifted animator and was
becoming a star within RWA, with fully one-third of the RWA showreel
being his work.[1] These longtime colleagues of Richard Williams (and others
who you can read about in the appendix) became the backbone of the the
Disney UK organization responsible for making *Who Framed Roger Rabbit*.

Andrew Ruhemann was twenty-five years old at the time of *Roger Rabbit*. He had been at Richard Williams Animation for a little over a year,
starting out as production manager and then assuming a role as executive
producer at RWA. Williams was at the Los Angeles office of RWA, which
they were in the process of shutting down, at the time Ruhemann took
Amblin's first call to RWA in London. He had to exhort Williams into accepting the assignment.[2]

In early 1986, both Williams and Simon Wells were working late at the
studio to meet a deadline on a commercial using a technique of drawing directly on the cel with a dipped pen when the telephone rang. Wells
answered and was astounded to find himself speaking with Chuck Jones.
Regardless of whether Jones's ambitions had been to direct *Roger Rabbit*
himself, he eventually told Spielberg that the only person capable of doing
justice to the animation aspect of the film would be Richard Williams. He
told Spielberg that Williams was fearless when it came to tackling tough
assignments. In the phone call, Wells could overhear Jones first imploring,
then cajoling, and then shouting at Williams to accept the assignment.[3]

Soon after, Spielberg and Zemeckis visited the studio on Soho Square.
In order to reach the boardroom, one had to pass a wall-sized display case
filled with the many awards RWA had won. It was meant to impress. As
they passed the display case, Spielberg and Zemeckis quipped that the
only award Williams did not have was an Oscar—before they looked down
in the corner and saw the Oscar Williams had won for *A Christmas Carol*.
That silenced them; this occurred before either of them had won their
first Oscars.[4]

Ruhemann was deeply involved with the negotiations between RWA
and Disney/Amblin. The arrangement was that Disney would establish a
new company, Walt Disney Animation UK Limited, which would take over
Williams's studio in London. The corresponding Amblin Entertainment
company, established for the *Roger Rabbit* production, was Toontown Limited. RWA was not just giving up assets and employees; Richard Williams

had established considerable goodwill within the European commercial animation community and the value of that goodwill was a key part of the negotiations. Williams intended to establish a new, smaller studio near the Disney UK location in order to continue work on the *The Thief* project.

The RWA employees would be transferred to the new entity on a secondment basis. Although all of the RWA employees assumed they would have a job on *Roger Rabbit*, not all of them were made offers.[5] Individual interviews and negotiations were conducted with Don Hahn, who had set up shop in the offices of 20th Century Fox on the opposite side of Soho Square.

Three RWA animators were not carried over on to the production of *Roger Rabbit*. Franchetti found out that she was pregnant near the same time as the plans for *Roger Rabbit* were revealed. She determined that she could not maintain the same torrid pace while pregnant and, consequently, did not take the offer to join Disney UK.[6] Williams told Hahn that he did not want Vincent Woodcock working on the picture. Work on *Roger Rabbit* began while the RWA team was still at Soho Square. Williams had given Woodcock a brief for the animated title of the Maroon cartoon. There was a lot on Williams's mind regarding the sale of his studio, so he was happy to entrust the initial work on the film to somebody he felt he could trust. Woodcock felt that he could improve on the title animation . . . and did not follow the brief. It was a sure way to catch the ire of Dick Williams. Woodcock was also a talented caricaturist and circulated a caricature he had done of Williams, looking scattered and disheveled . . . with his hair astray and the tag on his jumper (sweater) sticking out. When Williams saw the caricature, his face drained of its normal animation. Woodcock had taken too many liberties.

Vincent Woodcock and Clive Pallant eventually set up their own studio, called Illusion Animation, and started producing commercials primarily for the French market, where they had made agency connections while at RWA. They tried to develop an animated feature film of their own; an adaptation of Ray Bradbury's *The Halloween Tree*, but eventually contracted with Walt Disney Television Animation to set up DisneyToon Studio in Acton and were sequence directors on *DuckTales the Movie: Treasure of the Lost Lamp*.[7]

Max Howard was a child actor who switched to stage management and directing live theater. In 1981, Howard was in London managing *The Sound of Music* stage revival and Peter Schneider was in London as the stage manager with *One More Time*. Both productions were mounted by the same company, so Howard and Schneider got to know each other well. When it became clear that the animation for *Roger Rabbit* would be produced in London, Schneider called his friend there. Howard was interviewed by Dick Williams and, as he was waiting for the interview, was witness to Williams blowing up at Robert Watts.[8] Howard started in November 1986—his first days in Animation were spent with Sandy Rabins. She had moved from Paramount to Disney and was responsible for setting up the production subsidiary, Walt Disney Animation UK Limited. She would go on to become senior vice president of production and finance at Disney's Buena Vista Pictures before moving with Katzenberg to build the animation division of DreamWorks SKG and then becoming senior executive vice president of Sony Pictures Animation. At that time, though, Rabins worked for Marty Katz, who was executive vice president—at Disney—reporting to Jeffrey Katzenberg.

Williams treated Howard as an outsider throughout the production of *Who Framed Roger Rabbit*, but they developed a mutual respect and friendship over the course of the production. In a similar vein, Schneider didn't really know Don Hahn at this stage, and Howard was his eyes and ears in London at the start. But they were all professionals and soon learned each other's special skills and evolved to function as an effective management team. 20th Century Fox was the distributor for Disney's home video business in Europe, and Hahn was in the 20th Century Fox office at 31 Soho Square when Howard started working for Disney. Howard was there for his first two weeks with Disney.

RWA gave notice to terminate the lease on its location at 13 Soho Square, and a search was conducted for larger facilities suitable for the production. They found the Forum building in Camden Town using Allsop Estate Agents, whose offices were at 27 Soho Square—across Soho Square from Richard Williams Animation at 13 Soho Square.[9] There was no real role for Ruhemann once Don Hahn got involved in the *Roger Rabbit* project and arrived in London. He was not ready to be running around with a clipboard and looking over everybody's shoulders. Ruhemann spent about six months with the new organization, helping to organize the move to the new location in Camden Town, an area of central London northeast of Regent Park. He had spent almost a year on preproduction activities related to *Roger Rabbit* before he left Disney UK to run the new RWA studio at 138 Royal College Street, also in Camden Town.[10]

The Forum is located at 74–80 Camden Street in the Borough of Camden, otherwise known as Camden Town, in central London. It is a five-story Edwardian-era warehouse/office building with good access to tube stations and nearby residential areas. The studio eventually expanded to the third, fourth, and fifth floors of the building. Contracts were let to prepare the building and to build the specially designed animation desks. The RWA staff moved over from Soho Square and got themselves organized in their new digs. The Amblin production/financial controller, Bonne Radford, spent some time in the building, but soon took up residence in offices at Elstree Studios for the duration of the shoot.

Patsy de Lord took over from Andrew Ruhemann as the production manager at the Forum. Williams was suspicious of her being a Disney spy at the start. She had worked at ATV, for Sir Lew Grade, on *The Muppet Show* television series and she was the assistant to Jim Henson on *The Great Muppet Caper* and *The Dark Crystal*. She reported to both Don Hahn and Max Howard.[11]

The assistant production manager was Ian Cook, who had worked in that capacity at RWA for many years. It was the job of Cook and de Lord to keep the work flowing along the production pipeline. Their job was made very difficult by Richard Williams, who willfully disregarded the fast-approaching deadlines and the imperative to keep work moving. His focus was on quality, as the production manager's focus was on effective and efficient use of resources. Production oversight was often required in a "standing-over-the-shoulder-tapping-a-foot" manner that grated on artistic temperament, and Cook and de Lord occasionally had to play good cop/bad cop to coerce key animation required to keep the downstream production process effectively utilized. North American management was alarmed by the rapidly rising costs and rate at which the production was falling behind schedule. The whole thing may have come unraveled if it was not for the quiet and imperturbable presence of Don Hahn, who somehow managed to reconcile the artistic and financial aspects of the production and found ways of motivating people and gaining their respect. So started the production of animation for *Who Framed Roger Rabbit* at the Forum in Camden Town.

The Elvin family has a rich film pedigree, which was further enriched with the participation of Annie Elvin and her sons, Martin and Harry, on *Roger Rabbit*. Annie's father was a film editor at Gainsborough Studios and her husband had worked in the live-action film industry in Britain. Annie started as an actress. She had worked with Bob Hoskins in the theater. She also did voice-acting, but got her start in animation at the Larkins Studio. Over the years she had done the odd bit of Trace and Paint (the term often used for "Ink and Paint" in the UK) work at RWA. Annie started her own animation service company, doing mostly trace and paint work, in the early 1980s—Wicked Witch Studio was started on Halloween Day. A friend in the industry told her about Disney looking for somebody in the Matte and Roto group and she applied. She went to Camden Town to meet Don Hahn, who had already picked someone else to supervise the department but realized immediately that Annie had more experience. He selected Annie to replace the other person, who it turns out did not have the experience she claimed. Annie closed Wicked Witch down for the duration of the production, although it was reactivated for a time to handle some of the excess work towards the end of production.[12] Annie started on *Roger Rabbit* in April 1987 and began building and training the department.[13]

A number of senior RWA staff never signed the Disney contract, which ran twenty-six pages and included clauses that asserted Disney ownership of their work and ideas "throughout the known universe." Shelley Page and Chris Knott did not want to be "owned" by Disney. Page continued to do freelance work during the production of *Roger Rabbit*. Patsy de Lord had the task of going around on a regular basis throughout the production in an attempt to get them to sign their contracts.[14]

Ruhemann found Disney UK to be very corporate, with clocking-in and clocking-out. An early Walt Disney Animation UK office manual showed the following personnel under a *Who's Who* page:

Directors: Massimo Graziosi, Don Hahn, Harold Ross, Peter Schneider, Frank G. Wells
General Manager: Max Howard
Production Accountant: Ron McKelvey
P.A. to Hahn/Howard: Vanessa Aistrup
Receptionist: Gilly Fenn
Executive Producers: Steven Spielberg, Frank Marshall, Kathleen Kennedy
Producer: Robert Watts
Director: Robert Zemeckis
Animation Director: Richard Williams
Director of Photography: Dean Cundey
Associate Producer: Don Hahn
Production Manager: Patsy de Lord
Production Coordinators: Ian Cook, for Animation
                          Andrew Ruhemann, for PostProduction
Department Supervisors: Editing—Nick Fletcher
                          Special Effects—Chris Knott
                          Ink and Paint—Barbara McCormack
                          Camera—John Leatherbarrow
                          Matte and Roto—Annie Elvin

During the time that RWA was preparing the proof-of-concept test for Amblin, Ruhemann was the primary contact with ILM and, after the artwork, film, mattes, and exposure instructions were sent to ILM, Ruhemann visited ILM. It is likely for this reason that he is identified as the postproduction coordinator, although Ruhemann never saw the office manual and laughed at the title when told that this was how he had been identified. Ruhemann waited until Patsy de Lord had been installed in the position of production manager at Disney UK and then left to run the "new" Richard Williams Animation studio. He was there for six to twelve months until Mo Sutton, Williams's girlfriend at the time, took over. Andrew Ruhemann became the co-founder of Passion Pictures, a commercial studio that has grown to be a powerhouse in the field of commercials, documentaries, and short films.

Ruhemann is one of the many people who became prominent in the European commercial animation industry after having spent time at Richard Williams Animation. He describes working for Dick Williams as like riding a bucking bronco and that people with personal ambitions generally lasted at RWA for only two or three years before striking out on their own. He describes Dick Williams as an inspirational maverick, but says that he could also be mercurial.[15] That sentiment is expressed by most people who worked for him. They forgave the occasional tirade as part of the price of genius. They were more than rewarded by the training and insight they received from Williams. The RWA employees jokingly called themselves "the Soho Square Moonies."[16] Williams had a way of "love-bombing" you[17] when you first entered his sphere. Within a few weeks, he would go in the opposite direction and tell you that you were a complete waste of space. He would then build you up again, "in his image."

Williams was intoxicatingly enthusiastic and had a great reputation, so he was a terrific "rainmaker" for commercial contracts. He was an inspirational leader, but he was not the best organizer and manager. The processes associated with making small-scale commercials could accommodate his limitations, but the larger productions required organizational and management skills that Williams just did not possess. Williams was a "big picture" guy and sometimes the attention to detail and follow-up of a professional manager were what was called for. There were a few times that RWA was pulled out of the fire by the stalwart seconds-in-command, like Dick Purdum or Eric Goldberg. It could be a source of frustration.[18]

The other factor was that as the students developed mastery, and ego, they inevitably fell from grace. Following the pattern of other animators who aspired to more control and acknowledgment than what was available to them at RWA, Russell Hall left RWA early in 1987 to set up his own company. He was persuaded to work with Williams in the new Disney unit at the Forum and accepted a different contract than those who were seconded from RWA. He was given primary responsibility for the Jessica character.[19] Hall had his own large office in which he worked with his own assistants. It was clear to the others at the Forum that he and Williams often did not get along, but the two of them sort of "agreed to disagree"[20] and put their energies into this special project.

The list of animators who started their own studios after working with Dick Williams includes, but is not limited to: Dino Athanassiou (Stardust Pictures), Chuck Gammage (Chuck Gammage Animation), Eric Goldberg (Pizazz Pictures), Russell Hall (Russell Hall Films), Uli Meyer (Ulimation, Amblimation, Uli Meyer Animation), Dick and Jill Purdum (Richard Purdum Productions), Andrew Ruhemann (Passion Pictures), Rob Stevenhagen (Stardust Pictures, Pencil Pictures), and Tony White (Animus Productions).

Shelley Page was given a battlefield promotion to producer about a year before *Roger Rabbit* came into the picture. She was given the job of keeping the ninety-second Long Life Beer commercial, which was key to bringing RWA to the attention of Amblin, afloat while Williams was off doing other things. Desperate deadlines were a fact of life at RWA, and Williams joked that Page's special talent was that she did not seem to need sleep. She countered: "It's not that I don't need sleep, it's just that you never give me a chance to get any sleep." She went ten nights without sleep during the production of a commercial at RWA.[21] Nevertheless, Williams had an extraordinary charisma that attracted artists. He would look over their shoulder . . . then there would be an intake of breath . . . followed by silence. The artist would finally look around at Williams and say, "What!" Williams would then say, "Just do it . . . better!" What held the artists to Williams is that they ended up doing better work than they ever thought themselves capable.

There was no denying that the place ran on adrenaline, and that last-minute/all-hands-on-deck sessions lasting through to the next morning were a common occurrence. The thing is . . . it was *all* hands on deck and Williams would be there—doing his finest work. Roy Naisbitt would be there too—not animating, but doing whatever needed being done to help them get through the work, which often might include fetching them a drink or two. There is also no denying that Williams could have his moods. Franchetti had more sympathy for the outbursts after she, herself, fielded phone calls from a number of his ex-wives. Most people at RWA accepted the outbursts and they had a good sense of humor about it. One time,

Williams came into an office to talk to an animator about concerns over his timing on a particular commercial. He went to grab the timing sheet off the animator's desk, but the animator had it under a piece of heavy plastic that was screwed to the top of the desk and Williams was foiled and looked a bit foolish. He flew into a rage and began strangling a nearby desk lamp as he called out the animator's name. The outburst was soon over and he would again be . . . "charming" Dick. They could all laugh about it afterwards. What made it easier was that he was so generous with his talent and advice; he was generous in other ways, too. There are many examples of him keeping people on the payroll for extended periods of time when they were unable to work. It felt like being part of a family—with all the drama that sometimes entails—but at the end of the day they would often all take the ten-minute walk to the Marquess of Anglesay pub in Covent Garden to unwind and share their successes.[22]

Assembling the Crew

Sheridan College, near Toronto, had developed a strong animation program under the guidance of former Disney animator, Bill Matthews, and many of the graduates were working in Los Angeles in the late 1970s. The Motion Picture Screen Cartoonists union called a strike first in 1979 and then again in 1982. The central issue was "runaway production" to subcontracted studios overseas. One of the consequences of the strike was that the US O-1 work permits for Canadian animators were withdrawn and they had to find work elsewhere. Some went back to Canada and set up their own studios that were, in turn, contracted to produce animation for their former Hollywood employers.[23] Some became animation vagabonds, plying their craft around the world.

Chuck Gammage graduated from Sheridan College in 1978 and worked in Toronto at Nelvana. Tom Sito worked there with him during that time. In 1983, Gammage got a call from Roger Chiasson, a Sheridan graduate from the class of 1976, encouraging him to go to London to work on an animated sequence in *Highlander*. He then got a job working on commercials at RWA. Gammage started to work on *Roger Rabbit* while he was with RWA at 13 Soho Square.[24]

Uli Meyer had no formal training in art or animation. He was self-taught, making films as a kid with a Super 8 camera. At age nineteen, he was making £3,000 per week doing storyboards for the live-action film *Enemy Mine* (directed by Wolfgang Petersen, 20th Century Fox, 1985) in

Munich. He came to know Hans Bacher, a professor in Essen, Germany, and Harald Siepermann and worked with them in a co-operative they called MadTParty in Düsseldorf. Bacher had become a professional acquaintance of Richard Williams, a relationship that had been cemented by their mutual love of Milt Kahl's animation and their hobby as animation art collectors. Bacher had been privy to one of the earliest discussions of *Roger Rabbit* in Williams's Soho Square studio and had later extolled the talent of his young colleague. Meyer went to London in late 1986 at Williams's invitation. He was twenty-three years old at the time.[25]

RWA was renting overflow office space across the road from 13 Soho Square, where Uli Meyer, Chuck Gammage, and Bridgette Hartley worked on commercials and where Bacher and Siepermann came to work on *Roger Rabbit* storyboards. In late 1986, Williams sent Meyer to Los Angeles for three months to be trained by Art Babbitt, the former Disney animator who had animated the Chinese Mushroom dance in *Fantasia* and who had spent years working with Williams in London on *The Thief*. Babbitt was an excellent teacher, and Meyer was a quick student. They shared an office, in a suite of offices occupied by Filmfair, a small British animation company. Williams rented the office for Babbitt to work in while he was back in Los Angeles. Uli Meyer stayed with Andreas Deja while he was in Los Angeles. Meyer studied with Babbitt during the day and worked on commercials for RWA in the evenings.[26] When Meyer came back to London in early 1987, he had no place to stay, so he brought a mattress to Soho Square and lived at the studio, sleeping under his desk.[27]

Freelance work on commercials could be quite lucrative—that is, when one was working. When it came time for Uli Meyer to negotiate his contract with Hahn he had the experience of big freelance paydays . . . so the discussion arrived at an agreement of £750 per week, which did not strike Meyer as being excessive. He was young and indiscrete and mentioned his salary to Chuck Gammage, who had much more experience as an animator. It turns out that Gammage was only getting £450 per week and he stormed off angrily to see Hahn. As a consequence, Meyer's salary was reduced to £450 per week.[28]

Roger Chiasson and Rej Bourdages, another Sheridan College graduate, teamed up with Dino Athanassiou while they were all working in the Orient as itinerant animator/trainers. They worked together in the Philippines, setting up a studio for Bill Hanna. Athanassiou had been working in the London animation industry since 1981 and he had worked on *Asterix and Caesar* (1985), but he learned a great deal under the mentorship of Roger Chiasson. When they returned to London, Chuck Gammage snuck

Chiasson and Athanassiou into RWA at 13 Soho Square and showed them the *Roger Rabbit* proof-of-concept test. When Gammage started to work on *Roger Rabbit* while still at Soho Square, he recommended Athanassiou to Richard Williams. Athanassiou started on *Roger Rabbit* at the end of March 1987. He remembers having been working on *Roger Rabbit* for three weeks when Milt Kahl died on April 19, 1987.[29]

Chiasson was working at the Burbank Animation Studio in Sydney, Australia, when he got a call from Gammage about *Roger Rabbit*. It was May 1987. Dick Williams relied on Gammage's recommendation, and confirmation by Oscar Grillo, at Klacto Animation, where Chiasson had worked for a short time, and hired Chiasson. He started on *Roger Rabbit* in July 1987.[30]

Alvaro (Al) Gaivoto graduated from Sheridan College in the same class as Chiasson. He went to London in 1983 and worked as a freelancer, often at Richard Williams Animation. He went to work at the Hibbert/Ralph studio soon after it was established and was anticipating being made a partner, but Ralph blocked it. During a chance meeting with Williams, the two commiserated over their mutual complaints about Ralph. Graham Ralph had worked at RWA, but left with the RWA showreel and used it to get business for the fledgling studio he had started with Jerry Hibbert. Williams wanted Gaivoto to come over to Soho Square to attend the Art Babbitt classes and told him about the *Roger Rabbit* proof-of-concept test. Gaivoto left Hibbert/Ralph, after which Ralph sent Williams a letter saying, "Thank you for taking Al off our hands. Keep him on a short leash . . . he's not to be trusted." Williams asked Gaivoto, "God, are you fucking his wife?" "No," Gaivoto answered, " . . . the guy's a dick!" Williams said, "Do you want this?" and gave Ralph's letter to Gaivoto. Their mutual dislike for Ralph cemented an enduring respect and affection between Gaivoto and Williams. Gaivoto was hired for *Roger Rabbit* early on.[31]

Animators from Disney began to arrive at the Forum in April 1987. Dave "Spaff" Spafford was one of the first animators to be hired. Spaff had left Disney in 1979, along with Bluth, Goldman, Pomeroy, and the other animators. The studio environment that Bluth created was not to Spaff's liking and he left several months into the making of *An American Tail* (1986). He spent some time in Japan, working on *Little Nemo* (1989), and then came back to the US with the intention of doing freelance animation work. He went into Disney to interview for a freelance assignment and was surprised to be offered a full-time job. *Oliver & Company* (1988) was on hold while story issues were being dealt with, so the animators had little to do. Spaff had no seniority and wanted to keep busy in case the executives who now prowled the corridors caught on that nobody in that animation crew was doing any work. There was a rumor circulating in the studio about the *Roger Rabbit* project. Spaff was a big fan of Tex Avery and Warner Bros. cartoons, especially those of Bob Clampett, and was intrigued by what he was hearing about *Roger Rabbit*, so he just "assigned himself" to *Roger Rabbit*. He got hold of some of the Williams's early designs for the lead characters and busied himself with designing new characters and creating gag and story ideas. He even made maquettes of the lead characters. The walls of his office were plastered with drawings for *Roger Rabbit*. It was reminiscent of the *Seinfeld* episode in which George Constanza interviews for a job, but the interview is terminated abruptly before George knows whether he has been hired or not. Mr. Tuttle had been interrupted by an emergency phone call and had to leave the office. George decides that the best course of action is to just "show up" and pretend that he was hired.[32] Of course, things worked out better for Spaff than they did for George Costanza.

Zemeckis and Williams were visiting the Disney Studios in Burbank and happened to walk past Spaff's open door. Zemeckis had not wanted any of the *Roger Rabbit* animation to be done by Disney, or at Disney, so he was upset at seeing a room full of *Roger Rabbit* artwork and accused Disney of already working on the project. He was finally convinced that Spaff had just done this on his own and that it was not sanctioned—and both Zemeckis and Williams were immediately impressed by his initiative, his moxy, and, of course, his designs.[33] They asked whether he wanted to work on *Roger Rabbit* and then asked whether he would consider going to England. Spaff's answer was: "Are you kidding me?" Williams asked to see Spaff's portfolio. Spaff photocopied stacks of $20 bills and colored them with pencil. When Williams and Zemeckis opened his portfolio and the fake money fell out, they laughed and offered him the job.[34]

Williams had not met Andreas Deja yet and Bacher pushed for him. Deja was initially hesitant about leaving Los Angeles for England since he had come from Europe only a few years prior. He was making a name for himself within Disney and within the animation community in Los Angeles, but, ultimately, he could not pass up the opportunity to work with Williams and Zemeckis on a project that was already developing a mystique. He signed on for London.

Phil Nibbelink had started at Disney in 1978, in the same training class as John Lasseter and Chris Buck. He was made an assisting animator and was assigned to Randy Cartwright's unit. He worked on *The Fox and the Hound* and *The Black Cauldron*, but was in Story on *Oliver & Company* when

Eisner, Wells, and Katzenberg came to Disney. *Oliver & Company* was put on hold when the new management insisted on massive story changes. Nibbelink was disenchanted with the new Disney management at the time that Williams and Zemeckis visited the studio. Nibbelink and Deja were good friends, and Nibbelink let them know of his interest. He had family in England and he was ready for a change.

Nibbelink and Deja were allowed a shipping container for moving their things to England. Nibbelink had a VW camper van, which he crammed with all of his belongings, and drove it down to the Port of Los Angeles and into the shipping container. He even brought along his hand glider. The container was loaded on a ship that traveled to London by way of Cape Horn, at the southern tip of South America, so it was months before they saw their belongings again. Deja and Nibbelink ended up rooming together during the production.[35]

On the first day that Deja walked into the Forum he was handed a stack of photostats printed on orthochromatic Kodalith paper. It was the first scene shot: that of Eddie Valiant coming out from a visit to R. K. Maroon's office. Deja sat down and started animation on the ostrich (from *Fantasia*) and the frog (from *Song of the South*) that Valiant passes on the stairs.

Other animators arrived from all over the world. Alain Costa[36] and Jacques Muller[37] were from France, by way of Australia, and Brenda McKie came directly from Australia. Raul Garcia[38] was from Spain. Rob Stevenhagen[39] and Nicolette Van Gendt[40] were from the Netherlands. Marc Gordon-Bates was born in Wimbeldon (England) and grew up in Paris. His father was from South Africa and, with time spent in South Africa himself, he had a curious accent when speaking English, which was hard to pin down.[41] Philip Scarrold was from Rhodesia (now Zimbabwe).[42] A bunch were from Canada, many graduates of Sheridan College.

Nik Ranieri and Cal Leduc graduated from Sheridan College in 1984. Leduc saw an article in the *Hollywood Reporter* about Disney doing a 1940s film in London. Ranieri had a friend who had gone to Ireland to work at Bluth/Sullivan studio. With *Land Before Time* in production in Dublin and *Roger Rabbit* in London, Ranieri and Leduc decided to go overseas. They flew to Dublin on June 17, 1987. They visited the Bluth studio and were told to come back in three days. They left their reels and portfolios and filled in time in and around Dublin, limited by meager savings. When they returned, they were told that they still could not be seen and to come back in another week. They were asked to leave their reels, but since they had only one copy they took it with them and then left for London—never to return to the Bluth studio.

They went to London and made the rounds of all of the Soho commercial studios. By that time, RWA was no longer on Soho Square. They finally found their way to Richard Williams's new studio at 138 Royal College Street in Camden Town, meeting Andrew Ruhemann. He looked at their portfolios and said, "You look like you have a lot of abilities and your portfolios look good." Then they asked when the studio would be starting on *Roger Rabbit*. Ruhemann said, "Oh, I guess you want the Disney Studio," and directed them the 350 yards to the Forum . . . telling them, "Go over and see Don Hahn." Leduc did an in-between test, after which Hahn hired him. Hahn liked Nik's demo reel and wanted to hire him on the spot, but said he could not because Ranieri was not a British citizen. Ranieri's father worked at the Italian consulate in Toronto, and Nik had an Italian passport. He said, "You know that I'm EC [European Community]," and Hahn replied, "Welcome aboard!"

They were hired at the Disney UK studio on June 24, 1987, with a start date of July 13. They flew back to Canada to pack their things, say their goodbyes, and then flew back to London to look for an affordable place to live. Five months later, Ranieri got a recruiting letter from Sullivan/Bluth . . . asking him to send in his portfolio: they were just a bit late.[43]

It had not taken long after Nik and Cal were hired for Don Hahn to realize that Sheridan College would be a good source for animators who might have visas enabling them to work in London. On the recommendation of Nik and Cal, he contacted Glenn Sylvester, Rej Bourdages, Howy Parkins, and Irene Couloufis (later Irene Parkins). Joe Haidar, a 1982 Sheridan grad, was already in London. After working on a television series, *Raccoons*, at Atkinson Film Arts (also known as Bud Crawley Films) in Ottawa, he went to London and spent four years working freelance at several commercial studios, including Animation Partnership, Pizazz (with Eric Goldberg), and Klacto (with Oscar Grillo). Haidar heard about *Roger Rabbit* through the Soho grapevine and then saw an ad in *Variety*. He met with Don Hahn, who felt that Haidar should come in as an assistant to see "if the cream will rise." Haidar went on a vacation to the Canary Islands in the week before he was to start on *Roger Rabbit* and came back to start as an assistant with Phil Nibbelink.[44]

Word of the growing production in Camden spread through trade paper advertisements and talk in the Soho pubs. Animators Gordon Baker, Caron Creed, Gary Mudd, Alan Simpson, and Mike Swindall joined the crew. Richard Bazley,[45] Stella-Rose Benson,[46] Paul Chung,[47] Elaine Koo,[48] Rob Newman,[49] Silvia Pompei,[50] Bob Wilck, Julia Woolf,[51] and many other artists came on board as assistant animators throughout the production as the crew expanded to handle the vast amount of work required. Chris Knott was quick to identify other talented artists who had the discipline for the exacting work in the Visual Effects Department. Kevin Jon Davies,[52] Chris Jenkins,[53] Fraser MacLean,[54] Tim Sanpher,[55] Mike Smith,[56] and others joined the crew as the production ramped up.

Colin Alexander and Nick Harrop were attending Cornwall College to study scientific and technical graphics and needed to find a summer placement of relevant industrial experience. They headed to London and started to call potential employers. Andrew Ruhemann answered the phone when they reached the "R's," for Richard Williams Animation. He told them that the studio was closed but gave them the number for Walt Disney UK. It was May, and Annie Elvin was desperate to fill the Matte and Roto Department. The scuttlebutt at the Forum was that Matte and Roto had been budgeted for just Annie and one assistant. There ended up being about sixty tracers and painters, working overtime for much of the production—sometimes for as long as eighty-four hours per week.[57]

Stephen Cavalier's experience may have been typical of many of the London artistic contingent that joined the production. He had managed to get a toehold in the London animation industry by working in Paint and Trace on *When the Wind Blows* (1986) and on a freelance basis at some of the commercial studios. He was part of the London subculture of alternative lifestyles/alternative music/alternative art, and had a healthy cynicism and skepticism about politics and big corporations, but he managed to get an interview at the Forum and was blown away when shown some rushes. He was made an offer to work in Matte and Roto and during the production was assured that Disney was establishing this as a permanent studio in London. After existing on the artistic margins of society, this "big corporation" gig seemed pretty good. There was some culture clash between the "alt-creative" kids, the older British, "European art school" animators, and the "old" Disney animators who were brought in, but everybody dug in to get the job done. While the career animators relished the Disney crew jackets, Roger Rabbit alarm clocks, and "We Can Do It" buttons, the cynicism of the alt-creative British youth group kicked in. They would rather have had paid overtime . . . and also the time to spend it at local pubs like the Hawley Arms.[58]

Other support functions needed to be filled by people who were excellent artists in their own right. Tony Clark studied graphic design at Lincoln College of Art. He saw an advertisement for *Roger Rabbit* in the *Guardian* newspaper in August 1987. He rang up the Disney offices at Wardour Street, in Soho, and was directed to the Camden Town studio where he spoke with

Barbara MacCormack, the supervisor of the Ink and Paint Department. A Xerox Department operator had just handed in his notice, so Clark was invited to come to the Forum for an interview. He was interviewed by Maggie Brown, the assistant supervisor of Ink and Paint, and was offered a job on August 31, 1987. He started on *Roger Rabbit* on September 1, 1987, as a Xerox Department operator (aka, post punch assistant).[59]

The production had two Canon photocopy machines equipped with special acetate to avoid wrinkling. The acetates had paper backing to reduce the effect of heat on the cel, but the paper could not stop the cels from expanding with the heat of the machine. The cels had to be allowed to cool down before the peg holes were punched so that the animation drawing would register properly with the cel. If the cels were pegged up when still hot, the peg holes became misaligned with the animation paper holes. In his capacity as Xerox operator, Clark saw the raw animation drawings before they went on to the Ink and Paint Department and saw many of the unauthorized "call-outs" that the animators tried to slip into their drawings. Most of them were purged by the animation checkers or the Ink and Paint Department.

Annie Elvin had a son, Martin, who was hired as a camera operator working under John Leatherbarrow. Leatherbarrow also had his own company, Jigsaw, in the West End that took a hiatus during the production of *Roger Rabbit*—although it, too, was reactivated to handle some of the overflow shots on *Roger Rabbit* elements.

Annie's younger son, Harry, had all of two weeks of work experience when he was hired on to *Roger Rabbit* as a runner when he was fifteen.[60] A runner is an entry position in the film industry, similar to "starting in the mail room." In other places, he might be called a traffic boy . . . or a gofer. Warwick Davis had a short stint as a runner on *Roger Rabbit* during the live-action filming at Elstree. Humphrey, Robert Benchley's overly officious studio tour guide in *The Reluctant Dragon*, was a traffic boy. Burny Mattinson, the animator/storyman who directed and produced *Mickey's Christmas Carol*, started at the Disney Studios as a traffic boy. The runner on the sets at Elstree would take orders from the assistant director and duties included picking up the actors from their homes and dressing rooms, photocopying and distributing the call sheets and amended scripts, getting tea and coffee for the director and crew, getting dinners for the actors, and running errands for the actors and crew. At the Forum, the errand book was kept by Max Howard's office, where duties included picking up art supplies, doing odd jobs for the animators, delivering drawings and materials along the production pipeline, and many other tasks to keep things rolling.

There were three runners at the Forum for most of the production. Harry Elvin was very young and green. Another runner, Frazer Diamond, had been around film studios for much of his life. His father, Peter Diamond, had been the stunt coordinator on the initial trilogy of *Star Wars* films and Frazer and his brother were able to spend a lot of time on the set. He was seven years old in 1976 when the two of them got walk-on parts as Jawas on *Star Wars* (later retitled *Star Wars Episode IV: A New Hope*). Frazer was the little "don't shoot!" Jawa who held a gun on C-3PO. He was about twenty-seven years old when *Who Framed Roger Rabbit* began filming at Elstree. He was employed as one of the seventeen puppeteers in the master Ink and Paint Club shot. A couple of months later he was hired at the Forum as a runner. Toward the end of the production, as deadlines loomed and everybody pitched in to the extent of their capabilities, he even helped with line-testing and cel painting. He "acted" as one of the penguin waiters (or at least as its tray) and also painted some of the shadows and effects on the penguins.[61] In early 1988, Diamond left the production to work for the Monty Python production company, Prominent Features, on *A Fish Called Wanda*. Richard Leon came in to replace him for the balance of the production. He was young and very enthusiastic; he was a big animation fan.[62]

It was in late 1986 that Dick Williams called Hans Bacher in Düsseldorf and said, "You have to come to London—I want you to work on the film." Bacher and Siepermann worked in the RWA overflow offices across Soho Square from RWA when they visited London but they preferred to work in Düsseldorf. They were preparing storyboards for Toontown and designing the weasels and they had the storyboards that had been prepared by Joe Ranft and Mark Kausler.[63] Zemeckis and Williams wanted them "pushed" to a bit more of the Avery or Clampett style. Williams said, "Not funny enough." Arrangements were made to have hundreds of Avery and Clampett shorts sent over from Los Angeles and Bacher and Siepermann studied them. They were working in Düsseldorf and sending their work back to London. It was decided that they needed to hammer out the Toontown portion of the script with the writers, Seaman and Price, so Bacher and Siepermann were told to go to Amblin in Los Angeles. They arrived in Los Angeles on June 11, 1987.

The Amblin complex was built in Mexican hacienda-style. The building in which Zemeckis worked had a sign that read, "We Make Movies While U Wait." Bacher and Siepermann worked in a trailer next to Zemeckis's building for five weeks. They had meetings with Zemeckis, Seaman, and Price every second day. Spielberg took part in the meetings only twice during their five-week stay, but they got a sense of his authority within

Amblin and his power within the Hollywood community. Zemeckis described a sequence idea that sounded like one of Terry Gilliam's Monty Python animations. He wanted to have "the finger of God . . . you know, like Michaelangelo in the Sistine Chapel . . . come down out of the clouds and say something like, 'Damn the weasels,' and then smite them." Bacher thought that Spielberg would caution about whether "smiting" was a good thing to have in the film but, instead, he said, "Oh, I know whose voice that will be . . . Dustin [Hoffman] . . . Dustin will love it!" [64]

Bacher says, "The gags got crazy—too crazy to ever tell!" He says that Seaman and Price were hilarious. Their Toontown sequence storyboards were sufficient for sixty minutes of film time. In the end, only approximately fifty seconds worth of material was used in the film. Two examples will show the creativity of their ideas . . .[65]

Entry into Toontown

Eddie drives into Toontown along a canyon road. The canyon is in the shape of Jessica, and you see this huge "woman" emerge as the camera moves up to show Eddie winding down the cliff face. After Eddie gets down the canyon face, he stops the car and looks up. There is a whistling noise . . . and buildings are falling out of the sky and landing, with a thump, right next to him. One of the buildings is a school house—it just falls from the sky. Then the story starts and the scene is populated by fallen houses . . . birds start singing . . . and a new day begins.

Escape from Toontown

Eddie and Jessica flee Toontown in Benny the Car—they carom into a desert landscape when Casey Jones in a locomotive (from *The Brave Engineer* [1950]) crosses their path and then Mr. Toad (from the "Wind in the Willows" portion of *Ichabod and Mr. Toad* [1949]) crosses their path. As they zoom along a canyon road, they intersect the runaway trailer from *Mickey's Trailer* (1938) and several gags from that short are used. They careen towards a chasm as Pedro, the young mail plane from *Saludos Amigos* (1943), flies towards them. Benny jumps the canyon and Pedro and on the other side becomes caught in a chase with the giant cat and mouse from Tex Avery's *King-Size Canary* (1947), after which Droopy comes hopping along on his little horse—dressed as in *Northwest Hounded Police* (1947). Zeus (from *Fantasia* [1940]) is awoken in the clouds and hurls a lightning bolt at Benny—a near miss. The next bolt is aimed at Ichabod Crane (from *Ichabod and Mr. Toad* [1949]). Eddie is watching Ichabod on his horse and suddenly finds himself driving Benny up the tail of the dragon from *The Reluctant Dragon* [1941]), in a *Lullaby Land* (1933) landscape. The dragon whips them off his tail, sending them over a cliff and plunging into the sea. They surface and are chased by Monstro, the whale from *Pinocchio* (1940). Monstro swallows them, and as the darkness envelopes them—the light of the far end of the Toontown tunnel appears.

The Toontown portion of *Roger Rabbit* was drastically reduced due to time and cost constraints. In the end, the Glendale crew reworked animation straight from the Disney morgue for Eddie's entry to Toontown.

Bacher also designed the film's title logo. The title was not going to remain *Who Censored Roger Rabbit?* And, although it was being called *Who Framed Roger Rabbit* in its early Disney incarnations, Amblin had not settled on a title yet. Bacher did over sixty title designs, with different names and styles.[66] In addition to *Who Framed Roger Rabbit*, proposed titles included *Murder in Toontown*, *The Toontown Trials*, and the curiously named *Dead Toons Don't Pay Bills*.

Things were in full swing at the Forum in Camden Town when Bacher and Siepermann returned to London in the third week of July, 1987. London was working on the opening cartoon at the time.[67]

The animators had been hired, but the production needed assistants and in-betweeners. As the production grew more frenetic, it also needed additional animators. Don Hahn placed advertisements at the Association of Cinematograph Television and Allied Technicians (ACTT), in British trade papers and in international trade papers, such as *Screen International*. He wanted to attract local applicants, but many of the artists hired to the production came from far-flung parts of the world. Each of these animation gypsies took a different journey, and that they should all land as part of Richard Williams's crew on *Who Framed Roger Rabbit* is one of the fascinating and unique aspects of the film.

The United Kingdom had a system of colleges to meet regional needs in much the same way as community colleges in North America. Farnham School of Art was established in 1866, and Guildford School of Art was established in 1870. Farnham and Guildford are only about eleven miles apart in the west part of Surrey, approximately forty miles southwest of London. The colleges merged to form West Surrey College of Art and Design in 1969. In 2005, West Surrey College merged with colleges in Canterbury, Epsom,

Maidstone, and Rochester to form University for the Creative Arts, which was made a degree-granting institution in 2008. But, in 1987, the Farnham campus of West Surrey College of Art and Design was the only school in the UK offering a major in animation. The focus was on experimental animation and the avant-garde—the model being the National Film Board of Canada (with Norman McLaren and Caroline Leaf) and the animation from Yugoslavia. The college had neither the equipment typically used in commercial animation nor any staff with commercial experience.[68]

Neil Boyle and David Bowers were roommates. Boyle and James Baxter shared a strong interest in character animation. In the absence of staff with experience in the making of shorts and features based on story and character, Baxter and Boyle worked on their own and made a sixty-second student film. Baxter, Bowers, and Boyle had completed their first year when they heard rumors of the *Roger Rabbit* production. Some Farnham students had toured through Richard Williams Animation during the school year and had seen the proof-of-concept test.

Baxter and Boyle saw an advertisement for animators in *Screen International* magazine, saying that the Forum was open for applicants until 5 p.m. Production of a feature animated film in London was a rare thing in those days, so Baxter and Boyle grabbed the videotape of their sixty-second test animation and headed to London on a Friday afternoon. They arrived at where they understood the studio to be located just before 5 p.m., only to find that they were in the wrong end of central London. They ran across London, arriving at the Forum at 5:45 p.m. breathless and sweating. They talked their way past the old security guard at the desk in the small lobby and took the lift up to the second floor, where the studio receptionist's desk was located.[69]

Patsy de Lord happened to be walking by, balancing an immense stack of paperwork. Baxter and Boyle pleaded their case, but de Lord politely brushed them off. They were twenty-year-old students and veteran animators had not been carried over from RWA. They turned toward the lift and were about to press the button when they looked at each other and, in that look, conveyed that they would not be swayed so easily. They turned back and continued to plead their case, after which de Lord told them to leave the videotape of their student animation. On Monday they were invited back to take the in-betweener test. They passed the test and were put on a four-week trial period at half-pay. It was late June 1987. They were soon joined at Disney UK by their friend David Bowers and another classmate, Mick Harper.[70]

Bowers decided to call Disney UK and he was invited to come into London to do an in-betweener test. He did not pass, but he was given the opportunity to come back once a week for lessons from Andreas Deja. He took the test again two or three weeks later, and passed.[71]

Other students and graduates of West Surrey were at the Forum: Marc Ellis, Mike Pfeil, Dave Pritchard, Barney Russel, Dave Sigrist, and Amanda Talbot—all of whom joined the visual effects crew, led by Chris Knott. Some, like Talbot, had applied for an optical effects position,[72] and some, like Pritchard, had applied as a character animator but was taken on by Chris Knott following the entreaties of their mates on the visual effects crew. Pritchard came to the Forum just before Christmas of 1987, as pressure for the scheduled completion was peaking.[73]

Still more artists were needed, and the arrival of each new recruit was accompanied by an interesting story.

Peter Gambier joined the crew quite late in the production. He was a plasterer by trade and an artist by avocation. Brent Odell remembers him appearing at the Forum with a portfolio under one arm and a plaster bucket on his other arm. He was hired as an in-betweener. On his first day, he completed two or three drawings; the expectation was twelve drawings. He says that "Patsy de Lord stalked around the place looking for troublemakers." He was often told off by her for not being where he should have been—that is, the in-between pool.[74]

Three out of four of Lily Dell's siblings have been in the animation industry. Her brother is T. Dan Hofstedt, who worked for Bluth in Dublin and came to Disney on *Aladdin*. He suggested that she apply at Disney in London. She interviewed with Don Hahn and was put in the Matte and Roto Department. Before she actually started there, she was reassigned to the Visual Effects group, headed by Chris Knott . . . who she describes as a magnificent boss: kind, gentle, and nurturing.[75]

Roger Way was born in Ottawa, Canada. His mother was a wartime bride from England and worked as a maid in a big country house. He did not care for school and left at a young age. Way eventually found a job at Crawley Films in Ottawa, working on the *Wizard of Oz* television series in the Paint and Trace Department. He later worked at the National Film Board in Montreal. In 1964, at the age of twenty-four, he moved to England and found his way to Richard Williams Animation. He worked on titles for the films *Casino Royale* and *The Charge of the Light Brigade*, in addition to many commercials. He left RWA for a time and worked at many of the little studios around Soho. He worked on *Watership Down* (1978) at Halas and

Batchelor.[76] Fitzroy Tavern, a pub at 16 Charlotte Street in Fitzrovia, was a favorite meeting place for London's intellectuals, artists, and bohemians such as Dylan Thomas and George Orwell. In more modern times it became a favorite Friday night gathering place for Soho artists and animators. It was at this pub, and others such as the Star and Garter, at 62 Poland Street in Soho, that the animation community in London heard of opportunities and negotiated employment. Roger Way heard about *Roger Rabbit* on a Friday night at Fitzroy Tavern. He was called to start working on it in early August 1987.[77]

Pete Western grew up with animation; his father and mother worked with David Hand at G-B Animation, the studio set up by J. Arthur Rank. Western received his formal art training at Central St. Martins in London. At the time he graduated, in the early 1970s, he spent short periods at RWA and knew many of the people who had worked there.[78] The film union was strong in Britain, partly due to the power it held with the film laboratories, so Disney UK had to place trade magazine advertisements for assembling the crew. In addition, there had been rumors of *Roger Rabbit* within the London film community from the time of RWA's proof-of-concept animation test. It was while working at Hibbert/Ralph that Western saw a trade advertisement for *Roger Rabbit*. Western was turned down by Disney UK initially, but as pressure on production increased, he got a call from Don Hahn.[79] Uli Meyer had left the production a week before Western started, and Meyer's departure may have had something to do with the call from Hahn offering Western a position. It was near the end of June 1987, and Hahn had already realized that they weren't going to be able to finish the production on time if they didn't have more animators. Western started a short time before Colin White and a couple of weeks before Nik Ranieri and Cal Leduc.

Alex Williams was born in 1967 and got his first taste of working in animation as the voice of Tiny Tim in his father's 1982 production of *A Christmas Carol*. He was twenty years old and in his first year at the University of Oxford when production began on *Roger Rabbit*. He visited the Forum during the school break at Easter 1987 and asked Don Hahn whether he could work without compensation as an intern. After a couple of weeks of working for free, he asked if he could be paid. It was Patsy de Lord who asked him if he would consider staying on with the *Roger Rabbit* production rather than returning to Oxford. Williams was eager . . . and Oxford agreed to give him a year leave. Alex Williams started working on *Roger Rabbit* in April 1987 as part of the in-betweener pool . . . mostly at the service of Simon Wells. He then went on to be an assistant to Marc Gordon-Bates.[80]

And then, along came the Americans!

Greg Manwaring grew up at the US Army's Würzburg Air Base in Germany. Manwaring then went back to the United States and took the foundation program at the Otis-Parsons School of Art and Design. He then talked his way into the CalArts class of 1986, and may very well have bumped Andrew Stanton, a future principal at Pixar, from the class. After his sophomore year he got on to the crew of *Sport Goofy in Soccermania* at Disney. After his junior year, he got into the training program at Disney and on to *Oliver & Company*. He went on to work on "Family Dog," with Brad Bird, and did not return to CalArts. He got a call from Andreas Deja to go to Munich to work on the German production *In der Arche ist der Wurm drin* (*Stowaway On the Ark*); he remained there from March until June 1987. He visited Andreas Deja and Phil Nibbelink in London, during which time he bumped into Richard Williams, who asked him to do a Baby Herman animation test. He was hired on the spot and started on *Roger Rabbit* in July 1987.[81]

Tom Sito was born in Brooklyn. He attended the High School of Art and Design, the School of Visual Arts, and the Arts Students League. *The Adventures of Raggedy Ann & Andy* was being produced in New York City when Sito was in his first year of college. It was 1975, and it was too good an opportunity to miss; it was the first animated feature film to be produced in New York City since *Gulliver's Travels* had been started there before being moved to Florida. On *Raggedy Ann & Andy*, he got to work with people from animation's golden age: Hal Ambro, Art Babbitt, Corny Cole, Emery Hawkins, Irv Spence, and Art Vitello. Sito was nineteen years old and got to work with Grim Natwick, who was eighty-seven years old at the time. In addition, he formed friendships with people who would later also become involved with *Roger Rabbit*: Bill Frake, Eric Goldberg, and Richard Williams. Sito started in Ink and Paint and finished as an assistant animator. During this New York phase of his career, he also got to work with Shamus Culhane, who ran a small commercial operation out of his apartment.[82]

In 1978, Sito was in Los Angeles, working at Richard Williams's Los Angeles studio. He also spent time at the Lisberger Studio, working on *Animalympics*. He married Pat Connolly and they moved to Toronto in 1979 to work at Nelvana, along with Roger Allers and Chuck Gammage. Tom and Pat Sito were back in Los Angeles in 1982 to work on *Ziggy's Gift* in offices at the historic Crossroads of the World mall, again with Richard Williams and Eric Goldberg. When that production wrapped, he joined Ruby-Spears, after which he moved to Filmation, working on *He-Man and the Masters of the Universe* and other television shows. Tom and Pat then made a personal short animated film, *Propagandance*, which was shown at Annecy and the Sundance Film Festival in 1987.[83]

In October 1987, Tom and Pat decided to visit their friends Eric and Sue Goldberg in London and maybe work on a few commercials at Pizazz Pictures while they were there. While in London, Tom went up to Camden Town to have lunch with his old friend Chuck Gammage. They were near the Forum and Gammage suggested, "Why don't you come by to say hi to Dick?" At the time, Dick Williams had been feuding with some mutual acquaintances, one of them being Eric Goldberg, and Sito demurred, "I'm not quite sure how my reception would be," to which Gammage said, "It'll only hurt for a minute!"

They went to the Forum, and the instant Williams saw Tom Sito he said, "Oh, Sito, Sito . . . you must work on this film . . . Yes . . . you're hired." Sito told Williams that he was in London with his wife and that she was a checker, to which Williams said, "Oh, she's hired too!" Williams dragged Sito by the hand to Don Hahn's office, where he introduced Sito: "Don, this is Tom Sito . . . he's funny . . . hire him." Hahn shook Sito's hand and said, "You're hired!"; it was the first time they had ever met. It was also the first time Pat Sito had ever gotten a job without submitting a portfolio and the first time she had ever gotten a job that had not been advertised and to which she had not even applied.[84]

They started during the week of November 16, 1987. Pat Sito was brought into the small checkers office on the third floor and introduced to Julia Orr, and Atlanta Green and her brother, Cyrus Green. The checkers had started to work longer hours, but they were not behind in their work and had not requested additional personnel. They thought that the new American was a Disney spy. Pat was put in the room next door with Shelley Page and Jill Tudor. The next day, the final check supervisor was sacked, and Julia was promoted to supervisor. Pat took her desk in the checker room. She was sympathetic to the feelings of her new British colleagues and, when they found out that neither she nor Tom had ever worked for Disney before, they all became fast friends.[85]

On Tom's first day, he asked Dick Williams what he should work on, and Dick replied with a question: "What characters do you want to work on?" Sito knew that everybody was trying to get Roger shots and that it would be disruptive to compete with the established order, so he asked, "What do you really need?" Williams responded, "Weasels, nobody wants to do weasels!" [86] So, on Sito's first (part-) week, the week ending November 21, he animated 5–09 feet (89 frames or 3.7 seconds of screen time, for 35mm film) of weasels. For comparison, that week Simon Wells animated 16–08 feet (264 frames or 11.0 seconds of screen time) and Greg Manwaring animated 2–00 feet (32 frames or 1.3 seconds of screen time), although it is unfair to make this comparison without the context of the difficulty of the scene, the number of characters in the shot, and the amount detail the animator leaves to the assistant animators and in-betweeners.

On Thursday of the next week, November 27, American Thanksgiving was celebrated, and Max Howard took all of the Americans out for the evening for dinner at Charlie Palmer's restaurant and then to a theater in the West End . . . to see Barry Humphries's one-man show, as Dame Edna, in *Back with a Vengeance*. The Sitos were made to feel very welcome.[87]

Dave Bossert worked for six-to-eight months at Don Bluth Productions immediately after graduating from CalArts. Bluth was working mostly on video games at that time, but the market was changing and everybody was laid off. Bossert joined Disney in early 1984; *The Black Cauldron* was already in production. He moved on to development on *The Great Mouse Detective* when his work on *The Black Cauldron* was complete. He was also doing some early development work for *Oliver & Company*. There was not another project ready after *The Black Cauldron* was finished, but Disney did not want to let artists go in those days and carried a lot of them for significant amounts of time between productions. They would come to the office and they would be paid, but aside from a little bit of training or little oddball projects for the theme parks or television, there often was not much to do. The creative juices still flowed, and that energy was often directed to pranks and silly competitions . . . some of which were documented in Don Hahn's documentary *Waking Sleeping Beauty* (2009). Bossert was bored and left Disney to work on *Land Before Time* at Sullivan/Bluth Studios in Dublin. He resigned from Disney in December 1986 and started to work in Ireland in the Effects Department in January 1987. From the start, Bossert did not like the atmosphere at the Sullivan/Bluth Studios. He knew that he would not stay with Bluth for further pictures, but he made a commitment to stay on until the Effects were complete.[88]

In the meantime, Bossert had connected with Hahn, who had been a friend since Hahn had hired him at Disney in 1984, and visited London several times during the spring and summer of 1987 to visit Don. Each time, Hahn implored him to work on *Roger Rabbit*. Bossert was finally able to leave Dublin towards the end of September of 1987 and reported for duty with Chris Knott in the Effects Department at the Forum in late September 1987.[89] The Animation Department had a very international atmosphere, but the Effects Department was most decidedly British. They were an easygoing bunch, but they had a healthy dose of British cynicism for American "cheerleading" behavior and did not take it especially well when Bossert walked into the Effects room for the first time, wearing a Walt Disney Feature Animation sweatshirt, and announced, "It's okay now, the cavalry has arrived!"[90]

Dorse Lanpher entered the Art Center School in the fall of 1953; then, after three years there and at age twenty-one, he took his portfolio to Disney in Burbank and had an interview with Andy Engman. He was assigned to the Effects Department, under the supervision of Josh Meador. He worked on shorts such as *Paul Bunyan*, *Wind Wagon Smith*, and *Our Friend, the Atom* until he finally got on to *Sleeping Beauty*. He was drafted into the US Army before *Sleeping Beauty* was completed and came back to Disney in April of 1960.[91]

Vera Law became a friend of Lorna Pomeroy through a mutual interest in needlepoint. Lorna was part of the group working on *Banjo the Woodpile Cat* in Don Bluth's garage and suggested that Vera might be interested in helping out. Law learned about animation in those garage sessions and later got a job at Hanna-Barbera. When Bluth found out, he arranged for her to be hired by Disney and she started as a clean-up artist on *The Small One* . . . and was even the live-action reference model for Mary (Lanpher was the model for Joseph).[92]

Bluth had been trying to talk Lanpher into joining him when he walked out of the Disney Studios on his birthday in September 1979, but Lanpher was not quite ready to leave. Vera Law was one of the thirteen artists to leave with Bluth. The next day, Lanpher attended a meeting called by Ron Miller. It was intended to be a pep talk for the work to be done, but Miller started the meeting by saying, "Well, now that the cancer has been cut out . . ." It hurt Lanpher deeply that Miller should equate the interest in keeping Disney-quality animation alive with cancer. The feeling of "not belonging" grew and on November 8, he wrote a long resignation letter to Ed Hansen, giving his final date as November 23. It was a long letter, full of reasons and qualifications, and when Hansen finally looked up he just said, "Dorse, you had better get out of the studio right away." Lanpher went to work at Don Bluth Productions in Studio City on *The Secret of NIMH*, followed by an animated section for the film *Xanadu*, and then . . . video games. He had not completely broken with Disney, however; he maintained a good relationship with Don Hahn and did some uncredited freelance work on *Mickey's Christmas Carol* (1983) and *The Great Mouse Detective* (1986). It was during that time that Dorse and Vera got married.[93]

Bluth Group went bankrupt in 1984 and then co-founded Sullivan/Bluth Studios with moneyman Morris Sullivan in 1985. They initially set up a studio near the Van Nuys airport, but later moved everything to Dublin, Ireland. Lanpher negotiated a salary of $1,800 per week to move overseas and went to Dublin to work on *Land Before Time*. He and Vera had intended to do at least two pictures for Sullivan/Bluth, but Vera wanted to go back to California. They visited London periodically, while working in Ireland, and occasionally had dinner with Don Hahn, who prodded them into working on *Roger Rabbit*. Bossert had already come on board in September of 1987. They insisted on fulfilling their commitment to Bluth for completing *Land Before Time*. Vera would have been happy to go back to California right away, but Dorse talked her into another three months of tax-free income on *Roger Rabbit*. They took a three-week vacation to visit family in Los Angeles and then returned to London on January 1, 1988.[94]

Steve Hickner was also one of the international animation gypsies who worked at the Forum, although he first came on to *Roger Rabbit* as part of the Glendale unit in California. Hickner learned his craft in the television animation factories of the early 1980s. He worked at Filmation, Hanna-Barbera, and Ruby-Spears. He worked on *Ziggy's Gift* with Richard Williams and then was back at Filmation as an assistant supervisor on *He-Man and the Masters of the Universe*. In spite of having worked on many television shows, he only worked for ten weeks out of the year in 1982. He paid attention to the way the organizations functioned and to the traits of the leaders he admired. He wanted to improve his situation and spent a year working on his portfolio. When he was ready, he submitted his portfolio to Disney and was hired by Don Hahn as a trainee/in-betweener on *The Black Cauldron*.[95]

Soon after he came to Los Angeles in 1981, Hickner had met Darrell Van Citters and had seen the earliest *Roger Rabbit* animation test (in which animator Mike Gabriel played Eddie Valiant). Then, any news about *Roger Rabbit* dried up. Hickner worked on the reboot of *Sport Goofy in Soccermania* and then on Disney's Richard Dreyfuss-hosted Constitution television special, *Funny, You Don't Look 200: A Constitutional Vaudeville* (1987). It was during that production that Hickner heard there might be a Los Angeles-based unit for *Roger Rabbit*. He went to Peter Schneider at the end of July 1987 to ask whether he could be a part of it. Hickner ended up being the second person on the Los Angeles unit (also known as the Glendale unit), starting in August 1987. Ron Rocha was the first person assigned to the new unit . . . and the first task was to reconfigure a warehouse building on Airway, in Glendale, near the old Glendale airport terminal building and in the same general area that Disney Feature Animation was then located. Ron Rocha went to London in late September/early October of 1987, but did not want to stay there. Don Hahn asked Hickner to help out in London on Halloween of 1987 and on November 7, he was at the Forum.[96]

Early Days

The RWA crew moved to the Forum in Camden Town in early March 1987, and the Disney animators followed in early April. The other early arrivals showed up throughout March and April. The Forum had been prepared as an animation studio with the installation of animation desks designed and built by Chris Knott's partner, actor and carpenter Sam Sewell. Disney UK occupied the fourth and fifth floors of the five-story building at the start, but ultimately expanded to the third floor as more artists arrived through the summer of 1987. In August 1987, the Animation group (animators, assistants, and in-betweeners) consolidated on the fifth floor in a rabbit's warren of cubicles. A visiting food deliveryman was astounded, and commented that they were packed in like chickens in a roost. But in April, the Forum was only just starting to fill up and as the facility was being prepared, so was the crew—with drawing and acting classes by Walt Stanchfield, a former Disney animator who had conducted similar drawing classes at Disney for years. An important aspect of the training was to coach the animators on convincing human movement, especially in preparation for the work on Jessica Rabbit.

The fifth floor had large skylights that could flood the interior with light on sunny days, of which there were a few in London. The ambient light made it almost impossible for the artists to see through the many layers of paper on the animation desk backlit discs. In order to block some of the harsh light, brightly colored umbrellas were hung over the animator's desks. It gave the workplace a light and festive feel.

The earliest work was on the opening Maroon cartoon, on which work had actually started while still at 13 Soho Square. Roy Naisbitt prepared the complicated layouts. The backgrounds were animated, as had been done in Disney's *Three Orphan Kittens* (1935). After his work on the layouts was complete, Naisbitt spent most of his time at Richard Williams Animation's new location, a couple of blocks away at 138 Royal College Street. Live-action filming was still being done at Elstree Studios and on the Acme Warehouse set at White City as the animation crew was assembling. Some of the early animation crew were able to visit the live-action sets. The Los

Angeles live-action shooting had gone through editing by this time and the Kodalith photocopy backgrounds were starting to come through the ILM pipeline. When Andreas Deja arrived in early April, the first scene he was given was the ostrich ballet dancer that Eddie Valiant bumps into as he exits the R. K. Maroon studio. It was part of an extraordinarily long panning master shot full of special effects.

The pace of work was relaxed at the start of the production. The opening cartoon was straight animation, with no unusual surprises. It was when the live-action Kodalith backgrounds started to arrive that eyebrows raised. Although Richard Williams knew that the camera would be moving as in a typical live-action shoot, that fact was not generally known by the crew and they were shocked that their animation would be changing perspective in every frame. The impact that the moving camera would have on animation was also not likely fully understood by those who had prepared the production budgets. It did not take long after the crew started adding animation to the live-action scenes to discover the difficulty of meeting the established production budget. Each animator developed their own technique for pinning the animated character to the frame so that it would not appear to "float." As a consequence of the moving camera, there are very few "hold" shots in which only minor changes would be required for consecutive animation drawings. In order to make an animated character appear to hold still while the camera drifted, the orientation and perspective of the drawn character would need to be changed in each frame. The success with which the animators were able to accomplish this feat can be measured by how well the characters appear to be rooted in their real-world environment compared to Ralph Bakshi's live-action/animation combination film, *Cool World* (1992). There was a steep learning curve, and lessons learned would be passed on to newer recruits, but the pace of production did not proceed according to the budget.

Another factor was that Richard Williams seemed to have a compulsive need to "touch everything."[97] He would often draw, in ink, over animation drawings—requiring the animator to reproduce the entire drawing. For many of the animators, Williams's input was welcome. They had a lot to learn from a master animator and their having to redraw a scene was a small matter relative to the lessons they learned and the improvements to the scene. Williams almost always made time for this assistance and genuinely enjoyed sharing his experience and his draftsmanship. Nevertheless, he could be intimidating to the junior animators—although this was as much about them being awestruck by Williams as anything he might do.[98] Many of the more seasoned animators were not as accepting of what they viewed as Williams's interference. They considered it as meddling with their artistic choices. It ultimately resulted in two animators leaving prior to the conclusion of production.

Uli Meyer was an animation natural. Williams sent him to Los Angeles for training with Art Babbitt and when he came back to London he was producing excellent animation at a pace far exceeding that of most of the crew. At some point early in the production, he gave some design work on the Gorilla directly to Don Hahn—bypassing Williams. Williams was unhappy. Meyer had not intended it as a slight, but he now admits that he was a bit full of himself at that time. Williams had a meeting with Hahn. Even though Williams had a private office at the time, there was little privacy and both Meyer and Alain Costa overheard Williams saying, "I'm going to break his back . . . I can't work with him, I'm going to break his back."[99]

Meyer had wanted to animate a key scene with *Roger Rabbit*, but Williams assigned him the scene with Dumbo flying outside of R. K. Maroon's office window. Roger Rabbit and Baby Herman would have already appeared in the key scene in which they transitioned to their real-world toon selves from the opening Maroon cartoon, but the Dumbo scene was important in being the next appearance of an animated character and the first appearance of a Disney character. Nevertheless, Meyer was disappointed and upset with the assignment, and his upset was later compounded by Williams's suggestions and perceived meddling. Meyer chose to write Williams a letter with his concerns. He was angry when he wrote it, and now wonders whether his poorly written English at the time really served him well or whether he should have just sat on the letter for a while before reviewing it in a different frame of mind. Williams's response was to tell Meyer that he was planning to put him back as an in-betweener. Meyer was devastated and walked out.[100] Meyer was young and very proud, and at that time, he misunderstood how his own actions may have contributed to the situation. With the advantage of thirty years of hindsight, Meyer now admits that he wishes he had handled things differently.[101]

Another animator who left the production early was Dino Athanassiou. As early as May 1987, Williams was getting a lot of pressure from Katzenberg about the pace of the production. Williams said that the slow pace was due to the learning curve of dealing with the moving camera, but people were starting to realize that Williams himself was as much a cause of the production being behind schedule and over budget. At the start of June, Williams had just come back from a trip home to Canada, with a side trip to Disney and Amblin in Los Angeles. He was overheard telling his production coordinator, Ian Cook, that he needed to "shake things up a bit." Bridgitte

Hartley was assisting Gammage and was doing well, so Gammage gave her some scenes with Baby Herman to animate. When Williams found out, he screamed at her for doing animation without having gone through him. He ripped her apart and brought her to tears. When Williams finally relented, Athanassiou stared him down, as if daring him to try it again, then went directly to Don Hahn's office to resign.[102] Again, Gammage walked out, but he was convinced to come back. Hartley got along with everyone and it was hard to see her humiliated so publicly and so unreasonably.

Gammage had a bone to pick with Williams because Williams had also been changing his drawings. Gammage had been looking out for Meyer, almost as a big brother, and had quit in sympathy with Meyer, but Meyer convinced Gammage to go back to Williams shortly thereafter. Gammage continued to chafe at the perceived meddling with his drawings by Williams. A typical exchange between Williams and Gammage went like this:

DICK: Chuck, this scene . . . it's kinda not working.
CHUCK: That's it! I'm outta here!

Williams had high expectations of Gammage and was hard on him. They both pushed each other's buttons. Gammage quit several times, some might say frequently, and Williams would get him back after a cooling off period. He quit for good in late October 1987.[103]

Williams's tantrums were often a result of people not following his instructions, but they were also linked to him being away for a longer period of time than his instructions covered. If people took initiative, he was likely to be all over them. Nik Ranieri relates that his first work after being made up as an animator was a scene with Baby Herman. He thought that the poses given to him by Williams were just suggested layout poses and he did his own key animation poses. When Williams saw that his poses had not been followed he screamed, "You changed my drawings! My thirty-five years of experience against your five years of college and work!" Later, Ranieri was working on the scene with Roger Rabbit escaping from the weasels at the Terminal Bar. Williams was away and Ranieri had finished the work that Williams's instructions had covered. Ranieri chose to continue on with the scene, and when Williams finally returned—Ranieri was screamed at again[104] Williams's tantrums often included the exclamation, "This is the big times! . . . This is *Star Wars*!"[105]

In spite of issues that Russell Hall and Williams frequently had, Hall commented that while Williams could blow up, he was astute and could usually put his finger on what was not working . . . and that usually was a result of the person not following his clear directives.[106] Dave Spafford said, "When Williams blew up at you, it would be well-deserved."[107]

Russell Hall was also looked up to for the work he was doing on Jessica Rabbit. He was the only animator to have a private office, shared with his assistants Bella Bremner and Alyson Hamilton. Towards the end of the production, other animators were given Jessica Rabbit scenes, which had to be approved by Hall. Jacques Muller had the scene with Jessica and Roger hanging from a rope at the Acme Warehouse. Williams saw his drawings and drew corrections over them. After Muller made new drawings with the corrections, Hall saw them and had Muller change them back. This cycle was repeated several times until Don Hahn finally told Muller to submit the scene to Trace and Paint after he got Hall's approval. When the scene was finally painted, Muller noticed that it again had Williams's imprint.[108]

Life at the Forum

The relaxed pace from early in the production was soon replaced with a sense of urgency that escalated continuously through the balance of the production. When Disney representatives would visit the Forum, the crew would get a glimpse of the mounting pressure. As early as May 1987, Katzenberg was heard telling Williams, "Dick, we respect your work . . . we know you're great. You're used to working on fantastic commercials. Now, imagine that this is one big fucking commercial with one big fucking deadline. You have to meet that deadline or we're all dead in the water."[109] Katzenberg's visits always upset the London studio.[110] There were arguments between Schneider/Katzenberg, Zemeckis, and Williams about the rate at which Williams was progressing on the production.[111] At one point, Zemeckis was seen holding Williams by the lapels up against a wall at the studio.[112] He, as much as anybody, understood that movies were about illusion—western streets were usually just façades, and bustling seaports, castles on the hill, and space vehicles were usually just models or mattes. Sometimes, "good enough" had to be good enough. Katzenberg told Williams that he should only target 60 percent quality in order to get the film done. Williams responded that he was already doing only 60 percent quality, so Katzenberg told him to target 20 percent.[113] Nevertheless, Williams kept wanting to "touch" everything—making small changes on everybody's work. Don Hahn rarely confronted Williams, but his biggest task as associate producer in charge of animation was managing Richard

Williams. At one point, about six months into production, Hahn was looking for a replacement for Williams.[114] Eric Goldberg was one of the people
he contacted.

Hahn was generally well liked by the crew. He had a quiet, reassuring
way about him. When crunch time came, Williams would still insist, "Got
to be on ones, got to be on ones!" Hahn might come around quietly later
on and say, "Just put it on twos," if his assessment was that would not
harm the quality of the scene.[115] Hahn predicted to Max Howard that they
would need another animation unit, based on what he saw happening in
Camden Town. He started assembling it in advance. His mission was "How
to Manage Dick and Get His Genius into the Film." Williams was drawing
The Thief occasionally on *Who Framed Roger Rabbit* time, a practice that
had to be stopped.[116] Williams would frequently show up still dressed in
his tuxedo from a Dick's Six engagement the night before, although everybody would admit that Williams had incredible stamina and could work
crushingly long hours.[117] Hahn brought Stan Green to London for the last
six months of the production and placed him in Williams's office. Green
had been Milt Kahl's assistant for years and had earned Williams's respect.
Williams was less likely to draw in ink over the animator's finished scenes
or to yell when Green was present in the room.[118] Green was a charming
guy[119] and well-liked by the crew. He was a mentor for the young animators,
"like a kind uncle." [120]

On Max Howard's first day working for Hahn, Hahn telephoned him
from Los Angeles and said, "Max, we need a fax machine." Howard did not
know what a facsimile machine was at that time, but he went into the city
and came back to Camden Town with a fax machine—one with continuous
slick thermal printing paper, and no cutter. There was only one fax machine
in the Forum, and as time went on, that fax machine became a source of
"confidential" memos that would be intercepted on the machine. One such
memo from Katzenberg ended up being posted on the studio wall: "Use the
passion and integrity of the crew to get more quality and footage out of
them."[121] Another memo from Katzenberg to Williams read, "You can work
10 percent less well, and we'll get the job done." Yet another Katzenberg
memo, focused on controlling costs and speeding up production, exhorted
the London management team to get the artists to work longer hours
without overtime pay by "appealing to their artistic integrity."[122]

One practice that seemed to irk everybody was Williams's Monday
morning routing meeting. Each Monday morning the entire crew would
gather to watch Williams color in charts showing the progress of each

scene through the production pipeline. Some people may have thought that the feedback was useful, and it was a practice that may have been efficient at RWA on commercials, but most people on the crew found it a complete waste of time. The routing meeting would routinely last over two hours. Williams was also often prone to publicly ridiculing somebody's work. The routing meetings were not curtailed by Hahn until quite late in the production.

By the end of the production Hahn had developed an ulcer.[123] In spite of the aggravation, Hahn would be the first person to say that *Who Framed Roger Rabbit* would not have been the film it was if it were not for the involvement of Richard Williams. For any anecdote of awkward tantrums, there was an anecdote of Williams making a special occasion to praise outstanding work. People on the crew felt a "touch of genius." Williams had a "confidence" that he could *draw* his way out of any problem. He was always available for "drawing mechanics" instruction for junior and senior artists alike, and he was very encouraging of the growth of artists who he saw putting in extra effort. Simon Wells said, "Dick drew unbelievably well and unbelievably fast. It was like his 'brains were in his pencil'—almost as though he would just watch this *magic* coming out of his pencil."[124]

When asked to describe what they remembered most of their time at the Forum, most of the artists responded: "long, hard hours of endless work." The next thing they would describe was the food. Complaints about food have always been a focus of discussion amongst soldiers, prisoners, and airplane travelers, and so it was with the denizens of the Forum. Early in the production, people would go out for a pub lunch or go to a nearby pub for dinner if they were staying to work overtime. As the production progressed and the urgency ramped up, the studio started to provide meals in order to keep people at their desks, since pub dinners would take no less than an hour. The meals were typically a half-a-sandwich and an apple, but as time wore on and working late into the night became a standard practice, the evening meals became more substantial. Regardless, they curried every bit as much scorn and discussion. The Chef-in-a-Box meals came in plastic containers, designed to be spill-proof. That spill-proofing was tested when Raul Garcia decided to turn one over to make a photocopy image. Soon, one wall of the studio was covered by a mural of take-away meal images.[125] In spite of the many complaints, there were those who enjoyed the meals. Elaine Koo said, "The meals that were brought in were hot and lovely."[126] Koo was clearly a "cup half-full" person, but she had also worked in circumstances not nearly as professional and pleasant as what they had at the Forum. She said, "It was like sharing an apartment rather than a workplace." Indeed, they developed a special community. Many of the artists came from someplace else and had no special place to be—except for the work.

Beyond that, the British had a thriving pub culture, into which the local artists happily coached the newcomers. The local pubs were welcome havens at any time, but Friday night was pub night, and most of the crew would be out. There tended to be a hierarchy at the Forum, as there tended to be at all animation studios: the animators hung together, and the Effects and Matte and Roto departments tended to hang together, as well. This was as much because Animation took up the entire fifth floor of the Forum, and SFX and Matte and Roto occupied the fourth floor. There wasn't much "pipeline" connection between those floors, and wandering was discouraged. Xerox, Final Check, Editing, and Camera were on the third floor, with Trace and Paint and Rendering. Some of them had more occasion to be on the fourth and fifth floors and might have had a more extended social network. Regardless, they all had favorite local pubs.

St. Michael's Anglican Church was built in the Gothic Revival style in the late nineteenth century. It is located at the northwest corner of Camden and Pratt streets, across Pratt Street from the Forum. Across Camden Street from the church and half a block further west is St. Martin's Gardens, originally a cemetery built for St. Martin-in-the-Fields (on Trafalgar Square in the city), but now a public park. St. Martin's Tavern was located on Pratt Street, half a block south of the Forum. It backed onto St. Martin's Gardens and its old graveyard, so the tavern's nicknames were "Bone House" and "Pub of the Living Dead." Four blocks further along Camden Street, across from the Camden Town tube station, is the World's End pub. It was a raucous and busy and fun pub with a separate venue, The Electric Ballroom, located below. The Electric Ballroom featured live music and dancing. Three blocks further, across the Camden canal, is Dingwalls, also a live music hotspot. Dave Spafford used to play with a band at Dingwalls. Five blocks south on Pratt Street from the Forum, towards Regent's Park, is the Edinboro Castle, a quieter place that was a local favorite of Roy Naisbitt.

It was not uncommon for the animators to come back to the Forum to work after having spent some time at the pub. Spafford said, "The pub 'lubricates' funny ideas." It was after coming back from the pub that Spaff decided to have fun with his dueling pianos scene. Rather than just having Daffy Duck pounding away at the keys, he decided that it would be fun to have Daffy's hands come up over the soundboard holding odd objects— first there was an ice cream cone, then came a hammer, then boxing gloves, and then two dead chickens. The final thing was a single frame of Daffy holding a dead baby tied up with rope. On sober second thought, Spaff admitted that was "pretty gross" and took it out. Zemeckis was amused when he saw Spaff's other inventions—and the gag stayed in the film.[127]

In spite of the potential for lubrication of funny ideas, too much time in the pub was detrimental to productive work in the evening. Disney wasn't going to be able to eliminate the artist's activities, but they could try to temper and manage them. Therefore, a beer cart often accompanied the meal trolley when the crew worked overtime.[128] Every couple of weeks bins of Budweiser beer would appear—to give the Americans a taste of home.[129]

On September 16, 1987, the entire crew gathered in St. Martin's Gardens for a photograph. The photographer Bob Penn, captured a fun picture: the crew was caught mid-jump and with their hands in the air.

The crew was disciplined during the daytime, but production management would generally go home by 8 p.m., and the atmosphere between 8 and 11 p.m. was more relaxed. There would be more talking and socializing, especially after they knew that they would be able to complete the film on time. These after-hours work periods were also a time for release of pent-up energy that manifested itself in creative ways. The animators produced a couple of homemade films—*Revenge of the Killer Bhaji* (https://youtu.be/IQNDbV3vQk) was directed by Phil Nibbelink and starred Rob Newman, and *Dodgy Bhaji* starred Rob Stevenhagen. The plot of both films involved an onion bhaji, an Indian snack popular in London, attacking the neck of an animator in a way reminiscent of the rabbit attacking the knights in *Monty Python and the Holy Grail* (1975).[130]

There was also the old standard animator's game: rubber band wars. When the Forum was being refurbished after *Who Framed Roger Rabbit* in preparation for being taken over by Richard Williams for *The Thief*, an enormous collection of rubber bands was found up in the ductwork.[131]

As time went on and the pressure for production footage increased, Patsy de Lord (the production manager) and Ian Cook (the production coordinator) had the thankless task of pushing the artists and wrangling them when they strayed. The SFX crew was very tight and extremely loyal to their supervisor, Chris Knott. He was patient, kind, and empathetic, and universally described as the best boss any of them have ever had. All of the crew describes how Knott insulated and protected them from the pressure and the politics, and allowed them to do their work without distraction. That is not to say they could not create their own distractions and fun. Every day somebody in the SFX room would start clucking like a chicken or bleating like a sheep. Before long, everybody would join in for a full barnyard concert.[132]

The SFX crew left at noon to take Knott out for lunch at a nearby Indian restaurant for his birthday. The "lunch" lasted longer than normal and they didn't return to the Forum until 2:30 p.m. When the elevator opened on the fourth floor, there was Patsy de Lord standing with her arms crossed and her toe tapping. She looked at her watch and proceeded to ream them out. Knott told his crew to return to their work and then stayed for further tongue-lashing. The crew was upset and embarrassed, but there is no doubt that de Lord and production management were under enormous pressure at the time.[133]

The SFX crew was augmented with the arrival of Dave Bossert and Dorse Lanpher, both former Disney effects animators. The British crew knew that they needed the support, but there was a little clash of cultures. The closest McDonald's was five miles away on Tottenham Court Road. Lanpher used to pay for Bossert to take a taxi to bring back Big Macs.[134] The British animators thought it was outrageous yet endearingly American. Nevertheless, there were aspects to their new American colleagues that they marveled at. One time the crew ordered a pizza from Domino's for a late-night work party. It arrived late and cold. Bossert spoke to the delivery person and they did not have to pay for the pizza. The British animators were amazed . . . they would have never thought of asserting themselves in that way.[135] Beyond that, Bossert had a Sony Walkman CD player—something that the British had not previously seen and which they coveted. They appreciated the skill of the Disney animators and learned a great deal from them. Lanpher offered a glimpse at Disney glory days and was very easy to get along with. He was described as a midwestern gentleman.[136]

This was not the only clash of cultures at the Forum. As the pressure built, Don Hahn made up pin-back buttons reading, "We Can Do It." Later, he made up buttons reading, "We Did It." These, too, seemed very "American" and did not mesh with the typical British temperament.[137]

An inducement that was more readily accepted was crew jackets. Max Howard had a background in the theater, and it seems that crew production jackets were a British theater "thing." It was a novelty for animation crews at the time, although it has since become a staple of Disney film productions. The crew was pleased and proud to get the jackets. An issue of *Time Out London*, published after *Who Framed Roger Rabbit* was released, contained an article commenting, "Now we finally know who those people were who were walking around Camden Town in black jackets like some kids in an occupational army." The crew jackets were an external identifier of the crew's connection, but the shared experience of the Forum tied them like a military band of brothers.

Their common field of engagement was their workplace at the Forum and the pubs they would frequent. They had one memorable weekend outing in Surrey led by Al Gaivoto and Phil Nibbelink, both experienced ultralight aircraft enthusiasts. Everybody survived.[138]

There were also workplace romances. Irene Couloufis and Howy Parkins had been friends at Sheridan College in Toronto and had come to London together. They were eventually married. Caron Creed and Andrew Painter met at the Forum and were married after the production. Joe Haidar married Holly Russell, the Forum's receptionist, during the production. Dave Spafford and Debbie Lilly were dating during the production. Spaff was sent back to Los Angeles before work at the Forum was concluded, but he was back in London for the charity premiere at the Odeon Leicester Square theater in November 1988, and he and Debbie were married soon after. Back at home in North Hollywood, the Spaffords continued the tradition of Friday pub nights. They equipped their home with pub games and fittings, and it became the place to be on Friday nights for the Los Angeles animation community and any globetrotting animators who happened to be passing through.

The circumstances of the production also may have contributed to the failure of some marriages. It happened that some artists would be at the Forum for hours that were extraordinary even for this production. When they were told that they should attempt to find more balance in their lives, it would be discovered that their marriage was breaking up and they had no place else to go.[139]

There were some characters. Phil Scarrold seemed very angry much of the time and was hard to get to know. At one point, something got under his skin and he walked out of the production. He was gone for two weeks and his desk was empty, but the crew generally had so little interaction with him that nobody noticed that he was gone. He eventually came back of his own accord and it was as if nothing had happened. It is strange that he was often referred to as "the South African," although he came from Zimbabwe and it was Marc Gordon-Bates who had family links to South Africa.

Dave Spafford shaved off his long hair except for a tuft of hair high on his forehead that made him resemble Daffy Duck, the character he was animating at the time. He was "getting into his character," an earnest example of the "method school" of animation acting.[140]

Spafford was a keen student of the Warner Bros. characters. Early in the production, the animators were provided with reels of vintage cartoons from many Hollywood studios to better understand the ambiance of 1940s cartoons. Spaff coached Zemeckis on the nuances of Warner Bros. cartoons.

Who Framed Roger Rabbit was set in 1947, and Spaff was adamant that the design of the Warner Bros. characters should be faithful to the 1940s design model. Zemeckis shared that goal, but the Warner Bros. marketing department wanted to use the current (mid-1980s) character design models. Spaff insisted on animating using the 1940s model sheet, but Warner Bros. had approval for its characters and their insistence at the highest levels of the Disney organization trumped Spaff's authority. Spaff began to provide fake animation for approval, using the modern Warner Bros. model sheet, but would submit animation with the vintage Warner Bros. design for production. When Warner Bros. found out, they hit the roof and insisted that Spaff be fired. Disney was extremely upset with him, but Zemeckis supported him. He was ultimately reassigned to the Glendale unit, where he finished animating the duelling pianos scene, submitting the animation under assumed names. In his animation of Bugs Bunny in Toontown—falling with Mickey Mouse and Eddie Valiant—he had Bugs "flipping the bird" at "the Mouse."[141]

This certainly was not the only message that was slipped into the film by the animators. Spaff also managed to insert "SPAFF" into one frame of the cannon smoke during the duelling pianos scene. The most infamous scene, one that has provided fodder for much debate, is the no-panties scene, in which Jessica and and Eddie Valiant are ejected when Benny the Cab runs into a lamppost while they are escaping Toontown. At one point, Jessica's dress is hiked up above her waist and many observers insist that she is not wearing panties. Colin White animated Jessica in that scene. He claims that two frames were drawn of Jessica without panties, but he thought that the Checking Department would take them out.[142] Whether White intended Jessica to have no knickers or not, there is not much to distinguish the difference in a pencil drawing. The Xerox Department used to run extra copies of cels so that Barbara McCormack could suggest colors. The intent of the Trace and Paint Department was certainly for Jessica to be wearing knickers . . . and that they were to be pink.[143] That may have been an unfortunate color selection. It also may have been that the scene went through due the time/cost constraints at the end of the production. There was such pressure to complete the footage that some of the work might not have received the necessary level of oversight.[144]

Zemeckis had a real appreciation for vintage cartoons, especially after he was coached on cartoon history by Spaff. The very early animators knew that their films would only ever be viewed on a theater screen for a period of weeks . . . and likely never seen again. Nobody can perceive a single frame image as they flash by at twenty-four frames per second.

The early shorts were pumped out of the studios at a terrific rate and with little in the way of downstream checking departments, so the animators occasionally slipped in "irregular" frames. It often happened in the Fleischer Studio's Betty Boop shorts. Betty Boop was going to have a much larger role in *Who Framed Roger Rabbit*. She was supposed to have had an affair with Eddie Valiant in the past, and there are still remnants of a shared past between the two in the final film.[145] Zemeckis was determined to include an homage to the early animators by including a Betty Boop "nipple slip" frame. Roger Chiasson was told to animate one frame showing her nipples as she pulls on the hem of her dress. The drawing proceeded through Clean-up, Trace and Paint, and Checking with a note attached: "Bob Z. wants this boob shot for 1 frame."[146] It appeared in the theatrical presentation, but there was really not much to see, even with a subsequent frame-by-frame laserdisc examination. An interesting detail about Betty Boop is that her Xerox lines were black, while the Xerox lines for all other characters were brown.[147]

The inclusion of the Betty Boop nipple slip gave the impression to some people in the crew that their own personal inclusions might be acceptable. They surely were not! Kevin Jon Davies, an effects animator, put an almost imperceptible "KEV" in one frame of a shadow he drew of Roger Rabbit in the folds of Eddie Valiant's shirt during the scene in which Roger is hiding in the sink to avoid detection by the weasels. The cel got through Trace and Paint but Maggie Brown, the assistant head of the department, found it and pulled it and reported it to Don Hahn. Davies's continued future on the film was in jeopardy, but his boss, Chris Knott, went to bat for him and he stayed . . . a little chastened.[148]

The booby trap scene, in which a weasel reaches under Jessica's dress into her cleavage and comes out with his hand in a bear trap, almost had a nipple slip frame too. The frame was drawn and went through clean-up to Xerox. It was pulled from further processing, but a number of copies of the drawing survived.

When Roger Rabbit accepted a drink in R. K. Maroon's office, the alcohol caused him to go through a series of transformations concluding with him rocketing to the ceiling. In one frame, he was transformed into a penis shape. The frame was pulled from production.[149] Manwaring and Muller animated the scene with Jessica and Roger hanging from the rope at the Acme Warehouse. On the "It's the Dip!" close-up of Jessica, Manwaring's drawings showed hard nipples. Hahn told him that the nipples had to go. He also had Jessica's breasts heaving. Williams loved it, and called everybody over, exhorting them to "do boobs like Manwaring."[150]

Other animation irregularities were less vulgar; they usually just consisted of small personal call-outs. The checkers found the initials "G. M." discreetly hidden in one frame of Roger Rabbit's pupils. The checkers usually just reminded the animator of the policy, and that was that. It is impossible to know how many subtle call-outs managed to escape detection, but many were caught.[151] Some of the subliminal call-outs that have been described by the animators are so subtle that one would be hard-pressed to accept that they actually exist—like trying to "see" somebody else's interpretation of a fanciful cloud formation. For the animator, it was sufficient that their intent existed. The flip side of this argument is that people see subliminal messages in animated cartoons where no intent ever existed. The internet is full of false subliminal message outrage.

Of special interest are scenes that were intended, but ended up being deleted from the film. A scene deleted from the Ink and Paint Club sequence showed Bugs Bunny talking discreetly with Walt Disney in a booth. We would have caught Bugs saying, "Oh . . . okay, then I'm going to Warner Bros."[152] It was not put through animation . . . but it would have been a fun inclusion.

One scene did go through animation and although it was not deleted, it had to be completely redrawn. Brent Odell mostly animated "prop" scenes, such as the saw coming out of Judge Doom's arm, magnets, and eyeballs popping out.[153] He spent an arduous couple of weeks animating the chili bottle that fell off the kitchen shelf in the opening Maroon cartoon. The "camera" was drifting, zooming in and out, and the bottle was tipping and falling. Odell had to be extremely precise since a solid structure, like a bottle, would flutter and be perceived as an error by the audience if not done correctly. Spielberg was visiting the Forum at the time and leaned over Odell's shoulder to see what he was doing. He said, "I hate to tell you this, but we spell chili with one 'l.'" Odell had used the British spelling, "chilli," rather than the American spelling.[154] He also spent weeks animating a scene in which Eddie Valiant is caught in a mousetrap at the Acme Warehouse by Judge Doom. Valiant picks up a piece of stinky cheese and throws it at the trip mechanism to spring the trap and catapult him away from Doom. The scene was deleted after being animated.[155]

Another scene was deleted after being animated and progessing through Trace and Paint. Pete Western worked for months and months on the Pig-Head sequence: Eddie Valiant is kidnapped by the weasels and taken to Toontown, where he is *toonarooed*—painted with a Pig-Head. He is tossed out of the Toontown tunnel entrance and runs back to his office/apartment to shower off the toon head with turpentine. It was an extremely interesting sequence, with amazing effects, but Zemeckis felt that the scene leading up to it slowed down the story too much and ultimately decided that the scene had to be cut.[156] Western also worked on a scene with Valiant brandishing a toon gun. The animated gun was ultimately replaced by a toonish prop gun fabricated at ILM during the bluescreen shoot, so much of Western's animation was left on the cutting room floor.

A sequence that Zemeckis intended to cut was ultimately saved . . . and most people would agree that the film is better for its inclusion. When the weasels come to Valiant's apartment in search of Roger Rabbit, Valiant plunges Roger into the water-filled sink and pretends to be washing his socks. Roger comes up sputtering for breath while the weasels engage in Three Stooges-type schtick. He comes up again as the weasels leave and spits out a stream of water, wrings his ears dry while saying, "Jeepers, Eddie, you saved my life. How am I ever going to repay ya," and then plants a big cartoony kiss on Valiant's mouth. The sequence is packed with amazing special effects and wonderful acting by Hoskins. It was also animated by Andreas Deja, who loved being able to do the broad animation. It was one of his favorite scenes, and he was very unhappy that Zemeckis was considering cutting it. It was also one of the crew's favorite scenes, and the thought of cutting it almost caused a kind of palace revolt. Zemeckis ultimately agreed that it should stay.[157] This may be a sign of a good director: one who can consider well-intended critique. Then again, he was also going to take out the Michael J. Fox/Chuck Berry scene in Back to the Future.

Zemeckis was almost forced to cut the opening Maroon cartoon. The seven-minute cartoon had taken over six months but was still not completed. There was extreme pressure from Disney regarding time and budget. Neil Boyle's contract ran to the middle of April, but it was extended to May 4 so that he could add some dialogue to Roger Rabbit at the start of the Maroon cartoon. When he finally left, Williams was still there finishing the last scene.[158] Williams ultimately finished the Maroon cartoon at his own studio on his own time.[159]

The animators would check their work—the mechanics, acting, timing, fluidity, etc.—on a video line tester. In the old days, they would have used a Moviola. The line tester was essentially a video camera and a ¾-inch videotape machine. The operator was Angie Carroll, who in later years became Angie Dowd, a television fitness personality. She died in tragic circumstances in 2011, but in 1987, she was the master of the line tester. It had to run in "Forward" for ten seconds whenever a scene was stopped, because when it stopped, the videotape recorder would roll back ten-seconds worth of tape. The animators would need to have their scenes played repeatedly so that they could note areas for improvement. Neil Boyle's workspace was adjacent to the line tester, so his day was full of repeated ten-second clips of the animation voice track.[160] The line tester would not be as stressful a place for the animators as the "sweatbox" was in Walt Disney's time. Walt Disney had his telltale raised eyebrow when there was something he did not care for. Animators at the Forum would get something different if Williams was not pleased with a piece of animation. Williams saw Phil Nibbelink's early animation of a *Roger Rabbit* scene on the line tester. He said, "Boy, that's a great rabbit scene. Now—can you do it with Roger Rabbit?" [161]

The ¾-inch videotapes were sent back and forth between London and Los Angeles by FedEx for editing, along with daily phone calls. In April 2013, at a panel discussion during the AMPAS digital screening on the occasion of the celebration of the twenty-fifth anniversary of the film's release, Zemeckis said, "We had FedEx and ¾-inch tape—we thought we had technology by the tail."[162]

Of Williams, Max Howard said, "It was like trying to harness a typhoon."[163] Spaff said that Williams was one of the most enthusiastic people he had ever met.[164] Spaff got along extremely well with him. When asked whether there was any socializing with Williams, Spaff said, "Of course, are you kidding? Oh my God . . . I was in a band over there too. We did all kinds of stuff. I had a blast!" Williams would stew over ideas and then they would flood out in a torrent. He would often go with Roy Naisbitt to a local café for eggs and bacon and to talk about the production. Spaff would occasionally tag along. Williams would walk so quickly that Spaff would have to run along behind him. A lot of the animation on *Who Framed Roger Rabbit* was figured out at that café table.[165]

Williams could still throw in some surprises. One day, he came to see Shelley Page with a painted cel of Jessica. He said, "It's no good . . . make it better." It was a large head-and-shoulders shot, so Page thought that it was something for Publicity. She shaded the eyes with wax pencils, applied rouge and lipstick, and added gold flecks to the earrings. In all, she spent one hour on the cel—and Williams loved the result. One day later, Don Hahn stormed in to her office. It turns out that Williams wanted that level of detail on every Jessica cel in the film. In the scene that Jessica screams, "It's Dip!" on an extreme close-up, it took Page a full hour just to render Jessica's lips.[166] Williams had a sign over his desk:

> You can have it fast,
> You can have it cheap,
> You can have it good . . . choose any one.

A meeting was held in New York City on October 14, attended by Jeffrey Katzenberg, Peter Schneider, Marty Katz, Tim Engel, Frank Marshall, Bob Zemeckis, Steve Starkey, Ken Ralston, Robert Watts, and Dick Williams. Katzenberg was very blunt in sharing his views on how the production was progressing. Out of the meeting came a strategy for meeting the production deadline. The work-in-progress was screened for the first time in London on October 16. There was still a big "hole," with a notation on the screen saying, "Toontown Goes Here." The screening did not go well. The crowd was not enthusiastic. Zemeckis judged the audience response to be "horrible." The animators realized just how much more work would be required to complete the film . . . and it was unsettling.[167] The screening was held on the day after the Great Storm of 1987, when a violent extratropical cyclone hit England and France on the night of October 15. There were winds up to 134 miles per hour. Twenty-two people were killed in England and France, and there was an estimated two billion pounds (sterling) in damages. Trading on the London stock exchange was suspended and the Dow Jones average started to slide on Friday, October 16. It was the biggest single-day drop up to that time. October 19 was Black Monday: the global stock market crash. The crew was wondering whether it was all some portent of the future.

Even though one of the strategies that came from the meeting in New York was that a second animation unit would be geared up in Glendale, the pressure on the London crew and the long hours continued to mount. There would be fun times, though. Max Howard was sensitive to the needs of the artists. There was a weekly studio newsletter, *RABBITRABBITRABBIT*, which communicated upcoming events, help-wanted and personal columns, quizzes, and contests. The studio also organized movie screenings. A wine and cheese party was held on December 16 when Zemeckis, Marshall, and Katzenberg arrived in London to show off the first color composites. The next morning, the animators and management had a breakfast meeting in the Regency Suite at Le Méridien, a landmark hotel in Piccadilly Circus.

There were also celebrity sightings. Bob Hoskins was one of the favorite visitors. He was at the Forum in November when some rushes were being shown. He was surrounded by tall Americans muttering, "Well, Bob, we've got so much to do and time is running out." Hoskins replied: "Well, you don't want to rush it and fuck it up!" You could have heard a pin drop amongst the tall men.[168] Spielberg brought Christian Bale for a visit while *Empire of the Sun* was being filmed at Elstree Studios. Bale was eleven years old at the time, and he made a very positive impression on the artists. Greg Manwaring amused him with coin tricks and magic. Jim Henson visited the Forum in February, and Zemeckis brought Christopher Lloyd by in March. It was during Lloyd's visit that Nik Ranieri cemented his reputation as the crew's photo geek. He had missed an opportunity to have his photo taken with George Lucas on an earlier visit, so he always had a camera at the ready by his desk. Ranieri ran down the stairs to intercept Lloyd as he was leaving and asked for a photo. Zemeckis said, "It's up to you, Chris," to which Lloyd quietly said, "Okay." Hahn told Ranieri, "Go get your camera, Nik," and Ranieri sprinted up the stairs to retrieve it. He is sure that they were all rolling their eyes, but he got the photo.[169] Even though there was a no-camera policy at the Forum, it was allowed if the privilege was not abused. People like Nik Ranieri and Pete Western managed to take photos that have chronicled many of the people and events at the Forum. The photos have now been shared so broadly on the internet that it is difficult to ascertain their origins.

The other chronicle of the times at the Forum are the gag drawings. Many people on the crew were talented caricaturists. A caricature competition was held, with the objective of designing a caricature of Bob Zemeckis as a baby. The entries were to be submitted to Howard by mid-January 1988, to be judged by Williams and Hahn. Simon Wells won the competition and earned tickets to a show with Dame Edna. Of more historical interest are the gag drawings that captured the environment of the Forum, faux pas, and the anxieties of the crew. Tom Sito was a master. He created a wealth of memories for the crew. There was a caricature board, and at the end of the production, a special volume of the caricatures was made up as a gift to Bob Zemeckis.[170] Of course, many of the gag drawings lampooned the Chef-in-a-Box food and amusing gaffes made by colleagues. Other drawings reflect the more serious angst caused by the pressure of the production and the uncertainty for the future at the conclusion of the production.

It was viewed as a treat and an honor to be lampooned by Sito. Richard Leon was the young runner who had assisted at the Forum during the initial set-up and then came back into the Traffic group after the departure of Frazer Diamond. He was full of enthusiasm and questions. He was described as "überkeen." He was just jazzed to be there, but sometimes his enthusiasm could be a little irritating. Later in the production, the screening room became the catering staging area for overtime meals. The meals were not to be accessed until a given time, and Leon took his role as a gatekeeper very seriously. The artists were generally inclined to think of rules more as guidelines, and they could not give a fig for the strict access schedule, especially when they were hungry. The situation became a Tom Sito gag drawing.[171]

Chapter Five

THE GLENDALE UNIT

The Concorde Meeting

As the associate producer in charge of Animation, Don Hahn managed production at the Forum. Robert Watts had been splitting his time between *Who Framed Roger Rabbit* and his next project, *Indiana Jones and the Last Crusade*. Watts went to his office at the Forum on the morning of Tuesday, October 13, in anticipation of going to Spain later that day to scout locations for the *Indiana Jones* film. When he arrived, Patsy de Lord greeted him and said, "Robert, you're on the Concorde tonight." Watts and Hahn had been booked on the 7 p.m. Concorde flight to New York City.[1] In the front row of the plane were Princess Anne and Itzhak Perlman. It arrived in New York City at 5:30 p.m.—still on Tuesday, October 13.

Watts and Hahn had fitful sleeps and on Wednesday morning went to the Disney offices at 500 Park Avenue for the 7 a.m. meeting called by Jeffrey Katzenberg. In the boardroom were Jeffrey Katzenberg, Peter Schneider, Marty Katz, Tim Engel, Frank Marshall, Bob Zemeckis, Steve Starkey, Ken Ralston, and Dick Williams. Katzenberg is said to have "ripped everybody in the room," and, in response, fingers were being pointed every which way. At one point, Katzenberg said to the group, "Ya know what? Don Hahn will get this movie done, because if he doesn't . . . did you see that guy down on the street digging that ditch? If Don doesn't get this movie done, that guy will be Don Hahn!" Hahn later said, "He said it with a smile—one like the banditos flash in *The Treasure of Sierra Madre*."[2] Katzenberg confided that they would all be looking for jobs if they did not turn the production around. Michael Eisner was losing patience with the production delays and the ballooning costs.

Katzenberg reserved particular attention for Dick Williams. He told Williams that he was being too much of a perfectionist. According to Williams,

"He yelled at me. He's a tough corporate guy, but he's not going to go behind your back. He'll do it in front of everybody."[3] Later, when describing the meeting and his relationship with Katzenberg, Williams has said, "Do you want your throat cut by a professional or an amateur? If I'm going to be stabbed in the back, I'm just as happy to have it done by somebody who's happy to stab me in the front!"[4] But, he still had a grudging respect . . . sort of. Williams said of Katzenberg: "He's intelligent, and courageous enough to put his ass on the table" and "He's very tough and unpleasant, but he backed the picture because he knew it would be very successful."[5]

Hahn remembers that after the meeting he and Watts took a cab to the East River pier, where they boarded a helicopter to get them to their Pan Am flight back to London. It was not on the Concorde this time—they arrived back in London in the very early morning. Hahn recalls having an ominous feeling. During the flight, when Watts pulled his window shade down . . . it came off and fell into his lap. Watts recalls that he was in the office at the Forum on Tuesday morning and he was back in the office at the Forum on Thursday morning (October 15).[6] The night of October 15 was the Great Storm of 1987. London experienced wind gusts of over 100 miles per hour and twenty-two people were killed in the UK and France. It was the costliest weather event in UK history at the time. October 19 of the next week was Black Monday, when stock markets around the world crashed. The Dow Jones Average fell almost 23 percent.

Watts remembers the Concorde meeting as being very productive and that they succeeded in mapping out how they were going to complete the movie. The release date was linked to marketing programs with Coca-Cola and McDonald's, and it could not be postponed. It was determined that the London crew would not be able to finish the animation in time, and that another animation crew was needed. As it turns out, a satellite crew in Los Angeles had been considered for months and plans went into hyperdrive as an outcome of the meeting—there would be a Glendale animation unit.

The Leopard's Spots

It did not take long to realize that Dick Williams, ever the perfectionist, was not going to be able to meet the production deadline. The complication of animating in perspective, due to the camera not being locked down, made it difficult for the animators to make the budgeted footage. Beyond that, there were Dick's idiosyncrasies, eccentric behavior, and history of deadline trauma. Shelley Page, who worked with Dick at Richard Williams

Animation and then transitioned to the *Roger Rabbit* crew, described making commercials at RWA as "working on desperate deadlines, as we always were, thanks due to Dick's scheduling." She went ten nights with no sleep at all on one project. "It was another desperate deadline," she confided with affection.[7] There was no complaint in her observation; to the contrary, she was committed to Williams. She recognized his genius and she says that she accomplished more under his tutelage than she ever thought possible. Another animator, who worked for Williams for decades, observed "the 'lust for perfection' probably clouded his longer vision and obscured the practical aspects in this project." He described Williams as "by turns charming and funny, and an ogre; utterly professional, and an irreverent clown; a perceptive and discriminating plagiarist, and a stunning original artist; a visual visionary with vast scope, and a nitpicker . . . and a consummate, dedicated craftsman." He added, "I wouldn't have missed working with him for anything! If you were going to work in animation in London at that time, his was the place to be."

According to Richard Williams, "I had my own studio in 1958. After a while I got set up doing commercials. I made a little short [*Love Me, Love Me, Love Me*, 1962]—crudely animated, but very funny—and made a lot of money. I started another film, but had to scrap it. I ran out of money. It kept on like that. I had to shelve it and had to spend my time making commercials. So, I've lived in the commercial world as a chameleon—whatever they want, I do it. I get frustrated. On the other hand, they're paying money and I should honor it."[8] Commercials were always just a way for Williams to finance his personal projects, as was his involvement with *Roger Rabbit*. He has said, "The last thing I ever wanted to do was *Roger Rabbit*. I did the *Rabbit* in order to be bankable. The irony is that I always succeed when I'm doing someone else's laundry."[9]

The real irony is that someone else always seemed to be doing Dick's laundry. According to Carl Gover, Dick's business partner at RWA from 1972 until 1982, RWA had developed an excellent reputation with its commercials, and Gover was able to attract business from all over the world. The profits were always plowed back into Dick's dream feature, *The Thief and the Cobbler*. Part of the success was based on Williams giving clients a little more than they expected or paid for. It ensured a regular supply of work, but made for a stressful financial situation. Williams was very rarely satisfied and was always striving for perfection, which made it a struggle to balance the books. The quest for funding for *The Thief* was constant, but even with that, Williams seemed incapable of spending money wisely or even committing to some very lucrative commercial projects. He blew off a

big opportunity with the Royal Bank of Canada, as well as a personal project for Stevie Nicks of Fleetwood Mac and a Rupert Bear animated feature
with Paul McCartney. Williams finally agreed to direct *Raggedy Ann & Andy:
A Musical Adventure* (1977), believing that it could make him bankable at
last. The producers insisted that it be made in New York, so Williams had
to commute between London and New York while the Soho Square studio
churned out commercials as best they could. Williams brought in his friend,
Gerry Potterton, to help out on *Raggedy Ann and Andy*, but in the end the
producers hired Potterton to finish the production and fired Williams.[10]

Williams directed many successful projects, to be sure. He won an Academy Award for *A Christmas Carol* (1971), which was produced by Chuck
Jones. Williams said, "Jones let me choose which Dickens to adapt. Chuck
took all the heat for me—the best producer I ever worked for . . . the only
one who ever backed me. Blake Edwards was the same way—very clear instructions and then no interference. That's how you do your best work. We
made up everything as we went along . . . didn't even have a storyboard."[11]

Williams also directed a television special, *Ziggy's Gift* (1982), which
won an Emmy Award. Williams had opened a branch studio in Los Angeles and was dividing his time between London and Los Angeles. He was
overcommitted, and deadlines were being missed. Nevertheless, Williams
was easily distracted and was constantly drawn back to *The Thief*, which
often left RWA animator/directors such as Russell Hall, Dick Purdum, Eric
Goldberg, Shelley Page, and others to pick up the pieces.[12] Eric Goldberg
went to Los Angeles to "clean up Dick's mess."[13] Their relationship soured
during the making of *Ziggy's Gift*, although it has long since been repaired.

It is said that a leopard can't change its spots, and the situation with
Williams was little different at the Forum. Williams could not keep to
the budget footage pace of sixty feet per week. What was a producer to
do? Don Paul was a former Disney effects animator who was then working, unhappily, with Bluth in Ireland. In May 1987, Don Hahn met Don
Paul in London and asked Paul whether he could stay on to assist with
the effects work. Paul declined but said that he would happily take on
freelance work out of Los Angeles. Hahn soon asked him to lead a small
team in Los Angeles to take character animation from London and match
it to Los Angeles environments. Paul assembled a team of three animators and three additional artists who took on the task of adding shadows,
tone mattes, and reflections to scenes animated in London. The effects on
the later-deleted Pig-Head sequence were handled by Paul's team. It was
processing the footage at a rate of sixty-to-eighty feet per week.[14] In May
or June, Hahn also contacted Eric Goldberg, who was by then running his

own commercial studio, Pizazz Pictures, in London. Although Goldberg had been very interested in *Roger Rabbit* at the outset of the search for a director of animation, his own studio was developing an excellent reputation and he had no interest in bailing Williams out again.

Williams was very resistant to the idea of a second animation unit. He insisted that there was just a steep learning curve due to the complications in matching the animation to live-action filmed with a moving camera . . . and that the London crew would soon be achieving the necessary footage. As the pressure from Disney increased, he finally relented, but he wanted to supervise the additional unit. He eventually agreed that he might be able to work with Dale Baer. Since leaving Disney in 1976, Baer had freelanced on several Disney films and worked with Ralph Bakshi on *Lord of the Rings*. Williams had established his branch studio at 5631 Hollywood Boulevard in the same building as Quartet Films, a commercial studio co-founded by Art Babbitt. Baer worked at RWA (Los Angeles) for eighteen months during 1978 and 1979 before starting to produce his own commercials. He and Jane Baer incorporated themselves as Baer Animation Company and sold their house to finance a half-hour film, *A Special Thanksgiving*. They did a job for Disney, a short film called *Suited for the Sea*, part of an attraction at the Living Seas pavilion in EPCOT. Soon, the opportunities for freelance animators dried up and the Baers were running out of money. Sometime in late June, Baer got a call from Don Hahn, who asked, "Would you like to work on *Roger Rabbit*?" Baer did not have to think about it—he said, "Sure, tell me when!" Baer took a demo reel and *A Special Thanksgiving* to Amblin for a meeting with Zemeckis. Dale and Jane Baer were hired in July.[15]

Moving forward with a Los Angeles-based unit was contingent on the productivity of the London-based crew. Ron Rocha, the production assistant at Disney Animation prior to the arrival of Eisner, Wells, and Katzenberg, was the first person assigned to the Los Angeles-based unit. His first task was to reconfigure a nondescript warehouse located at 1400 Airway, adjacent to the Grand Central Terminal building at the site of the old Glendale airport. The second person in the Glendale unit was Steve Hickner, who started in August 1987. Rocha went to assist in London in late September but decided that he did not want to stay there and returned to be the production manager of the Glendale unit.[16] The Baers moved to the Airway site as soon as there was furniture for laying out portfolios to identify a potential animation crew. The earliest activity was the work of Don Paul's effects crew, which took on work from the London-based crew and animated the effects for the Pig-Head sequence.

The ACME Gag Factory

The ultimate participation of the Baers in the final production of animation was still up in the air in early September 1987. Nevertheless, the bluescreen shooting for the Toontown seqments was scheduled at ILM in mid-October, and the Toontown storyboards had still not been finalized. Although live-action filming started in Los Angeles in December 1986, the storyboards for the Toontown sequence still were not complete at that point. Hans Bacher and Harald Siepermann were at Amblin in Los Angeles, reworking the Toontown storyboards with screenwriters Seaman and Price in June 1987. The Story team had developed ninety minutes of gags, but there was a risk of the gags overpowering the story. The Toontown sequence ended up being shortened to less than six minutes of screen time.

The London crew was responsible for the Maroon cartoon that starts the film, but aside from that portion, there were no layouts and background in the work at the Forum. Although there were production illustrations done by David Russell and Marty Kline at Amblin to guide the live-action filming, the layout and backgrounds for the animators in London were the live-action Kodaliths.[17] Bill Frake was recommended to Don Hahn for head of Layout by veteran, Don Griffith. Frake was called by Hahn on August 11 and started at Airway on September 7, sitting at the desk next to Dave Spafford. Frake had started at Disney in 1981, but left the studio after *Great Mouse Detective*. He spent time at Marvel Studio and was at Hanna-Barbera when he got the call from Hahn. Frake respected his boss at Hanna-Barbera, Iwao Takamoto, and didn't want to leave him in the lurch. Takamoto's advice was: "Take the opportunity!"[18] It should be noted that Iwao Takamoto was Jane Baer's ex-husband, so he was very magnanimous in his advice for Frake to go and work for his ex-wife.

Frake was immediately told to come up with a look for Toontown even though there was not yet a completed script for this portion of the film. There was not much in the way of guidance for how Toontown should look, so the Glendale crew was free to come with the design and look of the place. Frake asked Jane Baer for concept work that had been done for Toontown previously. He was provided with drawings by Mike Peraza, from his short time at Amblin in December 1985, of a cartoon world in the style of the 1940s Fleischer Superman series. Zemeckis was looking for something different. It was the second week of September, and Dale Baer was feverishly boarding the script. Jane was impatient, nervous, high-strung, and angry. It could very well be that she felt the pressure of being in a competition with Dick Williams for their participation in *Roger Rabbit*, since Simon Wells had also done some Toontown storyboards and the Concorde meeting had not yet happened to consolidate the involvement of the Glendale unit. She brought in Dave Dunnet on September 15 to "help" Frake, although she still hadn't provided any direction for them. Dave Dunnet was a freelancer with whom Frake had worked on *The Black Cauldron*. He was known for fine renderings, the type of concept artwork that was common within Disney in the long lead-up process of establishing the look of a film. It was a luxury that few animation studios could afford. The Baers were still trying to come up with a budget, which required having a script/storyboard.[19]

In the week of September 21, a decision was made that the first view of Toontown, as Eddie Valiant exits the tunnel, would be a quilted landscape reminiscent of the 1933 Silly Symphony, *Lullaby Land*. It would give them an opportunity to root through the Disney morgue and populate the scene with vintage Disney characters in order to save cost and time. Jane Baer told Frake and Dunnet that rough designs for Toontown were needed for the end of the week. The concept was that the town itself should be a character. Zemeckis also told Baer that Disney intended to use the Toontown design for an alternate exit at Disneyland, which was being planned to manage the crush on Main Street, USA, at park closing.[20] Ultimately, that exit on the north side of Disneyland park was not built because the Frank Gehry-designed Team Disney administration building was constructed at that location on Ball Road. Toontown design concepts were eventually implemented in the Mickey's Toontown themed lands at Disneyland and Tokyo Disneyland.

At this time, though, the look of Toontown was not well defined. Dunnet worked at a couple of dark and moody concept drawings—fully rendered, as was his inclination and habit. On Monday, September 28, Jane told Frake and Dunnet that she needed all roughs and concepts by Friday, October 2, for a meeting with Zemeckis. On Tuesday, she said that she needed the drawings the next day. Frake stayed until late in the evening to complete his sketches. Jane was overwrought on Wednesday. She felt that the Glendale unit's further participation in the project hinged on the success of the meeting with Zemeckis. She was especially pleased with the clean quality of Dunnet's fully rendered and moody drawings. Zemeckis and Williams showed up at Airway at 3 p.m. on Friday. Jane Baer ushered Dunnet into the meeting to promote the "Disney-quality" concept work. Outside of the closed door, people could hear yelling. Suddenly Williams came out the door to the front lobby with some of Dunnet's Toontown concept art. Dunnet tended to work "clean," and his drawings looked impressive. Williams sat on the floor of the lobby and screamed, "We're not doing portfolio pieces here," and then proceeded to tear up Dunnet's drawings, crumple them, and throw them into a corner. He stormed out, and soon after, so did Dunnet.[21] Dunnet quit, and it took Dale Baer several days to find him and coax him into coming back. Baer pleaded with Don Hahn to bring Williams back to London. He was told that sending him to California had been a way of making more progress on the work in London.[22]

The incident has been retold, often as an example of Williams's temper and erratic behavior, but although the incident was regrettable and the behavior was questionable, Williams's underlying assertion was probably appropriate . . . and his anger might better have been directed at Jane Baer.

As it turns out, the drawings that Frake had prepared on his Tuesday night session were simple sketches, full of whimsy. Frake suggested pushing further the anthropomorphism of Toontown and gave personality to the street. Both Zemeckis and Williams loved them. Len Smith was hired to help out in Layout. Ron Dias was a talented freelancer who had worked with Disney many times. He was brought on to develop the look of the backgrounds. Beyond the final rendering of the anthropomorphic buildings, he developed the color palette and had to incorporate the live-action lighting into the cartoon environment. Michael Humphries and Kathleen Swain were hired to develop color keys and render the backgrounds. In all, between forty and fifty final backgrounds were rendered.[23]

The storyboards and layouts were required for the bluescreen shooting at ILM, and this aspect of the Glendale operation was necessarily going to proceed. Ultimately, the confidence generated in this process was critical to the decisions taken in the Concorde meeting in New York on Wednesday, October 14. "The hammer was ready to drop" for the Glendale unit, and following the Concorde meeting it moved into full production—two months after Don Paul was brought in as the start of the out-sourcing.[24]

The Glendale crew ultimately grew to seventy-six people. It did eleven minutes of animation, out of a total of fifty-six minutes of animation in the film. The Glendale unit was responsible primarily for the Toontown sequence and the Benny the Cab chase, as well as a few odds and sods throughout the film. The unit was established in a way that was separate and independent of Disney—sort of. By this time, Disney Animation had been moved off the main lot and was occupying buildings along Flower Street in Glendale, where Walt Disney Imagineering was located. The warehouse set up for the *Roger Rabbit* crew was on Airway, two streets east of

Flower. The building was not marked in any way. There was no mail delivery. Nobody, except those involved directly in the production, was allowed to enter, and the crew was told to keep it secret. In fact, it was not identified as a separate production unit in the film's credits, and in the narrative for the marketing of the film, it all but disappeared. The crew called itself the "Acme Gag Factory," but no sign to that effect ever graced 1400 Airway, Glendale, California.

There ended up being eleven animators on the Glendale crew, including Dale and Jane Baer. There was some downtime from *The Little Mermaid* at this time and several Disney animators were asked whether they would like the assignment. Matt O'Callaghan, Dave Pacheco, and Barry Temple jumped at the opportunity. Dave Spafford relocated from the London unit. Mark Kausler had worked earlier with Amblin on the Toontown storyboards. He was a talented freelancer and joined the production. Frans Vischer was working on *Quackbusters* at Warner Bros. when he heard about hiring for the Glendale crew. He had worked at Disney previously. He showed his portfolio to a friend on *Quackbusters*, to get some feedback from her. Later, as Dale Baer was going through the portfolio with him, they came to a double-screen scene, with Daffy Duck and Porky Pig on the phone on each side of the screen. Vischer was horrified to see that his friend had drawn a little penis on Porky. Baer either did not notice or was too gracious to comment . . . and he hired Vischer.[25] Bruce W. Smith had become an animator on *Pinocchio and the Emperor of the Night*, a Filmation production. He hired on to the Glendale crew, as did in-between artists and assistant animators: Carl Bell, Brenda Chapman, Kent Culotta, Eric Daniels, Mike Genz, Kent Holaday, Teresa Martin, David Nethery, Brett Newton, Bette Isis Thomson, and effects animators Randy Fullmer, Glenn Chaika, and Mac Torres. Ten other artists—painters and checkers—came from the Filmation production. A couple of animators left the crew prior to the end of production and did not receive a screen credit.

Toontown storyboards had been worked on by several teams at Amblin, but with the Toontown sequence now more fully edited and refined, it was up to the Glendale crew to prepare production storyboards and layouts. The rough layouts were fed to the animators as they were completed. The layouts were also required for the bluescreen shoot at ILM in mid-October. Dale Baer was busy with Benny the Cab animation, so Frake was sent to ILM for the ten days of shooting. His wife was pregnant with their second daughter. Frake brought his wife and young daughter to San Rafael and even to the set at ILM. Bob Hoskins would play with Frake's daughter on the set.[26]

Ken Ralston and ILM had the storyboard drawings, so they knew what kind of rigs to set up, but they had no idea what the animated background was to look like so that the cinematographer, Dean Cundey, could frame the shot and set the lighting, and so that Hoskins could be directed as to where to move and where to focus his eyeline. Frake came armed with the rough layout drawings. The VistaVision camera had a video port that could be directed to a monitor. A camera, similar to an Oxberry animation camera, was set up to view down on a sheet of tracing paper onto which Frake would sketch the background in perspective, based on the rough layouts for that particular scene frame. The background sketch could be composited with the video feed of Hoskins against the bluescreen to give an approximation of how the final shot would look. It would more often be Hoskins's stand-in, Sammy Pasha, who would be on the set for these set-ups. They would place marks on the soundstage, and stage technicians would hold targets on sticks to provide guidance for Hoskins. Hoskins's performance is all the more impressive knowing that he not only had to act against imaginary characters, but he had to move and act in an environment that did not exist.[27]

Hoskins had a terrific sense of humor and humility that endeared him to the crew. He doted on Frake's two-year-old daughter—missing his own daughter, Rosie, who was four years old at the time. He ate dinner one night at a nearby simple restaurant with the Frake family. A number of the out-of-towners went on a tour of Alcatraz Island one night. Hoskins was looking forward to accompanying them, but ended up deciding to stay at the hotel to work on the screenplay for *The Raggedy Rawney*, a film that he also directed.[28] A Diet Coke commercial was shot while they had access to Hoskins. A stage was dressed as a smoky film noir club, reminiscent of the Ink and Paint Club, and Charles Fleischer was brought up to ILM on Sunday, October 19, to play Roger opposite Hoskins's Eddie.[29] The animation for this would be some of the last animation done at the Forum.

For the scene in which Eddie Valiant tries to shoot Judge Doom with a toon gun, Frake was asked to provide a quick sketch. The sketch was whisked away to the ILM model shop and about ninety minutes later a toon gun appeared on the set for Hoskins to carry during the filming.[30] The magic at ILM was amazing, but it had an unfortunate impact for Pete Western, the animator in London who had been tasked with designing and animating a toon gun—weeks, maybe months, of work was made instantly redundant.

Over 130 bluescreen shots were done in the ten days of shooting at ILM, for about five-and-a-half minutes in the final film. Bill Frake filmed the scenes and the reference background drawings on an 8mm camera, winding up with over two hours of film. This included film of the shooting of the Diet Coke and McDonald's commercials that were done at ILM at the same time. This film, and his sketches, became very important to Arthur Schmidt, who otherwise would have had no reference for editing Hoskins against the bluescreen scenes. On a morning in mid-February 1988, Frake was still in bed after being in the hospital all night with his wife for the delivery of their second daughter when he got a call from the studio. He was upset that work had been at panic stations pace for months and . . . he couldn't even have a few hours off for his wife to have a *baby*? Frake had called back to Dale Baer in Glendale every day during the ILM shoot to give updates, but there were specific editing questions that only Frake could answer. Peter Schneider requested . . . or, "lightly demanded" . . . that Frake get out of bed and come in to the studio, even if it was only for half an hour. Frake redressed into his hospital scrubs and went in for the meeting.[31]

Dick Williams only came to the Airway location in Glendale a couple of times during the production. He typically shut himself in an office and had very little interaction with the animators. If an animator did show some completed work to him, he quite often drew over it in pen—requiring them to recreate the entire drawing. He made it clear to the crew that he was not happy the Glendale unit had been assembled. Jane Baer also made it clear that she was not happy with the oversight from Williams. She was very competitive and eager for the potential of work on future Disney productions. Bad-mouthing was going in both directions.[32] Many of the animators did not know or understand Jane's position or function. They were told that she was assisting Dale Baer, but they rarely saw her drawing. Jane would often make people change their animation after Dale had approved it. They knew that Dale and Jane had set up the unit, so they assumed that Jane could fire them and therefore had to treat her with a certain deference. She acted as a gatekeeper for Dale, who was happiest when he was busy animating.

The animators had the utmost respect for Dale and for his skill at animation. He was easygoing, and the atmosphere at Glendale was generally very upbeat. They all knew that they were working on something special. The Glendale unit was described as a wholesome mix of camaraderie and competitiveness.[33] The animators mostly remember being very busy, but they also remember the experience as being both fun and chaotic.

Williams was working with Dave Pacheco to find original animation in the Disney morgue that could be utilized in the Toontown and final sequences, although Williams's interest in the morgue may have had as much to do about a book on Milt Kahl that he and Andreas Deja were intending to write. On one visit to Glendale, he was accompanied by his son, Tim, who was about twelve years old at the time. The animators recall the photocopier being so heavily used by Williams's son that it broke down.

The animators appreciated Williams's talent as an animator, but they chafed at his sullen behavior and the belittlement of their work in the comparisons made with the London crew. Williams usually donned a V-neck sweater vest and often wore tuxedo trousers, with a satin strip. On his last visit to Glendale, several of the animators conspired to wear sweater vests and prompted Williams into a group photograph holding up the ILM crew jacket Bill Frake had from during the bluescreen work at Lucasfilm. It was a bit of a sore point, since the London crew received a jacket and there was no crew jacket for the Glendale unit. There was mugging and eye-rolling for the camera from some of the group and the exercise was intended to mock Williams, but he was oblivious to it.

It became apparent that Disney and Amblin had agreed to give Williams sole credit as director of animation. Baer had been promised co-credit, but that was changed two weeks before the film's release. Acknowledgment of a second, largely independent unit raised uncomfortable questions about who was responsible for the animation effort, and Williams was the face of animation in all of Disney's marketing and promotion. The Glendale crew was credited ultimately as "additional animation," with no reference to Glendale. The writing was on the wall, though, and the crew decided to take matters into its own hands. Their responsibility for the Toontown sequence would be recorded for posterity by embedding their names into the backgrounds in a similar fashion to the Windows on Main Street at the Disney parks.

The most recognizable name placement was meant as a gag rather than as a call-out. Graffiti on the wall of the out-of-order men's room Eddie Valiant enters in an attempt to escape Lena Hyena refers to Allyson Rubin, the production secretary. The graffiti reads, "For a good time call Allyson 'Wonderland,' the best is yet to be." As the receptionist, Allyson was the gatekeeper for contact with Bob Zemeckis. If anybody needed to contact Zemeckis, they would call Allyson to ask, "When is the best time to talk to Bob Z.?" She might say, "This is a good time to see him." It became an in-joke to say, "For a good time, call Allyson." Eddie Valiant's entry to Toontown through the tunnel was like "falling down a rabbit hole," so a reference to *Alice in Wonderland* seemed like an appropriate gag. Finally, the license plate frame on Allyson's car had the words . . . "the best is yet to be," which the animators thought odd and amusing. They took to calling her, "Allyson, the best is yet to be."[34] Urban legend has it that in the theatrical release a single frame of the film replaced "the best is yet to be" with Michael Eisner's home phone number. Indeed, in the theatrical release there was a phone number, but it was just a fictitious 555 area code number of the type commonly used in movies since the 1950s—not Eisner's.[35] Freeze-framing became a popular pastime with the advent of the laserdisc player. A frame-by-frame examination of the laserdisc and all subsequent video releases shows that the phone number has been removed.

Bill Frake and animator Dave Spafford sat next to one another in the Airway warehouse, and when Frake was designing the layout for this scene, Spafford said, "There has never been a urinal in a movie. I bet you a dollar that you don't do it in this one. I want you to put a urinal in the movie and have Bob Hoskins standing at it." Frake took the bet and put a urinal hanging on the wall, but he did not have Hoskins standing at it. In fact, there was no floor in the out-of-order men's room for him to stand on, so Hoskins defied gravity for a while, in a very cartoony way, and then plummeted.[36]

Other prominent crew call-outs included some posters in the dark alleys of Toontown: Bob Zemeckis ("Cartoony Bob Z. has a winner"); Dale Baer ("Br'er Baer, not too hard, not too soft, he's juuust right!"); and Greg Hinde ("Gregory and his Rubber Band . . . Coming Soon," with a caricature of Hinde as a band conductor). Hinde was famous within the crew for his prowess in rubber band fights. He could hit a fly in flight. Jane Baer earned a door sign: "Jane's Jade Jazz."

Other crew names are scattered throughout Toontown. David (Karp, or Craig, Dunnet, Goldberg, Spafford) and Laura (Craig) were on a bench. Giselle (Recinos) was on a building. Cindy's (Finn) and Christine's (Harding/Blum) were on store awnings. Mark's (Kausler) Cuts Barbershop and Marc's (Christenson) were on a poster, and Don (Paul), Randy (Fullmer), Sib "Eusebio" Torres, Mac (Torres), Scott (Santoro, or Scalise), and Allen (Blyth) were on another poster. A sign next to the Gag Shop was a call-out to Len Smith. Many of these people, in the more obvious locations, were associated with layout, painting, and effects. Attempts were made to have everybody on the crew named in Toontown; some names are on scattered newspapers in dark alleys while others are barely legible. Many names were at the fringes of the frame and were cropped out in the conversion from widescreen theatrical format to the home video format.[37]

In the scene where Eddie Valiant crashes into the overused gags truck in downtown Toontown, the animators were encouraged to insert gags and populate the scene with famous cartoon characters and chaotic action to enhance the otherworldliness of Toontown. The Glendale unit animators hated how Roger Rabbit's ears, as drawn in many of the London crew scenes, seemed to "float." It was a pet peeve, so they created an optometrist's store front in Toontown with a sign showing a rabbit with "floaty" ears. Ron Rocha, the production manager, had the gag removed at ILM after it had been approved by Baer. Regardless of how gregarious and nice a person might be, when they are a production manager they are rarely an animator's friend since they are the ones pressuring the animators for completion of work. Lori Noda was the production coordinator at the Glendale unit. The animators caricatured Noda as a little wind-up doll that moved through the scene until being destroyed by a falling bowling ball. The scene was kept away from Rocha—and when Rocha accompanied Dale Baer to show newly completed scenes to Zemeckis at Amblin, he was curious and anxious at not having previewed everything. Zemeckis loved the gag, and it stayed in the film.[38]

Bruce W. Smith was the last animator to join the crew. His first scene was Eddie Valiant's first view of Toontown upon exiting the tunnel. The countryside was reminiscent of the 1933 Disney short *Lullaby Land*. Smith animated the trees and other elements requiring new animation to fit the background. Although based on the 1932 Disney short *Flowers and Trees*, Smith added a lot of gags, including a tree doing an impression of Jimmy Durante. Barry Temple animated the hummingbirds, a reference to *Song of the South*.

The countryside was populated, in part, with the original animation from old Disney shorts and feature films. Dave Pacheco was one of the few Disney animators who transferred over for *Roger Rabbit*. Like many Disney animators, Dave is an avid Disney film historian and fan. During his lunch breaks when Animation was on the main Disney Studios lot, Dave would wander through the backlot or poke through the animation morgue. He developed an encyclopedic knowledge of the Disney films. He animated the weasels in the cab chasing Eddie and Roger in Benny the Cab. He even animated Bob Hoskins, as Eddie, in several frames of the car chase. Because of his knowledge of Disney films and his familiarity with the Disney animation morgue, it was Pacheco's role to raid the morgue for original animation to be added to the Toontown and the final sequences. The Disney Archives and the Disney Animation Library are a critical studio resource and revenue-generating business managed by professional archivists with art museum-level archival practices. At the time *Who Framed Roger Rabbit* was being made, the controls on access to the animation morgue had been tightened considerably from the old days—but it is astonishing that, in many cases, the original animation cels were clipped to remove any characters that were not to be reused in the *Roger Rabbit* sequence. Only the desired characters were kept, with sufficient celluloid to connect to the peg holes for proper registration.[39] The list of archival Disney characters (and animation) used in the Toontown opening scene is shown in Table 2. The films denoted with asterisks (*So Dear to My Heart*, *The Adventures of Ichabod and Mr. Toad*, and *Motor Mania*) are a bit of an anachronism, since they were released after 1947, the year in which *Who Framed Roger Rabbit* is supposed to be set. A similar anachronism involves the penguin waiters at the Ink and Paint Club, who appeared in *Mary Poppins* (1964). The rationalization is that the penguins were working as waiters in 1947, waiting for their big break into the movies in 1964.

Carl Bell was born in Toronto and studied at the Ontario College of Art. Dick Williams was a year ahead of him. In 1952, they both drove to Los Angeles in Williams's Morris Minor to visit the Disney Studios. Bell joined Disney briefly in 1958, until the layoffs following the completion of *Sleeping Beauty*. He worked at Disney briefly again in 1962 and then spent years at UPA, Bob Clampett, MGM, and Filmation. He was anxious to get into Disney again and went to see the Baers when he heard about *Who Framed Roger Rabbit*.[40] He was called in as an assistant animator when the pressure increased on the production. Matt O'Callaghan, Frans Vischer, and Carl were in adjoining cubicles; the partitions were high, so they could not see each other when they were seated at their desks. They generally worked quietly, but they would chat, joke, and share work ideas. One day they were talking about *The Mouse Factory*, a Mickey Mouse compilation television show with interstitials by celebrity guest hosts that aired during the early 1970s. It was created by Ward Kimball. The song that ran over the end credits was "Minnie's Yoo-Hoo," which was the theme song for the original Mickey Mouse clubs that met in theaters starting in 1930. They started singing the song, with O'Callaghan and Vischer feeling pleased with themselves when they managed to struggle through the first verse. They stopped, but were astounded to hear Bell merrily singing the second verse and continuing through every verse.[41] He was Disney through-and-through, in spite of having been away from Disney for twenty-five years. After the conclusion of *Who Framed Roger Rabbit*, Bell continued to work at Disney from *Oliver & Company* through to *Tarzan*.

Matt O'Callaghan had been storyboarding on *The Little Mermaid* but the story was being reworked and characters were being redesigned, which resulted in some downtime. He was only too pleased to be loaned to the

Table 2. Archival Disney Characters Populating Toontown Opening Scene		
Film	Year	Character
The Merry Dwarfs	1929	Merry Dwarfs
Flowers and Trees	1932	anthropomorphic trees
Lullaby Land	1933	quilted fields
Father Noah's Ark	1933	smiling sun
The Three Little Pigs	1933	Three Little Pigs
The Wise Little Hen	1934	Peter Pig
The Band Concert	1935	Peter Pig
The Tortoise and the Hare	1934	Toby Tortoise
The Tortoise and the Hare	1934	Girl Bunnies
The Tortoise and the Hare	1934	misc. pedestrians
Orphan's Benefit	1934, 1941	orphans
The Big Bad Wolf	1934	The Big Bad Wolf
The Big Bad Wolf	1934	Little Red Riding Hood
Who Killed Cock Robin?	1935	Jenny Wren
Elmer the Elephant	1936	Elmer Elephant
Snow White and the Seven Dwarfs	1937	Snow White
Snow White and the Seven Dwarfs	1937	Wicked Witch
Snow White and the Seven Dwarfs	1937	Seven Dwarfs
Pinocchio	1940	Jiminy Cricket
Fantasia	1940	black Baby Pegasus
Fantasia	1940	mushrooms
Fantasia	1940	cupids
The Reluctant Dragon	1941	Reluctant Dragon
The Reluctant Dragon	1941	Sir Giles
Chicken Little	1943	Chicken Little
Song of the South	1946	Tar Baby
Song of the South	1946	Bre'r Bear
Song of the South	1946	hummingbirds
Song of the South	1946	moles
Song of the South	1946	butterflies
So Dear to My Heart	1949*	Danny
The Adventures of Ichabod and Mr. Toad	1949*	J. Thaddeus Toad
Motor Mania	1950*	Mr. Walker
Mary Poppins	1964**	penguin waiters

Glendale *Roger Rabbit* unit. In the early Disney years, the Story Department and the Character Model Department were at the top of the heap for creative input to the feature films. In later years, especially after the death of Walt Disney, the top animators had license to design characters and modify story. It was actually the responsibility of animators to "tune" the acting in the scene and add gags that seemed appropriate as the acting unfolded. Therefore, the Disney-trained animators thought it was normal to "plus" their scenes. O'Callaghan was assigned the Lena Hyena character, who Eddie Valiant mistook for Jessica Rabbit. As she turns, she turns out to be nothing like Jessica Rabbit . . . and chases Eddie while exclaiming, "A . . . m-a-a-a-n!" Eddie Valiant falls from the out-of-order men's room, but Lena Hyena gets to the street first to catch and save him.[42]

The script called for Lena to give Eddie a big sloppy kiss on the side of his face. O'Callaghan thought that it would be funny to have Lena Hyena's tongue go into Eddie's ear and out the other side. He animated the scene, which the group thought was hilarious. They even recorded a slurping/smacking sound to punctuate Lena's tongue sucking back through Eddie's head. When the scene was shown to Zemeckis, he said, "Yeah, that's really funny, but it breaks the *rule*." The animators said, "What rule?" Zemeckis told them: "All of the things that are 'toony' happen to the toons and not to the live-action characters." Therefore, Lena's tongue going right through Eddie's head was not consistent with the *rule*. O'Callaghan then made the mistake of saying, "Bob, you have the elevator scene in which Droopy makes the elevator go down and up and Eddie ends up being as flat as a pancake." Beyond the impudence of the comment, Zemeckis did not like his storyboards being judged and edited by the animators.

About a week later, O'Callaghan was called into Don Hahn's office and told that Amblin wanted him off the project. In addition to having vexed Zemeckis, Dick Williams had taken a dislike to O'Callaghan and his drawing style. It always seemed to be something . . . the thickness of his pencil line, or whatever. He said he wanted every scene that O'Callaghan had animated to be redone. During O'Callaghan's meeting with Hahn, Hahn sort of smiled and said, "That's just not going to happen." He added, "Don't worry about getting taken off the movie because the reality is that there is only about two weeks left."[43]

Production in the Glendale unit was at a furious pace, as it was in London, and then it concluded quite abruptly. Most of the crew worked until late April 1988. Randy Fullmer was told that the production was very happy with his performance as an effects animator—and then he was laid off. He was let go on Wednesday, but he was hired by Disney on Friday to start on

Oliver & Company. He stayed at Disney for eighteen years, finishing as the producer of *Chicken Little.*[44]

Some people found their way straight into Disney, but others took a bit more tortuous path to get there. Many of the crew stayed together with the Baer Animation Company to produce several animated commercials linking the Chevy Lumina to the new Disney/MGM Studio theme park. Baer Animation Company received contracts from Disney to animate portions of *The Prince and the Pauper* and other films, and was also contracted to animate portions of *Rover Dangerfield* for Hyperion Pictures, which also produced *The Brave Little Toaster* (directed by Jerry Rees). Dale and Jane Baer, Mark Kausler, Bruce W. Smith, and Frans Vischer worked on the *Roger Rabbit* short *Tummy Trouble* in Glendale. Smith and Vischer then worked with Jerry Rees on some theme park animation attractions (Back to Neverland and Michael & Mickey) before working with Tom Wilhite at Hyperion Pictures on *Rover Dangerfield* and *Bébé's Kids.*

Chapter Six

EFFECTS MAGICIANS

Dave "Spaff" Spafford is a magician, illusion designer, and silhouette artist, in addition to being a gifted animator. He has been a fixture at the Magic Castle in Los Angeles.[1] The *Who Framed Roger Rabbit* production team included other magicians: Frank Marshall (aka Doc Fantasy, aka DJ Master Frank), Greg Manwaring, and Amanda Talbot.[2] There was magic in the leadership of Bob Zemeckis. There was magic in the way the crew was assembled from around the world. There was magic in the concept of the story and conversion to a screenplay that would work in the form of a movie. There was magic in the portrayal of Eddie Valiant by Bob Hoskins, but the suspension of disbelief that was necessary to sell the central conceit of the film—that cartoon characters existed and interacted with humans in the real world—would not have happened if it wasn't for the magicians in Effects.

The project would not have been given the green light if it had not been for a successful test-of-concept. One of the reasons Spielberg had been attracted to Dick Williams in the first place was the series of Fanta commercials done at Richard Williams Animation. In those commericals, Disney characters were shown interacting believably in a real-life environment. The effect was achieved by innovations developed by Chris Knott. He had directed a Kellogg's Tony the Tiger commercial, but found his niche when he started to specialize in visual effects (VFX) work. The live-action/animation combination technique used in the Kellogg's commercial was similar to the methods used in the making of *Pete's Dragon* (1977), *Bedknobs and Broomsticks* (1971), *Mary Poppins* (1964), *Dangerous When Wet* (1953), *Song of the South* (1946), *Anchors Aweigh* (1945), *The Three Caballeros* (1945), *You Oughta Be in Pictures* (1940), and the "Out of the Inkwell" series and *Alice Comedies* of the 1920s. The live-action film was back-projected and the the animation was shot on top. There was a loss of image quality and the combination looked contrived and false. The more sophisticated use of various types of mattes improved the illusion, but there was no getting away from a flat cartoon character being pasted into the live action.

Knott had an epiphany of two Big Ideas:

1. Even a thumbprint on a cel showed up as a black matte. Knott thought that it should be possible to split the compositing process into two stages . . . (1) a live dupe run, and (2) an animation run, which could be further split into "percentage" exposures. He could make a black "hold-out" matte by shooting the animation with backlight, then rewind the film and shoot with the animation top lit. The effect was to fill the black holdout with crisp animation. In postproduction, he could also prepare shadow mattes that would be shot at a percentage of the full exposure to produce a transparency or translucency. He could also add sculptural tone mattes to give the effect of "roundness."

2. Knott found that he could use very fine ground glass fog filters on the animation run to deliberately downgrade the image to more closely match it to the live action. He could also add highlights (rimlights) and other optical effects with filters and diffusers. He would conduct many exposure tests (also called "wedge tests") to balance the effect of matching the animation to the live action.

This was the technique used at RWA for the Fanta commercials.[3]

Knott was involved in the early meetings at 13 Soho Square when Spielberg, Zemeckis, Ralston, and others discussed how the project could proceed. A plan for the proof-of-concept was developed.

ILM had optical compositing equipment, but had no previous experience with tonal mattes in live-action/animation combination effects.[4] Knott would be a key figure in executing the proof-of-concept test.[5]

After a first effort of filming a simple interactive scene at ILM, a more complicated scenario was concocted. Roger Rabbit was to follow Eddie Valiant down a flight of stairs into an alleyway. Roger would trip and fall into a pile of boxes, then walk through a puddle of water, past a flashing neon sign, and behind a glass window pane. The actor would pick Roger up by the neck and place him on top of a trash can. Car headlights would flash on the scene, Roger would do a wild cartoon "take" and exit the scene. It is the first time that a crane drop shot had been used in a live-action/animation combination.[6]

Williams provided the animation for a fifty-second-long scene. Shelley Page did the airbrush shadows and three-way paint split on the animated character (Roger) to mimic the tone mattes that would be used in the film.[7]

There were thirty colors used on each cel. Another shorter-length extension of the test was done with Jessica, who was shown getting out of a car—using the technique of tonal and shadow mattes that was developed by Knott. There were additional animated sequin passes and rimlights integrated at ILM. The Jessica test demonstrated that her design needed to be changed, as did the way that she moved. The animation, film elements, and exposure sheets ("X-sheets") were sent to ILM.[8] Ed Jones, in charge of postproduction at ILM, sent a note to Knott complimenting him on the clarity of his exposure instructions.[9]

It took about two weeks for Richard Williams Animation to hear back from Zemeckis. He said, "I've never seen anything like it! This is it! You won't believe it! Spielberg's seen it in New York and he loves it! He said he's only seen film history twice in his life. The first time was with the tests that George Lucas did for *Star Wars*—and now he's seen it again . . . with this rabbit!"[10] The green light was given by Disney.

In the production of *Who Framed Roger Rabbit*, the London animation team would get the live-action Kodalith photostats, and Dick Williams would provide direction to the animators. The original animation drawings and the associated stats would come to Knott in the Effects Department. He would assign an effects animator and discuss how they should key-up the mattes providing the sculptural tone areas, shadows, and rimlights. The matte art would go to the Camera Department, headed by John Leatherbarrow. Each of the animated characters and their associated effects matte elements would be shot on a separate roll of high-contrast film. The color cels were shot "flip-flop"—that is, top-lit and then backlit.[11]

At ILM, the separate elements would be split and combined with live action in the optical printers, with high-contrast runs of tone, shadow, rims, and articulate mattes exposed at varying degrees of density and diffusion.[12] The details of light and shadow were made to match the lighting in the live-action shoot. There could be as many as twelve levels of effects animation for standard shots. Neutral density filters were used to graduate the edges. The tone pass might need to be sculpted and a soft edge was created on the tone mattes by putting it slightly out of focus.[13] An innovation, developed by Peg Hunter and Ed Jones at ILM, was a technique of "painting" the colored tones on the film. ILM created a palette of pastel colors on color print stock for each character. The colors were printed, with different types of diffusion, on the clear "hold-out" centers when adding the tone effects and shadows. It was, essentially, sculpting with color. Where the RWA technique provided a 2½-dimension effect, the ILM upgrade provided a 2¾-dimension effect.[14]

There were two key points in the film that were absolutely critical for going over-the-top with the animation effects: the opening transition from the Maroon cartoon to live action, including Valiant's exit into the Maroon Studio, and the first appearance of Jessica Rabbit at the Ink and Paint Club. The shot in which Valiant exits the Maroon Studio building required almost eighty passes on the optical printer to composite.[15] For Jessica's dress at the Ink and Paint Club, ILM included high-contrast elements, painted on a cel, to simulate sequins. It also included points of light-flash with filters and diffusion lenses. The final element was a pass shot through a plastic sandwich bag that had been rubbed with steel wool.[16]

What has separated *Who Framed Roger Rabbit* from other live-action/animation combination films is the extent to which interaction detail was added at times when "nobody is really looking." Kristian outlined three reasons why *Who Framed Roger Rabbit* has set the standard, not only for traditionally animated films but for CGI films, too. First, convincing eye-lines between human and animated characters; second, convincing physical interactions between the animated characters and the real world they inhabit; and third, convincing use of light and shadow.[17] Regarding the latter, the process of using tone mattes is described above, but the special magic of *Who Framed Roger Rabbit* is the extent to which the special effects animators provided detailed interplay of light and shadow that placed the animated characters convincingly in the real-world scene. This may have been demonstrated most persuasively in the scene in which Eddie, Dolores, and Roger are in the back room of the Terminal Bar, when Eddie is trying to saw off the handcuffs. Eddie accidentally bumps his head on the overhead light, which starts it swinging; therefore, the light source is constantly changing throughout the scene. London SFX animator Chris Jenkins, assisted by Fraser MacLean, not only created the set of tone mattes unique for each frame, which followed the changing light source and fully characterized Roger's underlying anatomy but, with ILM, altered the color of the tones and shadows as the quality of the light changed due to the swinging lamp. There was also a translucency in the painting of Roger's ears that is seen when his ears are directly in front of the overhead light.[18] The stunning but seemingly superfluous attention to detail might not be apparent to the ordinary moviegoer, but it went a long way to selling the combination concept at a subliminal level. Disney Animation even uses the term "bumping the lamp," when describing efforts to go above and beyond.

At the time of the *Roger Rabbit* project, ILM had ten people in the animation group and twenty people in the roto group. They would be put on teams for the duration of specific projects. *Willow* was going through ILM at the same time as *Who Framed Roger Rabbit*. Wes Takahashi was the supervising animator in the team assigned to the *Roger Rabbit* project. The other members of the team were Tim Björklund, Nick Stern, and Sean Turner. There had been rumors of the *Roger Rabbit* project floating around ILM for some time. John Armstrong, a senior ILM artist, even pigeonholed Ken Ralston to volunteer to direct the animation and have ILM do all of the film's animation, including the character animation. A copy of the novel *Who Censored Roger Rabbit?* was circulating at ILM, but at that point in time there was no idea of the scope of the project.[19] In fact, they were a bit cynical and doubtful about the potential for the *Roger Rabbit* project at the start due to their unsatisfactory experience on the film *Howard the Duck* and its poor performance at the box office.

The live-action film was processed at ILM to make the peg-registered Kodalith photostats of each frame that were sent to London. All of the animation and effects art was done in London. London would put the work under camera and send the negatives to ILM for processing.[20] It would go straight to the Optical Printer Department. Ken Ralston looked at the dailies and, if necessary, would go to the ILM animation group for embellishment with rimlights.[21] The Glendale unit sent the animation cels and effects art to ILM for camera work. Four optical printers worked full-time on the *Roger Rabbit* project.[22]

The ILM animation group prepared the extra rimlight effects requested by Ralston but they also did some special effects scenes themselves. Takahashi designed the effect in which the policeman reaches into a cartoon "hole" at the ACME Warehouse. The animation was rendered by Sean Turner.[23] Nick Stern did the shadows of the cartoon elevator on Bob Hoskins as he went up the skyscraper in Toontown. He also did the shadows for the flattened Judge Doom at the ACME Warehouse.[24]

The illusion of 1947 Hollywood was created with the help of effects supervisor Michael Lantieri. He and his crew dressed the Ren-Mar Studio, formerly the Desilu Studio, in Hollywood. They also dressed Hope Street in downtown Los Angeles, with signs and facades to evoke 1940s Hollywood. Richard Williams went to Los Angeles when he was fifteen years old to meet Disney animators. The year was 1948, and he stayed at the YMCA on South Hope Street. He says that the Hope Street exteriors created by Lantieri looked exactly right.[25] To complete the illusion, they laid down fake streetcar track and suspended phoney overhead electric cable for the streetcars. Two Pacific & Electric Red Cars were built by Dan Jefferies over bus frames.[26] Zemeckis was not happy about the look of the back projection when the scene of Valiant escaping the Toon Patrol was tested in the studio.

He wanted Hoskins to be driving a real vehicle on Hope Street. A special buggy was prepared for Benny the Cab from Honda four-wheel drive off-road vehicles. Robert Spurlock and Clay Pinney were brought in to oversee the conversion. The off-road vehicles were cut in half and articulated with air rams so that the front half would stretch out three feet and then the rest of the car would slide to catch up. The driver's seat also had air rams and four-way gimbals that would move Hoskins around in an exaggerated way.[27] The buggy was covered by the Benny the Cab animation, done mostly by Dale Baer. The driver of the buggy was underneath Hoskins's seat and was covered by spare tire animation. The Toon Patrol vehicle was operated remotely from the back of the van.[28] The cartoon interaction was enhanced with animated character reflections on the side of the Toon Patrol van.[29] Other in-camera effects in the Los Angeles shoot included creating footprints in dirt, moving bushes, and making splashes in puddles.[30]

In the shot where Eddie Valiant exits the Maroon Studio, a host of special effects were choreographed in a single-take panning shot. The most interesting was the stork mailman on a bicycle. They didn't have time to develop gyros that would keep the bicycle upright, and it would be difficult to disguise the mechanism under animation. Ultimately, they found that if they filled the tires with water, the bicycle would stay upright and its momentum, when pushed, would keep going in a moderately straight line and would crank the pedals. In the production take, it was pulled by a cable.[31]

In-camera mechanical effects were the key to the magic of cartoon interaction with the real world and George Gibbs was the mechanical effects supervisor in London. He had worked with Spielberg and Watts on the two *Indiana Jones* films. He read the script and noted what would require special effects. He scoped those out to provide Watts with a budget and the crew requirement. He ended up with a crew of six people conducting experiments and making robotic arms.[32] In addition, there was a crew of puppeteers, sometimes as many as seventeen, under the supervision of Dave Barclay. They operated marionettes, manipulated objects on rods from off-screen, and used their hands directly for movements on-screen, such as Roger moving under Valiant's overcoat at the Terminal Bar.[33]

A large special effects prop was the Dip Truck. It was a ten-wheel drive World War II bridge-building truck. It was to be used inside the ACME Warehouse set, so the diesel engine was replaced with a twelve-horsepower electric motor. A special gearing system and remote drive were added. They also added hydraulics, flashing lights, and a water cannon. Gibbs researched high-intensity water delivery systems and found a unique nozzle with flow straighteners. The design rectified the turbulence at the discharge of the nozzle, and with a pressure of 150 psi, he achieved a sixty-foot jet with no fall-off. The Dip was green fluorescent dye in water. Everything had to be washed down, dried, and placed back in position for continuity, before the next take. It would take hours between takes. The ACME Warehouse shoot required two crews working day and night. The London mechanical effects crew also built a model of the Dip Truck that was five-feet long and two-feet high.[34]

For the dueling pianos scene with Donald Duck and Daffy Duck, the piano keys were rigged to play the actual notes of Liszt's "Hungarian Rhapsody." Gibbs and the film's composer, Alan Silvestri, developed a computerized synclavier to play the keys at increasing speed as the duel escalated. The synclavier's digital impulses activated solenoids under each piano key.[35]

There were a number of effects that did not make it into the final cut of the film. The most notorious is the Pig-Head scene, which made it all the way through to Ink and Paint. At the conclusion of the scene, Eddie Valiant goes back to his office and showers with turpentine to remove the Pig-Head. Gibbs achieved the effect by lining a silicone rubber Pig-Head mold with Kleenex tissues and spun sugar. He made fine cuts in the Pig-Head mask, and when Hoskins poured "turpentine" shampoo on his head, the cotton candy and tissue dissolved. The process could be seen through the translucent shower curtain, and when Hoskins opened the shower curtain the dissolving "pink stuff" was dripping off him.[36] Another gag effect would have had the Toontown sign's eyes blink when blinded by the headlights of cars racing out of Toontown. Gibbs worked throughout the shoot in London to develop an exploding cigar that would peel back like a banana and blacken Hoskins's face. He perfected the prop, but it was not used.[37]

Several mechanical effects were also created at ILM. The ILM model department built a twenty-foot long Toontown entrance tunnel. It had a three-foot-by-three-foot transparency of a cartoon curtain at the Toontown end of the tunnel. The model was laid out by Jeff Olson. He made the tunnel ceiling in one-foot sections that were removed as the camera dollied through. A small Empire camera was rigged on the special dolly. The model shop also fabricated a miniature brick wall using 16,000 hand-made plaster bricks.[38] A miniature Dip Truck was driven through the prop wall. The breakaway portion was 6,000 bricks. A real truck was driven partially through a full-size wall. The model shop also built an eighteen-inch miniature Toon Patrol van, a period phone stand, and a .38-caliber toon handgun (to Bill Frake's design).[39]

In the London live-action shoot, Judge Doom was flattened by a steamroller. The location used to film the ACME Warehouse had a pit in the floor that was used for the effect. Christopher Lloyd lay on board placed at a ten-degree angle in the pit. His head was above grade and plywood covered up his body in the pit. A prop body, fabricated of tin and zinc, was placed in such a way that it appeared to be connected to Lloyd's head. The body was connected to springs that could be manipulated from underneath in the pit. The legs were made to writhe as the steamroller moved slowly towards Judge Doom and, ultimately, the legs and body were flattened. A flattened prop, with moving eyes and broken glasses that were rigged to fall off on cue, was fabricated. Gibbs also made a flat latex replica that was filled using a vacuum cleaner and rigged so that the hat would pop off when Judge Doom re-inflated himself.[40] Gibbs sent the full-sized flattened Judge Doom to ILM, where it was used as reference for the stop-motion animation done at ILM.

Tom St. Amand did the animation and Harry Walton set it up, lit it, and did the camerawork. Paula Lucchesi and Sheila Duignan made the Judge Doom puppets. Ken Ralston coordinated the group. They were given storyboards and the live-action film from London. The flattened Judge Doom peeled himself off the floor of the ACME Warehouse and moved unsteadily towards the gas cylinder. St. Amand and Walton used both stop-motion and go-motion techniques. Go-motion made up about 40 percent of the animated scene. The puppet was attached to the go-motion mover, which cycled through walking movements and allowed Walton to capture some motion blur. Stop-motion made up the remaining 60 percent of the scene. The puppet's head and body had a ball and socket armature. The legs were reinforced with aluminum wire so that they could be manipulated into the loopy pancake stride seen in the film. The first shot was twice as long as seen in the final cut of the movie. Judge Doom had some dialogue in the scene. St. Amand animated the dialogue with replacement mouths made of clay.[41]

The most critical ILM fabrication was the VistaVision camera. VistaVision was created by Paramount in the 1950s. It used a 35mm film with higher resolution and finer grain. The film ran through the camera sideways, so the frame was twice as big as on standard cameras. Most VistaVision cameras were used strictly for special effects work. The *Roger Rabbit* project needed a VistaVision camera due to the resolution required in the Kodalith photostat for the subsequent animation process, but no VistaVision cameras existed that could shoot dialogue. ILM had to build one. Mike Bolles and Greg Beaumonte designed and built the camera, which ILM called VistaFlex. It was equipped with reflex viewing, videotape playback, and an Ultimatte video system for the bluescreen shoot.[42] ILM used Kodalith 5297 daylight balance and Kodalith 5294 films for regular shooting, but used Kodalith 5247 film for everything that would have to be composited. They used Agfa 320 film when filming the ACME Warehouse scenes because the 5247 film was not fast enough.[43] Super 35 film was used in some off-the-street chase scenes.[44] Eastman 5245 black-and-white separation stock was used to make the photostat prints for the animators.[45]

Dale Baer was working furiously storyboarding the Toontown portion of the script in early September 1987. Bill Frake was hired and started to work in Glendale on September 7. He began working with Baer on storyboards and layouts. Towards the end of September, Frake and Dave Dunnet were developing the look of Toontown. The concept drawings were approved by Zemeckis on Friday, October 2. On October 7, Frake was told that he would be going to ILM, in San Rafael, to assist during the bluescreen shoot.

He arrived in San Francisco on Friday evening, October 9, and visited ILM with Dean Cundey on Saturday. On Monday, October 12, the blue-screen stage was being set up and the Optimatte video downshooter was being prepared for Frake. For each scene, Frake would draw a quick layout sketch on tracing paper to define the framing, the cartoon environment, positioning of the characters, and perspective lines. The drawing would be laid over a video monitor connected to the video tap on the VistaFlex camera. Hoskins or his double, Sammy Pasha, would be on the bluescreen stage or in a flying rig, and the video image would be matted on the layout drawing. Marks would be set up on the stage floor, positioning of eyeline spots would be established, and camera framing would be determined in preparation for the film takes. Frake adjusted the animation layouts as they worked through the shots, identifying the light sources for later synchronization with the background animation.[46]

Hoskins arrived in the afternoon of Tuesday, October 13, and five quick shots were done. 130 bluescreen shots had been completed by the time Toontown filming was concluded on October 20.

On October 14, they filmed the shot of Eddie Valiant falling from the skyscraper. He had escaped Lena Hyena by hiding in a men's room, only to find that it had no exterior walls . . . or floor. He plummeted, but managed to catch hold of a flagpole—only to have Tweety Bird pluck his fingers off the pole . . . as his "piggies went to market." Valiant is seen hurtling towards the ground, then the camera's point-of-view changes to the side-walk—with Valiant hurtling towards it. To make this shot, Hoskins was suspended sideways in a flying rig, with large fans blowing on his face. In the film, the shot would be shown in reverse as a very fast zoom towards the "plummeting" Hoskins. The problem was that the ILM stage was not big enough for the length of zoom required in the shot. Ken Ralston resolved the situation by bringing in an eighteen-wheel trailer to provide for the necessary dolly travel. The trailer was backed up to a loading door and the eight-perf camera, on a dolly, raced away from Hoskins—across the stage and into the trailer.[47]

The rules dictated that cartoons had to carry real guns when in Los Angeles and humans had to carry toon guns when in Toontown. On October 14, at about 9 a.m., Frake was asked to draw up a toon gun. The drawing was whisked away and by mid-afternoon the magicians in the ILM model shop had created the perfect toon-like gun prop.[48]

There were 1,031 optical composite shots completed during the making of *Who Framed Roger Rabbit*,[49] far more than for any other film made to that time—including the *Star Wars* films. *Return of the Jedi* contained about 300 optically composited shots. Some of the *Who Framed Roger Rabbit* composites were on the optical printer for ten hours at a time. It was a massive logistical undertaking. *Who Framed Roger Rabbit* was awarded the Oscar for Best Achievement in Visual Efffects. Disney and Amblin decided whose names would stand for receipt of the awards: Ken Ralston, George Gibbs, Ed Jones, and Dick Williams were selected, and there is no denying the magnitude of contribution that each of them made to the film. The noticeable omission was Chris Knott. It is not clear why Knott was not acknowledged for his contribution to the visual effects in the film by being included as a recipient of an Oscar. Knott had sent a full "How We Do This" manual of his optical combination developments to ILM at the onset of the *Roger Rabbit* project. It came back jacketed with an ILM logo.[50] Disney's behind-the-scenes documentary *Behind the Ears: The True Story of Roger Rabbit*, featured in the Vista series DVD release in 2003, and the television special *Roger Rabbit and the Secrets of Toontown* (1988) were edited to make it look as though the entire visual effects process was done at ILM. The lack of acknowledgment of the London effects team, and especially of the contribution of Chris Knott, remains a sore point for many artists who worked at the Forum.[51] Long after *Who Framed Roger Rabbit* had been released, Knott received a call from Don Hahn. Disney wanted to know what visual effects techniques had been developed specifically for the film, which Knott surmised was because Disney intended to apply for patents. Knott responded that he had developed most of the effects techniques used in *Roger Rabbit* while at RWA. He has great respect for Hahn and speaks highly of how Hahn managed the production in London, but he is disappointed that Hahn was made to be part of an effort to co-opt their intellectual property.[52]

Chapter Seven

WRAP UP

When the decision was made to produce the animation for *Who Framed Roger Rabbit* in London, the exchange rate was very favorable, and film production in England made good economic sense. As the crew at the Forum found its groove, there were certainly plans at Disney to make more animated films in London. Dick and Jill Purdum, formerly of Richard Williams Animation, were already developing *Beauty and the Beast*, and the talk was that it would be done in London.

Jeffrey Katzenberg and Marty Katz had been pushing hard in order to make the scheduled opening date for *Who Framed Roger Rabbit*. In addition to the monies already spent on promotion and arrangements for wide-circulation newsmagazine cover stories, there were marketing tie-ins with Coca-Cola and McDonald's, both of which were extremely time sensitive. At one point, Katzenberg was heard to say to Williams, "You can work 10 percent less well and we'll get the job done."[1] As time went on, Katzenberg told Williams that he should work at 60 percent quality. Williams said, "I'm already only doing 60 percent quality," to which Katzenberg responded, "It's too much . . . work at 20 percent quality."[2] These comments were clearly borne out of frustration with Williams and the desperation of pressure from Michael Eisner, but they inevitably became known to the crew and the comments were at odds with what "they" wanted for the film and diminished the value of their efforts—they took the comments personally. It was Katz's job to "shake the tree."[3] On December 16, 1987, an afternoon wine-and-cheese party was held at the Forum during a visit from Zemeckis, Katzenberg, Marshall, and Katz. During the event Katz told the animators that they needed to do "miracle work for no extra pay." Colin White's response was, "We're British . . . we don't care."[4] Dick Williams gave a speech to the entire crew at that time. He said, "Look, we're at crunch time now . . . this is really serious. We're really going to have to step up to the mark. Everybody has got to work for all the time that they have and with all of the energy they have in their bodies. You either do this, or you just leave! You just get out of this studio . . . you just leave right now!" Zemeckis jumped in to say, "What Dick means is . . .," as he saw the prospect of everybody walking when the production needed all hands on deck.[5] An inter-office memo to Hahn and Williams on Amblin Entertainment letterhead was intercepted and circulated amongst the crew. It was from Frank Marshall and read, "I have four important words for you. Get the footage up. Love, Doc Fantasy."

Technology didn't help the impression Katzenberg and Katz made on the animators. Fax machines were a new technology at the time and there was only one machine at the Forum. A "confidential" memo from Katzenberg to Hahn and Williams lay on the machine and it was not long before a copy circulated around the crew. It said, "We won't pay more overtime. Appeal to their [the animator's] artistic integrity," and it went over like a lead balloon.

The animators' opinion of Marty Katz was that he was intimidating and that he seemed like a character out of *The Sopranos* or *The Godfather*; they observed that he "dressed like a gangster." Of course, he was only doing his job, which was to get the animators focused on finishing the film on time, and, of course, there was a carrot . . . the "promise" of a future Disney film in London. During the event Katz said, "Your future is assured!"[6] That promise was reiterated at the breakfast meeting with Katzenberg that the animators were invited to at the Regency Suite in Le Méridien Hotel at Piccadilly on December 17—and at the Christmas party on December 18. Many of the veterans took comments like that with a grain of salt, but others in the crew perceived it to be a promise and some took out mortgages and made other large purchases on the assumption of continued employment. In addition to rumors of *Beauty and the Beast*, a second *Rescuers* film (*The Rescuers Down Under*) was being openly discussed.

It came as a surprise for some, and a shock for others, when layoff notices were distributed in mid-February for termination of the employment contracts in four weeks (i.e., mid-March 1988).

The wrap party was scheduled for Friday, March 18, at the Barbican Center—with the expectation that the animation would be complete and the film would have moved on to postproduction in California. The four workweeks of "termination notice" were often seven days a week and twelve-to sixteen hours a day. Many people had their contracts extended into early April in order to complete the animation. On March 18, most people had put in a full day of work at the Forum, without taking lunch . . . so they were ready for the break provided by the wrap party. Jacques

Muller rented a video camera and brought it into the Forum that day. His video provides an interesting glimpse into the rabbit warren of workspaces and the activity at the Forum.[7]

There was to be a work aspect to the wrap party. In the final sequence of the film the denizens of Toontown were to sing "Smile, Darn Ya, Smile!," and the producers wanted the London crew to do the singing. "Smile, Darn Ya, Smile!" was written by Charles O'Flynn, Jack Meskill, and Max Rich in 1931 and used in the Warner Bros. studio Merrie Melodies short of the same name. *Smile, Darn Ya, Smile!* starred Foxy, a character created by Rudy Ising, who made almost no effort to disguise that it was a complete knock-off of Mickey Mouse. Even Foxy's girlfriend looked exactly like Minnie Mouse. The song "Smile, Darn Ya, Smile!" was the nation's second most popular in 1931 and its publisher, and copyright holder, Crawford Music, made sure that it got plenty of exposure. It provided rights to use the song to Fleischer Studios and to Warner Bros. Studios. Fleischer used the song in the opening credits of *And the Green Grass Grew All Around* (1931), *My Wife's Gone to the Country* (1931), *That Old Gang of Mine* (1931), *Kitty From Kansas City* (1931), and *My Baby Just Cares For Me* (1931)—using the lyrics "sing, darn ya, sing." All of them were part of the Screen Songs series, which featured popular songs and the "famous bouncing ball." Betty Boop starred in *My Wife's Gone to the Country* and *Kitty from Kansas City*. Both of the Betty Boop shorts featured a mouse character that was indistinguishable from Mickey Mouse. Warner Bros. used the song in *Smile, Darn Ya, Smile!* (1931) and *Vitaphone Varieties* (1935). *Smile, Darn Ya, Smile* was directed by Rudy Ising and produced by Hugh Harman and Ising. It was drawn by Friz Freleng and Carmen Maxwell. It is a remake of the first Oswald the Lucky Rabbit short that was released, *Trolley Troubles* (1927), on which both Hugh Harman and Friz Freleng worked while still at the Disney Brothers studio.

Robert Watts suggested that there might be legal issues if the animators' voices were in the film without proper assignation of rights, so Toon Town Limited, the Amblin entity constituted for the production of *Who Framed Roger Rabbit*, prepared a contract for all of the participants to sign. Each person was given a £1 coin by Frank Marshall, out of a sock full of them, at their desks as they signed the contract on March 18th. The contract read [*sic*]:

From: Toon Town Limited   Dated: 18th March 1988
      Cannon Elstree Studios
      Shenley Road
      Borehamwood
      WD6 1JG

To: . . . .

Dear . . . .

"Who Framed Roger Rabbit?"

In consideration of the sum of £1 now paid to you by us and other good and valuable consideration (the receipt of which you hereby acknowledge):

1. You agree that if we film and/or record you at the party to be held at The Garden Room, The Barbican Center on 18th March 1988 and in particular your singing of the song "Smile Darn Ya Smile" we shall be entitled to include such film and/or recordings in our discretion in the feature film "Who Framed Roger Rabbit?" and/or the related documentary which we are producing (collectively "the Films").

2. You acknowledge that all rights whatsoever throughout the world in or in any way attaching to the Films or either of them and all the above-mentioned films and sound recordings in which you or your voice appear shall belong to us absolutely and that we may make or authorize any use of the same and may exploit the same in any manner but shall not be bound to do so.

3. You hereby give all such consents as are or may be required under the Performers Protection Acts 1958 to 1972 or any statute of like purpose of effect for the time being in force in any part of the world.

4. You acknowledge that the payment provided for in this letter constitutes full and adequate compensation for all services rendered and rights granted by you under this letter and that you are not entitled to any further or additional compensation whether by reference to any guild or union agreement or otherwise howsoever.

You agree that we shall be entitled to assign the benefit of this Agreement.

Yours faithfully,
[signed by Frank Marshall]

. . . .

for and on behalf of
TOON TOWN LIMITED
ACCEPTED AND AGREED:

. . . .

The crew members found their way to the Barbican Center for the get-together in the Garden Room. There was a free bar and there were hors d'oeuvres, although the video record shows decidedly more drinking than eating. The scene was very convivial, with people talking and laughing in small groups to piano accompaniment. People gradually drifted to an auditorium, where the song "Smile, Darn Ya, Smile!" was to be recorded. A sheet of lyrics was handed out and instructions were provided as the group assembled. They were to sing with their favorite cartoon voices. There was a practice run-through, followed by a lot more instructions. Two takes were recorded with the group sitting and then three takes were recorded with the group standing. Dick Williams did an impressive string of cartoon yells throughout the last take.

It was primarily the animation crew (animators, assistant animators, in-betweeners) who were invited to sing. Not all animators accepted the invitation, including many who were being laid off. Approximately sixty people took part in the recording. Those who did not sing consoled themselves at the bar while the recording was being done.

Following the recording session, everybody came into the auditorium. Frank Marshall did his "Doc Fantasy" magic act, which ended up with his falling into a big chocolate cake—a staple of his for end of production wrap parties. Then Bob Zemeckis took the floor to give a heartfelt thank you speech to the crew. He was heckled. A shout, "Show us your tits!" rang out, which indicates that there might have been a bit too much drinking prior to gathering everybody for the speeches. It was almost as though they were there for a celebration but a soccer match broke out instead. The dyed-in-the-wool Londoners had difficulty in considering themselves as part of "the Mouse" empire from the very start, but they invested much of themselves in the production and had high hopes for more work with Disney. They had put up with the Disney name badges, and the "We Can Do It" stick pins, and the upbeat cheerfulness, although these "very Disney, very American" things usually were far from popular in Britain.[8] There was always an underlying British cynicism—or, maybe better put, a healthy skepticism. They knew that they were lucky to be working on the film, but there was always an undercurrent of mocking it. The antipathy was never artist-to-artist—it was mostly aimed at the unseen Hollywood.[9] Many people later said it was unfortunate that Bob Zemeckis was on the stage, because the crew had no grievance with him. It should have been one of the other known Hollywood faces. Some thought that Zemeckis was just saying trite "American" stuff and got the brunt of the alcohol-fueled bitterness. Others thought that it was not mean-spirited but was "just the British letting off steam." They would say that the North Americans did not understand that the English people tease each other . . . and that it's not done in malice.[10] James Baxter thought, "I hope he's taking this the right way!"[11]

Zemeckis was confused and upset by the heckling and lack of respect from the crew. Several animators went up to him to apologize for behavior of the crowd.[12] Many others thought that it had been a grand night, and went back to the bar.

The ranks at the Forum thinned as March wore on. People left as their assignments concluded and their termination dates arrived. Some were given extensions into early April to finish the last of the work. Shelley Page was doing freelance work, after her time at the Forum was done, when she received a panicked call from Don Hahn saying that they had forgotten to do the airbrushed title card. He asked her to come back in to do it. She told him, "I've fulfilled my contract . . . this will be my freelance rate." She was paid three times her crew rate for the work.[13]

The last scene to be done was the dialogue with *Roger Rabbit* at the opening of the Maroon cartoon. Neil Boyle's contract was extended to May 4 to work with Dick Williams in finishing it. Williams was still there finishing it when Boyle left.[14] The contract for Tony Clark, the post-punch assistant or xerography technician, was extended to May 6 to move the scene along the pipeline.[15] When the scene was finished, the Ink and Paint Department was shut down and the studio was closed. Max Howard was the last person there when he got an emergency call from ILM. They had to reshoot the film's final scene. They had scoured the inventory of cels and three cels were missing. Howard found the animation drawings and called Barbara McCormack, the Trace and Paint supervisor. They inked and painted the three cels and dried them with a hairdryer. Howard then drove them to Heathrow airport and put them on a plane to Los Angeles.[16] Howard then relocated temporarily back to the 20th Century Fox offices on Soho Square, with the assistance of runner Richard Leon, after the Forum closed. They later relocated to offices on Euston Road.[17]

Glenn Sylvester worked long hours every day of the week from just after Christmas 1987 until when he finished with the production early the following April. He was totally wrung-out and went back to Canada to stay with his parents in Ottawa for a couple of months before looking for further work. He needed the decompression—and recalls just sitting, almost catatonic, on his parent's couch for the first four days after his return. He just could not think.[18] Nik Ranieri relates similarly that after he finished, he spent a full week just sitting on the couch in the flat he shared with Cal Leduc, watching snooker on television.[19] Many others have similar stories of the toll that the months of pressure took on them.[20] Many were so exhausted that they became ill at the conclusion of the production.[21] In the same meeting in which Dick Williams cajoled the crew to extend their efforts on the film, on December 16, he also said, "This project will be the project that defines your career. You will always be able to use it as currency with prospective employers."[22] Many people at the meeting thought that Williams was being terribly theatrical in saying such a thing, but most have found it to be true. Eventually, the exhausted crew picked themselves up and continued their careers.

The Disney animators, Andreas Deja and Dave Spafford, went back to the Disney fold in Burbank, although it was not so cut-and-dried for Spafford. He had already gone back to the US to work in the Glendale unit. As his time on *Roger Rabbit* came to an end, somebody at Disney said, "We're thinking of keeping you." Spaff went ballistic and said, "What do you mean you're *thinking* of keeping me—I'm a Disney employee!"[23] Others, such as Dave Bossert, and Dorse and Vera Lanpher found their way 'back' into Disney. A few others found their way into Disney in Burbank. James Baxter, Roger Chiasson, Joe Haidar, and Tom and Pat Sito joined Disney to work on the *Roger Rabbit* short *Tummy Trouble* before working on Disney features. Chris Jenkins and Nik Ranieri started on *The Little Mermaid* soon after the release of *Who Framed Roger Rabbit*. Cal Leduc started at Disney at couple of years later, on *The Lion King*, and Raul Garcia was in Burbank starting on *Aladdin*. Greg Manwaring joined the Florida crew on the *Roger Rabbit* short *Trail Mix-Up* and then worked on *The Lion King* and *Pocahontas*. Jacques Muller was retained by Disney as the manager for character art for merchandising in Disney Europe. He started in that function while still at the Forum and later moved to offices in Paris. In January 1989 he found his way to Burbank to join his colleagues on *Tummy Trouble*.²⁴

Max Howard went to the US with Disney and opened up the animation studio associated with the Disney/MGM Studio at Walt Disney World. London crew members Daniel Cohen, Bridgitte Hartley, Alan Simpson, Paul Steele, and Alex Williams ended up joining him there. Disney Television ultimately opened up a production in London . . . *DuckTales the Movie: Treasure of the Lost Lamp*, on which Caron Creed, Al Gaivoto, Fraser MacLean, Brent Odell, Andrew Painter, Dave Pritchard, and Emma Tornero worked.

Many animators went to Munich to work on *The Magic Voyage* for a time, including Rej Bourdages, Annie Dubois, Helga Egilson, Al Gaivoto, Peter Gambier, Cal Leduc, Irene Parkins (Couloufis), Howy Parkins, Silvia Pompei, Philippe Rejaudry, Rob Stevenhagen, Glen Sylvester, and Julia Woolf. *The BFG* was being produced in London, and Alain Costa and Gary French-Powell found work on it. Steven Spielberg established the Amblimation studio in London and more than forty-five artists and technicians from the Forum worked on productions there until it was finally wrapped into the newly formed DreamWorks Animation Studio. Simon Wells, David Bowers, Nick Fletcher, and Shelley Page had great impact at DreamWorks when they were brought to the United States. Many people from the Forum went to work at Andrew Ruhemann's newly formed Passion Pictures in London, and others went back to the commercial studios and freelancing they had done before *Roger Rabbit*. Within the year, Dick Williams was gearing up production on *The Thief* and moved from the house at 138 Royal College Street to take up residence back at the Forum. He attracted many *Roger Rabbit* alumni back with him.

There had been security at the entrance to the Forum, in the form of an elderly commissionaire at a table near the elevator. The primary function had been to control access of visitors, and unwanted visitors, to the production areas, but it was also the control point for materials exiting the building. No artwork was to leave the building, although many people did work at their homes when the crunch came. It is difficult to imagine that there would have been many bag checks and challenges from the commissionaires.

All of the art generated in the process of producing the film was the property of Disney, as is the case with all Disney films. In Burbank, selected concept art, drawings, and production cels are taken to the Disney Archives for cataloguing and storage. In the old days, cels were washed and reused. Animation veterans talk about "surfing" down the halls on mats of cels. Various studios routinely tossed animation cels in the trash and much artwork walked out the door with employees. Much of the animation art in the current auction market was 'saved' from garbage cans and dumpsters. Disney made animation cels available through Courvoisier Gallery from 1938 until 1946. Prices ranged from $5 to $50 for a multilayer cel set-up, with background, from films such as *Snow White and the Seven Dwarfs* and *Pinocchio*. At Disneyland, the Art Corner operated from 1955 until 1966, when it was closed for the expansion of Tomorrowland. Animation cels could be purchased for $1.47. Multilayer set-ups were available for $5. Even after the closure of the Art Corner, original Disney production cels could be purchased at the Emporium on Main Street in both Disneyland and Magic Kingdom in Walt Disney World for less than $25 for a multilayer cel set-up with a lithograph background.

Prior to *Roger Rabbit*, animation cels could be obtained through specialty auction houses, such as Hake's Americana and Collectibles, at reasonable prices, but Disney was not enjoying the value of the increasing prices for animation artwork. For *Roger Rabbit*, Disney intended to collect the production artwork, save some for the archives, destroy most of it, and sell the remainder to a growing animation collector market. The animation art at the Forum was collected in a room, but some of it "disappeared" before the intended disposition. In the course of the following twelve months the FBI was actively following up on *Roger Rabbit* cels and artwork that appeared in the gray collector market. Even crew members who had been gifted keepsakes or received them through official channels became aware of the situation when they inquired about the value of their keepsakes years afterward. Reputable animation art outlets would not handle the sale of any *Roger Rabbit* artwork that did not have the official Disney seal.[25]

The reason for a heightened level of vigilance became clear when the partnership of Disney and the Sotheby's auction house in New York was announced. On June 28, 1989, Sotheby's conducted "The Art of *Who Framed Roger Rabbit*" auction in New York City. On offer were 560 cels, each with a copy of its live-action or painted background, in 400 auction lots. Single set-ups would have one or more cel layers, depending on the number of characters in the scene. In addition, there were two-, three-, four-, and six-cel progressions, pan cels, and backgrounds. The pieces were exhibited at Sotheby's for several days prior to the auction. They were also presented in an auction sales catalogue, with a print run of 25,000, which soon became a collectible itself.[26]

What became several of the most iconic images from the film, often with Jessica and Roger together in a scene, were auctioned for the high end of the price range. Nevertheless, a two-cel progression with an incidental

TABLE 3. Sotheby's auction results

	Single set-up		2-cel progression		3-cel progression		4-cel progression		6-cel progression	
	Estimated, USD	Realized, USD	Estimated, USD	Realized, USD	Estimated, USD	Realized, USD	Estimated, USD	Realized, USD	Estimated, USD	Realized, USD
Weasels	700-900	1,000-1,800								
Baby Herman, Benny the Cab	1,000-1,500	1,600-2,400								
Roger Rabbit, Jessica Rabbit	1,200-1,800	1,800-11,500	1,800-2,200	4,100	2,800-3,200	11,500-14,500	4,000-6,000	11,000	5,000-7,000	8,800
Toontown Street scene	5,000-7,000	12,100								
Classic Disney and Warner Bros.	4,000-6,000	5,000	2,500-2,500	6,900						
Final scene pan shot -approx. 11" x 17"	4,000-6,000	7,150-10,450								
e.g. lots 258, 305, 379 -approx. 10" x 40"	10,000-15,000	27,500-33,000								
e.g. lot 226 -approx. 10" x 40"	15,000-20,000	50,6000								

character like the Stork (the mailman on a bicycle in the opening scene at the R. K. Maroon studio) realized $1,650, and a set-up from the closing images of Porky Pig and Tinkerbell realized $6,050 (compared with a pre-auction estimate of $2,000 to $3,000).

Premieres

The crews were invited to prerelease screenings of the film. The Burbank/ Glendale screening was held on June 14 at the Disney main lot theater. The London screening was held on June 19 at the Odeon Leicester Square theater. The Glendale crew invitation announced the film as a Touchstone Pictures and Steven Spielberg presentation. The London crew invitation did not provide that designation. Roy E. Disney's only involvement in *Roger Rabbit* was to say that *Who Framed Roger Rabbit* could not be released as a "Disney" film because of the adult themes. It was released under the Touchstone Pictures banner, although in the media mêlée in the popular and trade press everybody knew that it was a Disney film.[27]

An offer for attending the world premiere at Radio City Music Hall in New York City was extended to the London crew in the studio's weekly newsletter, *RABBITRABBITRABBIT*. The offer covered a flight to New York City on Continental Airlines out of Gatwick airport, four nights at the Best Western Milford Plaza Hotel near Times Square, and tickets to the premiere. The cost was £580 for a single-occupancy room, £491 for a double-occupancy room, £466 for a triple-occupancy room, and £453 for a quadruple-occupancy room. In a letter from Touchstone and Walt Disney Pictures' director of East Coast publicity, dated June 10, they were informed that there would be a special party for the animators, filmmakers, and cast following the screening. They also received a souvenir invitation that included a listing of the full cast and crew. The invitation referred to a cocktail reception to be held before the screening. It was a corporate event, and the letter informed the crew that they were not invited. The principal actors in attendance (Bob Hoskins, Joanna Cassidy, Charles Fleischer, and Kathleen Turner) certainly were.

At least thirty-five London animation crew members made the trip to New York on their own dime; many had not been there before. Several people from the Glendale crew also made it to New York. Tom and Pat Sito were the hometown tour guides for much of the group. They covered the Empire State Building, Times Square, the beach at Coney Island, and the Staten Island ferry. The official Disney representatives for the premiere found a Tiffany box/case on their bed when they arrived at their hotel room. Inside the box was a composited production cel and live-action background from the film, encased in a silver Tiffany frame; only a handful of these were created.[28]

The film premiere took place at Radio City Music Hall on Tuesday, June 21, at 7:30 p.m. Zemeckis, Watts, Marshall, Hahn, Howard, Schmidt, Ralston, and Katzenberg wore tuxedos and a blue bow-tie with yellow polka dots, in the manner of Roger Rabbit. Dick Williams wore an open collar white shirt and a sweater vest. Many of the animators wore tuxedos. Some people had not joined the Sito tour group, and apparently had not received the dress code memo. It was a scorchingly hot day, and Al Gaivoto had been touring New York with his wife, trying to find air-conditioning wherever they could. Gaivoto showed up at Radio City Music Hall for the premiere wearing shorts and T-shirt, and sporting a knapsack.[29]

Some of the animators complained about the seats they were given, but most were just happy to be there and delighted at the response from the crowd. When they went to go to the party after the screening, in a room underneath the theater, Dave Spafford said that some of them were not allowed in. They did not have the right color of ticket. Spaff was arguing with the doorman when a woman from Disney Publicity intervened. The doorman was saying, "I can't let you in with that." When the Publicity person asked what was the matter, Spaff said, "My ticket is green, and the only ones being allowed down here are yellow." She asked how many of them had yellow tickets . . . and it was most of them. For Spaff it was just another example of inequity in a career full of tilting at windmills.[30]

For the rest, it was a celebrity status that most had never previously experienced. Tom Sito took a group out on the town after the party. The tuxedos, and mention of their role in *Who Framed Roger Rabbit*, gave them head-of-the-line privileges for getting into the Blue Note Jazz Club on West Third Street. On the previous night (Monday), the *Roger Rabbit* card had been played to get them in to see Woody Allen playing at Michael's Pub on East Fifty-fifth Street.[31]

Who Framed Roger Rabbit had its general release on June 22 at the Ziegfeld Theatre and 1,200 other screens across North America. The response was tremendous. In Los Angeles, the admission line at the Cinerama Dome circled the block for days. For the crew, it was the first time they realized the significance of the project in which they'd been a part. They had felt that it was going to be something special, but an animated film takes a long time to develop and they spent most of that time seeing unfinished work. Although some had seen the transformation of the finished film at the crew screenings, it was not the same as seeing it with an audience. In a memo dated February 25, Don Hahn had warned the London crew to avoid speaking with the press about the film. The production was cloaked in secrecy, so it was a shock to be in New York City and see the movie theater windows and the toy display at Macy's. The crew members were giddier about picking up *Roger Rabbit* merchandise and souvenirs than the kids. As an example of the serendipity of the moment, Pete Western was walking over the Brooklyn Bridge to get a photograph of the Manhattan skyline when he was able to snag a $20 bill as it wafted by in the breeze.[32]

The film received extraordinary reviews.[33] The *Chicago Sun-Times* ran a review by film critic Roger Ebert on June 22 under the headline, "Runaway Hit from a Rabbit." Ebert wrote: "I stopped off at a hot dog stand before the screening of 'Who Framed Roger Rabbit,' and I ran into some other movie critics. They said they were going to the same screening. I asked them what they'd heard about the film. They said they were going to see it for the second time in two days. That's the kind of word-of-mouth that money can't buy. And 'Who Framed Roger Rabbit,' which opens today, is the kind of movie that gets made once in a blue moon, because it represents an immense challenge to the filmmakers: They have to make a good movie while inventing new technology at the same time. Like '2001,' 'Close Encounters' and 'E.T.,' this movie is not only a great entertainment but a breakthrough in craftsmanship—the first film to convincingly combine real actors and animated cartoon characters in the same space in the same time and make it look real. I've never seen anything like it before."[34]

A private preview screening of *Who Framed Roger Rabbit* was given in London, at the BAFTA theater in Piccadilly, on July 25. It was by invitation only (with the password for admission being, "Walt Sent Me") in order to market the use of *Who Famed Roger Rabbit* and the film's characters for promotional purposes. The rest of the United Kingdom would have to wait until November 21 for its premiere.

The premiere in London was a Royal Charity event in aid of the British Lung Foundation. Diana, Princess of Wales, was in attendance at the Odeon Leicester Square on that date. Diana was the last one to enter the theater—preceded by Bob Zemeckis, Steven Spielberg, Bob Hoskins, and Charles Fleischer. Spielberg was with his then-wife, Amy Irving, who provided Jessica's singing voice in the film.[35] Diana wore a pink satin ballgown with a white shawl collar, a choker of pink pearls, and pink pearl earrings. Spielberg introduced her to a *Roger Rabbit* costume character. She shook Roger's hand, but declined to give him a hug. The costumed character turned his back on the princess and shook, as if sobbing in dejection.

Several of the London crew managed to make it to the premiere. Annie Elvin, head of Matte and Roto, was there with her tuxedoed son, Harry, who was a runner at the Forum. Dave Spafford had come back from Los Angeles to visit friends. He and Debbie Lilly had maintained a long-distance relationship and would soon marry and live together in North Hollywood, where their Friday night parties became a required stop for the animation set. He joined Raul Garcia and several other London-based animators at the premiere. As with the New York premiere, Spaff complained that the animators were given short shrift by the Disney Publicity folks. In this case, it may have been atonement for the behavior during the wrap party eight months before. Spaff describes the situation: "The same thing happened . . . we had the crappiest seats . . . in the balcony, in the far corner, in the back row. When it was all over with, we're excited because Princess Diana is there. They held us all back, and then the one little section that they had roped off, with the 'real people who made the film,' was going upstairs to some special party. We thought they were clearing it in order to get her out safely and hoped we would be allowed in after the crowd had thinned. We made our point with Security and were directed to a side door, which we thought was a back way to the party room. No, it was the back door to the theater and all of a sudden we were in the alley. We all went to the pub instead."[36]

Oscars

The sixty-first annual Academy Awards show was broadcast on ABC. At this point, the Walt Disney Company had not yet acquired Capital Cities/ABC, Inc. The network advertised that an animated Roger Rabbit would be on hand for the live broadcast. There was a plan to have Roger and Jessica Rabbit as presenters for the Oscar telecast. *Who Framed Roger Rabbit* had been one of the year's biggest box-office hits. Dick Williams had already been voted to receive an Oscar for special achievement for directing the animation and for creating Jessica and Roger Rabbit, and the film had been nominated for six Oscars. The show's producer, Allan Carr, planned to use a special effects process, used the previous year to celebrate Mickey Mouse's sixtieth anniversary, for presenting the Oscar to Dick Williams. In the 1988 Oscar broadcast, Donald Duck, Daisy Duck, and Minnie Mouse were shown sitting in the audience. When Mickey Mouse appeared on the stage, dressed as the Sorcerer's Apprentice, he was challenged by Donald . . . who he magically put back into his seat. Mickey interacted with his co-presenter, Tom Selleck, and magically changed into a tuxedo. They presented the Oscar for Best Animated Short Subject. Carr spoke with Spielberg, Katzenberg, and Zemeckis, and found that it would be far too complicated to do the process properly with the tonal treatment used in *Who Framed Roger Rabbit*'s animation. It was estimated that the animation for the presentation would take nine months to complete and would be prohibitively expensive.[37]

Who Framed Roger Rabbit had been nominated for a Golden Globe as Best Motion Picture—Comedy or Musical, and Bob Hoskins had been nominated for Best Performance by an Actor in a Motion Picture—Comedy or Musical. He did not win in either category, but Disney and Amblin campaigned hard for Oscar nominations. Amblin and Touchstone Pictures ran ads in trade journals for consideration in Best Picture, Best Director (Robert Zemeckis), Best Actor (Bob Hoskins), Best Supporting Actor (Christopher Lloyd and Charles Fleischer), Best Supporting Actress (Joanna Cassidy and Kathleen Turner), Best Screenplay based on Material from Another Medium (Jeffrey Price and Peter Seaman), Best Cinematography (Dean Cundey), Best Original Score (Alan Silvestri), Best Make-Up (Peter Robb-King and Kenneth Chase), Best Costume Design (Joanna Johnston), Best Art Direction (Elliot Scott, Roger Cain, Stephen Scott, and Peter Howitt), Best Film Editing (Arthur Schmidt), Best Sound (Tony Dawe, Robert Knudson, John Boyd, and Don Digirolamo), Best Sound Effects Editing (Charles Campbell and Louis Edemann), and Best Visual Effects (Ken Ralston, Richard Williams, Edward Jones, and George Gibbs). Ultimately, they were nominated in the categories for Cinematography, Art Direction, Film Editing, Sound, Sound Effects Editing, and Visual Effects.

Several Disney animators, who had been on the London crew, were able to attend the Oscar show. Hans Bacher, James Baxter, Andreas Deja, Nik Ranieri, and Dave and Debbie Spafford rented a limousine, dressed in black tie, and walked the red carpet so they could be there to cheer for Dick Williams.

The ceremony was held on Wednesday, March 29, 1989, at the old Shrine Auditorium in Los Angeles. Bob Hope had hosted the Academy Awards show for the previous four years and a decision was made to not have a host for the show for the first time in two decades. Billy Crystal and Lily Tomlin bracketed an opening musical number. This opening number became notorious in Academy Award history. It ran for over eleven minutes and featured a newcomer, Eileen Bowman, dressed as Snow White. The theme was that she was a country girl coming to Hollywood to seek her fame and her new boyfriend, played by Rob Lowe, showed her the town.

They went through a number of set pieces with purpose-written lyrics sung to popular music. The primary anthem was Creedence Clearwater Revival's "Proud Mary." The audience did not know what to make of it. The next day, the Walt Disney Company filed suit against the Academy of Motion Picture Arts and Sciences (AMPAS) for copyright infringement in the use of the likeness of Snow White. AMPAS apologized and the lawsuit was withdrawn. The next year, AMPAS went back to having a host. Jeff Margolis continued to direct future Academy Award television specials, but producer Allan Carr never did. Billy Crystal hosted the Oscars for the next four years.

The first category *Roger Rabbit* was up for was Best Achievement in Sound and Sound Effects Editing. The award was presented by Jimmy Stewart and Kim Novak. The winner for Sound was *Bird*; the winner for Sound Effects Editing was *Who Framed Roger Rabbit*.

The third category *Roger Rabbit* was up for was Best Achievement in Art Direction. It was presented by Willem Dafoe and Gene Hackman. The winner was *Dangerous Liaisons*.

The fourth category *Roger Rabbit* was up for was Best Achievement in Visual Effects. It was presented by Lloyd Bridges and his sons, Beau and Jeff. The winner was *Who Framed Roger Rabbit*. Ken Ralston, Edward Jones, George Gibbs, and Richard Williams came to the stage to collect their Oscar statuettes. Ken Ralston did all of the talking. First, he recognized the hundreds of people in London and America who had made *Who Framed Roger Rabbit* possible. He thanked Bob Zemeckis and then several artists from ILM by name: Scott Farrar (visual effects camera operator), Steve Gawley (supervising model maker), Steve Starkey (associate producer), Wes Takahashi (ILM animation supervisor), Brad Jerrell (supervising stage technician), Bill Kimberlin (chief visual effects editor), and his wife, Robyn. He then suggested that the honor should go to animators and directors from the Golden Age of animation who had inspired *Roger Rabbit*. No specific mention was made of the Visual Effects team in London and its supervisor, Chris Knott, who had developed the tonal matte optical technique and created most of the artwork that was composited at ILM. Williams made no effort to balance the ledger, although the "leave the stage" music had already started to play.

Next up was the Special Achievement Oscar to Williams for Animation Direction and the creation of Jessica and Roger Rabbit. Robin Williams came onto the stage in a tuxedo, but wearing a Mickey Mouse hood and ears and large Mickey Mouse gloves. He gave a manic two-minute solo performance, then introduced Charles Fleischer. They continued with a manic repartee for another two-and-a-half minutes . . . finishing with a tag team rap-rhyming introduction to Williams. Williams thanked the Academy and made a specific call-out to Carl Bell. He then thanked Steven Spielberg, Jeffrey Katzenberg, and Bob Zemeckis. He then singled out Andreas Deja as his most stalwart animator. He called out, "The best is yet to come!" as the music played him off the stage.

The fifth category *Roger Rabbit* was up for Best Achievement in Cinematography. It was presented by Demi Moore and Bruce Willis. The winner was Peter Biziou, for *Mississippi Burning*.

The sixth, and last, category in which *Roger Rabbit* was nominated was Best Achievement in Film Editing, which was presented by Farrah Fawcett and Ryan O'Neal. The winner was Arthur Schmidt, for *Who Framed Roger Rabbit*.

The evening was a tremendous success for Disney, Amblin, and those who made *Who Framed Roger Rabbit*. The former crew of *Roger Rabbit* in London celebrated along with everybody else, but the celebration was tinged with a bit of regret. They were disappointed that Chris Knott had not been included as a recipient of an Oscar statuette, and they were especially disappointed that neither Ken Ralston nor Dick Williams had made specific mention of his contribution.

The next day, Williams invited anybody from the animation crews who were in the Los Angeles area to lunch at Chadney's restaurant in Burbank. The group included Leroy Anderson, Hans Bacher, James Baxter, Carl Bell, Roger Chiasson, Andreas Deja, Marc Gordon-Bates, Joe Haidar, Steve Hickner, Mark Kausler, Dorse Lanpher, Vera Lanpher, Jacques Muller, Joe Ranft, Nik Ranieri, Pat Sito, Tom Sito, Dave Spafford, Debbie Spafford, Frans Vischer, and Alex Williams. Williams's mother and young daughter were also at the gathering. They all got a chance to hold both of Dick's Oscar statuettes.[38]

Table 4. *Who Framed Roger Rabbit* Awards		
	Won	**Nominated**
Academy Awards	Film Editing	Cinematography
Oscar®	Sound Effects Editing	Sound
USA, 1989	Visual Effects	Art Direction
	Special Achievement-Richard Williams	
Golden Globes		Motion Picture - Comedy or Musical
USA, 1989		Performance by an Actor- Comedy or Musical
BAFTA Awards	Special Effects	Screenplay - Adapted
UK, 1989		Cinematography
		Editing
		Production Design
Academy of Science Fiction, Fantasy & Horror Films	Fantasy Film	Actor
Saturn	Director	Supporting Actor
	Special Effects	Supporting Actress
		Writing
		Music
American Cinema Editors		Best Edited Feature Film - Arthur Schmidt
Eddie		
USA, 1989		
Annie Awards	Individual Technical Achievement - Richard Williams	
Annie		
USA, 1989		
BMI Society of Cinematographers	Film Music	
USA, 1989		
Boston Society of Film Critics Awards	Special – Richard Williams	
USA, 1989		
British Society of Cinematographers		Cinematography
UK, 1989		
Chicago Film Critics Association Awards	Director	
USA, 1989		

	Won	Nominated
César Awards		Foreign Film
France, 1989		
David di Donatello Awards	Foreign Producer	
David		
Italy, 1989		
Directors Guild of America		Directorial Achievement in Motion Pictures
USA, 1989		
DVD Exclusive Awards		Menu design
USA, 2003		
Golden Screen	Best Picture	
Germany, 1989		
Grammy Awards		Original Instrumental Background Score
USA, 1989		
Hugo Awards	Dramatic Presentation	
USA, 1989		
Jupiter Awards	International Film	
Germany, 1988		
Kids' Choice Awards	Favorite Movie	
Blimp		
USA, 1989		
Los Angeles Film Critics Association Awards	Technical Achievement – Robert Zemeckis	
USA, 1988		
Motion Picture Sound Editors	Sound Editing / ADR	
USA, 1989		
Sant Jordi Awards	Foreign Film	
Spain, 1989		
Venice Film Festival	Special Mention (Children and Cinema)	
Italy, 1988		
Writers Guild of America		Screenplay Based on Material from Another Medium
USA, 1989		

Chapter Eight

COMMERCIALS, TELEVISION, SHORTS, AND SEQUELS

Commercials

Who Framed Roger Rabbit went into general release on 1,045 screens on June 22, 1988. It earned $11,226,239 on the opening weekend, which was good for first at the domestic box office. By the end of its theatrical run, the film had grossed $156,452,370 in North America and an additional $173,351,588 internationally—for a worldwide gross of $329,803,958, second only to *Rain Man* in 1988. In hindsight, its success seemed assured, but it was a huge gamble at the time. *Howard the Duck* had bombed at the box office. The *Roger Rabbit* story wasn't a well-known or popular property with a built-in fan base, and animated films had been little more than kiddie fodder for a very long time. The Walt Disney Company had spent about $45 million to make the film and another $10 million on promotion. It was a film whose popularity grew with buzz and word-of-mouth, but Disney had to get people to start talking about it. To ensure that it found an audience, Disney undertook marketing cross-promotions with Coca-Cola and McDonald's. A part of those marketing campaigns were two live-action/animation combination television commercials, one each for Diet Coke and McDonald's. Disney shared the $500,000 in television commercial production costs. The marketing value from the McDonald's advertising campaign was estimated to be $12 million and the value from the Diet Coke campaign was estimated to be $10 million.[1]

The McDonald's commercial related to the promotional offering of three different "supersized" plastic soda cups. It featured scenes from the film and then transitioned to new animation with Jessica and Roger going through a McDonald's drive-through in a big, black, vintage limousine.

Jessica reaches out to interact with the McDonald's employee in taking the items offered from the drive-thru window. The limousine speeds away and Jessica and Roger are thrown into the back seat.

In the Diet Coke commercial, Roger is seated at a table in a smoky film noir club reminiscent of the Ink and Paint Club. He is wearing a comically oversized trench coat and fedora, and he is holding a can of Diet Coke. He is watching Jessica on stage and has heart-shaped irises and hearts floating around his head. A penguin waiter walks past Eddie Valiant as he enters the club. Valiant sits at the table beside Roger and takes Roger's hat off while asking what Roger is doing there. Roger replies, "P-P-P-Please Eddie. I just came to see Jessica . . . and to have a Diet Coke!" Jessica blows him a kiss . . . that "flaps" over, as in the film. Roger catches it in his mouth and says, "She's enough to drive a toon loony." The live action for the Diet Coke commercial was filmed on October 19, 1987, at ILM, while Hoskins was available during the Toontown bluescreen shoot.[2] The new animation required for the commercials wasn't extensive, and was done by Simon Wells. Tony Clark recalls that the animation for the two commercials was done after the film was finished. His contract had concluded, but he was called back to do the Xerox and pegging work. Chris Jenkins was the only person left working in the Effects Department and there were one or two people left to ink and paint the cels.[3]

There were other television commercials related to the release of *Who Framed Roger Rabbit*. Of course, there were several trailers and commercials made specifically for television. Some of the early trailers/commercials, and many of the international commercials, contained clips of the later-deleted Pig-Head sequence.

The television commercial for the 1988 Disneyland Christmas Celebration features the Roger Rabbit costume character on a parade float. A television commercial promoting the opening of the Disney-MGM Studios theme park in 1989 included new animation of Roger Rabbit hopping off a cel on an animation desk. A 1989 Chevy Lumina television commercial series was also a cross-promotion for the opening of the Disney-MGM Studios theme park. The Lumina commercials used Baer Animation, the production company set up by Dale and Jane Baer for *Who Framed Roger Rabbit*. After the completion of its work on the feature film, much of the crew continued with animation contracts from Disney. Dean Cundey, the cinematographer, and Arthur Schmidt, the editor, also worked on the Lumina commercials. The commercials were filmed in December 1988, and the animation for the ten-spot campaign took three months to complete. They featured many of the classic Disney animated characters. The Lumina/

Disney-MGM Studios commercials debuted during the Oscar show on March 29, 1989, and ran through August 1989. These live-action/animation combination commercials cost between $300,000 and $500,000 and took fourteen weeks to produce, compared with typical television commercials at that time, which cost between $60,000 and $100,000 and took about ten days to produce.[4]

Disney was no stranger to using its animated characters to promote products in television commercials. In the 1950s, Disney had a commercial department that produced television commercials for American Motors, Jello, Cheerios, Trix, Peter Pan peanut butter, Baker's instant chocolate, and Lucky Strike cigarettes. It even created new cartoon characters for 7-Up (Fresh-Up Freddy), Ipana (Bucky Beaver), PG&E (Reddy Kilowatt), Frito-Lay (The Frito Kid), Mohawk Carpets (Tommy Mohawk), and Welch's (Pow and Wow). In the 1970s, Winnie-the-Pooh was used in Nabisco commercials, and Orange Bird was created for Florida Citrus Growers commercials. *Peanuts* characters were being used in Ford commercials in the 1950s and have been used in Metropolitan Life commercials since 1985. Richard Williams Animation and other commercial houses in London were doing brisk business with animated television commercials; in fact, RWAs own series of Fanta commercials, using Disney's classic characters, was one of the contributors to the *Who Framed Roger Rabbit* film being made. The film then spawned a blizzard of commercials using the same 2½-D live-action/animation look. The Lumina/Disney-MGM Studios commercials were put together by the Lintas Campbell-Ewald agency, but other advertising agencies also took advantage of the sudden enthusiasm for the *Who Framed Roger Rabbit* look. Many people who worked on *Who Framed Roger Rabbit* used the same techniques in commercials for years afterwards. An Ultra Pampers Plus commercial from 1987 used flat animated characters called Dry Bears, but the 1989 Ultra Pampers Plus "Disney Babies" commercial used the 2½-D technique.

Bell Atlantic used the technique in a 1989 commercial in which a cartoon *femme fatale* (modeled after Jessica Rabbit) and cartoon office workers create bedlam in an entrepreneur's new business office. The 1991 Weetabix "Big Shots" commercial featured toon bullets similar to the dum-dum bullets in *Who Framed Roger Rabbit*. It was produced by Passion Pictures and directed by Chuck Gammage. Uli Meyer Animation (Uli Meyer), Pizazz Pictures (Eric Goldberg), Passion Pictures (Andrew Ruhemann), Klacto Animations (Oscar Grillo), Felix Films (Mike Smith), Chuck Gammage Animation (Chuck Gammage), and Baer Animation (Dale and Jane Baer) grew in the aftermath of *Who Framed Roger Rabbit*.[5] The popularity of Nike's

Air Jordan commercials in 1992 and 1993, featuring Bugs Bunny, led to the *Space Jam* film that was ultimately released in 1996. Many members of the *Who Framed Roger Rabbit* Animation Department contributed to *Space Jam*, which had sequences produced in Los Angeles, Austin, Toronto, and London—at six different studios.[6]

In 1989, McDonald's ran a Halloween campaign that offered "Happy Halloween" certificates—a book of ten certificates for $1 that were redeemable for ice cream cones and sundaes at participating McDonald's. It also included a mail-in certificate for a Roger Rabbit plush toy with the purchase of the newly released *Who Framed Roger Rabbit* VHS videotape. Another television commercial for the VHS videotape was produced directly for Buena Vista Home Video. It contained new animation of Roger Rabbit poking out from a curtain to lean on his elbows beside a Santa-capped VHS box.

These VHS video promotions were focused at purchase for home viewing. In the UK at that time, the market was still mostly focused on video rentals. Buena Vista Home Video produced a ten-minute promotional film targeted to the British video rental industry. It featured Charles Fleischer giving a frenetic and comedic monologue. Disney's promotional offer included a "movie munchies" voucher booklet, redeemable for treats in participating movie theater lobbies. The VHS video was sold to rental agencies for £9.99. The film promoted post-rental sales of the video, at prices to be determined by the retailer. The VHS video was being offered to home consumers for $19.99 in the US.

Another, rather bizarre television commercial promoted a large pull-string Roger Rabbit plush toy. It starts with the large plush toy on a teeter-totter opposite a child. Roger is catapulted into the arms of a little girl. In the next scene, Roger is a passenger on a kiddie car riding on the sidewalk. He is catapulted again—this time, landing on the back of a poodle. In the last scene, a child clothes-pins Roger's ears to a laundry line and pushes him along the line. Roger careens through a venetian blind, leaving a "Roger-shaped hole" similar to the one left in R. K. Maroon's office in the film.

Television

The first time Roger Rabbit appeared on television was long before he appeared in film. One of the early series on the Disney Channel was *Walt Disney Studio Showcase*. An episode entitled *Backstage at Disney* was aired in April 1983. It was produced by Christopher D. Miller (Walt Disney's grandson) and written by John Culhane, a journalist and film historian who was caricatured as Mr. Snoops in *The Rescuers*. The episode is reminiscent of *The Reluctant Dragon* (1941), in which Robert Benchley, a famous humorist, explores the Disney Studios. John Culhane's exploration of the studio starts with the Sound Effects Department, as did Benchley's in the film. Culhane next visits Tim Burton and Rick Heinrichs, who describe their film project: *Vincent, Trick or Treat*, and *Hansel and Gretel*. He explores the Special Effects Department, which was making a massive animatronic puppet of a small dinosaur for the film, *Baby*, at the time, and then drops by the *Roger Rabbit* development unit. Culhane meets Marc Stirdivant (producer), Darrell van Citters (director), and Mike Giaimo (animator). Some pencil-test animation is shown: first, a scene with animated character, Captain "Clever" Cleaver (from the original novel), confronting Eddie Valiant and then Darrell van Citters describes the animation process and flips his pencil-test drawings, which morph into a scene with Jessica Rabbit enticing Eddie Valiant. Roger Rabbit makes a brief colored animation appearance at the end of the segment. The balance of the episode includes Joe Hale and Phil Nibbelink describing work on *The Black Cauldron*, Harrison Ellenshaw talking about matte painting special effects, and the orchestral music being recorded for Ray Bradbury's *Something Wicked This Way Comes* on the studio recording stage.

Roger Rabbit next appeared in the 1987 television special, *Sport Goofy in Soccermania*, which aired on May 27 on NBC, after a preview airing on the Disney Channel. *Sport Goofy in Soccermania* was released as a theatrical featurette in Europe. The early Darrell Van Citters version of Roger Rabbit is seen cheering in a crowd scene. This was Van Citters's last directorial work at Disney, although he did not receive credit. Disney felt that the featurette needed to be reworked and direction went to Matt O'Callaghan, with Ward Kimball assisting as a consultant. Disney ultimately decided not to release it theatrically in North America.

New *Roger Rabbit* animation was done for two network television specials. *Roger Rabbit & the Secrets of Toontown* was broadcast on the CBS network on September 13, 1988. It provided a general retrospective on animation history, with a focus on live-action/animation combination films. The television special was hosted by Joanna Cassidy. New animation has Roger Rabbit somersaulting into the title card (two minutes into the show) and joining Cassidy in a movie theater for some transitional segments. As a behind-the-scenes documentary, it was replaced by *Behind the Ears: The True Story of Roger Rabbit* in 2003 on the Vista series DVD release.

Roger Rabbit's next television outing was in the *Mickey's 60th Birthday* television special, broadcast as part of *The Magical World of Disney* anthology series on the NBC network. The special was shown on November 13, 1988. The premise is that a television show celebrating Mickey's sixtieth birthday is being shot. Charles Fleischer plays the stage manager and, while he is busy getting Mickey to the set, Roger Rabbit volunteers to wheel out the giant birthday cake. He puts a stick of dynamite, instead of a candle, on top of the cake and ends up destroying the set. Mickey reverses the destruction through the magic of the Sorcerer's hat, but the Sorcerer takes him on an odyssey to find his own inner magic. Roger Rabbit appears again later in the show . . . to find Mickey Mouse on Main Street in Disneyland.

In addition, Roger Rabbit appeared, with new animation, in the introduction of this installment of *The Magical World of Disney*. There have been many incarnations of the Disney anthology television series. In the first unbroken string it was *Walt Disney's Disneyland* on ABC from 1954 to 1959, *Walt Disney Presents* on ABC from 1959 to 1961, *Walt Disney's Wonderful World of Color* on NBC from 1961 to 1969, *The Wonderful World of Disney* on NBC from 1969 to 1979, and *Disney's Wonderful World* on NBC from 1979 to 1981. NBC canceled the show in 1981, but CBS picked it up from 1981 to 1983. At that time, the Disney Channel was starting up and Cardon Walker pulled the plug on the show (lest it cannibalize viewership in the new cable service). ABC picked up the anthology series again in 1986 as *The Disney Sunday Movie*, which ran until 1988. All of these incarnations had their own new introductory credits. The series moved again to NBC in 1988 as *The Magical World of Disney*. The opening featured clips from Disney films, television series, and the theme parks. In the magic of Disney cross-promotion, the camera swoops over EPCOT's Spaceship Earth, through Disney-MGM Studio's backlot street, and into a television control room window to see the back of Mickey Mouse's head in front of a control screen. A string of film clips concludes with a clip from *Who Framed Roger Rabbit* following the scene in which Roger drops the refrigerator on his head. The clip picks up Roger following the director, Raoul J. Raoul, off-screen, but as the camera pulls back new animation shows Roger move quickly to block a studio door from closing . . . which concludes the television show's opening credits.

Roger Rabbit had a cameo in an ABC television special *Best of Disney—50 Years of Magic*, which aired on May 24, 1991. The opening segment is a short film, *Michael & Mickey*, directed by Jerry Rees. The cinematographer was Dean Cundey. It is reminiscent of Eisner's introductory opening at the start of the *Mickey's 60th Birthday* television special. Eisner is at his office desk contemplating his affection for Disney films when Mickey Mouse appears. Eisner looks at the Mickey Mouse watch on his wrist and Mickey Mouse looks at the Michael Eisner watch on his wrist. It is announced that they need to go to a screening and they gather up the troops on the way to the screening room. Roger Rabbit is at the head of the boardroom table and scrambles over the table and down the hall. Michael and Mickey take seats in the second row and Mickey is frightened as Chernabog (from the "Night on Bald Mountain" segment of *Fantasia*) rears up. Eisner comes along with their popcorn and says, "Excuse me, will you sit down! You're blocking our view!" Chernbog excuses himself and meekly sits down as the projector rolls. This *Michael & Mickey* piece was also used in the Magic of Disney Animation attraction at the Disney-MGM Studio theme park.

Characters from *Who Framed Roger Rabbit* had cameos in at least two interstitial segments in the animated television series *Disney's House of Mouse*. The House of Mouse was similar to the Ink and Paint Club in *Who Framed Roger Rabbit* and, similar to the Ink and Paint Club, it had penguin waiters. Benny the Cab is shown as a member of the audience in two episodes: "Max's New Car," aired on November 3, 2001, and "Mickey vs. Shelby," aired on September 2, 2002.

The animated character, Bonkers D. Bobcat, appeared originally in segments of the *Raw Toonage* television animation series. Although Bonkers D. Bobcat is not a direct copy of Roger Rabbit, the concept for the television show has its roots firmly in *Who Framed Roger Rabbit*. At the time the show was being developed Spielberg and Eisner were well into their test of wills regarding the combined ownership of the *Roger Rabbit* characters, and Disney was not free to utilize the characters to fill out its television animation requirements. Bonkers is a former star of shorts at Wackytoon Studios and works in the Toon Division of the Hollywood Police Department. His boss and many of his colleagues are humans, but they are animated humans—therefore, the central conceit of *Who Framed Roger Rabbit* is somehow lost. A *Bonkers* episode, "Petal to the Metal," was released theatrically, with "Three Ninjas," in 1992. The *Bonkers* television series ran on *The Disney Afternoon* block from September 4, 1993, until February 23, 1994.

Jessica and Roger made a very small cameo appearance, with Genie, in *Aladdin and the King of Thieves*, a Disney direct-to-video film released in 1996.

Disney was not the only party to the shared ownership that utilized the *Roger Rabbit* characters. Many references to *Who Framed Roger Rabbit* and the *Roger Rabbit* characters appear in the Warner Bros. animated television series *Steven Spielberg presents Tiny Toon Adventures*, otherwise known as Tiny Toons—starting in the first episode, which was aired as a stand-alone special on September 14, 1990, on the CBS network. In "The Looney Beginning," an animator at Warner Bros. is threatened to come up with a new hit cartoon television show by the next day. He doodles through a couple of iterations of a cartoon rabbit at his animation desk and eventually comes up with a character that looks like a youthful Bugs Bunny. His doodles come to life on the animation paper, and his new creation asks for a "buddy." The animator doodles a young female rabbit, who does several impressions in order to find her voice. One of those impressions is a sultry Jessica Rabbit. The new cartoon stars are Buster Bunny and Babs Bunny. Later in the episode, Buster answers Babs in the affirmative by saying, "Roger, rabbit!"—to which Babs responds, "You've got the wrong bunny."

Other references *to Who Framed Roger Rabbit* in the *Tiny Toons* series include: a reference to Baby Herman in "The Wide World of Elmyra" (aired November 8, 1990); Buster being surprised at coming upon Bugs Bunny, as head of the university, to which Bugs says, "Eh, you were expecting maybe Roger Rabbit?" in "Looneyversity Daze" (aired November 20, 1990); an allusion to the title in "Who Bopped Bugs Bunny?" (aired December 14, 1990); Roger Rabbit appearing at an audition and hitting himself on the head with a frying pan in "New Character Day" (aired February 20, 1991); Babs doing an impression of Roger Rabbit in "Pledge Week" (aired September 16, 1991); Roger and Jessica Rabbit getting immediate access to Steven Spielberg in "Buster and Babs Go Hawaiian" (aired November 18, 1991); and Buster and Plucky doing impressions of Jessica Rabbit in "Thirteensomething" (aired September 14, 1992). In "Buster and Babs Go Hawaiian," Buster and Babs are trying to see Steven Spielberg and get held up by the studio guard. An ultra-long cartoon-style limousine pulls up and we see Jessica Rabbit's legs and Roger Rabbit's hand. They get immediate access to the studio. We also see a cameo of Robin Williams, as Peter Pan, and Dustin Hoffman, as Captain Hook. Interestingly, *Hook* premiered in theater a month after the airing of this *Tiny Toons* episode, showing that Steven Spielberg also had a knack for cross-promotion. Spielberg himself shows up in this episode as a cartoon representation of himself. Sherri Stoner was a writer on many of the *Tiny Toons* episodes. She had been the live-action reference for Ariel during the making of *The Little Mermaid*, and she and Deanna Oliver, who was the voice of Toaster in *The Brave Little Toaster*, wrote a script for a *Who Framed Roger Rabbit* sequel.

In thinking about how an idea or creation enters the public consciousness, consider how it is used by others in popular culture. *The Simpsons* debuted as bumpers on *The Tracey Ullman Show* in 1988, the year that *Who*

Framed Roger Rabbit was released. The show has continued, and remains popular, to the time of this writing—thirty years later. There have been numerous references to *Who Framed Roger Rabbit* in *The Simpsons*. In episode "The Boy Who Knew Too Much" (aired on May 5, 1994), the waiter's accident is similar to Roger's in the *Somethin's Cookin'* opening of the film. In episode "Treehouse of Terror IX" (aired on October 15, 1998), sharp objects fly towards Bart and Lisa, similar to *Somethin's Cookin'*. The title of "Kidney Trouble" (aired on December 6, 1998) is a parody of *Tummy Trouble*. In episode "Halloween of Horror" (aired on October 18, 2015), the continuing character Rainier Luftwaffe Wolfcastle (a parody of Arnold Schwarzenegger) is dressed as Jessica Rabbit in a *Rocky Horror Show* musical send-up. *The Simpsons Movie* (2007) opens with an Itchy and Scratchy short that segues into the film—itself a reference to the opening of *Who Framed Roger Rabbit*.

Roger Rabbit was also referenced in several *South Park* animated television series episodes: after the live feed is lost from *South Park*, they say they're going off to see *Who Framed Roger Rabbit* on television in the episode "Cartman's Mom is Still a Dirty Slut" (aired on February 25, 1998); Kenny dies like the weasels did in *Who Framed Roger Rabbit* in "Scott Tenorman Must Die" (aired on July 11, 2001); and Benny the Cab is one of the Imaginationland combatants in "Imaginationland: Episode III" (aired on October 31, 2007).[7]

Who Framed Roger Rabbit characters have also appeared in web-based shows. Roger Rabbit, Jessica Rabbit, and Baby Herman appeared in a *Robot Chicken* segment, entitled "The P-P-P-Perfect Crime" (aired on January 18, 2009), in AdultSwim.com's fourth season. The episode is a parody of the O. J. Simpson murder trial, as well as Alfred Hitchcock's 1951 film noir psychological thriller *Strangers on a Train*. A *Roger Rabbit* cartoon parody by Jared Winkler was posted to the web on September 11, 2013, as part of his *Cartoon Hookups* series at winkydinkmdoedia.com.

Shorts

Who Framed Roger Rabbit was a critical and financial blockbuster hit for Disney, and the studio intended to double-down on its success. The film's characters were the first new Disney characters in many years (even though they were actually co-owned by Disney and Amblin). Disney pursued its cross-marketing prowess with character merchandise, and giving its new star, Roger Rabbit, pride-of-place in Disney television specials and theme park presence. The fictional Roger Rabbit was a "B"-level star in R. K. Maroon's cartoon film shorts, so it seemed natural to provide new shorts in which he could star, thus extending his brand. Ultimately, Disney was actively considering a feature film sequel and wanted to build a library of *Roger Rabbit* shorts to keep the franchise alive.[8]

Bill Kopp graduated from CalArts after winning a student Oscar in both 1984 and 1985. His friend from CalArts, Wes Archer, called to say that Klasky/Csupo had been contracted to provide three thirty-second animated bumper segments per week for the *Tracey Ullman Show* summer replacement show. The bumpers were to be written by Matt Groening, creator of the comic strip *Life in Hell*, and M. K. (Mary) Brown, a frequent contributor to *National Lampoon*. Kopp brought in another friend, David Silverman, and the three of them did it all for the first season of four shows. Groening created *The Simpsons* segment, while Brown created the *Dr. N!Godatu* segment. The style evolved quickly over the course of those first four shows. Each of the three animators brought something to the look of the show: Kopp created Marge Simpson's tower of blue hair, Kopp and Archer brought manic/frenetic comic sensibility, Archer and Silverman brought the distinctive limited color palette and the efficient movement that added pace to the animation, and Silverman was an excellent draftsman who smoothed over the rough edges. They started a new segment each week, with each segment completed over a four-week time schedule. It was a wildly hectic situation made more intimidating when the popularity of *The Simpsons* segment gave rise to discussions about a series of its own.[9]

It was at that time that Kopp went to the Cinerama Dome movie theater to see *Who Framed Roger Rabbit* during its premiere week. He was very enthused with what he saw and thought that he would be ready for an "old-school" cartoon with that level of animation. Two weeks later, he got a call from Disney with an offer to work on *Roger Rabbit* shorts. It was very different from Klasky/Csupo; at Disney, they were allocated almost a year to do storyboards for a seven-minute cartoon. Bill Kopp, Kevin Harkey, and Pat Ventura made up one of the story units. There was no script . . . just a year to hone a storyboard. The story units made their pitches to Spielberg, Katzenberg, and Zemeckis, and the Kopp/Harkey/Ventura story for *Tummy Trouble* was selected for the first *Roger Rabbit* short.[10]

The *Tummy Trouble* unit was set up in the Airway Building, the same location that Dale Baer's Glendale unit had occupied. Under the stewardship of Rob Minkoff, the crew filled out with a mix of new talent and veterans of *Who Framed Roger Rabbit*. Some animators from the London and Glendale units were offered contracts with Disney Feature Animation, either to help finish *The Little Mermaid* or to join the new *Beauty and the Beast* crew. Andreas Deja, Tom Sito, and Glen Keane were part of a small *Beauty and the Beast* development crew headed by Dick and Jill Purdom. Disney felt that the tone was too dark and the story was reworked, with the involvement of Howard Ashman (and Alan Menken). The delay in production allowed James Baxter, Roger Chiasson, Jacques Muller, and Tom and Pat Sito to join the *Tummy Trouble* crew. Chiasson and Muller started at Disney in Los Angeles in January 1989.

Joe Haidar had asked Max Howard to bring his portfolio to Disney at the conclusion of the *Who Framed Roger Rabbit* production in London, but he did not hear anything back from Disney. Haidar was back in Canada, working at Animation House in Toronto, when he got a call from Nik Ranieri, who was already working at Disney in Los Angeles, saying that Haidar's name was on the board to receive scenes on *The Little Mermaid* and that if he did not show up, he risked losing the assignment. The confusion was sorted out, but Haidar ended up being assigned first to the *Tummy Trouble* crew.[11]

Tummy Trouble is essentially an "ordinary" cartoon. It is only in the thirty seconds before the final credit roll that the cartoon switches to the live-action/animation combination, therefore the animation and production was relatively straightforward—except for the wild Tex Avery-style takes. Tom Bancroft and his twin brother, Tony, were in their sophomore year at CalArts in 1989 when Disney came to campus to look at portfolios for an internship at the Los Angeles Disney Studios in preparation for staffing up the new studio in Florida. Twenty interns were selected, from all over the US. Ultimately, twelve artists would be selected to move to the Florida studio and start there for the opening day. Both Tom and Tony Bancroft were selected.[12]

The interns were also located at the Airway Building in Glendale. Bancroft describes seeing *Who Framed Roger Rabbit* in the theater as a revelation . . . especially the *Somethin's Cookin'* short that leads off the film. He thought that the watercolor backgrounds and the animation done on "ones" made it the most beautiful cartoon he had ever seen, and it is certain that his fellow interns felt the same way. Bancroft was astounded to be sharing space with many of the artists who had made it only eighteen months after he had been a student animator wannabe in the theater. The interns used to stay late and study the *Tummy Trouble* animation drawings in the evening when everybody else had left.[13]

Eisner, Wells, and Katzenberg loved all of the acclaim being heaped on *Who Framed Roger Rabbit* and that the audience seemed genuinely thrilled to see the classic Fab Five Disney characters (Mickey Mouse, Minnie Mouse, Donald Duck, Goofy, and Pluto) on the big screen again. Katzenberg had put *The Prince and the Pauper* into production. It was originally intended that the first production at the new animation studio in Florida would be another featurette, *Mickey's Arabian Adventure*, which Burny Mattinson was slated to direct. In fact, very early visitors to the Disney-MGM Studios theme park were able to see development work from the featurette in the Magic of Disney Animation staging area. As it turns out, the production of *Aladdin* was ramping up, and it was decided to avoid having two projects using essentially the same source material.[14] Disney was intending to make a sequel to *Who Framed Roger Rabbit*, and releasing *Roger Rabbit* shorts would add to the anticipation of the eventual feature film. It was decided to make *Roller Coaster Rabbit* the Florida studio's first major project—and thus take advantage of the cross-marketing opportunity.

At the conclusion of making *Who Framed Roger Rabbit*, Max Howard was called to go to Los Angeles, where he was offered the job of overseeing the Disney animation studios outside of Los Angeles. Disney had acquired the former Hanna-Barbera studio in Sydney, Australia, earlier in 1988, and was in the throes of buying the Brizzi brothers' studio in Paris. Gary Krisel, head of Disney's Television group, had grand plans, intending to set up a studio in London, finalize the acquisition of the studio in Paris, and establish a studio in Tokyo. Ultimately, Disney Television, with the burgeoning number of animated television series, and with its direct-to-video mandate, would also open animation studios in Toronto and Vancouver.[15] Howard accepted the job, with the first order of business being to establish the Disney animation studio at the Disney-MGM Studios theme park in Walt Disney World. It took some time to make arrangements for his family to emigrate to the United States, so he leased an office in the Capitol Records office suite on Euston Road in London. In the meantime, he helped to set up the Disney Television group studio for the *DuckTales: The Movie* unit at Kings Cross in London. Howard moved to the US on September 30, 1988.[16]

The studio in Florida was to be a working animation studio and an attraction at the Disney-MGM Studios theme park at Walt Disney World. As an attraction, it was called the Magic of Disney Animation. Access to the park area was through a large "studio arch," off the hub in front of the replica of Grauman's Chinese Theater, and onto a forecourt. The attraction entrance opened into a staging area with Disney Animation awards and development art from upcoming animation projects. The guests moved into a theater to see Jerry Rees's *Back to Neverland* film, then moved on to see the working studio. A video presentation, on a series of overhead monitors, described the animation process and functioned to move guests along the elevated corridor. The working area was at a slightly lower elevation and was separated from the guests by floor-to-ceiling glass. Guests may have thought that it was one-way glass and that they could not be observed, but the animators could see and hear the guests—although their own awareness and sensitivity to "being on display" diminished over time. The animators called the public area of the studio the "fishbowl." Everybody had their turn working in the fishbowl, but as time went on, the more senior artists earned private offices and newer artists were on display.[17] The new animation desks and furniture were sourced from Artek Design in Calgary, Alberta, Canada. They were an updated version of the Kem Weber design. The same desks were used to equip the new Disney Animation studios in Toronto and Vancouver as well. The Florida studio was modern and well-equipped, but what makes a studio are its people—and the new studio would be staffed by a mix of animation veterans and fresh young artists.

Tummy Trouble was released on June 23, 1989, with *Honey, I Shrunk the Kids.* The next *Roger Rabbit* short *Roller Coaster Rabbit*, had already been storyboarded in the Airway Building and was ready to go.[18] Barry Temple was the first animator from California to move to Florida. He arrived in Florida in April 1989, with others following quickly.[19] Dave Stephan signed on for a two-year contract.[20] Aaron Blaise was another selection from the intern program. He had grown up in Naples, Florida, and had studied at the Ringling School of Art and Design in Sarasota, so he was going home . . . and started at the Florida studio on April 17, 1989.[21] To describe the experienced animators who moved to Florida as veterans might evoke an image of grizzled old-timers bent over a desk—but they were quite young, eager to be part of a studio startup. Barry Cook, Mark Henn, Mark Kausler, Alex Kupershmidt, Dave Stephan, and Barry Temple came from Disney in California. Bridgitte Hartley and Alan Simpson came from London, fresh off their experience on *Who Framed Roger Rabbit.* Alex Williams (Dick's son) had been an assistant on *Who Framed Roger Rabbit* while taking a hiatus from university. He went back to Merton College and the University of Oxford, but joined the Florida crew during his school break for the summer of 1989.[22] The official opening of the Disney-MGM Studios theme park was May 1, 1989.

Max Howard was instrumental in establishing the working tone at the studio. He was approachable and well-respected by the artists, as well as the distant Disney management. He encouraged team work and social connections. Seventy-five percent of the staff were young and green . . . and from someplace else. They became fast friends and went to each other's weddings, birthday parties, children's births, and funerals.[23] For those who came later . . . and weren't part of the early bonding . . . it sometimes felt like "everybody knew everybody else's business."[24]

Tom Bancroft recalls many celebrities being toured through the studio in his first year. One of them was former president Jimmy Carter, along with his Secret Service detail. One of the Disney artists had drawn a $100 bill as a student illustration exercise. He had pinned it to his work station bulletin board. One of the members of the Secret Service detail wanted to arrest the artist for counterfeiting. Max Howard smoothed the situation over, but the illustration was shredded. The artists were also proud of their skill at figure drawing, and many had their drawings of nudes on their boards. Tourists complained—and the drawings had to be taken down.[25]

The production pipeline and organization was being developed on the fly as they did *Roller Coaster Rabbit*. Mery-et Lescher applied after being given a heads-up by Alex Kupershmidt, a friend from college, and started at the studio in April 1989—initially setting up the state-of-the-art Mechanical Concept animation camera.[26] Rob Bekuhrs got a call from his college friend, Bill Kopp, saying that the new studio needed a computer effects animator. Bekuhrs worked on *Tummy Trouble* (the laser blast in the operating room) in Los Angeles for about two weeks, arriving in Florida a week after the studio opened.[27]

Bill Kopp and Pat Ventura had storyboarded two *Roger Rabbit* shorts, *Beach Blanket Bunny* and *Jolly Roger*, before *Roller Coaster Rabbit*, but it was decided to produce *Roller Coaster Rabbit* first. Bill Kopp was slated to be the director. It was a big jump from a three-man renegade unit churning out *The Simpsons* bumpers to directing a Disney film. *Roller Coaster Rabbit* didn't have a producer assigned to it at the start of production. The crew was green, and the production pipeline and studio organization had not been fully established. It was a tough situation for an inexperienced director. The film wasn't moving forward as it should have been, and the early reels were not looking good. Kopp was also a bit of a character. Suffice it to say, things did not work out and Kopp returned to California.[28] Rob Minkoff, the director of *Tummy Trouble*, was brought in to direct *Roller Coaster Rabbit*. Thirty percent of the animation had been completed. It was all scrapped, with Minkoff making a fresh start. Of course, there was an expectation of adherence to budgets and the other standard performance metrics of a working studio, but it was also a theme park attraction and contributed to that aspect of a revenue stream for Disney. Neveretheless, *Roller Coaster Rabbit* ultimately took over nine months to produce and cost over $8 million[29]—big numbers for a seven-minute cartoon.

The rollercoaster track and ride car in Roger's wide rollercoaster ride were animated with computer assistance. The shapes were rendered as wire-frame drawings and printed on a Hewlett-Packard plotter. Early on, the algorithm describing a scene in which the rollercoaster spirals "to infinity" wasn't adequately considered (and limited). The complex drawing was left to plot overnight. When Bekuhrs arrived back to the studio in the morning, he found the plotter still working away on an infinitessimally small spiral—and a hole torn through the plotter paper.[30]

The plot of *Roller Coaster Rabbit* adheres perfectly to the formula. Mother leaves Baby Herman in Roger's care, Baby Herman wanders off during a moment of inattention, and Roger suffers catastrophe upon catastrophe as he valiantly tries to protect Baby Herman from harm due to his infant naïveté. The plot is amazingly similar to that of *Thrill of Fair*, a Popeye cartoon made by Famous Studios in 1951. In essence, the mother has the same role at Olive Oyl, Baby Herman the same role as Swee'Pea, and Roger the same role as Popeye.

Roller Coaster Rabbit was released on June 15, 1990, with Warren Beatty's *Dick Tracy*. *Tummy Trouble* had been released with Disney's *Honey, I Shrunk the Kids,* and many people felt that a large portion of that film's box-office success was due to its association with the *Roger Rabbit* short. It was Spielberg's understanding that the next *Roger Rabbit* short would be released with *Arachnophobia*, an Amblin Entertainment/Disney production that was to be the first title released through Disney's new Hollywood Pictures film division. In addition to that, it was Frank Marshall's first turn at directing a full-length feature film. In the meantime, Beatty was making *Dick Tracy*, a production fraught with intrigue and cost overruns. The production cost was climbing above $45 million and Michael Eisner decided to prop up the *Dick Tracy* release with *Roller Coaster Rabbit*. *Dick Tracy* eventually made $163 million, but production and promotion costs ultimately reached $100 million. On the other hand, *Arachnophobia* fared relatively poorly at the box office, making $52 million, despite receiving great reviews. Spielberg was upset at the slight and later asserted his position and privilege, as co-owner of the character rights, by denying approval for production of the next *Roger Rabbit* short, *Hare in My Soup*, to proceed.[31]

Hare in My Soup was intended to be the next *Roger Rabbit* short, and it might have been released with *The Rocketeer* if things had gone according to schedule. The suits at Disney headquarters in Burbank wanted more

Baby Herman. The story was adjusted to have Baby Herman follow a frog that was trying to "save its legs" by escaping a French restaurant. Roger played a waiter. Kupershmidt and Blaise animated the frog trying to escape the restaurant. Chris Bailey was slated to be the director. The project went through several crews.[32] It was ultimately killed when Spielberg withheld his approval. The notes and input from Disney creative executives had resulted in story changes that had started to stray from the formula, so Spielberg's position may have been a sound creative judgment. It is likely that his decision was also a shot across the bow for Eisner.

At one time or another, as many as twelve different shorts were in various stages of completion. Different crews would be given shots at working on them. *Beach Blanket Bunny* and *Jolly Roger* were amongst the titles. One of the other shorts was very "videogame-ish," and the story got lost in the focus on effects. As Katzenberg geared up the production schedule for animated feature films to one film release each year, the Florida studio picked up scenes in the animated features, contributing to *The Rescuers Down Under* (1990), *Beauty and the Beast* (1991), and *Aladdin* (1992). The Florida crews would keep busy with work on a *Roger Rabbit* short during slow periods between features. One short film project that did reach fruition was *Off His Rockers*, the pet project of Barry Cook. Cook started at Disney after being referred by a friend as an effects animator on *Tron* in 1981. He came up with *Oilspot and Lipstick*, featuring Disney's first computer character animation. It was made in 1986 by the Disney Computer Animation Late Night Group, a group of volunteers, including Randy Cartwright, Mike Cedeno, Barry Cook, and Tina Price, who worked on the film during their own time. Similarly, *Off His Rockers* was a bootleg project for which the small production group was allowed to use studio equipment and resources. The film shows a young boy fixated and lost in playing a video game and the struggles of his rocking horse in trying to catch his attention. The boy was rendered in traditional animation, but the backgrounds, props, and the rocking horse were computer-generated. Rob Bekuhrs did the computer animation. It was Tom Bancroft's first "test" as an animator. Cook directed a core group of six people that eventually expanded to over seventy-five people when Disney decided to release the short with *Honey, I Blew Up the Kid. Off His Rockers* was not submitted by Disney to SIGGRAPH or Oscar consideration.

Off His Rockers ultimately led to the third *Roger Rabbit* short, which is thought of very fondly by those from Florida who worked on it. *Trail Mix-Up* was conceived at the Florida studio, although much of the storyboarding was done by Pat Ventura, who had storyboarded the previous *Roger Rabbit* shorts. *Trail Mix-Up* was directed by Barry Cook. After having worked on several feature animation projects requiring subtle acting, the animators enjoyed the opportunity to do broad cartoony animation.[33] Tom Bancroft enjoyed the scenes that Cook gave him to animate. He felt that Cook may have been favorably inclined due to Bancroft's early contributions on *Off His Rockers*.[34] Mark Kausler had moved back to Los Angeles, but he worked on Jessica remotely.[35]

The crew had fun in making this film and took liberties with inside jokes, as in the old days. When Roger Rabbit and Baby Herman are in the sawmill and zoom rapidly towards camera as they start their flume ride, a skull and crossbones can be seen in the irises of Roger Rabbit's eyes, while a Mickey Mouse silhouette can be seen in the irises of Baby Herman's eyes. In the bumble bee sequence, Roger spits out a number of bees he has swallowed. On close inspection, some of the bee heads include: Tinker Bell, Mickey Mouse, Evinrude (from *The Rescuers Down Under*), Genie (from *Aladdin*), and Ric Sluiter (background artist and art director for *Trail Mix-Up*).[36] At the start of the short, Roger is demonstrating how to start a fire. Jessica, as a park ranger, drives up in a Jeep and stands over Roger. The fury with which he turns the stick on the stone and self-immolates is an allusion to masturbation. When Katzenberg said that the scene must be deleted, Cook sent a note to him to convince him into letting it stay . . . he finally agreed . . . *but* he maintained that Jessica's "buttons" had to go. The breast-pocket buttons on Jessica's park ranger uniform were just too obvious an invitation to censors and undesired ratings.[37] Being housed in trailers during the production of *Trail Mix-Up* may have contributed to the animators' high jinks.

At the conclusion of the short, the Old Predictable Geyser blasts a giant boulder and log (and Roger Rabbit, Baby Herman, the beaver, and the bear) towards Mount Rushmore. Mount Rushmore is animated into a wild Tex Avery-style "take" immediately before contact. The film cuts to a very large sculpted miniature of the wild take, which is destroyed in a real-life explosion. The miniature was sculpted by Bob Spurlock and his crew from Stetson Visual Services. It was set up at Disney's Golden Oak Ranch, off Placerita Canyon Road in Newhall, California, and then blown up.[38] Spurlock had worked on the mechanical effects during filming of *Who Framed Roger Rabbit* in Los Angeles.

Trail Mix-Up was released on March 12, 1993, accompanying *A Far Off Place*.

Sequel

Hollywood sequels were not always part of the movie landscape. In the past, remakes were more prevalent—either to take advantage of new social circumstances (*Scarface* [1932]—alcohol and prohibition; *Scarface* [1983]—cocaine]; clever new situational circumstances and new leading actors (*The Thomas Crown Affair* [1968]—bank robbery/Steve McQueen; *The Thomas Crown Affair* (1999)—art theft/Pierce Brosnan); clever use of a continuing soft spot for an automobile (*The Italian Job* [1969]—Mini; *The Italian Job* [2003]—Mini); "clever" use of shot-for-shot capability (*Psycho* [1960]—Alfred Hitchcock; *Psycho* [1998]—Gus Van Sant]; or because of sheer power and audacity (*The Ten Commandments* [1923]—Cecile B. DeMille; *The Ten Commandments* [1956]—Cecile B. DeMille]. Remakes sometimes brought foreign films into the English sphere—*The Magnificent Seven* (from *Seven Samurai* [Japan]) and *Fistful of Dollars* (from *Yojimbo* [Japan]).[39]

There have been movie franchises, including those revolving around James Bond (starting in 1962), Superman (starting in 1978), *Star Trek* (starting in 1979), Indiana Jones (starting in 1981), and Batman (starting in 1989). There have been sequels based on genre properties that have captured audience imagination, including such works in science fiction as *Star Wars* (1977), *Mad Max* (1979), *Alien* (1979), *The Terminator* (1984), *Back to the Future* (1985), and *RoboCop* (1987) and such works in horror as *Halloween* (1978), *Friday the 13th* (1980), *Troll* (1986), *Critters* (1986), *Child's Play* (1988), and *Maniac Cop* (1988).

There have been sequels based on popular films, among them *A Fistful of Dollars* (1964, a remake itself of a Japanese film), *The Godfather* (1972), *Death Wish* (1974), *Jaws* (1975), and *Smokey and the Bandit* (1977). But, for the most part, sequels were a 1980s phenomenon: *Porky's* (1981), *Rambo—First Blood* (1982), *The Beastmaster* (1982), *Beverly Hills Cop* (1984), *The Karate Kid* (1984), *Police Academy* (1984), *Class of Nuke 'em High* (1986), *Iron Eagle* (1986), *Crocodile Dundee* (1986), *Honey, I Shrunk the Kids* (1989), and *The Mighty Ducks* (1992).[40]

Many of these sequels fell into the bailiwick of Spielberg and the "Disney" of Eisner, Wells, and Katzenberg. It almost goes without saying that the critical and box-office success of *Who Framed Roger Rabbit* would bring thoughts of a sequel and a franchise. *Who Framed Roger Rabbit* was released in June 1988, and a costumed Roger Rabbit character was presented to Lady Diana, Princess of Wales, at the London premiere in November 1988. The *Roger Rabbit* short *Tummy Trouble* was in production in January 1989, and Disney already had a slate of *Roger Rabbit* short storyboards at that time. A sequel was in active development, although it was actually a prequel . . . providing the background leading up to the *Who Framed Roger Rabbit* plot. Tom Cruise was being discussed openly for the part of the young Eddie Valiant.

It is not known how many *Roger Rabbit* sequel screenplays were submitted. Jerry Rees, who is himself part of the *Roger Rabbit* legend, submitted a screenplay to Amblin. Nat Mauldin wrote a screenplay entitled, *Roger Rabbit II: Toon Platoon*. It was a prequel set in 1940 that described Roger Rabbit's journey to Hollywood in search of his mother, how he met his future wife (Jessica), and his involvement in World War II. Eisner already had Spielberg's back up by releasing *Roller Coaster Rabbit* with *Dick Tracy* instead of *Arachnophobia*. Spielberg had already vetoed *Hare in My Soup* after it was well into production. By that time, Spielberg was developing *Schindler's List* and (re)discovering his Jewish heritage. *Toon Platoon* involved the unmasking of the manager of Jessica's radio station as a Nazi spy. Spielberg did not want to lessen the menace of Nazis by having them as the villains of a *Roger Rabbit* comedic animated film, so he vetoed further development based on the Mauldin screenplay.[41]

Spielberg gave approval for the development and release of *Trail Mix-Up*, released in late 1993, which Eisner took as a peace feeler. Eisner authorized a rewrite of the Mauldin screenplay. Sherri Stoner and Deanna Oliver, writing partners on Spielberg's *Tiny Toons Adventures*, were brought in to retool the premise on which the screenplay was based. They pushed it back to the Great Depression, in New York City. They retained the idea that Roger Rabbit was looking for his long-lost mother, but he got to Hollywood in a different way. Jessica was appearing in a Broadway show and Roger took a job as a stagehand in order to woo her. One night, he was stranded on stage when the curtain raised and . . . he became a Broadway and film star. Instead of Nazi intrigue, it became more of a Busby Berkeley-style musical. Disney was sufficiently keen to send the script to Alan Menken, who wrote five songs for the film and offered to serve as executive producer. Eisner also hired Kathleen Kennedy and Frank Marshall as producers. Jeffrey Katzenberg had left Disney by this time, and was now a partner in DreamWorks SKG. In spite of the illwill and lawsuits between Katzenberg and Eisner, Spielberg approved the script for development. Disney brought in Rob Minkoff and Floyd Norman to develop it further.[42]

The difficulty of the special effects achieved in *Who Framed Roger Rabbit* was still very much on everybody's mind—and, by this time, computer-generated special effects were a staple of Hollywood films. Eisner ordered a test of CGI effects for the *Roger Rabbit* sequel. In the spring of 1998, a CGI test was conducted, with Jim Pentecost as the producer and Eric Goldberg as the director. Goldberg designed a new animation model sheet for a young Roger Rabbit. The test included three scenes shot in live action by Frank Marshall at the Raleigh Studio.[43] The first portion of the test contained two scenes with the toons rendered by traditional animation techniques. In the first scene, two weasels burst into the office of a Hollywood agent to "persuade" him to schedule an audition for Roger. They are carrying tommy guns. The tommy guns and the breaking table were generated with computer animation.[44] The second scene was designed to determine whether a live-action prop could be transitioned to CGI in a convincing way. Barry Temple did the traditional animation. The live actor was carrying a whiskey bottle, but Roger thought it was a bottle of apple juice. Roger grabs the bottle from the actor's hand, drinks from it, and goes off like a rocket.[45] Goldberg said, "It was invisible! They did a fantastic job! You would never know that it was a CGI replacement bottle."[46] The second portion of the test was designed to evaluate whether Roger could be convincing in CGI character animation. It had Roger appearing out of a top hat and leaping over to the agent's desk, knocking the telephone off the desk and doing a cartoon loop-the-loop before announcing himself. The scene was initially animated by Tom Bancroft using traditional animation. He put "extra business" into the scene to test the CGI animators—"funky motion" and blur/smear.[47] As advanced as the special effects were intended to be, the telephone was pulled off the desk with wires. Bancroft had indeed set the bar high; in fact, there was no computer technology yet available to reconstruct the organic smears easily done using traditional animation. Eric Guaglione and his team of several computer animators worked for almost a year to have the CGI animation match the traditional animation.[48] They were successful, but the test readjusted the budget for a sequel to in excess of $100 million. *Pearl Harbor* had just cost $135–140 million to make. The animated film *Treasure Planet* was said to have cost $180 million, but brought in only $38 million at the box office.[49] At the same time, other CGI live-action/computer animation combinations, such as *Monkeybone* and *Adventures of Rocky and Bullwinkle*, had failed at the box office. Eisner canceled any further work on the *Roger Rabbit* sequel.[50]

Roy Disney had championed the evaluation of CGI animation for the *Roger Rabbit* sequel. While it did not lead to a *Roger Rabbit* sequel, the computer animation technology gains achieved by Guaglione and his team were important to the Disney organization. The same computer animation techniques were used by Eric Goldberg for the Genie (from *Aladdin*) in the Magic Theater attraction at Tokyo Disney Sea.[51] Making Roger Rabbit appear convincing in the test required very organic computer modeling. Pixar had been making CGI animated films of inanimate and nonhuman subjects. The Pixar film in development at the time was Brad Bird's *The Incredibles*, with cartoony humans . . . and similar animation issues as Roger Rabbit. Eric Guaglione did a joint Disney/Pixar presentation at SIGGRAPH that year.[52] Disney acquired Pixar Animation Studios in 2006. Ed Catmull became the president of animation for Disney and Pixar, and John Lasseter became the chief creative officer.

Chapter Nine

AT THE PARKS

Even as Bill Frake was starting to lay out Towntown and develop its look for the film, there were plans to use the design for a second entrance to Disneyland.[1] The main entrance, facing south towards the parking lot (now Disney California Adventure), is connected to the hub by Main Street, USA. In order to relieve congestion at closing and to provide access to another parking area, a new entrance on the north side of Disneyland would lead to West Ball Road and quick access to the Santa Ana Freeway (I-5). The route from the new entrance to the attractions would have shops for guests to purchase souvenirs before leaving the park, similar to Main Street. The route was to be "themed," much like Toontown. This entrance ultimately gave way to other plans.

Mickey's Birthdayland was a popular "homegrown" attraction at Walt Disney World. It had been developed in 1988, to celebrate Mickey Mouse's sixtieth birthday, as a fixed-costume character meet-and-greet location, both to cater to a growing demand for guest-character interactions and to better manage those interactions—especially the safety aspect. Stories abound of the abuse Disney employees, in character costume, received from "energetic" young guests.[2] Mickey's Birthdayland was located on some unused land east of the 20,000 *Leagues Under the Sea* attraction and was accessed through Fantasyland. It was closed temporarily in April 1990 and remodeled, to be reopened in May 1990 as Mickey's Starland. In 1996, it was remodeled again and turned into the "permanent" attraction, Mickey's Toontown Fair.

Walt Disney Imagineering (WDI) was not involved in the development of Mickey's Birthdayland at Walt Disney World, but Disneyland had the same interest in a character meet-and-greet zone and went to WDI for the design.[3] Joe Lanzisero was selected to lead the project, while Dave Burkhart was the show producer. Lanzisero had just completed the Splash Mountain project for Tokyo Disneyland. His Mickey's Starland team included Don

Carson, a young Imagineer who had worked with him on Splash Mountain,[4] Marcelo Vignali, who had been working on the Walt Disney World Muppetland project (which had been canceled after Jim Henson died), Hani El Masri, who had been working on a Mickeyville concept for Tokyo Disneyland, and Jim Shull.[5]

The group visited Mickey's Starland in Walt Disney World. It had been built as a temporary attraction . . . and felt that way. The backdrop was painted plywood flats.[6] Disneyland's Mickey's Starland was intended to be a much larger project, a themed "land." In the original concept, there would be a transition from Fantasyland by means of a Winnie-the-Pooh ride. The meet-and-greet elements would be in Mickey's house and Minnie's house. Attractions in Goofy's house and Donald's boat, plus other features such as a gas station and shops, would make up Mickey's suburban neighborhood.

Mickey's neighborhoods, as depicted in the 1950s film shorts and comics, were basically . . . Pasadena.[7] The popularity of *Who Framed Roger Rabbit* made it natural to consider its inclusion in a new character land. Michael Eisner was enthusiastic about cross-promotion and bringing popular Disney film elements into the theme parks. Disneyland's Mickey's Starland layout would include Mickey's suburban neighborhood and a downtown Toontown.

Global Van Lines' western region headquarters was located on South Harbor Boulevard at the Santa Ana Freeway. Global Van Lines was an early Disneyland sponsor. In 1985 Disney purchased the land from Global Van Lines. At that time, the Disneyland administrative building was located outside the berm near the Grand Canyon Diorama. It was overcrowded, and many of the business groups were already working out of leased office space off the Disneyland park site. Staff was increasing due to park expansion plans; in fact, the park administrative office building was going to give way to those expansion plans. A new Team Disney Anaheim building was to be built along Santa Ana Freeway in the area formerly occupied by Global Van Lines.

Disney owned property west of Disneyland on Walnut Street north of the Disneyland Hotel complex. At one time, it had been used as a Disney picnicking area called Holidayland. Disney acquired the Disneyland Hotel and property and assets at Long Beach in 1988, after the death of Jack Wrather. Additional property was assembled west of Disneyland for a new park, with separate admission, to be called Westcot.

Neither Westcot nor a marine-themed park at Long Beach were built, although much of the design work for the Long Beach park was later utilized at the Tokyo Disney Sea park. The land west of the Disneyland park was utilized for freeway access ramps and for a giant multi-level parking structure, which replaced and enhanced the parking lost to Disney California Adventure.

Although the plan had been to have a new Team Disney Anaheim building in place by 1991, an architect was not selected until 1992. Frank Gehry was chosen to design the building. The result was a schizophrenic structure, with a long straight length facing the freeway and the opposite side, facing the park, having Gehry's signature complex curvature.[8] The freeway side has a ground-level buttress that Gehry described as a "cow catcher," but Disney cast members call it "the Zipper Building." Gehry was later commissioned by Disney to design an ice rink complex in Anaheim, just north of Ball Road. He also designed the Walt Disney Concert Hall complex in downtown Los Angeles, although it was not a project of the Walt Disney Company.

The four-story Team Disney Anaheim building was opened in 1995. A five-story-high cast member parking structure was built adjacent to it. The parkade looks down over Disneyland maintenance shops and service areas. These service areas were always hidden from guest view by the Disneyland railroad and the associated berm and trees. The tall parkade and administration building would need to be blocked from view to preserve the otherworldliness of Toontown.

The Team Disney administrative complex resulted in a scaled-back downtown Toontown. At one time, Toontown was to have been much larger than the current size. Downtown Toontown was to have additional buildings to the east. The Jolly Trolley was to go from Mickey's neighborhood area to downtown Toontown, and then proceed up a downtown Toontown street (between the existing structures and the additional buildings).

Although WDI explored the theme of a Mickey Mouse environment characterized by the suburban look of the 1950s shorts and comics, theming quickly focused on exploiting the popularity of *Who Framed Roger Rabbit*. The squash-and-stretch cartooniness of the film's Toontown was a natural for this new themed land. Joe Lanzisero scoped out the overall design concept for what was to be called Toontown. Although the film's Toontown guided the concept, the atmosphere in the film was generally dark and foreboding. The WDI team wanted a sweeter version of Toontown. Their first thought was for the buildings to actually squash and stretch, but the engineering and mechanics would be extraordinarily expensive and difficult, and the polymeric exterior materials would break down quickly in the hot California sun, high UV radiation, and constant flexing cycles. The buildings were then changed to having a sculpted look. One rule was agreed on: none of the buildings would have faces with googly eyes, as that was deemed too frightening for little children.[9]

In late 1990, Hani El Masri worked on a project called Mickeyville that was intended as a new land for Tokyo Disneyland. The architectural theme was reminiscent of Mickey's 1930s- and '40s-era "medieval" cartoons, like *Ye Olden Days*, *The Brave Little Tailor*, and *Mickey and the Beanstalk*, with a large nod to the architecture of Pinocchio's village. Early designs for Minnie's Candy House and Donald's Dock House were more cartoony. Masri moved on to the Toontown project and ended up designing Minnie's House and Goofy's Bounce House.[10] Jim Shull designed Mickey's House and Donald's Boat. Don Carson led the development of downtown Toontown and designed the shell for the Car Toon Spin ride. Marcelo Vignali provided design concepts for several Toontown buildings, including the firehouse and train station. Andrea Favilli—a sculptor who had previously designed the Disney Legends statue and award, as well as the Cameraman statue that has been placed at several Disney parks—designed the exterior for the Roger Rabbit's Car Toon Spin ride building.[11]

Don Carson had full access to the Disney Archives for the background paintings used in the 1950s Mickey Mouse film shorts and *Who Framed Roger Rabbit*. The look of downtown Toontown was to be guided by the anthropomorphism and animation of the film. Mickey's neighborhood was to be complementary and consistent with that theme. The WDI designers agreed that the buildings should slump and sag as though they were made of cake that had fallen in the oven.[12]

The design work was done in a fraction of the time usually allotted for park projects; site preparation was being done even as the building concepts were being developed. The overall layout was decided, with building footprints assigned, and then the buildings would have to be designed to fit. Toontown was going to be much larger than what was finally built. In addition to having a more extensive Toontown area, it was going to spill into the area in Fantasyland where the Princess Fantasy Faire theater later resided . . . for a transitional area themed as Winnie-the-Pooh's Hundred Acre Wood. There was also going to be a bumper car ride called Donald's Deals, a kind of a used-car lot. It would have been located where the Five and Dime store was eventually placed.[13] There was originally going to be a Winnie-the-Pooh tree ride, located where Roger Rabbit's Car Toon Spin ended up. It was to have been a multi-story ride, with "hunny"-pot ride vehicles ascending the tree.[14]

The building concepts were created, followed by color sketches and color elevations. A Toontown model was created, with the buildings sculpted in foam. The buildings were not designed with the aid of computer modeling, which could break out the design of complicated structural elements and engineering load calculations, as Frank Gehry's Guggenheim Museum in Bilboa, Spain, and the Walt Disney Concert Hall in Los Angeles had been. The type of structures being considered could not be found in any building code, so the Toontown buildings were essentially concrete bunkers with a decorative metal structure overlay. The metal structure would be draped with wire mesh and covered by sprayed concrete. The architects were stymied in translating the concept sketches to architectural drawings, so Carson overlaid design drawings on the structural architectural drawings.[15]

The Toontown model was used as reference throughout construction. Much of the exterior metal overlay was fit in the field, with that portion of the model taken to the construction site. A construction contractor employee was assigned to guard the model piece against potential damage. In addition, Carson spent long days on site to ensure that the exteriors were faithful to the original concept drawings. He would spray-paint the rough exterior design on the concrete base, over which the exterior finishers would sculpt and carve.[16] Ron Esposito was the "rockwork" expert who led the concrete spraying and exterior "concrete painting." At one time, there were as many as thirty WDI imagineers involved in the downtown Toontown team.

It was after design work had started on Toontown that WDI was made aware that the Team Disney Anaheim building was to be built behind the attraction. Carson drew the task of designing the viewblock. He experimented by carving simple stylized hills out of foamboard. The WDI shops had just recently installed an OSHA-approved spray paint booth, and its paint cabinet had a myriad of colors. Carson required three different shades of the same color to show depth in the viewblock for downtown Toontown, and the only color in the cabinet with three reasonable distinct shades was red. He used shades of grey and green for the rolling hills behind Mickey's neighborhood. These viewblocks were intended only as tests and were meant to be temporary. All of the Disney park color themes required the approval of the "King of Color," John Hench, who was the venerable former animator/designer and the creative guru at WDI. Hench happened to be visiting the park at the time of the test viewblock installation. Although the colors were selected more by happenstance, Hench loved them . . . and the temporary viewblock stayed in place.[17]

Joe Lanzisero came to WDI from an animation background and wanted to be more involved with the *Roger Rabbit* components of Toontown, but as overall project creative lead, he had his hands full. His original design for the *Roger Rabbit* fountain remained, through to construction, as his design contribution. He had prepared the first rough storyboard for the ride. Lanzisero and Vignali fleshed out the concepts with color story drawings. As Lanzisero's time came to be directed to other aspects of the Toontown project, Vignali took over the leadership of Roger Rabbit's Car Toon Spin ride portion of the project.

The Winnie-the-Pooh tree ride was scrapped, but the concept of winding up a ride path was retained in the early Car Toon Spin ride design.[18] The ride vehicles were to come outside of the building on the second floor. The intent was to have the themed Benny the Cab vehicles and delighted guests act as "weinies" for the ride and for Toontown. "Weinie" is the WDI term for a design feature that draws the guests towards the desired "imagineered" path. Vignali initially considered the Omnimover ride system (used for the Doom Buggies in the Haunted Mansion attraction) to move guests through the attraction. The Omnimover is driven by a moving chain onto which the ride vehicles are clamped. The vehicles move at a steady speed. A bus-bar ride system allows for independent vehicle movement, which would add a dynamic element to the ride experience to reinforce the story points of skidding in spilled Dip and escaping Weasels. The ride vehicles would have a three-wheeled chassis in order to bank the corners and climb the elevation to the second floor. When this ride system finally reached the WDI engineering group it was determined that the bus-bar system would be unable to climb as required. Use of the bus-bar system would require ramps with low grades that would fill up most of the floor area allocated for the ride building. They had to eliminate the ride's second floor, which would essentially cut the area available to tell the story by half.[19]

Of the many challenges, the smaller footprint resulting from the elimination of the second floor was the greatest. In addition, the footprint needed to accommodate an interior queue to protect guests from the rain and hot sun. It was to be a "dark" ride on a spinning ride vehicle, so the storyline could not be complex. Vignali wanted a linear and kinetic story. He studied other rides at Disney parks for what worked and what didn't. He wanted to maintain the film noir aspect of the film, so he settled on a story involving a kidnapping, chase, and rescue. The "chase" takes the guests on their adventure through Toontown. The queuing area sets up the story and provides the atmosphere. It can't be assumed that the guests are familiar with the *Roger Rabbit* film storyline or the dangerous nature of Dip, for example. The queue winds a tortuous path of instruction, then intrigue, which ultimately finds Jessica tied up in the trunk of a car and kidnapped by the Weasels.[20] This was the first precursor of a queue being considered as Act I of a WDI attraction.[21] Vignali worked with a WDI CAD (computer-aided design) engineer to weave the ride track in clever ways to optimize the use of the building footprint. Lanzisero had done the original storyboards for the Car Toon Spin ride. Vignali and his team tightened up the story and designed the set pieces in such a way that the optimized ride path was only a few feet shorter than the original two-story plan. They also went with a two-person vehicle design that ultimately increased the total ride capacity beyond the original budget.[22]

Vignali worked with show writer, Art Verity, to flesh out the story, write the dialogue, and add humor. Vignali even "appears" in the attraction— voicing Bongo, the Gorilla, asking for the password to the Ink and Paint Club in the queue area, voicing the bull in the china shop, and appearing as one of the laughing jacks-in-the-box in the warehouse. The other jack-in-the-box was voiced by Lanzisero, and the jack-in-the-box clown faces are caricatures of Lanzisero and Vignali—one box is marked "J," for Joe, and the other is marked "M," for Marcelo. It was Lanzisero who thought of the guests escaping through a portable hole. Andra Favilli recommended a world-class magician, Jim Steinmeyer, to help make the illusion of the portable-hole escape work. Favilli worked closely with Vignali to bring the set pieces to life.[23] The team also included Judy Chin and WDI model builders Daniel Singer and Kent Elofson.[24]

The final design concept for the film's version of Toontown was conceived and decided on relatively quickly by the Glendale unit and Zemeckis. There weren't many concept and development drawings, and Vignali didn't have access to them. He was given a VHS copy of *Who Framed Roger Rabbit*, which he watched over and over again—scrolling forward and back, especially over the Toontown portion. He made sketches from the monitor screen, and since there were relatively few backgrounds, he had wide latitude in his designs. His intent was to capture the essence of Toontown and use it in the design of new Toontown elements to service the ride's storyline.

Another aspect of optimizing the ride layout design required that the vehicles spin. The WDI team installed a Mad Hatter's Teacup ride teacup onto the Haunted Mansion's Omnimover system. The Haunted Mansion Doom Buggies have predetermined turns to support the ride story. The test with the teacup was intended to determine whether rider-determined spinning would enhance or diminish the ride experience. "Tactical" turning might allow the guest to focus on certain ride elements, which could allow them to "catch" elements that would enhance their connection to the ride story, but would more likely cause them to "miss" other elements that would result in diminishing their connection with the ride story. But, the imagineers' expectation was that many (young) guests would choose to spin the vehicle as quickly as possible . . . and lose all sense of the story. One part of the Omnimover test involved the imagineers spinning the teacup at "neck-breaking" speed, and it confirmed that almost no aspect of the Haunted Mansion story would be assimilated. More than that, the experience at Disneyland was that guests on spin rides, who concentrated on fast spins, occasionally get sick. It is relatively easy to shut down the Mad Hatter Teacup ride for a short time to clean up the ride. Guests making themselves ill on a dark ride would quickly become an operations nightmare. The imagineers experimented with gearing down the spin ratio on the teacup. Ultimately, the spin ratio on the Car Toon Spin ride vehicles has been geared down so much that it is very difficult to spin the vehicle quickly enough to generate any significant centrifugal force. The vehicles are "locked" in place until their tires get to the Dip spill. They lock again when the Weasel tries to spray Dip at the end of the ride.[25]

The full-size sculptures for the ride vehicles were farmed out to outside vendors in order to control costs, but Vignali remembers his delight at first seeing the fiberglass sculpts at WDI's MAPO engineering/fabrication site in Tujunga. Roger Rabbit's Car Toon Spin ride was initially budgeted at $40 million. After the disappointing opening of EuroDisneyland and because of the deepening recession in North America, the ride budget was cut in half and the cost ultimately proved to be approximately $22 million.[26]

Jess Harnell provided the voice of Roger Rabbit in Roger Rabbit's Car Toon Spin ride. He was often the voice of Roger Rabbit during the periods that Charles Fleischer wasn't available. Harnell was also the voice of Br'er Rabbit in Splash Mountain. Jim Cummings provided the voice of Baby Herman, while June Foray portrayed the Weasels.

There were bigger plans for Roger Rabbit at Walt Disney World (WDW). Roger Rabbit's Hollywoodland was to be located in Disney-MGM Studios (now Disney's Hollywood Studios), where Rock 'n' RollerCoaster is situated on Sunset Boulevard. The area was to include three rides, Red Car Transportation and Terminal Bar, Toontown Diner, and Maroon Studios. The rides would have been Roger Rabbit's Car Toon Spin, Baby Herman's Baby Buggy rollercoaster, and the Toontown Trolley.

Roger Rabbit figured prominently in promotions for Disney-MGM Studios theme park while it was still under construction. Both Roger Rabbit and Mickey Mouse accompanied Michael Eisner in a photo showing him in a director's chair with the studio gate, in front of Animation Courtyard, in the background. Jeffrey Katzenberg is shown in a director's chair, accompanied by Roger, on the New York street.

When Disney-MGM Studios theme park opened on May 1, 1989, *Who Framed Roger Rabbit* had been a bona fide blockbuster the previous year and had picked up four Oscars in March. The first film short, *Tummy Trouble*, was ready for release, and the second short was slated to be produced at the new animation studio associated with Disney-MGM Studios theme park. Not only was it a working animation studio, but it was a theme park attraction, too. Park guests entered from the Animation Courtyard into a staging area with displays of Disney Oscars and development art for upcoming animated feature films. The guests proceeded to an auditorium to see *Back to Neverland*, a film directed by Jerry Rees that explains animation in a very entertaining fashion. The film featured Robin Williams and Walter Cronkite. Animator Bruce W. Smith made an on-screen appearance, and Rebecca Rees could be seen in a Walt Disney World crowd scene. The film was produced for Disney by Bob Rogers and Company (BRC Imagination Arts), a boutique entertainment company that started with a project for film and interactive aspects at EPCOT's World of Motion and has developed technological and creative expertise for themed "experiences." The *Back to Neverland* project was moribund when it was handed to Rees. He reconceived the presentation and brought in members of the *Who Framed Roger Rabbit* Glendale unit: Frans Vischer, Bruce W. Smith, Mark Kausler, Ron Dias, Annamarie Costa, Kristine Brown, and Kathy Barrows-Fullmer. Following the film, the guests moved into a viewing area (the "fishbowl"), where they could look down through glass partitions into the animation studio. The Florida animation studio was producing the new *Roger Rabbit* short, *Roller Coaster Rabbit*, and Disney-MGM Studios theme park guests could witness the making of the film. In addition, Disney was working actively on a potential feature film sequel at the time.

A billboard promoting Maroon Studios and featuring Baby Herman, Roger Rabbit, and Jessica Rabbit is installed atop the back face of a Hollywood Boulevard building, facing Echo Lake. Below it, on the second floor, is the window for Eddie Valiant's office. In the film, Roger Rabbit escaped through R. K. Maroon's office window, not Eddie Valiant's office window, but as a tribute to the film Roger Rabbit's silhouette is cut through the blinds of the adjoining window.

The film is also referenced in the Red Car and automobiles used in the film, which are along the tram route in the the backlot tour. The Dipmobile was initially located, bursting through a wall, at the head of the New York street. It was later relegated to the backlot portion of the tram tour route. Guests could also interact with a recreation of the Acme Gagworks, featuring the Toon Patrol's paddy wagon and the steamroller. There were shops selling gifts and a photo-op with a Jessica Rabbit standee.

Roger Rabbit was everpresent as a costume character. He wasn't the same scale, relative to humans, as in the film. Instead, he was one of the taller costume characters—similar, in height, to Goofy. (However, Roger was a bit shorter in stature in his Tokyo Disneyland incarnation.) Roger was featured in all of the costume character show productions at the theme parks. He was also given prominence in parade floats. He was featured in the music float in the Magic Kingdom's SpectroMagic parade.

Roger Rabbit was present as a giant inflatable character float in Disneyland's thirty-fifth-anniversary Mardi Gras parade in 1990 and was the grand marshal, and an inflatable character float, in Walt Disney World's twentieth-anniversary parade in 1991. That same year, Disney had a traveling show to promote WDW's twentieth anniversary. Roger Rabbit was the front man, with an image of him as a magician with a top hat emblazoned on the tour caravan trailers—promising Disney magic in celebration of WDW's first twenty years. A costume character show traveled the USA to promote WDW's "Surprise Celebration." On either side of the stage were giant character balloons of Roger Rabbit and Mickey Mouse.[27]

When EuroDisneyland Resort opened in 1992, Roger Rabbit was again present. He led the character parade atop a massive articulated Benny the Cab float, which elongated and contracted, as in the film, with a middle bellows. In 2013, Roger Rabbit re-emerged at Disneyland Paris as part of a character show. The unique aspect was that Jessica appeared for the first time as a costume character. She had a breast-enhancement bodysuit with a sequined dress and a face mask. The effect was somewhat grotesque. Roger Rabbit and the same Jessica costume character were part of the Disneyland Paris twenty-fifth-anniversary celebration in 2017.

When Shanghai Disneyland opened twenty-five years later, in 2016, the only reference to Roger Rabbit was Benny the Cab's taxi garage in an alley off the entry shopping boulevard.

Pop Century Resort was opened in Walt Disney World in 2003. It celebrated cultural icons of bygone decades. A giant sculpture of Roger Rabbit, atop a barrel of Dip, adorned a courtyard in the 1980s complex, along with the Rubik's Cube and the Sony Walkman.[28]

Jessica Rabbit had her own store at WDW's Pleasure Island that sold Jessica-themed jewelry and other *Who Framed Roger Rabbit* merchandise. The iconic neon Jessica sign above the store was designed by a freelance artist, Mark Marderosian, who had been designing images for Jessica T-shirts and pins as part of a large effort to produce merchandise prior to the store's opening. He created a pose in a drawing that captured Jessica's look perfectly and Disney decided to use it for the store's sign. Somebody in Disney Merchandise had the idea to put a mechanism in the sign to make one of the legs swing back and forth. The store opened with Pleasure Island in May 1989. The store was repurposed as the Music Legends store in 1992, at which time the Jessica sign was incorporated into the "Pleasure Island tonight!" sign that hung over over the West End Stage. The sign was taken down in 2006 and remains in storage.[29]

Chapter Ten

MERCHANDISING THE RABBIT

From the day that Walt Disney accepted $300 for allowing Oswald the Lucky Rabbit to be featured on a children's stencil set, merchandising has been a large aspect of Disney's operations. The first merchandising contract was with George Borgfeldt & Company, for the manufacture of figures and toys in the likeness of Minnie and Mickey Mouse. Merchandising contracts brought in much-needed revenue to the fledgling studio and promoted Mickey's short films. In 1932, Herman "Kay" Kamen signed with Disney and took Disney Merchandising to a whole new level. Kamen's marketing campaign for *Snow White and the Seven Dwarfs* was the first of its kind. He inundated the market with *Snow White* merchandise.[1]

In later years, Disney Marketing became masters of cross-marketing, using its television shows, theme parks, and VCR/DVD/Blu-ray releases to promote each other and the Disney films. The Disney name is ubiquitous in merchandise associated with the release of each new animated feature film and animated television series.

Disney had spent about $45 million to make *Who Framed Roger Rabbit* and an additional $10 million on promotion. There was buzz within the film industry, but some of the word-of-mouth sounded similar to *Snow White and the Seven Dwarfs* having been called "Disney's Folly." Disney needed to ensure that the film found its audience, so it undertook marketing cross-promotions with Coca-Cola and McDonald's. Disney shared the $500,000 production cost of a television commercial for each, but the marketing value from the McDonald's advertising campaign was estimated to be $12 million and the value from the Diet Coke campaign was estimated to be $10 million.[2] The McDonald's promotion included the release of three different "supersized" plastic soda cups.

The release of a full slate of character merchandise preceded the release of the film. Topps released a set of *Who Framed Roger Rabbit* trading cards in 1987. At that time, trading cards came in waxed paper packages and

Table 5. Disney Comics			
Roger Rabbit			
Issue No.	Release Date	Roger Rabbit/Rick Flint Story Title	Roger Rabbit Story Title
1	Jun-90	The Trouble With Toons!	Good Neighbor Roger
2	Jul-90	The Color of Trouble!	Gym Dandy
3	Aug-90	Roller Coaster Riot	20,000 Leaks Under the Sink
4	Sep-90	Little China in Big Trouble	Cotton-Tailspin
5	Oct-90	Justifiable Hamicide!	Nuts 'n' Volts
6	Nov-90	Taxi Turmoil!	Candy Cane Mutiny
7	Dec-90	Djinn Game	Dial M for Roger
8	Jan-91	The Spies of Life	Top Bun
9	Feb-91	Your Hare's on Fire!	Toro! Toro! Toro!
10	Mar-91	The Case of the Tuned-In-Toons!	Constructive Criticism
11	Apr-91	Who Framed Rick Flint?	Movin' to the Music
12	May-91	Somebunny to Love	Warren Peace
13	Jun-91	Stork Raving Mad!	Hare Apparent
14	Jul-91	Who Fired Jessica Rabbit?	Dry Run
15	Aug-91	The Great Toon Detective	Football Follies
16	Sep-91	See Ya Later, Aviator!	Toon Alone
17	Oct-91	Flying Saucers Over Toontown	Play Safe
18	Nov-91	I Have Seen the Future, and It is... Rutabagas!	Movie House Madness
Roger Rabbit's Toontown			
1	Aug-91	A Story Called: ... Called: ...Called: ?	Baby Herman in... Shopping Spree
2	Sep-91	Pre-Hysterical Roger	Jessica Rabbit in... The Kissing Bandit
3	Oct-91	The Lumberjack of Tomorrow	Jessica Rabbit in... TeeVee Jeebies
4	Nov-91	The Longest Daze. or. How NOT to Fire a Cannon	Baby Herman in... Life in the Pen
5	Dec-91	Party Panic	Baby Herman in... Rome-Ant Rampage

still included a piece of bubble gum. PVC collector character figures were released by Applause. These included clever "portable-hole" PVC character figures. "Animates" action-figures and "Flexies" bendable character figures were released by LJN Toys. Milton-Bradley released a board game and the "Dip Flip" game.[3]

Golden Book released a hardcover *Who Framed Roger Rabbit* movie storybook and a children's *Roger Rabbit* storybook, *A Different Toon*, in 1988. Golden Books also published several *Roger Rabbit* coloring books. Marvel Publications released a graphic novel, *Who Framed Roger Rabbit*, in 1988 and followed it up in 1989 with a second graphic novel, *The Resurrection of Doom . . .*, which included the *Tummy Trouble* story as an added feature. Disney Movie Book No. 1, *Tummy Trouble*, was published in 1989.

The Disney Comics imprint began in 1990, and a *Roger Rabbit* comic book series was included, with other titles coming mostly from the *Disney Saturday Afternoon* television block. The first issue finds Roger working at the Maroon Studio, now run by R. K. Maroon's brother, C. B. Maroon. Roger tries to hire Eddie Valiant for some detective work, but Valiant is too busy to take the case and refers Roger to Rick Flint, a former police detective. The comic books included a full story involving Roger Rabbit and Rick Flint and a second, more-cartoony story with Roger and other toons. The comic series ran for eighteen issues, from June 1990 until November 1991. It spawned a five-issue comic series, entitled *Roger Rabbit's Toontown*, which ran from August 1991 until December 1991. Its format involved a full story starring Roger Rabbit and a second story starring either Jessica Rabbit or Baby Herman.

Starting in the August 1991 issue of *Roger Rabbit*, the second feature followed a Maroon cartoon format, with the story starting at the conclusion of the characters filming a Maroon cartoon short. The plug was pulled on the *Roger Rabbit* comic series much sooner than the other Disney Comics series that started at the same time. In spite of a fervent core following, sales of the *Roger Rabbit* comics just didn't meet Disney's expectations.[4]

Disney Adventures was a children's entertainment and educational magazine published by Disney Publishing Worldwide. A Fall 1990 preview issue was published and then regular issues were released monthly starting in November 1990. Its last cover date was November 2007. It provided educational material, entertainment news, sports coverage, celebrity profiles, puzzles and games, and comics. In the early years, Disney-based comics were featured, promoting broadcast, syndicated, and Disney Channel animated television series: *DuckTales*, *Chip 'n' Dale Rescue Rangers*, *TaleSpin*, *Darkwing Duck*, *Goof Troop*, *Gargoyles*, and *Bonkers*. It also featured comics derived from Disney animated feature films and in later years included non-Disney comics. A *Roger Rabbit* comic was published in the first (November 1990) issue; it was *Good Neighbor Roger*, a reprint from the first (June 1990) Disney Comics issue. *Who Framed Roger Rabbit* characters were featured on five *Disney Adventures* covers. *Roger Rabbit* comics appeared in *Disney Adventures* magazine until the May 1993 issue. Although many early comics were reprints from the Disney Comics series, *later Disney Adventures* issues contained original *Roger Rabbit* comic stories.

Roger Rabbit's last hurrah in Disney Comics was a 1992 one-off issue, *Roger Rabbit in 3D*, as part of a Disney Comics in 3D series. It was republished in November 2013.

Disney released *Who Framed Roger Rabbit* in VHS format on October 12, 1989. It was released in laserdisc format in 1994. Laserdisc permitted high-definition images while advancing frame-by-frame. In the old days, animators routinely inserted risqué frames, knowing that theatrical films had a very finite screen life and that the single frames would never be "seen" in a movie theater. VHS videotapes and consumer videotape players provided poor resolution when a frame was held, so mischievous animators had little concern—if they even thought about the consequences of the risqué frames. Keen-eyed fan sleuths found the risqué frames on laserdisc.[5] The scenes most often discussed include Benny the Cab careening into a lamppost and Jessica's dress hiking up when she and Bob Hoskins are thrown from the vehicle; Baby Herman extending his middle finger upward as he jumps under a woman's skirt; and Betty Boop's exposed nipple at the Ink and Paint Club. The frames were removed or modified in subsequent laserdisc and other video format releases. It was rumored that Michael Eisner's home phone number was included in the film's initial theatrical release but that it had been deleted from the laserdisc version. That rumor has been debunked by those involved in making the film.

The film was released in DVD format on September 28, 1999. On March 25, 2003, Disney released a Vista Series DVD, which included a documentary, *Behind the Ears: The True Story of Roger Rabbit*, and the three Roger Rabbit shorts. On March 12, 2013, Disney released *Who Framed Roger Rabbit* in Blu-ray format for the film's twentieth anniversary. It was digitally restored by Prasad Studios.

Amiga released a PC video game, entitled *Who Framed Roger Rabbit*, in 1988, with animation by Eric Daniels, who had been an assistant animator in Dale Baer's Glendale unit. *Hare Raising Havoc* was released in 1991 by Blue Sky Software for Amiga and DOS platforms. Capcom released a *Who Framed Roger Rabbit* video game on Nintendo in 1989 and on Game Boy in 1991. The Japanese video game, *The Bugs Bunny Crazy Castle*, was released by Kemco for Nintendo. It inexplicably features Roger Rabbit in one version and Mickey Mouse in another version.

Jessica Rabbit had her own store at Walt Disney World's Pleasure Island that sold Jessica-themed jewelry and other *Who Framed Roger Rabbit* merchandise. The iconic neon sign was designed by a freelance artist, Mark Marderosian, who had been designing images for T-shirts and pins . . . part of a large effort to produce merchandise prior to the store opening.[6] Disney presented a *Roger Rabbit* package to its merchandise licensees. It contained folders with design ideas, the pantone color palette used in the film, character poses, preproduction art, and promotional videotapes. Licensees were flown to Los Angeles for the presentation—Steven Spielberg and Michael Eisner were scheduled to be at the après-presentation cocktail party. The date of the presentation sticks in Wendy Gell's memory . . . October, 19, 1987—Black Monday—in the week following Jeffrey Katzenberg's Concorde meeting.[7]

Gell was a successful designer of whimsical jewelry. Her work had caught the interest of Disney and they offered her a license during the early days of the Disney Store. She designed dimensional character pins, brooches, and other jewelry, often covered in pavé crystals, sequins, and rhinestones. Her work was among the very first Jessica Rabbit items to be released and were extremely popular at Disney Stores and at the Jessica Store in Pleasure Island, Walt Disney World.[8]

Pinback badges had always been available at the Disney parks, and some of the earliest *Roger Rabbit* pins were pinback buttons celebrating Spring break. Pinback buttons were released for Spring break 1989, 1990, 1991, and 1992. Other pinback buttons showed characters from the film with a quote from the film, such a Bongo the Gorilla peering through the door slot at the Ink and Paint Club, with the following text: "Walt sent me." Pins have long been traded amongst competing sports teams and at large international congresses, such as Boy Scout Jamborees and the Olympics. The popularity of cloisonné pins grew at the Disney parks over time. The collecting of Disney pins was a hobby enjoyed by many Disney park visitors and Disney created many pins featuring characters, attraction logos, park buildings, icons, special events, and seasonal themes. Pins related to the *Who Framed Roger Rabbit* film were available, but a lot of creative energy went into making Jessica pins and other merchandise for the store at Pleasure Island. Interest in *Roger Rabbit* merchandise eventually waned, and the Jessica store closed in 1992, after which there was a drought of *Roger Rabbit*-themed pins. In 1999, as part of the Millenium Celebration, Disney Pin Trading was officially promoted at Walt Disney World and the number of pin designs exploded. With that came a resurgence in interest for Jessica

Rabbit pins, often with seasonal themes. Rachel Sur started at Disney in 2004 after graduating with a degree in graphic design. She created many of the Jessica pins that continue to be very popular with collectors.[9]

Jessica had always been intriguing and popular, but even after general interest in the film waned there remained a corps of Jessica fans. One of the first official Jessica statuettes was a 1997 sculpture by Henry Alvarez. The figure was to be released in a painted-resin-and-bronzed version, but it was never put into production. In 1999, Kent Melton sculpted a Jessica and Roger set entitled, "Dear Jessica, How Do I Love Thee," which was released as part of the Walt Disney Classic Collection for the tenth anniversary of the film's release. A Jessica "beanie" plush doll was also available in 1999. Mattel's release of a Jessica doll in 1999 was more complicated, since it was intended for a general youth audience rather than the older fan base. Since the rights to Jessica were owned by Disney and Amblin, both parties had right of approval. Lisa Temming, Mattel's senior project designer on the Jessica doll, recalls the development process. A prototype was made internally at Mattel and "the guys" were very enthusiastic about it. It was on-model and had the right proportions and attitude. Disney approval was by a male artist who was delighted that the doll was on-model and "on-character." The Amblin approver was a woman who felt that the Jessica doll, as designed, would help to perpetuate negative body issues in young girls. The resultant breast reduction surgery caused the figure to be "off-model" and lose some of its character, at least for some of its fan base.[10]

In 2001, Markrita produced a statue with Roger and Jessica that was sold exclusively at the Art of Disney gallery stores. In 2002, Armani produced a thirteen-inch Jessica statuette. Mediacom Toy produced stunning vinyl figures of Roger Rabbit and Benny the Cab in 2002, and produced a nine-inch vinyl Jessica Rabbit figure in 2003. Kent Melton sculpted another Jessica figure in 2004, entitled "I'm Not Bad, I'm Just Drawn That Way," as part of Disney's Leading Ladies series. In 2005, Cody Reynolds sculpted the twenty-four-inch Big Figure Jessica statue that was available exclusively at Disney parks. Jim Shore sculpted a Disneyland Paris exclusive for Enesco, entitled "Haute Couture, Jessica Rabbit von Roger," which was released in 2007. Also in 2007, Disneyland Paris released another, more classic Jessica figure, called the "Kiss" statue as a consequence of Jessica standing on an open-mouthed "kiss" pedestal. Tracy Lee was a clean-up artist on *Roller Coaster Rabbit* and *Trail Mix-Up*. When Disney's Florida studio was closed, Lee started Electric Tiki and got a Disney license. Electric Tiki produced a *Roller Coaster Rabbit* mini-maquette in 2009 and a *Trail Mix Up* mini-maquette in 2011.[11] Both pieces were available through Sideshow

Collectibles. Disney sold a "Gallery of Light'"Robert Olszewski figure of Jessica in 2010. In 2011, Ryuji produced a manga-styled Jessica Rabbit statuette. In 2012, Jim Shore again sculpted Jessica, as a 10 ¼-inch figure by Enesco, entitled "Drawn This Way," for the Disney Traditions collection. A Premium Format series Jessica, by Ficchi Illustration, made a big splash at the 2013 Comic-Con. Also in 2013, Costa Alavesos sculpted a Jessica figure to commemorate the twenty-fifth anniversary of the film's release. Romero Britto, a pop designer, produced a Jessica bust and a 9½-inch Jessica figure in 2013 for the Disney Showcase collection. Rubén Procopio was a longtime Disney animator and maquette sculptor. He later worked with Electric Tiki, and in 2009, with Grand Jester Studios, he designed a 8 ¾-inch figure of Jessica, produced by Enesco, for the Disney Showcase collection. Grand Jester Studios released a new version of the 8 ¾-inch Jessica figure in 2015 . . . this one sculpted by Patrick Romandy-Simmons. Romero Britto released figures of Roger Rabbit and Benny the Cab in 2017.[12]

Sotheby's conducted its first auction of "new" Disney animation art on June 28, 1989. It consisted of 394 lots, and the auction catalogue became an instant Disney collectible. The film created a wider general interest in animation and helped to spawn a new "silver age" for animation. It also contributed to a tremendous increase in the value of animation art. Similar to the interest and market for serious Jessica Rabbit sculpted figures that grew in the 2000s, a market developed for serious artistic interpretations of Disney animation characters. A number of Jessica paintings have been released through the Disney Fine Art program, by former Disney artists and other fine artists such as Steven Chorney, Chris Dellorco, Manuel Hernandez, Mike Kungl, Guido Mena, James Mulligan, and Tim Rogerson. Rogerson worked as a Disney show artist, at Walt Disney World, while he attended Ringling School of Art and Design. He was later asked to contribute to the Disney Fine Art program and was named the official artist for Disney's first ever D23 Expo, at which he created a piece called "In the Company of Legends." He has created two Jessica Rabbit pieces.[13]

High-end *Who Framed Roger Rabbit* collectibles, such as ornate snow-globes, have been produced through the years. Most of them have focused on Jessica Rabbit. Between 1988 and 2003 the availability of Jessica merchandise was scarce. That began to change as Jessica developed a near-cult following and the character's popularity grew in the Disney pin market. In 2007, Disneyland Paris offered a surprising array of new Jessica merchandise—not only the figures mentioned above, but a clock, shirt, chalkboard, apron, and additional pins. Tokyo Disneyland also got into the act in 2007, with the release of a line of Jessica stationery. Although the release of new Jessica merchandise has diminished, the Days of Christmas store at Walt Disney World has offered Jessica tree ornaments and Hallmark has continued to offer new Roger and Jessica tree ornaments. In 2011, Disney Parks sold an "I'm Not Bad . . . I'm Just Drawn to Chocolate" chocolate bar. When new collectible figures are introduced, such as the Funko Pop! series, *Who Framed Roger Rabbit* characters are often among those included.[14]

Chapter Eleven

THE STORY CONTINUES

The story of *Roger Rabbit* started with Gary K. Wolf's novel *Who Censored Roger Rabbit?*, but he wasn't finished with *Roger Rabbit* yet. In 1991, Villard Books published his second *Roger Rabbit* novel, *Who P-P-P-Plugged Roger Rabbit?* The success of the film and the relatively small print runs of the book had skewed the public awareness of the characters to the film versions. Wolf has been sanguine about the need to modify the characters and premise of his story to suit the particular needs of a cinematic presentation, and he adjusted the representation of his main characters to align more closely with the film versions in his second novel. The delay in the publication of the second *Roger Rabbit* novel was partly due to the on-again/off-again situation at the Disney Studios regarding a sequel to the film. Disney consented to the use of its version of Roger Rabbit on the book's cover. The artwork was done by Dayna Stedry, who worked with Jeff Killian, the creator of the "period" Maroon cartoon film posters that adorn R. K. Maroon's office in the film. The cover shows Eddie Valiant in a fedora, this time with his back to the camera, watching Roger's antics at what appears to be a radio show microphone stand. Wolf introduced a new character, Joellyn, Jessica Rabbit's twin sister—almost identical, except only six and half inches tall. On the cover, Joellyn is perched on Eddie Valiant's shoulder, also watching Roger. It is not exactly clear what Roger is doing, but what emanates from the rear of his pants is either his rabbit-y powder puff tail or a devastating cartoon fart. It was not Wolf's shoulder on which Joellyn was standing, but Wolf is shown on the back cover, dressed in a red vest, bow tie, and fedora at a drive-in theater, sitting in Benny the Cab and accompanied by Roger Rabbit. In an interview given in 1995, Wolf was asked whether he would reprise his role as Eddie Valiant on future book covers. He replied that he expected there to be more opportunities.[1]

By 1995, Wolf had a third *Roger Rabbit* novel almost ready for publication. It was to be called *Roger Rabbit's Gossipy Guide to Toontown*. The book was to feature Roger taking Gary Cooper on a tour of Toontown, during which they would uncover a murder and work together to solve it. The book was not finished . . . mostly due to the continuing uncertainty of a film prequel or sequel.[2]

Wolf published *Roger Rabbit* short stories occasionally. He donated *Hare's Lookin' At You, Babs (Barbara Walters Interviews Roger Rabbit)* to a Brookline, Massachussetts, library fundraising book project.[3] "Stay Tooned, Folks!" was published in *Amazing Stories* magazine in 2004.[4] Wolf wrote a *Roger Rabbit* story in 2012 that was published in *Penumbra*, an e-magazine dedicated to speculative fiction.[5] A collection of short stories was published by Smashwords Editions in 2012 as an e-book, entitled *The Road to Toontown!* It contained fifteen Gary K. Wolf short stories, four of which were linked to Roger Rabbit: "A Riverworld Run Through Toontown," "Hare's Lookin' At You, Babs," "Stay Tooned, Folks!," and "Which Witch is Which?"[6]

In late 2013, Wolf published his third *Roger Rabbit* novel, *Who Wacked Roger Rabbit?*, as an eBook through Musa Publishing. In the book, Eddie Valiant gets a job as Gary Cooper's bodyguard while Cooper scouts a location for his next film, *Hi, Toon!* The film is to be shot in Toontown, and Gary Cooper's co-star is Roger Rabbit. A hoodlum, a pig named Willy Prosciutto, threatens to kill Cooper, and trouble ensues. Wolf has said that he started writing *Who Wacked Roger Rabbit?* in 1991.[7] There appear to be a number of similarities with his description of the unfinished novel, *Roger Rabbit's Gossipy Guide to Toontown*, which Wolf says may yet be completed and published, although the perceived similarity may be due to the presence of Gary Cooper in each story. (Wolf is an ardent fan of the actor.) The artwork for the cover of *Who Wacked Roger Rabbit?* was done by Jacques Muller, an animator who worked on the London crew of *Who Framed Roger Rabbit*. This time, Wolf does reprise his role of Eddie Valiant on the front cover. *Who Wacked Roger Rabbit?* was available online in .pdf format, although Musa Publishing also released a limited printing of a softcover book edition.

Wolf also promoted a concept for a new *Roger Rabbit* film that he had presented to Disney in 2013. *The Stooge* was based loosely on the (Dean) Martin and (Jerry) Lewis film of the same name. Mickey Mouse was to play the straight man, Martin, and Roger Rabbit was to play the zany pal, Lewis. Both Walt Disney and Orson Welles would be brought to life with computer graphics as Roger and Mickey interacted with the real world. The proposal was written by Wolf, with Erik von Wodtke, and concept art was prepared by Douglas A. Sirois. The art consisted of posters for the proposed film and posters for *Roger Rabbit* short film parodies: *Roger Rabbit Returns, Rear Window Rabbit!*, and *The Birds*.[8]

Who Censored Roger Rabbit? was also available through Musa Publishing in 2013 in .pdf format. *Who Censored Roger Rabbit?* was rereleased in a limited printing in 2018 by Centipede Press. The cover art was done by British illustrator Wayne Anderson. Gary K. Wolf remains a colorful character and lives true to his philosophy: "I color my cows blue, and make people happy!"[9]

When *Who Framed Roger Rabbit* was released in June of 1988, it was fresh, unique, and magical. Roger Ebert, the great *Chicago Sun-Times* film critic, said, "What you feel when you see a movie like this is more than appreciation, it's gratitude." *Who Framed Roger Rabbit* was also enduring—as it happened, Roger Ebert died after a long battle with cancer on April 4, 2013, the same day that the Academy of Motion Picture Arts and Sciences hosted a twenty-fifth anniversary "Toontown Reunion" and the film's first digital screening. Rich Moore, the director of *Zootopia* (2016) and *Wreck-It Ralph* (2012), hosted a panel discussion following the screening. The audience was polite and mature, although many of them hadn't been born when the film was released. Most were aware that *Who Framed Roger Rabbit* was partly responsible for the resurgence in interest in animation that ushered in a "silver age" of feature animation. There was a camaraderie and enthusiasm for the film that had the earmarks of cultishness.[10] In many quarters there remains great enthusiasm for more of Roger Rabbit.

Eric Carter's 1992 catalogue of theatrical film releases showed the title *Who Discovered Roger Rabbit*, which was set for release at Christmas 1993. It was to be directed by Rob Minkoff, with screenplay by Nat Mauldin.[11] In 2014, Minkoff said that he had, indeed, been attached to the *Roger Rabbit* project for a year after he had directed the first two *Roger Rabbit* shorts.[12] Roger started off in New York City and found his way to Los Angeles in search of his mother. It was a rags-to-riches story that turned into something like *Sunset Boulevard*. Floyd Norman described getting the script from producer Jim Pentecost in 1996 and working for months on story concepts. Alan Menken wrote five songs for what was to be like a Busby Berkeley musical.[13] Spielberg and Eisner could not come to an agreement and the project was shelved, but that did not end interest in bringing *Roger Rabbit* back to the big screen. Frank Marshall said that he was "open" to the idea of a sequel in 2007.[14] Zemeckis hinted at a *Roger Rabbit* sequel during an interview on MTV in 2009.[15] In late 2012, Zemeckis said that he had a script, written by Seaman and Price (the screenwriters on the original film), that he was very happy with.[16] In early 2013, Zemeckis's colleague and associate producer of *Who Framed Roger Rabbit*, Steve Starkey, said "This sequel is going to get made. Trust me. Yeah, we have a great script and we're just trying to pull it together and see if we can pull it off. But we're ready to go. If somebody says 'go,' we're there."[17]

It's not clear whether the Eddie Valiant character would have been part of the sequel, but Bob Hoskins retired from acting in 2012 after a long struggle with Parkinson's disease. He died from pneumonia, at age seventy-one, on April 29, 2014, in London. Don Hahn stated, "We probably won't be returning to Toontown any time soon," during a *Roger Rabbit* panel discussion at Comic-Con in San Diego on July 19, 2013. Zemeckis explained, "The current corporate Disney culture has no interest in Roger and they certainly don't like Jessica at all," in late 2016.[18]

That news has not dampened the enthusiasm of many of the *Who Framed Roger Rabbit* fans. Doug Walker plays the Nostalgia Critic, a bitter and sarcastic critic who reviews films and television shows from his childhood, usually with comically exaggerated outrage. He "remembers the movies, so that you don't have to." Walker reviewed *Who Framed Roger Rabbit* in his *Nostalgia Critic* web series in 2012 and followed up with a *What You Never Knew About . . .* segment on *Who Framed Roger Rabbit* in 2015. He was enthusiastic, yet solemn and respectful, in his reviews—and proclaimed it "absolutely awesome." [19] He gave it a definite high-five.

The film was titillating and clever, with historical and cultural references and adult double entendres. Even if today's youth might not remember the details of the film or catch the nuances of the cultural references, they certainly remember Jessica Rabbit. The "memory" tends mostly to the titillating aspect. The recent and most common manifestation of *Roger Rabbit* is the co-opting of the Jessica Rabbit character, in particular, by amateur artists. The images range from cute and clever to hard-core pornographic. Many images reside on the deviantart.com website, but any internet search will pull up an almost unlimited number of Jessica Rabbit images.

Cosplay is a contraction of "costume play," and is a term that was coined by Nobuyuki Takahashi, of the anime publishing house Studio Hard, after he attended the 1983 World Science Fiction Convention in Los Angeles. Cosplay is "the practice of dressing up as a character from a film, book, or video game, especially one from the Japanese genres of manga or anime" (Oxford Dictionary), and Jessica Rabbit has been a popular cosplay character. Comic cons started in 1970 as San Diego's Golden State Comic-Minicon. There were one hundred attendees. In 2016, there were over 130,000 attendees. The comic conventions have expanded beyond their focused roots to include all aspects of entertainment and media, and there are over one hundred large comic cons held in North America annually. Again, a quick internet search will find countless images of women, and sometimes men, dressed as Jessica Rabbit. Perhaps the epitome of Jessica Rabbit cosplay was achieved by the famous model Heidi Klum at her annual Halloween costume party at the Lavo nightclub in New York City in 2015. Her transformation into Jessica Rabbit took nine hours and required a team of professional make-up artists. Klum wore rubber face prosthetics with heightened cheekbones, plumped lips, and elongated eyelids with two-inch eyelashes. She also wore body enhancements that included an enlarged chest and bottom.[20] The effect was extraordinary.

A major auction of film costumes and props was held by the Prop Store in London on September 26, 2017. Bidders put in a long day waiting until it got to the "W's" for *Who Framed Roger Rabbit*, but bidding was enthusiastic. The lots included items such as an Elstree Studios *Who Framed Roger Rabbit* clapperboard, set dressing items, Acme Warehouse props, Eddie Valiant and Judge Doom costumes, Judge Doom's cane, and foam stand-ins for Roger Rabbit and Smart Ass Weasel. Over $130,000 was paid for the twenty-seven lots up for bid. One floor bidder won 70 percent of the lots and paid $100,000 for their *Roger Rabbit* memorabilia.

In late 2017 a line of clothing with *Roger Rabbit* iconography was introduced by the Hundreds, a streetwear brand inspired by California culture. It added animation themes to previous punk, hip-hop, skateboarding, and surfing themes.

Most of the artists who worked on *Who Framed Roger Rabbit* feel a very special connection with it. In many cases it was their first major feature film. Many of them have gone on to become leaders within the animation industry, and most have enjoyed steady employment, in part due to that pedigree. The circumstances of the production, and the response to it, created a bond amongst them that has remained special—for an industry in which paths often cross fleetingly and move on. A tenth-anniversary crew reunion was held in Burbank on June 23, 1998, and was attended by between forty-five and fifty people. On September 20, 2008, the Ottawa International Animation Festival held a gala screening of *Who Framed Roger Rabbit* to mark its twentieth anniversary and paid tribute to Richard Williams in an event hosted by John Canemaker. Many of Williams's cohorts from the past, including the *Roger Rabbit* days, traveled to Ottawa to be part of that moment.

The Elstree Project held a *Who Framed Roger Rabbit* reunion event on November 22, 2012, in anticipation of the film's twenty-fifth anniversary.

On April 4, 2013, the Academy of Motion Picture Arts and Sciences hosted "A Toontown Reunion" at its theater in Los Angeles to commemorate the twenty-fifth anniversary of the release of the film. The event coincided with the film's anniversary Blu-ray release, representing its first digital screening. A panel discussion followed the screening, introduced by Bill Kroyer and hosted by Rich Moore. The panel consisted of Joanna Cassidy, Andreas Deja, Charles Fleischer, Don Hahn, Jeffrey Price, Peter Seaman, Steve Starkey, and Bob Zemeckis. At least twenty-five members of the crew were in attendance and most of them were able to stay after the program for a group photo on the stage.[21] A tribute to Richard Williams, on the occasion of his eightieth birthday, was held at the Edinburgh International Film Festival on June 29, 2013, and served as an opportunity for a small reunion. A twenty-fifth-anniversary *Roger Rabbit* panel discussion was held at the 2013 Comic-Con in San Diego on July 19, 2013. The panel was comprised of James Baxter, Dave Bossert, Andreas Deja, Charles Fleischer, Don Hahn, Nik Ranieri, and Tom Sito. An informal crew reunion was held at the King's Head Pub in Sherman Oaks, with about twenty people able to attend. Richard Williams was feted with a tribute at AMPAS on October 4, 2013, and at the twentieth Cartoon Art Trust Awards in London on November 22, 2016. The occasions provided opportunities for crew reunions on both sides of the Atlantic.

The London-based animators of Soho formed a tightly knit community. They have long arranged get-togethers at their favorite Soho pubs, such as the Star & Garter. On September 25, 2015, a reunion was organized at the Edinboro Castle, a pub the animation crew used to frequent, during the production of the film, in Camden Town. More than thirty people attended the event.

A thirtieth-anniversary charity screening was organized by the Los Angeles Conservancy in the grand Los Angeles Theater on Broadway in historic downtown Los Angeles, only blocks from where *Who Framed Roger Rabbit* live-action filming was done on Hope Street. At least a dozen animators who worked on *Roger Rabbit* attended the June 16, 2018, screening, then adjourned across the street to Clifton's to reminisce.

Who Framed Roger Rabbit remains a special film and a very special experience for those who were involved in its making. But it was also special to a generation of filmgoers and it has since developed a following in younger generations. The making of *Who Framed Roger Rabbit* was a unique undertaking. The stars aligned to bring together people with extraordinary talent from around the globe. It holds a special place in animation history and in film history.

Richard Williams Animation 1986
Christmas card (front) by Errol Le Cain
(permission of © Richard Williams)

Richard Williams Animation 1986 Christmas card (inside) by Errol Le Cain (permission of © Richard Williams)

The Forum, 74–80 Camden Street (permission of Peter Western)

The Forum entrance, June 24, 1987 (permission of Nik Ranieri)

Great Storm of 1987, October 16, 1987 (permission of Nik Ranieri)

The Forum, October 21, 1987: L-R: Sue Baker, Dave Spafford, Nik Ranieri, Andreas Deja (permission of Nik Ranieri)

The Forum, November 12, 1987: L-R: Nik Ranieri, Robert Watts, Bob Hoskins, Bob Zemeckis, Frank Marshall, Jacques Muller (permission of Nik Ranieri)

The Forum, December 16, 1987 (wine and cheese party): L-R: Jeffrey Katzenberg, Frank Marshall, Tom Sito (permission of Nik Ranieri)

SFX crew—Chris Knott birthday card, drawn by Lily Dell (permission of Lily Dell)

The Forum, February 5, 1988: L-R: Nik Ranieri, Irene Couloufis (Parkins), Jacques Muller, Steven Spielberg (permission of Nik Ranieri)

The Forum, March 1988, fifth floor: Glenn Sylvester (permission of Nik Ranieri)

The Forum, March 14, 1988, third-floor lobby: Nik Ranieri, Christopher Lloyd, Robert Zemeckis (permission of Nik Ranieri)

The Forum, March 21, 1988, route meeting: L-R: James Baxter, Annie Elvin, Maggie Brown, Ian Cook, Patsy De Lord, Chris Knott, Steve Hickner (with camera), Don Hahn (with camera), Dick Williams (permission of Pete Western)

Wrap party, the Barbican Center, Garden Room, March 18, 1988 (permission of Nik Ranieri)

Wrap party, the Barbican Center, recording of "Smile, Darn Ya, Smile!," March 18, 1988 (permission of Nik Ranieri)

Gag drawing by Tom Sito (permission of Tom Sito)

Gag drawing by Tom Sito (permission of Tom Sito)

Gag drawing by Tom Sito (permission of Tom Sito)

Gag drawing by Tom Sito (permission of Tom Sito)

1400 Air Way, Glendale, California (permission of Ross Anderson)

Sweater Vest gag, Glendale, California: L-R: Dave Spafford, Dave Nethery, Kent Holaday, Frans Vischer, Richard Williams, Dave Pacheco, Matt O'Callaghan, Bill Frake (permission of Matt O'Callaghan)

Motivational pin-back buttons (permission of Ross Anderson)

Signed Radio City Music Hall premiere program (permission of Tom Sito)

Radio City Music Hall, New York City premiere, June 21, 1988: L-R: Nik Ranieri, Richard Williams, Stan Green, Roger Chiasson, Alex Williams, James Baxter (permission of Nik Ranieri)

Radio City Music Hall, New York City premiere, June 21, 1988: L-R: Richard Williams, Robert Watts (permission of Anthony Clark)

Radio City Music Hall, New York City premiere, June 21, 1988: L-R: Bob Hoskins, Robert Zemeckis (permission of Anthony Clark)

London crew reunion card, September 26, 2015 (permission of Ross Anderson)

st of luck with
e book Ross.
Rob Newman

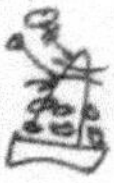

Crazy Canadian!
Thanks for the
memories!

Fantastic job getting us
together Ross !!!
Tony Clark

28 YEARS LATER, THE CREW
REASSEMBLE
THANKS ROSS!

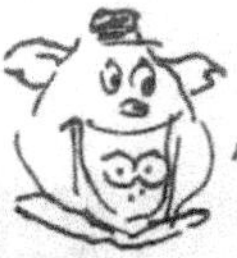

"PIGHEAD PETE"

ROGER RABBIT REUNION

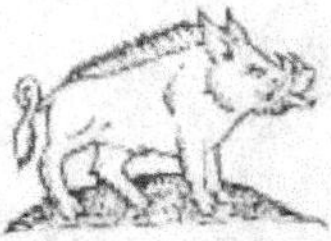

THE EDINBORO' CASTLE

SEPTEMBER 26, 2015

To Ross
– What a wonderful
idea! Thankyousomuch!
love
Graeme

Wonderful stuff!!
Good man Ross!!
xx Nick Langf

GREAT TO MEET
YOU Ross &
KATE

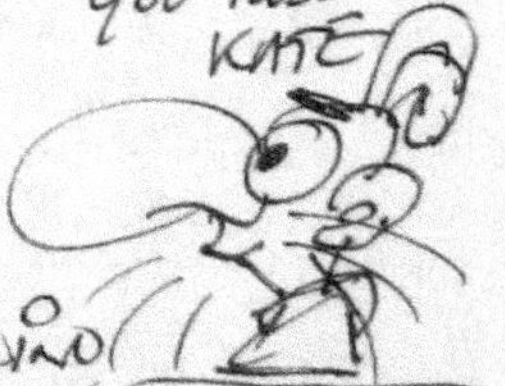

Dino

I FRAMED HIM

Lots of love
Emma Tarnero x

Arthur Schmidt's Oscar statuette (permission of
Arthur Schmidt)

London charity premiere, November 21, 1988: Republic of Niger stamp, with
Diana, Princess of Wales, and Roger Rabbit

ACKNOWLEDGMENTS

This book grew out of a hobby interest in animation, particularly Disney animation, and a world-class collection of books on animation and anything Disney. When I was young—when there were only a handful of books published on animation—I contacted the Disney Studios directly and ended up meeting a handful of the Nine Old Men. Shortly after *Who Framed Roger Rabbit* was released, I moved to Oakville, to the neighborhood adjoining Sheridan College. The graduation class photos were on display near the college administrative office in those days, and I noticed a number of names that were familiar from the film's end credits. I contacted Disney Studios and came to know Nik Ranieri, an animator on *Who Framed Roger Rabbit* who has gone on to be a supervising animator on many classic Disney animated feature films and non-Disney films. My interest in *Who Framed Roger Rabbit* was more focused on the early development group within Disney. I contacted Darrell Van Citters at Renegade Animation. He and Mike Giaimo were very generous in sharing some of their thoughts on that early work in their careers.

I have found that most dedicated animators are also amateur animation historians. Darrell had a strong connection with the *Mr. Magoo's Christmas Carol* television special, produced by UPA, which was broadcast on NBC in December 1962. He wrote the book *Mr. Magoo's Christmas Carol: The Making of the First Animated Christmas Special* (Oxberry Press, 2009), which I recommend highly. I transited through Los Angeles on a work trip shortly after his book was published, and stopped by Renegade Animation to visit him. During the visit, I asked whether he would consider writing a book about his experience with *Roger Rabbit*. The *Roger Rabbit* project at Disney was Darrell's first opportunity to develop a feature film property, so he was especially attached to it and it was a blow when the project went elsewhere. He has strong opinions about the final film. He put my question back at me, saying that he would provide detailed information about the early development period if I wanted to undertake the writing of a book. There has been very little written about the Disney Animation Studio of the 1980s, so I took up the challenge. Coincidentally, at the very time that I started to map out the task, Don Hahn and Peter Schneider were preparing their documentary film on the animation renewal at Disney, *Waking Sleeping Beauty.*

With the help and encouragement of Nik Ranieri, I made my first research trip to Los Angeles in September 2009. I made a couple of research trips to Los Angeles after that, as well as trips to Florida and London. The more people I spoke with, the more help, encouragement, and introductions, I received, and with that . . . the scope of the book expanded to be a comprehensive coverage of *Roger Rabbit* from his origins in the imagination of Gary K. Wolf to the present. I delved into the Disney Studios of the 1970s and '80s—how else to provide context and explain the decisions that were ultimately made in getting the film to the screen?

Along the way, I have met many wonderful people. Most of them are around my age, and most of them were exposed to the same influences that piqued my interest in animation at a young age. Many of them, I am glad to say, have become friends. For many of them, *Who Framed Roger Rabbit* was the biggest film project they ever worked on . . . and as Dick Williams predicted . . . it has been the foundation of many careers ever since. I received a great deal of encouragement about the project from the people I spoke with—and there were many of them. I am extremely grateful for that interest and encouragement, and this book is ultimately my gift to them.

It took me over eight years to finish writing the book. I must admit that I extended the "research" portion of the work because I was having too much fun doing it. The "writing" portion is more work, and a full-time job with lots of associated travel was an easy excuse for how long it took to finish. In this regard, I must acknowledge the sage advice of Tom Sito, who told me two things. At the six-and-and-a-half-year mark he said, "Don't sweat taking time to write the book. It took me an average of seven years each to write my two [books]. Ya gotta make a living."

Then, at the seven-year mark, following some more of my excuses on the slow progress, Tom said, "Just write the damn book!"

My thanks go to my kids, Chris, Elise, and Scott. They have encouraged me throughout. I must acknowledge the long-suffering patience of my wife, Kate. The time and expense of this project came directly from time that could have been spent with family and money that should have been in the household coffers. Kate has been generous and forgiving, and very encouraging . . . I love you. She has also been a wonderful companion on several of the research trips. We transited through London in September

2015 and arranged a reunion in Camden Town for people who had worked on *Who Framed Roger Rabbit*. I think the real reason that many of them continue to speak with me is so they might see Kate again on a follow-up visit.

Many of the people I've spoken with have shared more than just memories. I appreciate the generosity of all of those who shared ephemera saved from their time working on *Roger Rabbit*.

My thanks to Didier Ghez, author of the *Walt's People* book series of interviews and many other animation books, for reading an early version of a partial manuscript and providing much-needed constructive criticism. My thanks, also, to Christopher Tremblay, professor at Western Michigan University and author of *Walt's Pilgrimage: A Journey in the Life of Walter Elias Disney*, for the thorough proofreading of the manuscript.

I would like to thank the people at the University Press of Mississippi for their parts in making this book happen. Vijay Shah provided great encouragement after finding out about the project. Peter Tonguette did a wonderful job with the copyediting. Everybody with whom I interacted was helpful and professional. It made the process very special for a first-time author.

DISNEY STUDIOS: 1966 TO 1984

Disney without Walt

The team of Walt and Roy Disney was more than the sum of what each one could do on his own. Roy was the older brother who had looked after and over Walt all his life. Walt was the dreamer, and Roy did what was required to make those dreams come true. The relationship was based on mutual respect, trust, balance, and brotherly love.

Walt Disney died in the morning of December 15, 1966. Prior to his death, Walt had presided over the secretive Project X and the surreptitious assembly of land in central Florida. On November 15, 1965, in the Cherry Plaza Hotel in Orlando at a press conference with Gov. Haydon Burns flanked by the Disney brothers, the announcement of what would become Walt Disney World was made. The first comments from Walt related to how his big brother had looked after him and provided the appropriate balance in their organization. He was careful to not pin a name on their Florida endeavor during the press conference.

At a luncheon a little over two months before he died, Walt was asked what would be the fate of the Florida Project if he got hit by a truck after lunch. Walt replied, "Absolutely nothing. My brother Roy runs this company. I just piddle around." A week after Walt died, Roy spoke to a group of Walt Disney Productions executives and creative staff in a projection room at the Disney Studios. He was going to postpone his retirement. "We are going to finish this park [in Florida], and we're going to do it the way Walt wanted it," Roy stated firmly. "Don't you ever forget it. I want every one of you to do just exactly what you were going to do when Walt was alive." One of his first decisions was that the Disney World project would be officially renamed Walt Disney World.[1] In the five years until Walt Disney World officially opened on October 25, 1971, the halls of Walt Disney Productions resonated with the question, "What would Walt do?" Roy O. Disney fulfilled his commitment and presided over the opening of the park in Florida, but he died unexpectedly two months later, on December 20, 1971.

The leadership of the company fell to Donn Tatum, a "Roy" man; and after him, to Card Walker, a "Walt" man. During those years, the question "What would Walt do?" remained constant.

Disney Animation

Sleeping Beauty was released in early 1959, and at that time over 500 people were employed in Disney's Animation Department. In previous decades, studio staff could be moved onto the production of the next feature, into the production of shorts, or into development work for future features. In the 1950s, people may have even been moved into the production of television specials or the short-lived television commercial department. Several people were moved onto Walt's personal bankroll to work on developing Disneyland attractions—a small group that grew to eventually become WED (for *Walter Elias Disney*) Enterprises, later to be called Walt Disney Imagineering (WDI). Trusted artists and storytellers with film experience were conscripted to Walt's service. This group included Herb Ryman, Harper Goff, John Hench, Ken Anderson, Marc Davis, Bill Justice, and X. Atencio.

Unfortunately, the projects in Animation could not sustain the crew that had been assembled to make *Sleeping Beauty*, and the department was trimmed to about 125 people. A cadre of talented animators were known as the "Nine Old Men," a name chosen after the nickname for the members of the US Supreme Court. The group was made up of Les Clark, Marc Davis, Ollie Johnston, Milt Kahl, Ward Kimball, Eric Larson, John Lounsbery, Woolie Reitherman, and Frank Thomas. They were the supervising/directing animators, and as the Animation Department contracted and the Shorts Department was phased out . . . there were few animator positions to which assistant animators or in-betweeners could aspire, and fewer still directing positions. Many highly talented artists were in a holding pattern and many of those with higher ambitions left the studio to exercise their creativity elsewhere.

If Walt Disney had a genius, it was as a story man who thoroughly understood his audience and was able to communicate his vision to the people who could execute it. Even though other people held the nominal titles of director or producer, there was no mistaking that the product of the studio was a Walt Disney film. It would be unfair to say that the directors and producers were simply functionaries, because they included highly creative people, but Walt provided the overall creative leadership. Walt had been distracted by Disneyland and, then, by the planning of the Florida Project, and the feature films suffered in his relative absence. Nevertheless, he was the final arbiter and if there was any question about what Walt would do—well, he could be asked.

After Walt's death and Roy's determination that everyone should "do just exactly what you were going to do when Walt was alive," the Nine Old Men became part of a studio brain trust, the Animation Board, which managed the direction of Disney Animation. Woolie Reitherman had become the *de facto* leader amongst the Nine Old Men during the 1960s, and after Walt's death, he took on the leadership mantle. He was comfortable with command. During World War II, he was vice air commander of the Burmese Air Lift. He was a great action editor, but he was not as concerned with content.[2] The Nine Old Men were great "sequence" guys, which was fine when Walt was there to ride herd on them, but with Walt gone the focus seemed to be on sequences structured around animation *tours de force* rather than being in service to the overall story. As a consequence, the Disney animated films of the 1960s and 1970s contained inspired animation by animators at the top of their form, but the films are generally viewed as amongst the weakest in the Disney canon.

Ward Kimball retired in August of 1973, and by that time the rest of the Nine Old Men were approaching forty years of service. Even the "B" squad of animators was exceeding thirty years of service, as were the skilled assistants. It became clear that it had been a mistake to have not provided opportunities for growth and to have not hired new staff regularly throughout the 1960s.

Studio Management

E. Cardon "Card" Walker started at Disney as a mailroom clerk in 1938 and became a unit manager for short subjects. In 1941, he joined the US Navy, eventually serving as the flight deck commander of the USS Bunker Hill aircraft carrier. After World War II, he returned to the Disney Studios and had become vice president of advertising and sales by 1956. He was elected to the board of directors in 1960. After Walt's death in December 1966, Walker became executive vice president and chief operating officer. When Roy O. Disney died in 1971, Walker became president. In November 1976, Walker took over from Donn Tatum as CEO and retained the position of president, until it went to Ron Miller in 1978.

Ron Miller attended University of Southern California and played varsity football; he met Walt Disney's eldest daughter, Diane, on a blind date. They were married on May 9, 1954. Five months after the wedding, Miller was drafted into the US Army. Following his army service, he played a season as a tight end with the National Football League's Los Angeles Rams.

After his marriage to Diane and prior to his army service, Miller spent several months in 1954 as a liaison between Disneyland and Walt's company, WED Enterprises. At the conclusion of his first season in the NFL, Walt convinced Miller to work for him at the Disney Studios. He sponsored Miller into the Screen Directors Guild and Miller started as a second assistant on *Old Yeller* in 1957. He eventually directed Walt in some of his introductions for the weekly television series and Miller rose through the producer ranks. He became president of Walt Disney Productions in 1978, and CEO in 1983.

Ed Hansen had started at the Disney Studios in 1952 as an animation effects artist on *Peter Pan* and worked his way up to assistant director on *Robin Hood*. He made the move into management in 1972 and was the administrative head of animation by 1975.

Tom Wilhite joined Disney in 1976 as the publicity director. Miller promoted Wilhite to be vice president in charge of development and head of Live-Action Production in 1979. Wilhite and Hansen would have a strained and uneasy working relationship.

Walt Disney World had opened in 1971 and was a runaway success, thus taking more of executive management's attention. Disney animated films were being viewed more as a source for characters and character merchandise to the theme parks than as the life blood of the company. The Animation Department was largely left to do what it had been doing, without a great deal of oversight. The expectations were not high, and neither was the motivation. The filmmaking was left in the hands of a group of lesser artists who had been waiting in the wings for decades. They were insecure about their standing. They hadn't been trained as leaders, and their response was to circle the wagons.[3] It was into this environment that new blood started to appear.

New Hires

The number of animators involved in making the Disney animated features released after *Sleeping Beauty* (1959) was surprisingly few. *The Jungle Book* (1967), *The AristoCats* (1970), and *Robin Hood* (1974) used no more than twelve animators. *Robin Hood* was the first animated feature to include assistant animators in the film credits, and five key assistant animators received credit. It is difficult to make meaningful comparisons between the credits received on films because the criteria for granting credit has changed over time and some productions may have participants because of the studio gearing up with training programs or holding for development on other projects; nevertheless, *The Rescuers* (1977) had fifteen animators and eleven assistant animators, *The Fox and the Hound* (1981) had thirty animators and twenty-two assistant animators, *The Black Cauldron* (1985) had thirty-one animators and twenty-nine assistant animators, and *Beauty and the Beast* (1991) had thirty-nine animators and sixty-two assistant animators.

From 1970 to 1977, Disney hired only twenty-one people—most of them in 1977.[4] Pete Young was one of the earliest of the new hires of the 1970s. He was hired in 1970, and after serving time as an effects animator, he moved into the Story Department. Dale Baer was hired in 1971, followed three months later by Don Bluth. Bluth was not, in fact, new to Disney Studios. He had first been hired in 1955 and had been an assistant to John Lounsbery on *Sleeping Beauty*. He left in 1957 to do missionary work, as a part of his Mormon faith, before getting on again at Disney.

Dale Baer had graduated from Chouinard and started in the animation industry at Filmation, where he worked with Don Bluth. Bluth was friendly, but controlling.[5] Baer was unsatisfied at Filmation and was put in contact with Andy Engman, then head of personnel at Disney Animation. He was the first person hired from outside the studio into the new Training Program. At that time the studio was like a gentleman's club and people still actively wondered, "How would Walt do it?" The studio had a total of just fifteen to twenty animators. In fact, active consideration was given to eliminating Animation at Disney.[6] Roy O. Disney had seen some early work from Hanna-Barbera's *Charlotte's Web* (1973) and thought that Disney should emulate it. Disney could make almost as much money on the scheduled cycle of rereleases as on a new production (i.e., when Disney rereleased *Snow White and the Seven Dwarfs* in 1975 it made $11 million--all profit). Nevertheless, new hiring was made into the Training Program, including Gary Goldman, Heidi Guedel, and Richard Rich in 1972, Andy Gaskill and John Pomeroy in 1973, and Ron Clements, Glen Keane, and Tad Stones in 1974.

Acceptance into the Training Program was based on an animation test that would be reviewed by the Animation Board. Successful candidates would be assigned to animators and attended classes given by animation veterans. They would also work through the tasks of clean-up and in-betweening before moving on as assistant animators. The studio got busy again after *Robin Hood* was released in 1974. The trainees would do incidental animation on crowd scenes and objects. During the production of *Winnie the Pooh and Tigger Too*, some scenes would be given to trainees to animate—usually, the same scenes given to several trainees. The best ones might be selected for production.[7] Andy Engman retired as head of personnel in the Animation Department in 1972, and Ed Hansen, who had been assistant director on *Robin Hood*, took over.

Randy Cartwright, Ed Gombert, Ron Husband, and Dave Spafford were hired into the Training Program in 1975. Don Hahn, Steve Hulett, Vera Law, and Rebecca Lodolo were hired in 1976. Randy Cartwright and Dave Spafford had spent time working at Disneyland as character performers prior to being hired into the Training Program.[8]

Ward Kimball had retired in 1973, Les Clark retired late in 1975, John Lounsbery died early in 1976, and Milt Kahl retired at the end of April, 1976. Frank Thomas and Ollie Johnston (also known, collectively, as Frank 'n' Ollie) were beginning the hand over of their assignments to other animators and were starting to think about capturing their knowledge of animation in a book. (*Disney Animation: The Illusion of Life* was finally published in 1981.) The responsibility for the Training Program went to Eric Larson, who had a wonderful way about him with the trainees. He wouldn't push himself on them, but he was always accessible. He was patient and had the ability to diagnose and provide feedback in a way that was both instructive and confidence-building.

Don Bluth was the first person to graduate from the new Training Program. He was a full-fledged animator within one year. At the time Heidi Guedel came into the program in 1972, she described Bluth as being "the fair-haired boy" at the studio.[9] Bluth cultivated a following. He was charismatic; some called him messianic. He felt that Disney wasn't remaining true to its traditions and its standard of animation production values. He talked about the self-indulgence of the animators, especially in *Robin Hood*—saying, "The story had no soul."

Heidi Guedel graduated from Chouinard and started at Disney in June 1972. She shared an office with Jane Takamoto, who had returned to the studio in 1973. Guedel had known Dale Baer at Chouinard and was mentored by him at Disney. She described Baer as self-conscious and shy to a debilitating degree. Nevertheless, he overcame his shyness enough to marry Jane Takamoto in 1975.[10] Baer had always had a strained and challenging relationship with Don Bluth. Largely as a consequence of that, he left Disney in 1976. He left on good terms with Ed Hansen, and was soon working on a freelance basis on *Mickey's Christmas Carol*.[11] Jane Baer left the studio in 1976 as well.

The California Institute of the Arts was formed following the merger of the Chouinard Art Institute and the Los Angeles Conservatory of Music. Walt Disney coordinated the merger and ensured its formation with a large bequeathal. The relationship between Walt Disney and the Chouinard Institute stretched as far back as 1929. Many Disney animators were sent for training classes at Chouinard and, later, one of its faculty members, Don Graham, became the Disney in-house instructor. CalArts had an experimental animation program, headed by Jules Engel, but a character animation program was not developed until the mid-1970s. The first graduating class was in 1979, but Disney made attractive offers to promising candidates and several students hired on to Disney before graduating. The character animation program was headed by Jack Hannah, a longtime Disney animator. His initial animation classes involved exercises of in-betweening. This was totally unsatisfactory to the precocious early students, who wanted to be animators rather than in-betweeners; in other words, they wanted to make films.

Glen Keane is the son of the cartoonist Bil Keane, the creator of *The Family Circus* comic strip. Glen applied to the CalArts School of Art, but his application was somehow diverted to the Film Graphics Department and he was accepted into what would later be called the experimental animation program. With his selection of options, he graduated in the character animation program before it really existed and began at Disney in 1974. In the early days of the Disney Training Program, the trainees would learn from each other after Eric Larson's tutelage. Keane became an animator on *The Rescuers*. Some of his assistants had been at the studio for decades. His observation was that having long-service and talented artists being assistants to young animators was built-in trouble.[12]

Darrell Van Citters was the first student to graduate from the CalArts character animation program (excluding Glen Keane), due to his advanced standing from the University of New Mexico. He was hired by Disney in 1976. Brad Bird, John Musker, and Jerry Rees were made offers they couldn't refuse and left CalArts before graduating and starting at Disney in 1977. Also going to work in 1977 was Henry Selick, who had studied in the experimental animation program under Jules Engel and then stayed on to get a master's degree in character animation.

Brad Bird visited the Disney Studios for the first time when he was eleven years old. He told those he met on the tour that he was going to be an animator. They didn't doubt it, but they were surprised when he visited again three years later, at age fourteen, with a fifteen-minute short.[13] Milt Kahl took Bird under his wing and he spent summers interning at the studio. The special bond Bird developed with Kahl, and the liberties Bird took with his visits and intern arrangements, did not endear him to intermediaries such as Ed Hansen, then-personnel manager for the Animation Department. This would prove to be an issue in the future.

Don Bluth was cultivating a following. Ron Miller was trying to make a connection with the new animators, but he did not really understand animation or what to do with it. "Old hands," such as Ted Berman and Art Stevens, were not enthusiastic about the future of animation at Disney and they were not enthusiastic about the films they were doing. They had inherited the leadership mantle when their animation leaders had retired, but they did not know how to lead. Art Stevens had been John Lounsbery's assistant and right-hand man for years. When Lounsbery died on the operating table during heart bypass surgery, Stevens took over. Lounsbery had been doing director duty on *The Rescuers*, and Stevens stepped into that role. He chafed at the direct and unvarnished feedback that Woolie Reitherman tended to give in public.[14] Stevens felt suppressed by Reitherman and advocated for Reitherman's removal as both director and producer. Art Stevens, Ted Berman, and Richard Rich were slated to be co-directors on *The Fox and the Hound*. Ted Berman's pep talk at the announcement of *The Fox and the Hound* completely underwhelmed the new hires from CalArts—"They expect us to make a movie, so we're going to make a movie. I don't think the plant will be open long enough for us to finish it, but we'll start making the movie, I guess."[15] There was nobody with leadership and vision, at a film level, except for Don Bluth.[16]

Don's brother, Toby, had written a story and Don soon began rounding up animation personnel to work in his garage on his personal project. The film was called *The Piper*, but it was never finished. Bluth fancied himself as a latter day Art Babbitt, conducting an off-site training program in traditional Disney-style animation. Another garage project was started, *Banjo the Woodpile Cat*. Many people worked with Bluth on the project on their own time, including Don Hahn for a short time—having his first go at animation. Bluth soon had an entourage. He seemed like a reasonable choice for the future of the studio, given the other choices available at the time. He had a Rasputin-like quality and people fell under his spell. Heidi Guedel was infatuated with him—puppy-love, or more.[17] Not every woman was besotted with him—Rebecca Lodolo described him as "creepy."[18] One time, Bluth observed Heidi Guedel in the Disney parking lot making plans for a date with another animator. Bluth called Guedel and told her that everybody was required to be at his house for work on *Banjo the Woodpile Cat*. Guedel broke the date and showed up at Bluth's house to find that she was the only one there.[19] It had been a test of loyalty.

Trouble in Paradise

John Musker started at Disney in May 1977, during the same week that *Star Wars* opened—a film matching the sensibilities of the younger animators and one that many people felt that Disney should have produced. The early CalArts hires were frustrated with the situation at the studio. There is no doubt that the CalArts guys were cocky. They were continuing as they had done at CalArts, anxious to animate and make films . . . and happy to set their own agenda. They happened to be a very talented group.

They were also very loyal to Eric Larson, who was very generous with his experience and knowledge. It had been understood that Eric Larson would be directing the upcoming special film *The Small One*. Concept art and story drawings were pinned up in the story room on Friday evening and on Monday morning the drawings were gone and Don Bluth had been named as director. The CalArts guys felt that Bluth had conspired to depose Larson.[20] Another view is that Larson himself was not sure if he could handle it.[21] Dave Spafford felt that Larson was slowing down and seemed to be "aging quickly" at this time. Regardless of how or why it happened, the relationship of the CalArts group with Bluth was very strained. At some point, Bluth came into the office shared by Musker, Rees, and Bird to air his grievances. The conversation did not go well and as things escalated, Bluth said, "This place is a rats' nest of innuendo and rumor!" The group thought that was a badge of honor, and Andy Gaskill presented them with an air-brushed sign saying, "RATS' NEST," which was proudly placed above their door.[22]

The factions got further apart. Bluth said, "You guys are green! You have no right to complain!" He did not stop with the CalArts group. He said, referring to the old-timer faction, "Cliff [Nordberg] is the bottom of the barrel."[23] Randy Cartwright remained neutral in the battle of the "Bluthies" versus the "Ratsnesters." Bluth was pushing hard. He had pushed to the point that other contenders, such as Dale Baer and Dick Sebast, had already left the studio. He wanted to fire Brad Bird, but he did not have the authority. Bird did not shy away from providing his opinion about the state of the studio, often in loud and disruptive ways. He did not have the protection of Milt Kahl, now that Kahl was retired, and he had already incurred the pique of Ed Hansen from his student days. He was eventually fired. During the production of *The Small One*, Cartwright would often find Bluth's office door closed, with a sign reading, "Meeting in Progress." He would push his work for Bluth's approval under the door. He had a sense that Bluth, Goldman, and Pomeroy were not limiting their discussions to *The Small One*.[24]

While Bluth was directing *Pete's Dragon*, and then *The Small One*, *The Fox and the Hound* was begun with co-directors Art Stevens, Ted Berman, and Rick Rich. Bluth realized that he was not going to get the total authority that he craved. On Bluth's birthday, September 13, 1979, Don Bluth, Gary Goldman, and John Pomeroy handed in their resignations. The next day, eight more people resigned: four animators, Lorna Pomeroy, Heidi Guedel, Linda Miller, and Emily Jiuliano, as well as four assistants, Vera Law, Sally Voorheis, Frank Jones, and Dave Spafford. Two days later, Diann Landau, an effects animator, also resigned.[25] For his part, Spafford was less an acolyte of Bluth than an admirer of Pomeroy. He felt that Pomeroy's departure was going to leave a huge hole at Disney, and chose to cast his fortune with Pomeroy.[26] Following the departure of Bluth and his coterie, Ron Miller held a meeting with the Animation staff and started his speech, "Now that the cancer has been excised . . ." Dorse Lanpher, an outstanding, longtime effects animator, left shortly thereafter.[27] As a parting shot, it was later found that an animation drawing of the widow in *The Fox and the Hound*, drawn either by Bluth or Spafford, was made with her middle finger inexplicably extended—metaphorically "flipping the bird" at Disney.[28]

The New Generation

Ron Miller became president of Walt Disney Productions in 1978. He knew that a movie like *Star Wars* should have been made at the Disney Studios. The studio had struck it big in 1964 with the special effects extravaganza, *Mary Poppins*. A key contributor to the success of that film was matte painter, Peter Ellenshaw. Peter's son, Harrison, was being passed the matte-painting baton at Disney in 1970, after a stint in the US Navy. While working at Disney, he took on some outside projects and wound up doing the matte paintings for *Star Wars*. Disney had planned for a science fiction adventure as early as 1974, but had not followed through with it. After the success of *Star* Wars, the project, now called *The Black Hole*, was put into production. It would feature major visual effects and was the first time that Harrison had collaborated with his father, who came out of retirement to work on the film. There was a corporate inertia that would be impossible to overcome with the people who were in place in the studio. In spite of the awe-inspiring visual effects, there was a certain clumsiness because Disney did not have motion-control camera capability at the time. The film did not have a star-laden cast and the characters seemed shallow and a bit corny. The film was released in late 1979, and Tom Wilhite was put in charge of finding a way to market it. He had the marketing for *The Black Hole* focus on the visual effects. The film was only a modest success, but it did move Disney away from the staid period films and corny family comedies that had been the staple for decades. Miller promoted Wilhite to be vice president in charge of development.

Steve Lisberger was running a small studio in Boston. He developed a concept, *Animalympics*, for bringing attention to the upcoming Olympics in Moscow (in 1980) by using animals as athletes. He was also developing a project, called *Futurebowl*, about gladiatorial warriors battling on an electronic game grid. In 1978, he moved his studio to Venice Beach, California, bringing with him animator Roger Allers and recent Sheridan College graduates Dave Stephan and Darrell Rooney. Work continued on the development of the electronic world concept, which was now called, *Tron*. When President Jimmy Carter boycotted the 1980 Moscow Olympic Games to protest Russia's invasion of Afghanistan, NBC would no longer be televising the Olympic Games, leaving Lisberger with no place to show *Animalympics*. The pressure was on to sell *Tron* in order to keep the studio afloat.[29]

Lisberger took the script for *Tron* to Disney and Wilhite liked it. Wilhite convinced Miller, and Disney bought the script and contracted Lisberger's organization to set up *Tron*. Earlier on, during the introductory meetings Lisberger had at Disney, he recruited Bill Kroyer to work on his developing projects. Now, Kroyer was back on the Disney lot. Jerry Rees was dissatisfied with the limitations being put on him during production of *The Fox and the Hound* by directors he felt were unimaginative and derivative. He was curious about the new group setting up offices up in the third floor of the Animation Building and asked Wilhite if he could look around. Rees was hired into the new group to do storyboards with Kroyer.[30]

Kroyer and Rees worked in a trailer parked in the Disney backlot. At the time *Tron* was made there was no software available for making things "move." Rees had taken FORTRAN computer programming in high school but had no experience with animating on a computer. The computer programmers had never done story-based animation. It was new for everybody and they developed methods for communicating their needs. Four computer firms were used on the film: Information International, Inc. (Triple-I) animated Sark's Carrier, the Solar Sailer, and the Master Control Program; Mathematical Applications Group, Inc (MAGI Synthavision) animated the Light Cycles, tanks, and Recognizers; Robert Abel & Associates created the opening title sequence; and Digital Effects provided a digital simulation of Bit and Tron's formation in the opening sequence. MAGI had two 80 MB hard drives; there was insufficient capacity to store a rendered frame, so the footage was rendered onto film. Very few of the CGI effects resulted from computer simulations; most of the animation was computer rendering of carefully charted movements graphed and drawn by Rees. For a time, Disney rented a VistaVision projector to look at CGI dailies. One of the first CGI scenes to be rendered and shown in this way was a Light Cycle sequence. John Lasseter was curious about what his friends were up to and was one of the first people to see these images. He has said that the event changed forever the direction of his career.[31] While working on *Tron*, Rees conceived of a "Computer Oriented Production System" (*COPS*) for managing computer usage for character animation. He even met Ed Catmull and Alvy Ray Smith, who led a group within Lucasfilm that would eventually become Pixar.[32]

Tron was a departure for Disney; although the studio had made live-action/animation combination films before—such as the *Alice Comedies* shorts, *Song of the South*, *So Dear to My Heart*, *Mary Poppins*, and *Pete's Dragon*—the studio organization was simpler, and when Walt was present there was less turf protection and egotistical behavior than in the early 1980s. Furthermore, *Tron* was essentially an outside production on the Disney lot; something that is typical nowadays and was normal at other studio lots, but was new at Disney.

The summer of 1982 turned out to be a banner year for movies, but by 1982 the Disney television series *The Wonderful World of Disney* did not have the ratings it once enjoyed, especially in its prime demographic—namely, children, from ages seven to twelve.[33] Disney produced a half-hour show, *Computers Are People, Too!*, which was intended to generate interest in *Tron*.[34] Nevertheless, the Disney marketing group that had been used to working with products like *The Boatniks* (1970), *The Apple Dumpling Gang* (1975), and *The Unidentified Flying Oddball* (1975) was now charged with promoting *Tron*.[35] *Tron* actually received a lot of media coverage, although an expected cover article in *Time* magazine was pulled for coverage of the resignation of President Ronald Reagan's secretary of state, Alexander Haig. Its marketing budget was meager compared to the norm for Hollywood films.[36] *Tron* was released in July 1982. It was not well understood and reviews were mixed. The film lost a bit of money on its initial release, although it developed a loyal following that grew through its release on VHS cassette and, later, DVD. Disney produced a long-awaited sequel, *Tron: Legacy*, in 2010, as well as an animated television series *Tron: Uprising*, which was shown on the Disney XD cable channel in 2012. In addition to this, *Tron* brought an additional legacy to the Disney Studios—when the *Tron* production group folded up its tent at the Disney Studios, Disney retained two key animators, Barry Cook and David Stephan.

The hiring into the Disney Training Program continued in order to complete *The Fox and the Hound* following the Bluth walkout at the end of 1979. Like many of the new animators, Tony Anselmo had written to the Disney Studios as a youngster and had been lucky to have attracted the interest and encouragement of veteran animators. Disney arranged to send him to CalArts after he finished high school. They called him to start work at the studio in 1980, after his junior year. By 1984, Anselmo was not only an animator, but he was being prepared by Clarence "Ducky" Nash to carry on as the voice of Donald Duck. Mark Henn and Brian McEntee were also hired in 1980 from CalArts. Joe Ranft left CalArts to join Disney after his sophomore year. Other key new hires in 1980 included Phil Nibbelink, who had graduated from Western Washington State University and spent a year studying in Italy; Bill Frake, who went to the Art School of Virginia and then finished his formal education, studying illustration at the Fashion Institute in New York City; and David Pacheco, who worked for Hanna-Barbera for two years after high school and then brought his portfolio to Disney.[37]

Barry Cook had also interned at Hanna-Barbera following high school. He was hired by Disney in 1981 as an effects animator on *Tron*.[38] Dave Pruiksma had gone to the Pratt Institute in New York and then transferred to CalArts. Frans Vischer and Matt O'Callaghan were also at CalArts, and the three young animators were hired into the Training Program in 1981.[39] The 1981 Disney annual report focuses on the theme parks, with the cover showing Walt Disney World cast members commemorating the tenth anniversary of the opening of the Magic Kingdom and several pages devoted to the preparations for the opening of EPCOT in late 1982. Deeper in the annual report is a photo showing Joe Hale speaking to a group of young animators that includes Anselmo, Frake, Pruiksma, and Vischer in the Animation Building hallway. The caption reads: "The first eight-week session of the Disney School of Animation (DSA), a program specially designed to meet the Studio's growing demand for quality animators, reached a successful conclusion in October with all fourteen candidates moving directly into production work on a variety of animated Studio projects. A second session is scheduled to begin February 1 (1982) with still a third planned for June."[40]   Work was winding down on *The Fox and the Hound*. The CalArts alumni were a creative bunch, and if those urges could not be satisfied in their work, they would make their own films. An early, primitive effort was *Doctor of Doom*, made in 1979 and co-directed by Jerry Rees and Tim Burton. It was a modest amusement, with nonsense overdubbing similar to Woody Allen's *What's Up, Tiger Lily?* The gang lent a hand . . . Chris Buck, Randy Cartwright, Mike Giaimo, Harry Sabin, and Darrell Van Citters were also involved. Cartwright was a UCLA grad and, not to be outdone, he acquired a movie camera and decided to film a "home-movie" tour of Disney Animation. Of course, it was contrary to the rule dictating no cameras in the studio, and seconds into Cartwright's on-camera introduction outside the Animation Building, Ron Miller walked out of the building and through the frame. He had some pleasant words to say and went on his way. Cartwright started his journey through the halls of the Animation Building, conducting impromptu interviews with whoever he came across. His cameraman was John Lasseter. Although only intended for personal use, the film is a remarkable record of life in the Disney Studios at the time and clips were later used in the documentary *Waking Sleeping Beauty* (2009), directed by Don Hahn and Peter Schneider.[41]

A volleyball court was set up on a lawn near the backlot. It was within sight of the trailers in which Rees and Kroyer were working on *Tron*. The animators would play volleyball during lunches and breaks. On January 15, 1980, Darrell Van Citters issued a challenge to Ron Miller:

Dear Ron,
     The volleyball players of the Animation Department cordially challenge you and your boys to a best 2 out of 3 volleyball match for ownership of Walt Disney Productions and is affiliates.
     As the challengee, you may pick the date and time; generally we play at lunch.
     Looking forward to hearing from you. Good luck

The game was played on May 14, 1980. The producer team included Ron Miller and house producers Marc Stirdivant, Jerry Courtland, Jan Williams, Tom Leetch, and Kevin Corcoran (who played Moochie in many Disney films and television shows in the late '50s and early '60s). The Animator team consisted of Chris Buck, Tim Burton, Mike Gabriel, Jay Jackson, Jerry Rees, and Darrell Van Citters. John Musker provided a spirited commentary.[42] The producers even raided Wardrobe for uniforms, but it was all for naught: they lost 15–2 and 15–6. Ownership of Walt Disney Productions was not ceded to the animators, but Miller ponied up for pitchers of beer at Don's Place, a local watering hole, afterward.

In 1982, Tim Burton and Jerry Rees co-directed a more ambitious short film, *Luau*. It is an intentionally cheesy surf-movie parody. Appearing in the film were Tim Burton, Randy Cartwright, Mike Gabriel, Brian McEntee, John Musker, Joe Ranft, Jerry Rees, and many others.

The Black Caldera

Life was not all fun and games on the Disney lot. Art Stevens was advocating for himself that Woolie Reitherman was standing in his way. In *The Fox and the Hound*, Stevens moved into the director's chair, and Reitherman's involvement was limited to producing as he eased into retirement in 1981. The directors selected for the next animated feature, *The Black Cauldron*, were Art Stevens, Ted Berman, and Richard Rich. Joe Hale was selected as producer. He had good analytical skills and he had worked well with Henry Selick on *A Watcher in the Woods* (1980). It was felt that he would provide a good link between the veteran directors and the young animators.[43] As it turns out, he had neither enough weight in the organization nor the conviction to take a firm stand. He decided to listen to Stevens and Rich. Rick Rich wanted to make *Sleeping Beauty II*.[44] The other directors wanted *The Black Cauldron* to be more like *Star Wars*.[45] There was a high level of tension in the building and the directors were acting independently.[46] The series of books on which the film was based, *The Chronicles of Prydain*, was being left behind. The directors had not read the books. Burny Mattinson complained that they had not even read the initial script, which he prepared with Mel Shaw.[47] Ron Miller would put his foot down on certain things, but other things—particularly at the studio—he just "let go." [48]

Joe Hale had come through the Ward Kimball unit, and his tastes tended to be a bit quirkier than most of the more traditional Disney animators.[49] The question arose as to "what to do with Tim Burton?" Everybody agreed that he had an odd, but enticing, creativity, but he seemed unable to animate . . . or even draw . . . in the Disney style. It was decided to put him in an office with Andreas Deja in hopes that Deja's facility with the Disney style might rub off a bit. Deja grew up in Germany. He had drawn Disney characters since he was in kindergarten, and after he saw *The Jungle Book* when he was ten years old, he knew that he wanted to be a Disney animator. He wrote to the studio and received replies encouraging him to work at life drawing, not just cartooning. He went to art school, taking graphic design because there were no courses in animation. He analyzed 8mm clips from Disney films that were available at the time and taught himself to animate. After graduating from art school Deja was invited to join the Disney Studios in 1980.[50]

The time spent with Deja did not seem to improve Burton's drawing skills, but it was a productive time for him to work on drawings of his own initiative. John Lasseter had seen Burton's sketch books and told John Musker, "He does these amazing sketches . . . like stuff from *The Rocky Horror Picture Show*." Musker had been drafted as the fourth director by Tom Wilhite, to better represent a youthful perspective. They went to Joe Hale, who was enthusiastic and put Burton onto concept work for *The Black Cauldron*. The other directors were aghast: "These can't be part of a Disney movie!" they said. The Story Department had included Musker, Ron Clements, Pete Young, Steve Hulett, Vance Gerry, Burny Mattinson, and Mel Shaw, all of whom really liked the books on which the film was to be based. The other directors did not particularly care for the books, so there was a schism—and Musker was always the odd man out. The writers wanted a younger protagonist, but the older directors wanted a quasi-*Star Wars* thing. Musker said, "they flattened out the characters and made it less entertaining . . . it wasn't good film-making."[51] Joe Hale went to Ron Miller and said, "We could do it this newfangled way, if you want to go that way. You can do it 'UPA,' which the CalArts guys want to do, or you can do it the traditional way, the way that Art and Ted and Rick want to do—but I'm really getting pulled in these two different directions. Ron, what movie do *you* want to make?" Phrased in that way, Miller's choice was clear. Miller replied, "I look at the returns of *Lady and the Tramp* [which was being rereleased in France at the time] and they're great. Why would I want to do something different than that? That's what I want to do." Musker became very frustrated.[52]

The concept work by Burton would not be considered and he walked off, refusing to work within the Disney mainstream. Wilhite recognized the frustration of the younger animators since he was nearly the same age. John Musker said that when Wilhite was moved from Disney Public Relations into the production side of the studio he was viewed as "the Irving Thalberg of Disney," the "Boy Wonder—the young guy."[53] He had the ear of Ron Miller. *The Black Cauldron* was being touted as "the young people's movie," and he felt that a young director was required to bring that sensibility. It was Wilhite who drafted Musker to be a co-director. Ed Hansen was the Animation Department manager and did not want Wilhite involved at all. Wilhite saw the waste of young talent and did what he could to satisfy their creativity and retain them at the studio. He was the head of Live-Action and Television and greenlit projects that showcased the talents of young Animation Department artists. Hansen felt ignored and trampled on. Musker characterized him as "an old-school middle manager."

Wilhite brought Tim Burton and Rick Heinrichs into the Live-Action Department, where they made *Vincent* and *Frankenweenie. Fun with Mr. Future* was a special project being developed to promote EPCOT at Walt Disney World by Darrell Van Citters.

Lasseter had become intrigued with the nascent computer animation ever since he had seen the dailies for *Tron.* Lasseter brought Thomas Disch's 1980 novel *The Brave Little Toaster: A Bedtime Story for Small Appliances* to Wilhite's attention as a story that would be especially suitable for computer animation. The intent was to have it be the world's first CGI animated feature film. A test-of-concept was done: a piece using Maurice Sendak's short story *Where the Wild Things Are.* Glen Keane did the character animation and Lasseter coordinated the computer work with MAGI. Shortly after, the *Where the Wild Things Are* test and storyboards were pitched to Ron Miller. *The Brave Little Toaster* was being developed under the auspices of the Live-Action Department, which was very threatening to the Animation Department management. Miller felt compelled to support Hansen, and not long afterwards . . . Hansen fired Lasseter.[54]

Brad Bird had been fired already and, after *Tron,* Jerry Rees joined him in San Francisco to put together, and get financing for, an animated film based on *The Spirit*, a masked crimefighter created by comic book cartoonist Will Eisner. A number of friends from the Disney Studios contributed work on storyboards and animation, including John Musker. He was frustrated and upset with his situation on *The Black Cauldron* and was ready to quit Disney and join Bird and Rees on *The Spirit* if they could get it off the ground. Wilhite recognized Musker's dissatisfaction and moved him into Story on a new project, *Basil of Baker Street.* He was also going to direct it. He and Joe Ranft worked on it for six months and they gave it a "Monty Python/Goon Show" sensibility. When they showed it to Ron Miller, he said, "What! Start over . . . I don't get this at all." Eventually, Musker was combined with Ron Clements, as co-directors, a writing and directorial team that continues to this day, and a veteran, Dave Michener, was added to provide some balance. It is Musker's opinion that "you can't exceed the creativity level of your chief executive, unless he defers to someone that he empowers that way. Wilhite eventually got disenfranchised because his live-action films didn't do that well. Richard Berger was put in his place."[55]

While he was still in Miller's good graces, Wilhite filled the pipeline with *Something Wicked This Way Comes*, based on Ray Bradbury's book, *Never Cry Wolf*, and *Return to Oz*. He also acquired a script for a romantic fantasy movie called *Splash*,[56] and the film rights for an as-yet-unpublished novel called *Who Censored Roger Rabbit?*

Sheridan College (located near Toronto) was turning out excellent animation program graduates under the tutelage of Bill Matthews. Hanna-Barbera hired a number of Sheridan graduates and encouraged them to recruit classmates, most of them Canadian. By 1979, between twenty-five and thirty Canadian animators were working at the Hanna-Barbera studio on West Cahuenga Boulevard in Hollywood. Hanna-Barbera was making the animated feature film *Heidi's Song* at the time. Animators on the film, many of whom would later be prominent in the story of *Roger Rabbit*, included Hal Ambro, Bronwen Barry, Roger Chiasson, Barry Cook, Alvaro Gaivoto, John Kimball, Duncan Majoribanks, Dave Pacheco, and Iwao Takamoto. The number of Canadians working in Hollywood was not an issue with the Motion Picture Screen Cartoonists (MPSC) union, but the major issue for union members was "runaway production"—offshore production at subcontracted studios. The union took a stand and called a strike in 1979. During the strike, Bill Matthews, the co-founder of the Sheridan animation program who was now back working at Disney, had the disquieting experience of carrying a picket sign reading, "American Jobs for American People!" The Sheridan graduates, themselves, were obliged to be on the picket line. Unfortunately, as a consequence of the agreement reached with the producers, the work permits for the Canadian animators were withdrawn. Roger Chiasson, Chuck Gammage, Alvaro Gaivoto, Duncan Marjoribanks, and many others had to leave the US and find work elsewhere.[57] Many of them set up studios in Canada themselves and received contracts from their former employers in Hollywood.

The issue of runaway production reared its head again in 1982. The producers had deals with startup animation studios in Taipei, South Korea, and Canada. The producers typically did their hiring for the upcoming television seasons in March or April, but in 1982 nobody was hired until late in July—so that the animator's savings would be depleted. Production schedules were then accelerated in order to build an inventory of shows. There were rumors that Hanna-Barbera was pulling up stakes in Hollywood and moving everything overseas.[58]

The members of MPSC, Local 839, went out on strike on August 5, 1982. Lou Scheimer, head of the Filmation studio, had kept all of his animation work in Hollywood and decided to walk the picket line in front of his own studio.[59]

Dave "Spaff" Spafford had always liked Ron Miller and felt that Miller was generally well liked on the Disney lot. He said, "I loved Ron Miller. He wasn't a great studio head, but he did a great job being head of a studio that already had 500 balls rolling."[60] Miller had interceded when Spaff had a disagreement with Ed Hansen about not being afforded the same opportunities for training and development as the recent CalArts graduates. They became friends and Miller used Spaff as a sounding board for what was happening in the Disney Animation Department. Spaff was not especially fond of Bluth, but he was very close to John Pomeroy and felt that the CalArts faction viewed him as a Bluth sympathizer. When Bluth, Pomeroy, and Goldman left Disney in 1979, Spaff followed—not only because the hole left by Pomeroy would be too big for Disney to recover from, but because he felt that he would be marginalized by the CalArts faction if he stayed. Nevertheless, Spaff's departure with Bluth hurt Miller deeply.[61]

Spaff felt that Disney (i.e., Ron Miller) had strung out the 1982 strike partially to hurt the Aurora/Bluth studio by causing Bluth to lose investors for the project after *The Secret of NIMH* Spaff almost lost his house as a consequence of the strike and he was upset. One day Bluth strikers, all of them former Disney animators, showed up at the studio gates dressed as characters from *The Secret of NIMH*, the film they were making at the time. Spaff carried a sign reading, "Miller = 🏈 " Miller went ballistic. Spaff leaped onto the hood of Miller's car and gave Miller "the bird" with both hands, shouting, "Up yours, Football Boy!" Miller jumped out of his car and had to be restrained. Spaff recalled, "As Miller came for me I thought, I'm going to get my ass kicked by a millionaire. That's not something that just anyone can say."[62] Spaff regrets the way he behaved that day.[63] The entire incident is very reminiscent of a confrontation between Art Babbitt and Walt Disney during the 1941 strike.

Richard Williams's ABC television special, *Ziggy's Gift*, came within one week of falling under a *force majeure* clause and becoming an insurance loss. It was finally completed and won an Emmy award. The Aurora/Bluth studio also came very close to folding.

A Disney lawyer identified an obscure codicil, called "financial core," in its union contracts and bylaws that provided a way for its union members to resign legally from their union. Disney artists began resigning in droves.

After ten weeks, the picket lines collapsed and MPSC, Local 839, members returned to work on October 16, 1982.[64]

By 1984, Baer, Bird, Burton, Gaskill, Kroyer, Lasseter, Rees, and Selick had left the Disney Studios. Tom Wilhite would leave within the year. In 1977, Roy E. Disney, Walt Disney's nephew, quit his executive position and resigned from the Disney board of directors. By 1984, he was fed up with the direction of the company and the management of Disney Animation and he initiated a set of events that would see Ron Miller deposed as CEO before the end of the year and see the installation of Michael Eisner as CEO and Frank Wells as president. Eisner would be followed to Disney from Paramount soon afterwards by Jeffrey Katzenberg. The Disney Animation management team, at the time Eisner and Wells arrived, was as follows:

Ed Hansen, vice president, Animation Production;
Joanne Phillips, Hansen's secretary/assistant, who functioned at the department coordinator;
Don Hahn, production manager;
Ron Rocha, production assistant;
and Joe Morris, who manned the supply closet.

SHORT BIOGRAPHIES

Colin Alexander attended the Falmouth School of Art and Design at Cornwall College, taking a degree program in scientific and technical graphics. In the summer of 1987, between his third and fourth year, he was required to arrange for a relevant work placement. He called Walt Disney UK, was put in contact with Annie Elvin, and was hired straight away.

After *Who Framed Roger Rabbit*, Alexander continued working with Annie Elvin at her Wicked Witch studio, mostly doing trace and paint for commercial studios in the Soho area. A year after *Roger Rabbit* finished, the Amblimation studio was established in Acton, West London. Alexander was the production coordinator at Amblimation until it closed down in 1995, Alexander moved back to Newcastle-upon-Tyne, obtained a teaching certificate and has been teaching graphics, design, and technology since then.

Dino Athanassiou worked in the Orient as an itinerant animator/trainer. When he returned to London, Chuck Gammage recommended Athanassiou to Richard Williams and Athanassiou started on *Roger Rabbit* at the end of March 1987. Athanassiou worked on *Roger Rabbit* for only about eight weeks—leaving at the start of June 1987.

After *Who Framed Roger Rabbit*, Athanassiou founded Stardust Pictures. He was a story artist for DreamWorks' *Sinbad: Legend of the Seven Seas*, *Shark Tale*, and *Madagascar*. He worked on *Happily N'Ever After* (Vanguard) and was animation director on the *Thomas & Friends* television series (2008) and the *Thomas & Friends* direct-to-video releases in 2009 to 2013.

Hans Bacher was in the same class at Folkwang School in Essen, Germany, as Andreas Deja. They made commercials in their spare time. While students, Bacher accompanied Deja on a road trip to meet Eric Larson at the Hamburg port-of-call on his North Atlantic vacation cruise.

Bacher was a partner in a commercial agency, MadTParty, in Düsseldorf, and developed a professional relationship and friendship with Richard Williams. He was involved in early concept work on *Who Framed Roger Rabbit*. He later developed the Alfred J. Kwak character and television series with

Harald Siepermann. Bacher was the production designer for Amblimation's *Balto* in 1995 and for Disney's *Mulan* in 1998. He was a visual development artist on Disney feature films from *Beauty and the Beast* to *Brother Bear*.

He did freelance work in the Philippines and has been teaching at Nanyang Technological University in Singapore since 2011.

Dale Baer graduated from Chouinard and started in the animation industry at Filmation. He contacted Andy Engman, then head of personnel at Disney Animation, and became the first person hired from outside the studio into the new Training Program.

Baer left Disney under friendly terms during *Pete's Dragon*, and did a lot of freelance work on Disney films. He and his wife, Jane, were developing projects for their own studio when they were called about the *Roger Rabbit* project. They established an animation unit in Glendale, and after *Who Framed Roger Rabbit*, they formed the Baer Animation Company, doing commercials and contracted film segments for major studios, including Disney. He did some work on *The Lion King* (1994) and returned to Disney, as an employee, in 1998, working on *Tarzan* and the feature films through to *Winnie the Pooh*. He also worked on several shorts, including *The Ballad of Nessie* and *Get a Horse!* Since retiring from Disney Baer worked on Eric Goldberg's Disney-themed couch gag for *The Simpsons* (2016) and concept work on *Zootopia*.

Baer received the Winsor McCay Award in 2016.

Jane Baer was born in Winnipeg, Canada, as Jane Shattuck. She joined Disney in 1956 and worked on *Sleeping Beauty*. She married Disney animator Iwao Takamoto in 1957, and they both left Disney to take jobs with Hanna-Barbera in 1961, where Iwao became a key character designer. Jane and Iwao divorced, and Jane Takamoto came back to the Disney Studios in 1973. She married Dale Baer in 1975. Dale left Disney in 1976. He was soon working on a freelance basis on *Mickey's Christmas Carol*[10] Jane Baer left the studio in 1976 as well. Thereafter, she worked periodically for Disney, and was an assistant animator on *The Black Cauldron*. The Baers were developing projects for their own studio when they were contacted about *Roger Rabbit* and established an animation unit located in Glendale.

Although the intent of the Glendale unit was to be at arm's length from Disney, it was a symbiotic relationship at best and really functioned as a Disney unit. Dale was the animation director and creative lead, while Jane was the business manager in the partnership. Both of them were looking towards a continuing relationship with Disney after *Who Framed Roger*

Rabbit and viewed Richard Williams as both colleague and "competition." Jane was aggressive in promoting the unit.

After *Who Framed Roger Rabbit*, they established the Baer Animation Company and completed many Disney contracts, including the short *The Prince and the Pauper*. They also did several Chevy Lumina commercials using classic Disney characters.

Tom Bancroft and his twin brother, Tony, were selected as interns at the Disney Studios in Glendale in 1989, after their sophomore year at CalArts in 1989. Tom and Tony Bancroft were selected to move to Florida for the start-up of the animation studio at the theme park.

Bancroft worked at Walt Disney Feature Animation—Florida until 2000, during which time he worked on the *Roger Rabbit* shorts and *Beauty and the Beast*, *The Lion King*, *Aladdin*, *Pocahontas*, and *Mulan*. He worked on *Veggie Tales* at Big Idea in Chicago, but came back to the Disney Studios in Florida until it closed in 2003, during which time he worked on *Brother Bear*.

He wrote the books *Creating Characters with Personality* (2006) and *Character Mentor* (2012) and started an online animation training site, TaughtByaPro.com. He and his brother conduct interviews on *The Bancroft Brothers Animation Podcast*, and Tom is artist-in-residence for the animation program at Lipscomb University in Nashville, Tennessee.

Dave Barclay assisted on *The Empire Strikes Back* (1980) at nineteen years old and performed as both Yoda and Jabba the Hutt in *Return of the Jedi* (1983). He performed in the Jim Henson productions *The Dark Crystal* (1982) and *Labyrinth* (1986), and would, in future years, perform in *The Muppets Christmas Carol* (1992), *The Muppets* (2011), and *The Muppets: Most Wanted* (2014). In addition, he was a featured puppeteer on Jim Henson's *Fraggle Rock* television show (1983–87). He performed in the pilot episode of *Spitting Image*, the award-winning British satirical political puppet show that featured caricature puppets of celebrities and politicians. The episode was filmed the day before the first call he received requesting his involvement in *Roger Rabbit*. Barclay was the chief puppeteer who, along with Mike Quinn, put the puppeteer crew together. They had previously done the auditioning for the Henson films, which were also filmed at Elstree Studios. George Gibbs used to jokingly introduce him on the *Roger Rabbit* set—saying, "This is Dave Barclay. He's getting me my next Oscar."

He has since worked on feature films such as *Cats and Dogs* (2001) and *Where the Wild Things Are* (2009).

James Baxter heard about *Who Framed Roger Rabbit* being produced in London after having completed one year at West Surrey College of Art and Design. He was made an in-betweener for Andreas Deja. He had a good spatial sense, and says that his brain seems to be wired to understand how movement breaks down frame-to-frame. He was soon made a clean-up animator for Marc Gordon-Bates, who he says was very patient with him. Deja advocated for Baxter to be given more scope and responsibility, and showed Baxter's "Thumper" test to Dick Williams. Williams thought he should be given more time to develop, but finally relented and gave Baxter some shots with hands turning the key to the Dipmobile. His first animation, as an animator, was of a weasel stomping on the accelerator when starting up the Dipmobile. Deja also championed Baxter being hired by Disney after the completion of *Who Framed Roger Rabbit*.

Baxter moved from Disney to DreamWorks after *The Hunchback of Notre Dame* and worked on DreamWorks features *The Prince of Egypt* through to *Madagascar*. He set up his own animation company in 2005 and provided the animation in Disney's *Enchanted* and the animated opening credits for *Kung Fu Panda*. He returned to DreamWorks in 2008 and has worked on *How to Train Your Dragon* and *The Croods*.

Richard Bazley had been working in London for a couple of years when he saw an ad in a magazine that Disney was looking for animators. Bazley had no animation training, but he put together a portfolio of life drawings and took it to the Forum. It was early in the production and he was told that they were looking for experienced animators only. Bazley taught himself the basics of animation from the Preston Blair books. Jill Brooks, from Stuart Brooks Animation, was sufficiently impressed that she arranged an appointment for him at Disney and it was agreed that he could come in for an in-betweener test. He went to Pizazz to see Eric Goldberg, who provided some coaching, and got on to the *Who Framed Roger Rabbit* crew.

Bazley worked at Disney in Burbank on *Pocahontas*, *Hercules*, and *Tarzan*. He worked at Warner Bros. on *The Iron Giant*, *Osmosis Jones*, and *Harry Potter and the Prisoner of Azkaban*. He directed *Centurion Resurrection* (2014), a live-action short.

Rob Bekuhrs attended CalArts with Bill Kopp. Kopp told him that the new Disney Florida studio needed a computer effects animator. Bekuhrs worked on *Tummy Trouble* in Los Angeles for about two weeks, and arrived in Florida a week after the studio opened. In *Roller Coaster Rabbit*, the rollercoaster track and ride car in Roger's wild rollercoaster ride were animated with computer assistance. Bekuhrs worked on *Off His Rockers* (1992), an early CGI short done at the Florida studio. He worked at Disney in Florida until the studio was closed in 2003.

Since that time, he has worked on feature films such as *The Wild*, *Coraline*, *ParaNorman*, and *John Carter*.

Carl Bell studied at the Ontario College of Art. He joined Disney briefly in 1958, until the layoffs following the completion of *Sleeping Beauty*. He worked at Disney briefly again in 1962 and then spent years at UPA, Bob Clampett, MGM, and Filmation. He was anxious to get into Disney again and went to see the Baers when he heard about *Who Framed Roger Rabbit*. He was called in as an assistant animator when the pressure increased on the production.

After *Who Framed Roger Rabbit*, Bell was hired by Disney and worked on *Oliver & Company* through to *Tarzan*.

Stella-Rose Benson graduated from West Surrey College of Art and Design and was working as a freelance artist in Soho when she heard about *Roger Rabbit* by word-of-mouth. Bob Wilck suggested to her that she should apply. She had worked at RWA a couple of times prior to *Roger Rabbit*. Benson was on the film for nine months, starting in April 1987. After *Roger Rabbit*, she worked as a freelance animator. One of the projects she worked on was the television short *The Snowman and the Snowdog* (2012).

She keeps busy as a story illustrator and gardener.

Aaron Blaise grew up in Naples, Florida, and studied at the Ringling School of Art and Design in Sarasota. He was part of the Disney Burbank internship program for staffing the new studio in Florida. He was selected and started in Florida on April 17, 1989.

He worked on the *Roger Rabbit* shorts produced at the Florida studio, as well as some of the shorts that were ultimately not completed. He worked on the feature films to which the Florida studio contributed (*Beauty and the Beast*, *Aladdin*, *The Lion King*) and *Mulan*, for which Florida was the primary production studio. Blaise directed *Brother Bear* (2003), the last project at the Walt Disney Feature Animation—Florida studio. Since the closure of the studio, Blaise has developed a number of film projects and has pursued his love of wildlife art.

Don Bluth was first hired at Disney in 1955 and was an assistant to John Lounsbery on *Sleeping Beauty*. He left in 1957 to do missionary work in Argentina, as a part of his Mormon faith. He started working at Filmation in 1967 and joined Disney again in 1971. He left in dramatic fashion, on his birthday in 1979, taking eleven other artists with him to finish *Banjo the Woodpile Cat*, a project he'd been doing while at Disney using volunteers from the studio, and to start up Don Bluth Productions. He produced the animated video games *Dragon's Lair* and *Space Ace*. He directed and produced *The Secret of NIMH*, *An American Tail*, *The Land Before Time*, and *All Dogs Go to Heaven*. In 1985, the new Sullivan/Bluth Studio moved to Dublin, Ireland. His affiliation with Steven Spielberg lasted until 1989.

He directed *Anastasia* and *Titan A.E.* for Fox. Bluth and Gary Goldman started a crowdfunding campaign in 2015 to raise money for development of a feature film based on his video game, *Dragon's Lair*.

Bluth received the Winsor McCay Award in 2004.

Dave Bossert graduated from CalArts and joined Disney in early 1984. *The Black Cauldron* was already in production. He moved on to development on *The Great Mouse Detective* when his work on *The Black Cauldron* was complete. He resigned from Disney in December 1986 to start work on *Land Before Time* at Sullivan/Bluth Studios in Dublin, Ireland, in January 1987. He visited Don Hahn in London and was asked to join the *Roger Rabbit* crew. He moved to London for *Roger Rabbit* and was rehired by Disney in Glendale after *Roger Rabbit* was complete.

Bossert worked as an effects animator on *The Little Mermaid*, *Beauty and the Beast*, *Aladdin*, *The Nightmare Before Christmas*, *The Lion King*, and *Pocahontas*. He was the visual effects supervisor and artist coordinator on the *Runaway Brain*, *Lorenzo*, and *The Little Matchgirl* shorts and on the feature, *Fantasia 2000*. He was the associate producer on *Destino*.

Bossert produced the True Life Adventure DVD collection and directed *The Cat That Looked at a King* and *One by One*, special features on feature film DVD releases. He also directed the *Pumbaa and Timon—Wild About Safety* DVD series for Disney Educational and was the artistic supervisor of the Disney Restoration Team.

Bossert created the *Disney Animated* iPad app that won a BAFTA Award and directed *The Tunes Behind the Toons* (2014) and *Cartoon Camera* (2016). He is also the author of *Remembering Roy E. Disney, An Animator's Gallery,*

Dali and Disney—Destino, The Art of Tennessee Loveless—10X10XTEN, Oswald the Lucky Rabbit—The Search for the Lost Cartoons, and *Kem Weber: Mid-Century Furniture Designs for the Disney Studios*. He has become the classic example of somebody who is busier in his retirement than when he was "working."

David Bowers went to West Surrey College of Art and Design, leaving school after first year to work on *Who Framed Roger Rabbit*. He worked in the newly established Amblimation studio in London after the completion of *Roger Rabbit* and was taken on by DreamWorks SKG when Amblimation was closed. He worked on the early traditional animation DreamWorks feature films, but was assigned as storyboard supervisor on *Chicken Run*, a joint DreamWorks/Aardman production. He directed the animated feature films *Flushed Away* (Aardman) and *Astro Boy* (ImagiAnimation), as well as the live-action *Diary of a Wimpy Kid* (2011) film series.

Neil Boyle submitted his portfolio at the Forum in the summer after completing his first year at West Surrey College of Art and Design. He started as an in-betweener in August 1987, and after a four-week trial became Dick Williams's assistant at the age of twenty.

When *Who Framed Roger Rabbit* was completed, there was a two-month break before they started on *The Thief and the Cobbler*. Boyle was an animator on the film and later animated the title sequence on Williams's *Animator's Survival Kit* DVD series.

Boyle wrote, directed, and produced the animated short *The Last Belle* (2011) and *Made Up* (2016). He was the lead animator on *The Simpsons* couch gag (Sylvain Chomet, 2014) and worked on *Ethel & Ernest*. He is attached to be director on *Kensuke's Kingdom* (Lupus Films), based on Michael Morpurgo's 1999 children's novel.

Maggie Brown worked in the Trace and Paint Department on *Watership Down*. She freelanced in the London commercial studios, working at RWA several times until she was hired full-time. She moved on to *Who Framed Roger Rabbit* as the assistant head of Trace and Paint, liaison with the Camera, Xerox, Checking, and Animation departments.

After *Roger Rabbit*, she went back to freelancing and then worked on *The Thief and the Cobbler* as head of Trace and Paint.

Chris Buck studied for two years at CalArts, part of the very talented initial character animation class. He joined Disney in 1978 and was an animator on *The Fox and the Hound*. He was involved in several special projects in the early 1980s, including early development and experimental animation for *Roger Rabbit* (1981–82), animation on *Mickey's Christmas Carol*, storyboarding for Tim Burton's *Frankenweenie*, and story and animation on *Sport Goofy in Soccermania*.

He left Disney and worked on *The Brave Little Toaster* and *Bébé's Kids* for Wilhite's Hyperion Pictures. He worked on Warner Bros.' *Box Office Bunny*, directed by Darrell Van Citters. He also worked on Brad Bird's "Family Dog" episode of *Steven Spielberg's Amazing Stories* and directed the "Family Dog" television series (1993) that followed. He was back at Disney for *Pocahontas* and co-directed *Tarzan*. He worked on *Home on the Range*, but left to join Sony to write the screenplay and direct *Surf's Up*. John Lasseter convinced him to come back to Disney in 2008, where he developed a project entitled "The Snow Queen," which he eventually directed as *Frozen*. He is directing the sequel, *Frozen 2*.

Don Carson worked at Walt Disney Imagineering on many Disney theme park projects, including Toontown at Disneyland and Tokyo Disneyland. He later went on his own, establishing Don Carson Creative, doing concept and 3D design contracts for WDI, Jim Henson Co., Universal Studios, and for corporations such Microsoft and Coca-Cola.

Randy Cartwright graduated from UCLA in 1974 and started at Disney in 1975. He graduated from the Training Program and became an in-betweener under Ollie Johnston on *The Rescuers*. He was soon made Ollie's assistant and was then made full animator on *Pete's Dragon*. He worked with Ollie on *The Fox and the Hound*, and when Ollie Johnston and Frank Thomas both retired in 1978 to write their book, *Disney Animation: The Illusion of Life*, Cartwright was made a supervising animator. He did experimental animation for the *Roger Rabbit* development team.

Cartwright left Disney in 1983 to work on *Little Nemo: Adventures in Slumberland* for TMS in Japan and *The Brave Little Toaster* for Hyperion Pictures in Taiwan. He was back at Disney in 1986 and was the artistic lead on the Disney/Pixar CAPS digital ink and paint system, for which he won an Academy Scientific and Technical Award. He was an animator on *Beauty and the Beast* and *The Lion King*. He did the computer animation on the Magic Carpet in *Aladdin* and worked in Story on *Hercules*. He worked at DreamWorks as head of Story on *Antz* and *Shrek* and at ILM as an animator on *Pirates of the Caribbean: The Curse of the Black Pearl*. He was back at Disney on *The Princess and the Frog* and worked as a storyboard artist on the *Sofia the First* television series (2013–14).

Joanna Cassidy's breakout role was as Zhora in Ridley Scott's *Blade Runner* (1982). She was in *The Fourth Protocol* (1987). She played Dolores in *Who Framed Roger Rabbit*. Recent recurring roles in television series have included *Six Feet Under* (HBO, 2001–2005) and *Body of Proof* (ABC, 2011–13).

Stephen Cavalier worked at Amblimation as an animator following the completion of *Who Framed Roger Rabbit*. He wrote and directed the short *Daddy* (2001). He is the director of animation for *The Hive* television series and directed the 2016 TV movie, *The Hive Summer Special: The Buzz Double*. He is the author of *The World History of Animation*, published by University of California Press in 2011.

Roger Chiasson was born in Edmundston, New Brunswick. When he was about to enter high school, his family moved to Toronto. Roger was supposed to be registered into Northern Secondary School, which had a commercial arts program and was the same high school that Richard Williams attended. Instead, he attended North Toronto Collegiate Institute, another public high school located less than half-a-mile away. After finishing his sophomore year, Chiasson went to Sheridan College to study Art Fundamentals.

The Nelvana studio was just starting up in Toronto when Chiasson graduated in 1976. He was looking for a bit of adventure, though, and was hired as an intern at Halas and Batchelor that summer, staying with an uncle who lived in London. He was soon animating and shortly thereafter was actually paid as an animator. John Halas was very impressed with Chiasson and talked him into returning to Toronto to establish a satellite studio. Halas put up the money and Chiasson got Duncan Marjoribanks and Mark Simon to come in with him. They worked in Toronto for about twelve months and did a few commercials, but the real product of their year was a very nice showreel.

After that year, he went to Hanna-Barbera (H-B) in Los Angeles at the invitation of a Sheridan classmate, Al Gaivoto. H-B had to let "foreign" workers go as part of the settlement of the 1979 Screen Cartoonists strike. Chiasson stayed around Los Angeles for a while, working freelance, then made arrangements with H-B to set up a studio in Toronto to work on various H-B television series, including Scooby-Doo. Chiasson started traveling for H-B to coach and supervise at its overseas studios in Spain, Japan, South Korea, the Phillipines, and Australia. He worked with Raul Garcia while in Spain on *Lucky Luke* for H-B. Chiasson would go back to London between overseas assignments to pick up other work.

On a trip to London, Chuck Gammage snuck Chiasson and Dino Athanassiou into RWA at 13 Soho Square and showed them the *Roger Rabbit* proof-of-concept test. When Gammage started to work on *Roger Rabbit* while still at Soho Square, he recommended Chiasson and Athanassiou to Richard Williams.

After *Roger Rabbit*, Chiasson was hired by Disney in Glendale and worked on the *Roger Rabbit* short *Tummy Trouble*. He worked on *The Rescuers Down Under* before leaving to work on *FernGully: The Last Rainforest* at Kroyer Films. He was back at Disney for *The Hunchback of Notre Dame*, *Hercules*, and *Tarzan*, before working on *Osmosis Jones* (Warner Bros.) and *Curious George* (Universal).

He has worked at Yowza! Animation, a studio in Toronto founded by his brother, Claude Chiasson.

Paul Chung was born in Hong Kong. He moved to London in 1981. He went to film school and received training in live-action film and graphic design, but had no formal training in animation. At the time Chung started in the industry, it seemed to him that every "foreign" animator had been trained at Sheridan College. The few schools in the UK that offered programs in animation didn't really train students to work in a commercial environment. That sort of training was available only through courses offered by veterans such as Harold Whittaker or apprenticing at an animation studio. Chung had done some freelance work for RWA in the past and was working for Tony White at Animus when he got a phone call from Disney. He was invited to come in to take an animation test. He had worked as an animator for several years by that time, so the request set him back and he refused to take the test. Eventually, he considered the opportunity of working with Richard Williams and Disney and the international crew on a feature production and went to the Forum, where he was hired as an assistant animator. He started in May 1987, shortly after Uli Meyer had walked out of the production. He worked primarily with Rob Stevenhagen, with whom he became lifelong friends. His name was on a list of assistants to be promoted to animator, but he was shy and quiet and Williams kept forgetting him—even though others further down on the list were promoted. Chung never made a fuss about it, although it concerned him that Williams couldn't remember him even though he had shouted at Chung many times.

He worked at Passion Pictures after *Roger Rabbit*, but moved to Dream-Works, where he worked on *Shrek*, *Shrek 2*, *Madagascar*, *Over the Hedge*, *Shrek the Third*, *Bee Movie*, and *Megamind*. He joined Moving Picture Company (MPC) and worked on *Wrath of Titans*, *Godzilla*, *Guardians of the Galaxy*, *Exodus—Gods and Kings*, and *The Jungle Book*.

Tony Clark studied graphic design at the Lincoln College of Art. He worked in a nearby factory after graduation, but was intrigued when he met somebody who had a part-time job painting animation cels. Clark moved to London and got a job in the Vintage Magazine Shop photo darkroom. He saw an advertisement for *Roger Rabbit* in the *Guardian* newspaper in August 1987. He rang up the Disney offices at Wardour Street, in Soho, and was directed to the Camden Town studio where he spoke with Barbara McCormack, the supervisor of the Ink and Paint Department. A Xerox Department operator had just handed in his notice, so Clark was invited to come to the Forum for an interview. He was interviewed by Maggie Brown, the assistant supervisor of Ink and Paint, and was offered a job on August 31, 1987. He started on *Roger Rabbit* on September 1, 1987, as a Xerox Department operator (aka, post punch assistant).

He has worked at Passion Pictures since *Roger Rabbit*, but has also worked on films such as *Lost in Space* (1998). He contributed to the documentary *The Making of* The Hitchhiker's Guide to the Galaxy (1993).

Daniel Cohen started in the Soho animation community as a runner at Gingerbread Animation. He started to freelance as an inker/painter and did a little animation while at Moo Movies. There was a rumor going around Soho about a movie in which Bob Hoskins is handcuffed to a rabbit. A colleague encouraged Cohen to call Disney and, when Cohen demurred, placed the call himself and thrust the handset into Cohen's hand when he got a ringtone at Disney. Cohen was called in for an interview and took a paint test. His hand was shaking and he was sweating, which he chocked up to nervousness. It turns out that he had chicken pox. He was called to start working at the Forum in late July 1987. He was taken on as a painter, but after a week he was made an inker and then went into the Checking Department.

Cohen worked at commercial studios in London, but eventually found his way to the US and worked at the Walt Disney Feature Animation studio in Florida until it closed in 2003. Since then he has worked in digital visual effects and is a senior producer with FuseFX.

Barry Cook started at Disney after being referred by a friend as an effects animator on *Tron* in 1981. He came up with the idea for the short *Oilspot and Lipstick*, featuring Disney's first computer character animation. It was made in 1986 by the Disney Computer Animation Late Night Group, a group of volunteers, including Randy Cartwright, Mike Cedeno, Barry Cook, and Tina Price, who worked on the film during their own time. Similarly, *Off His Rockers*, produced at the Walt Disney Feature Animation studio in Florida, was a bootleg project for which the small production group was allowed to use studio equipment and resources. Cook directed *Off His Rockers* and the *Roger Rabbit* short *Trail Mix-Up* in Florida. He directed the Disney feature film *Mulan*, for which he received an Annie Award.

He spent years at WDFA-F developing a project based on Oscar Wilde's *The Canterville Ghost*. His original working title was *The Ghost and His Gift*, but it went through many name changes (*My Peoples*, *Elgin's People*, *Once in a Blue Moon*, and *A Few Good Ghosts*) and a shift from traditional animation to CGI before being canceled with the closure of the Florida studio.

Cook directed *Arthur Christmas* (Aardman) and *Walking With Dinosaurs* (2013).

Alain Costa grew up in France, where he and his brother, Jean-Manuel, taught themselves animation. Both Alain and his brother worked on *le Roi et l'Oiseau* (*The King and the Mockingbird*, 1980) with director Paul Grimault. Alain was an animator, and Jean-Manuel, a painter. Alain Costa moved to Australia and got a job at Burbank Films Australia. Costa and Jacques Muller worked together at Burbank Studio in Sydney on *A Christmas Carol* (1982), *Great Expectations* (1983), and *Sherlock Holmes and the Baskerville Curse* (1983).

Costa moved to London and saw a Disney recruiting advertisement in the newspaper. He sent his reel to Don Hahn and met Hahn at the Forum; nobody else was there. When he came back to the Forum to start work, Phil Nibbelink had just arrived.

Costa has worked for Disney, Bluth, Warner Bros., and ILM and has taught animation in France. He lives in Dublin, Ireland, where he paints animals and landscapes. Jean-Manuel does stop-motion animation.

Howy Parkins and **Irene Couloufis** were dating at Sheridan College. He is a British citizen by birth, so some time after his graduation, they went to London to find work. They worked around the commercial studios for a while, but were keen to get into feature animation. They got a call from Don Hahn in the early summer of 1987.

After *Roger Rabbit*, they—along with many of the crew—worked on *The Magic Voyage* in Germany. Back in North America, Couloufis worked on *FernGully*, *Cool World*, and *The Pagemaster*. She worked on *Cats Don't Dance* as Irene Parkins.

She worked at DreamWorks on *The Prince of Egypt* and subsequent films until she moved to Sony for *Open Season*. She worked on *Beowolf* at Warner Bros. and then *Bolt* at Disney. She went back to DreamWorks and has worked on *How to Train Your Dragon*, *The Croods*, *Home*, *Trolls*, and *The Boss Baby*.

Caron Creed (Painter), (1961–2014), had worked at RWA and moved on to be an animator on *Who Framed Roger Rabbit*. It was while working at the Forum that she met her future husband, Andrew Painter. After *Roger Rabbit*, they worked on *DuckTales the Movie: Treasure of the Lost Lamp* (1990) and then worked at Hibbert/Ralph and Passion Pictures and other boutique animation houses in London. Both Caron and Andrew later concentrated on character design and illustration.

Dean Cundey is a cinematographer known for his frequent collaborations with Bob Zemeckis and John Carpenter. He worked on *Halloween* (1978), *Escape From New York* (1981), *The Thing* (1982), and *Big Trouble in Little China* (1986) with Carpenter. In addition to *Who Framed Roger Rabbit*, he worked on *Romancing the Stone* (1984), *Back to the Future* (1986), *Back to the Future Part II* (1989), *Back to the Future Part III* (1990), *Hook* (1991), and *Death Becomes Her* (1992) with Zemeckis. He also worked on Jurassic *Park* (1993), *Looney Tunes: Back in Action* (1993), *The Flintstones* (1994), *Garfield* (1994), *Apollo 13* (1995), *Flubber* (1997), *The Parent Trap* (1998), *Camp Rock* (2008), *Walking With the Enemy* (2014), and *Where is Daniel* (2017). He shot *Honey, I Shrunk the Audience*, a 3D film shown at the Disney theme parks.

He directed the direct-to-video film *Honey, We Shrunk Ourselves* (1997).

Eric Daniels was an in-betweener in the Glendale crew on *Who Framed Roger Rabbit*. After *Roger Rabbit*, he worked for Baer Animation on commercials and on *Rover Dangerfield* and *Tom and Jerry: The Movie*.

Daniels worked at DreamWorks on *Over the Hedge*. He was the CGI lead animator at Disney on Treasure Planet and has animated at Disney on *Meet the Robinsons*, *Bolt*, *The Princess and the Frog*, *Tangled*, *Wreck-It Ralph*, *Winnie the Pooh*, *Frozen*, *Big Hero 6*, and *Moana*.

Kevin Jon Davies got into an art college pre-foundation course at age sixteen and was then accepted at the London College of Printing. At eighteen, Davies found himself walking down a basement corridor in a building housing some overflow from the BBC's main offices and heard the bleeping of R2-D2. He poked his head into the office and saw two BBC editors preparing a clip to be used in the BBC children's program, *Jim'll Fix It*, hosted by the now notorious Jimmy Savile. He was able to speak with the producer, who was impressed by Davies's knowledge of science fiction and who had just received notice of *The Hitchhiker's Guide to the Galaxy* television series. It was 1980, and Davies got his first job in the film industry working on *The Hitchhikers Guide to the Galaxy* television series. He started to freelance in 1981 and worked for Gerry Anderson—famous for the Supermarionation science fiction television series, *Thunderbirds*—on the *Terrahawks* puppet show pilot. Davies did the titles and graphics.

A friend sent him a recruiting advertisement for the *Roger Rabbit* production. He applied and was one of the first half dozen people hired to the Effects Department. After *Roger Rabbit*, Davies tried to put together his own animated film for a television series on robots. It was to be called "Thingy and Whatsit." He recruited a number of friends from the Effects Department with the inducement of curry lunches, if they would work for free. Nothing much came of it. He followed Chris Knott to Passion Pictures and worked there for several years. He directed a documentary, *The Making of* The Hitchhiker's Guide to the Galaxy (1993), as well as numerous television documentaries over the years, many of them related to *Doctor Who* and other science fiction topics.

Andreas Deja grew up in Germany. He had drawn Disney characters since he was in kindergarten, and after he saw *The Jungle Book* at age ten, he knew that he wanted to be a Disney animator. He wrote to the studio and received replies encouraging him to work at life drawing, not just cartooning. He went to art school, taking graphic design because there were no courses in animation. He analyzed 8mm clips from Disney films that were available at the time and taught himself to animate. He sent drawings to Eric Larson, who by this time was head of the Disney Training Program, and Larson would reply with critiques and encouragement. Larson went on a northern European cruise vacation, and Deja (with his friend and mentor, Hans Bacher) drove for six hours to meet him at a stopover in Hamburg, Germany. After graduating from art school, Deja was invited to join the Disney Studios in 1980.

Tim Burton was put in the same office as Deja, in hopes that Burton could develop the Disney style. It didn't work. Deja worked on *The Black Cauldron*, *The Great Mouse Detective*, *Who Framed Roger Rabbit*, *Oliver & Company*, *The Little Mermaid*, *The Prince and the Pauper* [short], *Beauty and the Beast*, *Aladdin*, *The Lion King*, *Runaway Brain* [short], *Hercules*, *Fantasia 2000*, *The Emperor's New Groove*, *Lilo & Stitch*, *Home on the Range*, *How to Hook Up Your Home Theater* [short], *Enchanted*, *The Princess and the Frog*, *The Ballad of Nessie* [short], and *Winnie the Pooh*. He has also been a Disney emissary/consultant at the satellite Disney studios in France and Australia.

Deja is a noted Disney animation art collector and historian. He has been sharing his experience and knowledge on his *DejaView.com* blog since 2011. He is directing a personal animated film, *Mushka*, due for release in 2019.

Deja received the Winsor McCay Award in 2006.

Three out of four of **Lily Dell**'s siblings have been in the animation industry. Her brother is T. Dan Hofstedt, who worked for Bluth in Dublin and came to Disney on *Aladdin*. Lily worked as a silhouettist and caricaturist at Disneyland in the mid-1970s. She grew up in California, then moved to Hawaii and eventually moved to Australia, where she met her husband. He was originally from London, so they decided to move to England at his urging. She had been a reasonable artist in her youth. She had learned to handle pressure and be quick from her work at Disneyland. Her brother was already working with Bluth in Dublin at the time and suggested that she apply at Disney in London. She interviewed with Don Hahn and was put in the Matte and Roto Department. She eventually joined the Effects Department.

After *Roger Rabbit*, she returned to Australia and eventually joined the Disney Australia animation studio in Sydney, where she worked on the theatrical releases *A Goofy Movie*, *Return to Neverland*, and *The Jungle Book 2*. She worked on television series such as *Bonkers*, *Aladdin*, *The Shnookums and Meat Funny Cartoon Show*, *Quack Pack*, *Timon & Pumbaa*, *Jungle Cubs*, *101 Dalmatians: The Series*, and *The Legend of Tarzan*. She worked on the Disney short *Redux Riding Hood* (1997). Dell also worked on many direct-to-video releases: *The Return of Jafar*, *Aladdin and the King of Thieves*, *Beauty and the Beast: The Enchanted Christmas*, *The Lion King 2: Simba's Pride*, *Winnie the Pooh: Seasons of Giving*, *An Extremely Goofy Movie*, *The Little Mermaid 2: Return to the Sea*, *Lady and the Tramp 2: Scamp's Adventure*, *The Lion King 1½*, *Mickey, Donald, and Goofy: The Three Musketeers*, *Tarzan 2*, *Lilo & Stitch 2: Stitch Has a Glitch*, *Bambi II*, *Brother Bear 2*, *The Fox and the Hound 2*, and *Cinderella III: A Twist in Time* (2007), when the studio was closed.

She lectures at Design Center Enmore in Sydney.

Patsy de Lord took over from Andrew Ruhemann as the production manager at the Forum. Williams was suspicious of her being a Disney spy at the start. She had worked at ATV, for Sir Lew Grade, on *The Muppet Show* television series and she was the assistant to Jim Henson on *The Great Muppet Caper* and *The Dark Crystal*. She was secretary to Steven Spielberg on *Indiana Jones and the Temple of Doom*. She reported to both Don Hahn and Max Howard on *Who Framed Roger Rabbit*.

After Roger Rabbit, she was the production coordinator on films such as Air America, Four Weddings and a Funeral, Mission: Impossible, The Mummy, 102 Dalmatians, and Hannibal Rising.

Roy E. Disney (1930–2009) was the son of Roy O. Disney, and the nephew of Walt Disney. He graduated from Pomona College in 1951 and joined Disney after a short time with Jack Web's *Dragnet* television series, which was filmed on the Disney lot in Burbank. He worked mainly with the *True-Life Adventure* television series at Disney. He did some photography for the feature film *Perri* (1957).

He organized the ouster of Ron Miller in 1984 that brought Michael Eisner and Frank Wells to Disney, after which he was named chairman of the Disney Animation Department. He organized the "Save Disney" campaign to oust Michael Eisner in 2005. He was named a Disney Legend in 1998.

Disney was a trustee of CalArts. He was a large shareholder in the Walt Disney Company and invested in many other enterprises through his company, Shamrock Holdings. He was a competitive sailor, competing many times in the TransPacific Yacht Race. He was the Grand Marshall of the 2000 Tournament of Roses Parade.

Roy E. Disney received the Winsor McCay Award in 1993.

Dave Dunnet started his career doing layout at Filmation in 1980. He moved to Hanna-Barbera in 1982, doing layout on the Smurfs. He was at Disney as an assistant layout artist on *The Black Cauldron* and as a layout artist on *The Great Mouse Detective*. He was a layout artist on *Who Framed Roger Rabbit* and was the layout supervisor on *The Little Mermaid* and *The Prince and the Pauper*. He was with Hyperion Pictures on *The Itsy Bitsy Spider* and *Bébé's Kids*, and was art director and layout supervisor on *The Brave Little Toaster Goes to Mars* and *The Brave Little Toaster to the Rescue*.

He worked on *Tarzan* at Disney as the location designer. He was the layout designer on *An Extremely Goofy Movie*, the *Mickey's House of Villains* video, and the *Disney's House of Mouse* television series (2001–2002).

Dunnet was the background designer on *The Powerpuff Girls* and *Star Wars: Clone Wars*. He was the background designer on the *Foster's Home for Imaginary Friends* television series (2004–2009) and the location designer on *Kick Buttowski: Suburban Daredevil* (2010). He was the development artist and location designer on *My Little Pony: Friendship is Magic* (2010–2011).

Hani El-Masri (1951–2015) won the National Award for Best Illustration of a Children's Book in Egypt in 1979. He moved to America in 1987 and worked freelance until being hired by Walt Disney Imagineering in 1990. In 1995, he was hired by DreamWorks as a visual development artist, working on *Prince of Egypt*, *The Road to El Dorado*, *Spirit: Stallion of the Cimarron*, and worked on *Osmosis Jones* at Warner Bros.

He moved back to Egypt in 2005, where he illustrated children's books.

Annie Elvin (1938–2014) started as an actress. She had worked with Bob Hoskins in the theater. She also did voice-acting, but got her start in animation at the Larkins Studio. Over the years she had done the odd bit of Trace and Paint work at RWA.

Annie started her own animation service company, doing mostly Trace and Paint work, in the early 1980s—Wicked Witch Studio was started on Halloween Day. Most of the Wicked Witch crew was rolled into service on *Roger Rabbit*. Elvin was head of the Matte and Roto Department on *Roger Rabbit*. Two of her sons, Martin and Harry, were also on the *Roger Rabbit* crew in Camden Town. After *Roger Rabbit*, she worked at Amblimation on *American Tail: Fievel Goes West*. She worked on *The Magic Sword: Quest for Camelot* and *The Rugrats Movie* (Nickelodeon), and was the colorist on *Corpse Bride*.

Andrea Favilli is a sculptor. He created the Disney Legends Award. Larger versions of it are located at the Walt Disney Company headquarters in Burbank and at Disneyland Paris. He created the Cameraman sculpture located in Disney's Hollywood Studios at Walt Disney World. He sculpted Roy O. and Edna Disney; the statue is located on the grounds of St. Joseph Hospital, across from the Disney headquarters in Burbank.

Charles Fleischer grew up in Washington, DC, and got his start in show business doing comedy bits as a nine-year-old at Camp Kewanee, in La Plume, Pennsylvania. He later studied acting at Goodman Theatre in Chicago. Jonathan Winters was his comic idol, and Fleischer's comedy has always been a bit manic like his mentor. Fleischer received national attention when he put his trumpet mouthpiece on a piece of Sears Tower piping and "played" the building like a musical instrument.

Fleischer was doing a stand-up comedy routine at the Comedy Store in Los Angeles in the early 1980s. Zemeckis remembered him and asked him to come in to audition for a part in *Romancing the Stone*. Fleischer got a call from Zemeckis in early 1986 to voice Roger Rabbit in the screen tests for the part of Eddie Valiant. He continued to play that role in the film.

In his stand-up gigs, and anywhere else he can, Fleischer talks of "moleeds," which he describes as the primary particle of the universe, with a property of being multiples of "37." He presented "All Things are Moleeds" during a TED Talk.

Nick Fletcher was an assistant editor at Richard Williams Animation for five years prior to working with Williams on *Who Framed Roger Rabbit*. After *Roger Rabbit*, Fletcher worked at Amblimation in London and went to DreamWorks in Glendale when Amblimation was closed. He was the lead editor on *An American Tail: Fievel Goes West, We're Back! A Dinosaur Story, The Prince of Egypt, Spirit: Stallion of the Cimarron, Shark Tale, Bee Movie, Shrek Forever After, Madagascar 3: Europe's Most Wanted, Home*, and *Trolls*.

Bill Frake went to the Art School of Virginia and then finished his formal education, studying illustration, at the Fashion Institute in New York City. He worked on the *Schoolhouse Rock!* television series in 1973 and on *Raggedy Ann & Andy: A Musical Adventure* in New York. He was hired into the Disney Training Program in 1980. He worked on *The Black Cauldron* and *The Great Mouse Detective* as a layout artist. He was working at Hanna-Barbera when he got the call to be head of Layout and set design on *Who Framed Roger Rabbit*.

Frake worked at both Warner Bros. and Disney after *Roger Rabbit*: at Disney on *Pocahontas, Hercules,* and *Fantasia 2000*; and at Warner Bros. on *A Troll in Central Park, The Pebble and the Penguin, Quest for Camelot,* and *The Iron Giant*.

He moved to Blue Sky Studios as story artist on *Gone Nutty* [short] and *Ice Age, Robots, Ice Age: The Meltdown, Horton Hears a Who!, Ice Age: Dawn of the Dinosaurs, Rio, Epic, Rio 2,* and *Spies in Disguise*.

He is lending his talents on layout and story to Chris Williams's short *The Sketchbook*, set during World War I.

Randy Fullmer graduated from CalArts in 1974 with a Bachelor of Fine Arts degree. He rattled around the animation business, developing his skills doing medical, scientific, and educational films. He worked on animated segments for *Sesame Street*. Fullmer worked at Don Bluth Studios in 1983–84, doing effects on the video games *Space Ace* and *Dragon's Lair*. He also worked at John Dykstra's FX house, Apogee, and at Filmation.

In 1987, he was given a three-month contract to work on the Toontown segment of *Who Framed Roger Rabbit*, which extended to nineteen years of employment at Disney. He worked in Effects on *Oliver & Company*, *The Little Mermaid*, and was effects supervisor on *The Rescuers Down Under*. He was artistic coordinator on *The Lion King* and *The Hunchback of Notre Dame*. He was the producer on *The Emperor's New Groove* and *Chicken Little*.

In 2006, he founded Wyn Guitars. He is the sole luthier and makes guitars that are works of art.

Al Gaivoto graduated from Sheridan College in Canada and worked at Hanna-Barbera in Los Angeles in the late 1970s. After the 1979 strike, he became an international animation gypsy, working in Europe and the Far East. After *Who Framed Roger Rabbit*, he took over some of the directing duties on the German production *The Magic Voyage*. He worked in London on *DuckTales the Movie: Treasure of the Lost Lamp*.

Gaivoto teaches and operates the Old Rectory in Altersberg, Austria, as a bed and breakfast.

Peter Gambier came late to the production of *Who Framed Roger Rabbit*. He was a plasterer by trade and an artist by avocation. Brent Odell remembers him appearing at the Forum with a portfolio under one arm and a plaster bucket on his other arm. He was hired as an in-betweener.

Gambier worked on *The Magic Voyage* and *Asterix in America* in Gemany and *Quest for Camelot* in London.

He is a lime plasterer.

Chuck Gammage graduated from Sheridan College in 1978. He worked at H-B for a year, until his work permit was pulled as a consequence of the 1979 MPSC strike. He worked in Toronto at Nelvana for a few years after that. Tom Sito worked with Chuck Gammage at Nelvana during that time.

Chuck Gammage snuck Chiasson and Dino Athanassiou into RWA at 13 Soho Square and showed them the *Roger Rabbit* proof-of-concept test. When Gammage started to work on *Roger Rabbit* while still at Soho Square, he recommended Athanassiou and Chiasson to Richard Williams.

After *Roger Rabbit*, he worked at Passion Pictures and later founded Chuck Gammage Animation back in Canada, where he directed a segment of *Space Jam* (1996). He does commercial and contract work on films and television shows. He did *The Stanley Dynamic* in 2017.

Raul Garcia was born in Spain and became entranced with animation by the Disney television shows that would pull back the curtain on animation magic. He got hold of the Preston Blair book *How to Animate Film Cartoons* and taught himself animation. At nineteen years old, Garcia went to RWA in London, where another Spaniard, Oscar Grillo, worked at the time, to ask for a job. He wasn't hired, so he went back to Spain and worked at the Hanna-Barbera studio on *The Smurfs*, *Lucky Luke*, and *The Flintstones*. The H-B studio had brought over a number of Canadian animators and Garcia joined that group, moving from production to production. He worked on *Asterix and Caesar* and *Asterix in Britain* before moving to Los Angeles for six months, then to South Korea for thirteen months, working on *The Chipmunk Adventure*. On the way back to Spain from Korea, he picked up a book at the airport for light airplane reading—it happened to be *Who Censored Roger Rabbit?* He thought that it might make a good animated film. During the stopover in Los Angeles, he bought a *Premiere* magazine, in which he saw a tiny notation that *Roger Rabbit* was to be produced in London. During the stopover in London, Garcia went to RWA at Soho Square instead of continuing directly to Madrid. It was too early; the RWA unit was only just about to move to Camden Town. Garcia went to Dublin, Ireland, and worked at the Bluth/Sullivan Studio on *Land Before Time* for nine months before he got a call from the Forum. He says that the atmosphere at Bluth was oppressive, as though it was a religious cult, whereas the atmosphere at the Forum was very nice.

After *Roger Rabbit*, Garcia worked at Amblimation on *An American Tail: Fievel Goes West*. He later went to Los Angeles and worked at Disney on *Aladdin*, *Pocahontas*, *The Hunchback of Notre Dame*, *Hercules*, *Tarzan*, and *Fantasia 2000*. Garcia and several other Disney animators had the chance to work with an idol, Chuck Jones, on a couple of Warner Bros. shorts, *Chariots of Fur* and *Another Froggy Evening*. They jumped at the moonlighting opportunity but used aliases. Garcia was credited as Ralph E. Newman, an alias he also used for some animation work on *Mrs. Doubtfire* (1993).

Garcia wrote and directed the shorts, *The Tell-Tale Heart* (2005) and *The Fall of the House of Usher* (2012), and the feature animated film *Extraordinary Tales* (2015). He was the animation director on *Americano* (2016).

Michael Giaimo graduated from CalArts and joined Disney during the turmoil of the early 1980s. He worked on *The Black Cauldron*, but was happy to move into special projects. He was part of the Darrell Van Citter/Chris Buck team for *Fun with Mr. Future*, *Roger Rabbit* development (1982–84), and *Sport Goofy in Soccermania*. He left Disney to work on *The Brave Little Toaster*, the Warner Bros. short *Box Office Bunny*, and Kroyer's *FernGully: The Last Rainforest*. He was back at Disney for character design and visual development on *Pocahontas* and, later, on *Home on the Range*. He came back to Disney again, to serve as art director on *Frozen*.

George Gibbs got his start in show business in 1966, as a special effects assistant on Gerry Anderson's science fiction puppet television series *Thunderbirds*. He had worked on many films, including *Superman* (1978), a couple from the Pink Panther series, Monty Python's *The Meaning of Life* (1983), *Brazil* (1985), and *Labyrinth* (1986). He had won an Oscar for *Indiana Jones and the Temple of Doom* (1984), but he had also managed to be attached to the problem-plagued film *Ishtar* (1987). Compared to *Ishtar*, *Who Framed Roger Rabbit* was a dream assignment, mostly because of Zemeckis's passion for the film and the clarity with which he communicated his vision. Gibbs ended up with another Oscar.

Since *Roger Rabbit*, Gibbs has worked on films such as *A Fish Called Wanda*, *Indiana Jones and the Last Crusade*, *Aliens 3*, *Patriot Games*, *101 Dalmatians*, *The Saint*, and *The League of Extraordinary Gentlemen*.

Eric Goldberg majored in illustration at the Pratt Institute in Brooklyn then got on to the crew of *Raggedy Ann & Andy: A Musical Adventure*, which was directed by Richard Williams. He later went to London to work at Richard Williams Animation as a director-animator on commercials and film titles. Goldberg eventually left the studio, but Williams got him back to work on *Ziggy's Gift* in Los Angeles. Goldberg moved to Los Angeles to work on the 1982 Emmy Award-winning television Christmas special. Goldberg returned to London after completing *Ziggy's Gift* and co-founded Pizazz Pictures, developing a worldwide clientele with smart commercials done using a wide variety of techniques.

Goldberg was coaxed to Disney with being offered to animate the Genie in *Aladdin*. He was the co-director of *Pocahontas*. He had an abiding affection for Warner Bros. characters and took the opportunity to work with Chuck Jones by moonlighting on *Chariots of Fur* as "Claude Rains." Meanwhile, he directed and animated two segments of *Fantasia 2000*:

"Rhapsody in Blue" and "The Carnival of the Animals." He left Disney to be the animation director on *Looney Tunes: Back in Action* and spent time at Warner Bros. developing *Where the Wild Things Are*. He did the animation in the Disneyland Main Street Cinema attraction, *Disneyland: The First 50 Magical Years* and the *Gran Fiesta Tour Starring The Three Caballeros*, and he worked with Kurtz & Co. on the titles for *The Pink Panther*.

Goldberg came back to Disney for *The Princess and the Frog* and has worked on *Winnie the Pooh*, as well as special hand-drawn projects such as the short *Get a Horse!* and the title animation for *Moana*. He is responsible for a Disney-themed couch gag for *The Simpsons* (2016).

Goldberg received the Winsor McCay Award in 2010.

Marc Gordon-Bates was the first graduate of the Gobelins film school to be a Disney animator. He worked in Paris on the Asterix films, *Asterix and Caesar* and *Asterix in Britain*. Chuck Gammage introduced Gordon-Bates to Dick Williams. Williams asked Gordon-Bates to help with finishing a couple of scenes for a Frankenberry commercial before bringing him on board the *Roger Rabbit* crew at the Forum. Gordon-Bates designed the Dum-Dum Bullets and animated primarily on the weasels.

Gordon-Bates has remained active in the animation industry. He worked as a director for the *W.I.T.C.H.* television series (2004–2005) and was a storyboard artist for the *Wibbly Pig* television series (2009–2010).

Stan Green (1921–1997) joined Disney in the 1950s and worked on *Sleeping Beauty*. Green worked at a number of different studios when Disney downsized the Animation Department. He was production designer and one of the directors on *The Lone Ranger* television series (1969) at Halas and Batchelor. Art Babbitt and Bill Tytla also directed several of the episodes. Green was the designer on the television movie *Hey, Hey, Hey, It's Fat Albert* (1969) for Campbell-Silver-Cosby. He did layout at Hanna-Barbera on the *Josie and the Pussycats* (1970) and the *Pebbles and Bamm-Bamm Show* (1971) television series. Green returned to Disney and was the key assistant animator to Milt Kahl on *Robin Hood* and *The Rescuers*.

After *Roger Rabbit*, he was a character assistant on *The Prince and the Pauper*. He went to Germany to work on *The Magic Voyage* and was a key animator and sequence director. Similar to his role on *Roger Rabbit*, he was an animation consultant on *The Magic Sword: Quest for Camelot*. An opportunity to direct on another project came his way just before he died in 1997.

Eric Guaglione worked for Dream Quest Images (DQI), a visual effect company in Santa Barbara, with credits including *Twilight Zone: The Movie* (1983), *Gremlins* (1984), and *Indiana Jones and the Temple of Doom* (1984). DQI was eventually purchased by Disney and merged into its own computer visual effects group as the Secret Lab. The organization worked on *Dinosaur* (2000) and a few of other films before being shut down by Disney. Guaglione worked at Santa Barbara Studios (SBS) on the film *Star Trek: Generations* (1994) and on various *Star Trek* television series: *Star Trek: The Next Generation* (1994), *Star Trek: Deep Space Nine* (1992–94), and *Star Trek: Voyage* (1995–96).

He moved to the Disney Studios in Florida to provide digital visual effects and computer animation. He worked on *Mulan*, *The Magic Lamp 3D*, *Lilo & Stitch*, and *Brother Bear*.

After the Florida studio was closed, he worked with Animal Logic on *Legend of the Guardians*. He relocated to Helsinki, Finland, with Rovio, as supervising director on the *Angry Birds Toons* and the *Angry Birds Stella* (2013–16) television series.

Don Hahn grew up near Disneyland, but his family moved up to Burbank when he was in high school. He got a summer intern position at the Disney Studios in the mid-1970s, working in the animation morgue. The pace at the studio was slow, and the creative talent wasn't always challenged; some left. Hahn was hired at Disney in 1976. One of his first jobs was working for Woolie Reitherman, fetching coffee and being Woolie's "man Friday," a runner, or traffic, position. Before long, Hahn was sitting in on production meetings and eventually became Reitherman's assistant director on *The Rescuers*. As production scaled back, he rolled over to become Don Bluth's assistant director on *Pete's Dragon*. So, by the time that Peter Schneider was looking for somebody with experience to guide him in discussions about live-action/animation combination with Amblin, Hahn was the last man standing. He did an excellent job as associate producer in charge of animation on *Who Framed Roger Rabbit* and went on to great things in Disney.

Hahn produced *Beauty and the Beast*, *The Lion King*, *The Hunchback of Notre Dame*, *Fantasia 2000*, *Atlantis: The Lost Empire*, and *The Haunted Mansion*. He produced the shorts, *Lorenzo*, *One by One*, and *The Little Match Girl*. He produced and directed the documentary *Waking Sleeping Beauty*. He founded his own production company, Stone Circle Productions, and has been executive producer on the Disneynature film series, *Frankenweenie*, *Malificent*, and Beauty and the Beast. He has been busy directing and producing many documentary films. His 2017 documentary film, *The Gamble House*, was nominated for an Emmy award.

Hahn has written several books: *Dancing Corndogs in the Night*, *Animation Magic*, *Alchemy of Animation*, *Drawn to Life*, and *Brainstorm*. He has received honorary doctorates from St. Xavier University (2011), Laguna College (2012), and Chapman University's Dodge College of Film and Media Arts (2017).

Joe Haidar grew up in Scarborough, a suburb east of Toronto, and graduated from Sheridan College in 1982—in the same class as Roger Chiasson's brother, Claude—and got a job at Atkinson Film Arts, also known as Bud Crawley Films, in Ottawa. Atkinson was doing service work for US companies at the time. Haidar left because he wanted to work on a feature film and got on to *Care Bears Movie II* at Nelvana in Toronto. He then went to London in the hopes of getting work doing storyboards but it proved difficult because he wasn't in a film union. Six months later, he got a call from Allen Cameron for storyboarding on *Highlander* (1986). As Sheridan College graduates began to fill the ranks of the *Roger Rabbit* crew, Haidar got a call.

After *Roger Rabbit*, Haidar went to Disney in Glendale on *Tummy Trouble* and then worked on *The Rescuers Down Under*, *Beauty and the Beast*, *Aladdin*, *The Lion King*, *Pocahontas*, *Mulan*, *Atlantis: The Lost Empire*, and *Home on the Range*. He was one of the Disney animators who moonlighted on Chuck Jones's *Chariots of Fur*. Haidar used the pseudonym Margaret Trudeaux. He also worked on *Looney Tunes: Back in Action*.

He worked on *Curious George*, *Enchanted*, and as a storyboard artist for Illumination on *Hop*. Haidar wrote, directed, and produced a live-action/animation combination short *Animated American* (2008).

Russell Hall received art training at Leeds College prior to starting at RWA. He was apprentice to Ken Harris, the famous retired Warner Bros. animator who Williams brought over to London to develop the skills of the artists at RWA and to work on *The Thief*. Hall also worked on *The Thief* when there was any downtime between commercials. He was the person primarily responsible for the Discovery Train commercial for the government of Canada in 1977 and for the Count Pushkin Vodka commercials. He was becoming a star within RWA, with fully one-third of the RWA showreel consisting of Hall's work. Following the pattern of other animators who aspired to more control and acknowledgment than what was available to them at RWA, Hall left RWA early in 1987 to set up his own company. He was persuaded to work with Williams in the new Disney unit at the Forum and was given primary responsibility for the Jessica character. Hall had his own large office in which he worked with his own assistants. It was clear to the others at the Forum that he and Williams often didn't get along, but the two of them "agreed to disagree" and put their energies into this special project.

After *Roger Rabbit*, Hall operated his own studio, doing commercials and contract film projects. He worked on *The Magic Sword: Quest for* Camelot and *The Iron Giant*. He worked on a television movie, *The Cunning Little Vixen* (2003).

Alyson Hamilton was at the University of Newcastle upon Tyne when she heard that Richard Williams's Dick's Six jazz band was coming to perform. She took her portfolio to the performance, where Williams offered her a job. She worked at RWA as Russell Hall's in-betweener for eighteen months prior to the move to the Forum. Hamilton and Bella Bremner shared Hall's office during the production of *Who Framed Roger Rabbit*.

Hamilton worked on *The Thief and the Cobbler* and *The Magic Sword: Quest for Camelot*. She did freelance work on commercials, but worked on another film, *Miss Potter*, for Passion Pictures in 2006.

She then left the animation industry to focus on her first love: garden and landscape design.

Bridgette Hartley (1963–1992) moved to Florida in 1989 to be part of the startup of the Disney Studios in the Disney/MGM theme park at Walt Disney World. She worked on *Roller Coaster Rabbit, The Prince and the Pauper*, and *The Rescuers Down Under*. She died of cancer in 1992. She was much loved by her colleagues at WDFA-Florida. Max Howard managed to get approval for construction of a garden used as a cast break area at the studio. Much of the construction and planting was done on a volunteer basis by the crew. Max Howard and Roy E. Disney were on hand for the dedication of Brigitte's Garden in November 1994.

Mark Henn graduated from CalArts and joined Disney in 1980. He started out on *The Fox and the Hound* as an in-betweener to Glen Keane. He worked on *Mickey's Christmas Carol, The Black Cauldron, The Great Mouse Detective*, and *Oliver & Company*. He was interested in going to London for *Roger Rabbit*, but only a limited number of Disney animators were asked to go and all were bachelors. Henn had started a family by that time. He worked on *The Little Mermaid*, then moved to Florida in 1989 as part of the startup of the new Disney studios at Walt Disney World. He was featured in the "The House Meets the Mouse" episode of the television series *Full House* in 1993.

Henn directed the short *John Henry* (2000) while in Florida. He was brought back to Disney-Burbank when the Florida studio was closed and did some work on *Home on the Range* as well as consulting on direct-to-video productions from the international Disney animation studios. He worked on *Meet the Robinsons, Enchanted, The Princess and the Frog, The Ballad of Nessie, Winnie the Pooh, Wreck-It Ralph,* Tinkerbell in *Saving Mr. Banks, Get a Horse!, Frozen, Big Hero 6,* and *Zootopia.*

Henn is an accomplished sculptor, specializing in bronzes of historical and western themes. He received the Winsor McCay Award in 2012.

Steve Hickner learned his craft in the television animation factories of the early 1980s. He worked on such series as *The Kid Power Hour with Shazam!, The New Adventures of Zorro,* and *Blackstar* at Filmation; *The Little Rascals, Pac-Man,* and *The Dukes* at Hanna-Barbera; and *Saturday Supercade* at Ruby-Spears. He worked on *Ziggy's Gift* with Richard Williams and then was back at Filmation as an assistant supervisor on *He-Man and the Masters of the Universe.* He wanted to improve his situation and spent a year working on his portfolio. When he was ready, he submitted his portfolio to Disney and was hired by Don Hahn as a trainee/in-betweener on *The Black Cauldron.*

Hickner worked on the reboot of *Sport Goofy in Soccermania* and then worked on Disney's Richard Dreyfuss-hosted Constitution television special, *Funny, You Don't Look 200: A Constitutional Vaudeville* (1987). It was during that production that Hickner heard there might be a Los Angeles-based unit for *Roger Rabbit.* He went to Peter Schneider to ask whether he could be a part of it. Hickner ended up being the second person on the Los Angeles unit (also known as the Glendale unit), starting in August 1987. Don Hahn asked Hickner to help out in London and on November 7, he was at the Forum. He organized the final toon crowd scene, which was a logistical nightmare. He was back in Los Angeles, working on *The Little Mermaid,* at the time of the London wrap party.

Hickner joined Amblimation when it started up in London and was producer on *American Tail: Fievel Goes West, We're Back! A Dinosaurs Story,* and *Balto.* He moved to DreamWorks in Glendale when Amblimation was closed, and was director on *The Prince of Egypt,* the television show *Father of the Pride,* and *Bee Movie.* He was also a story artist on *Kung Fu Panda, Mr. Peabody & Sherman,* and *Home.*

Hickner is the author of *Animating Your Career* (Brigantine Media, 2013).

Bob Hoskins (1942–2014) was born in Bury St. Edmunds, in Suffolk, where his mother was living for safety from the London Blitz of World War II, but he was raised in London. He had an interesting coming-of-age, which included a job as a fire-eater in a circus. He spent two years in Syria, living amongst Bedouin tribes, and he spent six months on a kibbutz in Israel. As an actor, he often played an archetypal "Cockney bully hiding a heart of shining gold." He played a sleazy rock 'n' roll artist's agent in the film based on Pink Floyd's album *The Wall*. In 1986/87, he received the BAFTA and Golden Globe Awards, as well as an Oscar nomination for Best Actor for his work in *Mona Lisa*.

Hoskins directed *The Raggedy Rawney*, a World War II gypsy drama that was released in 1988. He was writing the screenplay while he was in San Francisco filming bluescreen Toontown scenes for *Roger Rabbit* at ILM. He has also written plays under the name, Robert Williams.

Hoskins's film credits include: *The Wall* (1982), *Brazil* (1985), *Mona Lisa* (1986), *Who Framed Roger Rabbit*, *The Raggedy Rawney* (1988), *Mermaids* (1990), *Hook* (1991), *Super Mario Bros.* (1993), *Nixon* (1995), *Enemy at the Gates* (2001), *A Christmas Carol* (2009), the Neverland television mini-series (2011), and *Snow White and the Huntsman* (2012).

Max Howard was a child actor, from the age of eleven, and then switched to stage management and directing live theater. He came to know Peter Schneider, who was also managing a theater production in London. Schneider was hired as the president of Disney Animation in October 1985. About a year after having started at Disney, when it became clear that the animation for *Roger Rabbit* would be produced in London, Schneider called his friend in London, Max Howard.

At the conclusion of *Who Framed Roger Rabbit*, Max Howard was called to go to Los Angeles and was offered the job of overseeing the Disney animation studios outside of Los Angeles. Howard accepted the job, with the first order of business being to establish the Disney animation studio at the Disney-MGM Studios theme park in Walt Disney World.

Howard was appointed as president of Warner Bros. Feature Animation in 1995. He shepherded *Space Jam*, *The Magic Sword: Quest for Camelot*, and *The Iron Giant*. He moved to DreamWorks and was executive producer on *Spirit: Stallion of the Cimarron*. He was president of Exodus Film Group and produced *Igor* (2008). He was an executive producer on *Saving Santa* (2013). Howard operates a very active consulting business. In 2015, he started working with the DeTao Group in China to develop feature animated films with Chinese content.

Howard received an honorary doctorate from Teesside University in UK in 2010.

Michael Humphries studied at the Art Center College of Design in Pasadena. He was a caricature artist at Disneyland in the 1970s. He worked as a background artist on many television series at Hanna-Barbera both before and after *Roger Rabbit*. He worked on *Jetsons: The Movie* in 1990. At Disney, he worked on *The Lion King, Fantasia 2000*, and *The Princess and the Frog*. He was the production designer on *Open Season* at Sony and visual development artist on *The Simpsons Movie* at 20th Century Fox. He worked on *My Little Pony: The Movie*.

He is very busy as an illustrator and fine artist.

Chris Jenkins grew up in Wales and came to London to study scientific illustration at Middlesex University. He took a brief class in animation in his first year, with Andrew Brownlow. While at Middlesex University, he met Alan Lee, a master of fantasy illustration and, later, the concept artist for the *Lord of the Rings* film trilogy and subsequent *The Hobbit* films, and developed an interest in fantasy illustration. A student friend from his first year mentioned hearing some scuttlebutt about the *Roger Rabbit* production. Jenkins was at a student art exhibition in London when he bumped into Andrew Brownlow, who was already on the *Roger Rabbit* crew. Brownlow arranged for Jenkins to get an interview with Chris Knott, and he was hired in the Effects group on the spot.

After *Roger Rabbit*, he was brought to Disney Feature Animation in Glendale, where he worked as an effects animator on *The Little Mermaid, The Prince and the Pauper, Beauty and the Beast, Aladdin*, the *Roger Rabbit* short *Trail Mix-Up, The Lion King, Pocahontas*, and *Hercules*. He was the visual effects supervisor on *The Hunchback of Notre Dame*.

Jenkins moved to Sony Pictures Imageworks, where he was writer and producer on *Surf's Up* and then spent some time at Blue Sky Studios, developing *Rio*. He moved to DreamWorks in 2011, where he produced *Home*. He worked in Story on *The Ark and the Aardvark* (2018) for Unified Pictures, and wrote and directed *Duck Duck Goose* (2018) for Original Force. He worked on *Ralph Breaks the Internet: Wreck-It Ralph 2* (2018).

Ed Jones started at ILM as a laboratory technician on *The Empire Strikes Back* (1980) and *Raiders of the Lost Ark* (1981). He worked in optical line-up at ILM on films such as *Star Trek II: The Wrath of Khan* (1982), *Star Wars: Return of the Jedi* (1983), *Indiana Jones and the Temple of Doom* (1984), and

Young Sherlock Holmes (1985). He was the optical photography supervisor on *The Witches of Eastwick* (1987) and executive in charge of postproduction on *The Hunt for Red October* (1990).

Jones was the visual effects supervisor for Universal on *The Public Eye* (1992), and for Warner Bros. on *Space Jam* (1996) and *Cats & Dogs* (2001). He was an executive producer on *Happy Feet* (Warner Bros., 2006).

Marty Katz served in Vietnam and later worked at ABC, Quinn Martin Productions, and Paramount. He joined Disney in 1985 at senior vice president of motion picture and television production. He started his own production company in 1992. It was initially located at the Disney Studios, but he moved to independent offices in 1996.

Jeffrey Katzenberg worked for the New York mayoral campaign of John Lindsay at the age of fourteen. He started at Paramount in 1974, soon thereafter becoming assistant to Barry Diller. He became president of production under Michael Eisner. Eisner brought Katzenberg to Disney, where he was charged with turning around Feature Animation. Things went sideways after the death of Frank Wells in a helicopter crash in 1994. Katzenberg was not promoted to president of Disney, as he had expected. He left and co-founded DreamWorks with Steven Spielberg and David Geffen.

Katzenberg promoted CGI and switched DreamWorks to CGI productions exclusively. DreamWorks Animation was spun off in an IPO in 2004. It was acquired by NBC Universal in 2016.

Katzenberg received the Winsor McCay Award in 2009.

Mark Kausler was an assistant animator on *Yellow Submarine* (1968). He worked with Bakshi on *Heavy Traffic* and *Coonskin*. He worked on *The Rescuers* at Disney and worked freelance on *The Black Cauldron* and *The Great Mouse Detective*. He animated on the "Family Dog" episode of *Steven Spielberg's Amazing Stories* and on *Sport Goofy in Soccermania* in 1987. He worked at Warner Bros. in 1988. He worked with Jerry Rees on the Disney theme park productions *Back to Neverland* and *Michael and* Mickey.

Kausler worked on *Tummy Trouble* in Glendale and then moved to Florida in 1989 for the opening of the new Disney studio, where he worked on *Roller Coaster Rabbit* and other unproduced *Roger Rabbit* sequels. He worked on Disney features while in Florida and worked on the *Roger Rabbit* short *Trail Mix-Up* after he'd moved back to California.

Kausler wrote and directed *It's the Cat (2004)* and *There Must Be Some Other Cat* (2013).

Kathleen Kennedy graduated from San Diego State University in telecommunications and film and was hired by Steven Spielberg as his secretary in 1978. She was an associate on *Raiders of the Lost Ark* (1981), an associate producer on *Poltergeist* (1982), and a producer on *E.T.—The Extra-Terrestrial* (1982). Kennedy, along with Spielberg and her husband Frank Marshall, founded Amblin Entertainment in 1981. She was president of Amblin until 1992, when she and Marshall formed the Kennedy/Marshall Company. She stepped down from Kennedy/Marshall in 2012.

In October 2012, Kennedy became president of Lucasfilm, now a subsidiary of Disney, and brand manager of the *Star Wars* franchise.

Marty Kline has been a storyboard artist and illustrator since 1977, when he worked on John Dykstra's *Apogee*. He worked on a freelance basis for many years, finally joining Sony Imageworks in 1995. He has been on his own since 2007.

Chris Knott was born in Yorkshire and went to a polytechnic school in London for psychology. He met Sam Sewell, who was to become his life-long partner. Their flatmate worked at Halas and Batchelor, and Knott often helped with work she brought home. He showed a real aptitude and found it more satisfying than his studies, so after two years he left school and went to work at Halas and Batchelor. He ultimately found his way to Richard Williams Animation, where he eventually became the special effects guru. He was the animation special effects supervisor on *Who Framed Roger Rabbit*. After *Roger Rabbit*, he worked at Passion Pictures and on *The Thief and the Cobbler*.

Elaine Koo was born in Hong Kong, but her family moved to England when she was in high school. She went to art college in the early 1980s and worked on the 1982 production of Briggs's *The Snowman*. She also worked on Paul McCartney's *Rupert, the Bear* and spent some time at RWA, working periodically on *The Thief*. As with many animators from the Soho commercial community, she was asked to take the in-betweener test for *Roger Rabbit* to ensure that she could fit into the style they were looking for. After *Roger Rabbit*, she worked on *Freddie as F.R.O.7*.

Bill Kopp graduated from CalArts after winning a student Oscar in both 1984 and 1985. His friend from CalArts, Wes Archer, called to say that Klasky/Csupo had been contracted to provide three thirty-second animated bumper segments per week for *The Tracey Ullman Show* summer replacement show. The bumpers were to be written by Matt Groening, creator of the comic strip *Life in Hell*, and M. K. (Mary) Brown, a frequent contributor to *National Lampoon*. Kopp brought in another friend, David Silverman, and the three of them "did it all" for the first season of four shows. Groening created *The Simpsons* segment and Brown created the *Dr. N!Godatu* segment. The style evolved quickly over those first four shows. They started a new segment each week, with each segment completed over a four-week time schedule. It was a very hectic situation made more intimidating when the popularity of *The Simpsons* segment gave rise to discussion about a series of its own.

Kopp was one of the writers of the *Roger Rabbit* shorts. He created, wrote, and produced the television series *Eek! The Cat* (1992), *The Shnookums and Meat Funny Cartoon Show* (1995), and *Mad Jack the Pirate* (1998).

Dorse Lanpher (1935–2011) entered the Art Center School in the fall of 1953 and in 1956 went to Disney in Burbank with his portfolio under his arm. He had an interview with Andy Engman and was assigned to the Effects Department, under the supervision of Josh Meador. He worked on shorts such as *Paul Bunyan*, *Wind Wagon Smith*, and *Our Friend, the Atom* until he finally got onto *Sleeping Beauty*. He was drafted into the US Army before *Sleeping Beauty* was completed and came back to the Disney Studios in April of 1960. His stint in the army saved him from the general layoffs that happened after *Sleeping Beauty* finished. He worked on effects in *101 Dalmatians* and even did some character animation in *The Sword in the Stone*. He took on freelance work as often as he could, and eventually left Disney. He was back at Disney in 1975, on *The Rescuers*.

Lanpher left Disney in September 1979, along with Bluth and company and worked on *Banjo the Woodpile Cat*, *Xanadu*, *The Secret of NIMH*, *An American Tail*, *Land Before Time*, and the video games *Space Ace* and *Dragon's Lair*. Lanpher and his wife, Vera, came to London for *Roger Rabbit* from Sullivan/Bluth in Dublin. After *Roger Rabbit*, Lanpher went to Disney in Glendale to work on *Oliver & Company*, *The Little Mermaid*, *Beauty and the Beast*, *Aladdin*, *The Lion King*, *Pocahontas*, *The Hunchback of Notre Dame*, *Hercules*, *Mulan*, *Tarzan*, *Fantasia 2000*, *The Emperor's New Groove*, *Atlantis: The Lost Empire*, and *Home on the Range*. He also did effects on the WDFA-F *Roger Rabbit* shorts *Roller Coaster Rabbit* and *Trail Mix-Up*.

His wrote an autobiography, *Flyin' Chunks and Other Things to Duck* (2010).

Vera Law (later Lanpher) became a friend of Lorna Pomeroy through a mutual interest in needlepoint. Lorna was part of the group working on *Banjo the Woodpile Cat* in Don Bluth's garage and suggested that Vera might be interested in helping out. Law learned about animation in those garage sessions and later got a job at Hanna-Barbera. When Bluth found out, he arranged for her to be hired by Disney and she started as a clean-up artist on *The Small One* and was even the live-action reference model for Mary.

Law left Disney in 1979, along with Bluth. She, along with husband Dorse Lanpher, left Sullivan/Bluth in Dublin to work on *Who Framed Roger Rabbit* in London. After *Roger Rabbit*, she moved with Dorse to Disney in Glendale and was an assistant animator on many of the same films. She married another Disney artist, Dave Pacheco, in 2003. Vera Pacheco was clean-up supervisor on *Chicken Little*, *The Princess and the Frog*, and *Winnie the Pooh*.

Michael Lantieri has a long filmography that includes *Blue Thunder*, *Last Starfighter*, *Star Trek: The Voyage Home*, *Who Framed Roger Rabbit*, *Indiana Jones and the Last Crusade*, *Back to the Future Part II*, *Back to the Future Part III*, *Hook*, *Death Becomes Her*, *Bram Stoker's Dracula*, *Jurassic Park* (for which he received an Oscar), *The Flintstones*, *Casper*, *Congo*, *Mars Attacks!*, *The Lost World: Jurassic Park*, *Mousehunt*, *Wild Wild West*, *The Astronaut's Wife*, *A.I. Artificial Intelligence*, *Jurassic Park III*, *Minority Report*, *Hulk*, *The Terminal*, *The Polar Express*, *Superman Returns*, *Pirates of the Caribbean: Dead Man's Chest*, *Beowolf*, *Get Smart*, *A Christmas Carol*, *Alice in Wonderland*, *Mars Needs Moms*, *Flight*, *San Andreas*, and *Jurassic World*.

Joe Lanzisero graduated from CalArts and was an animator at Disney from 1979 to 1986, working on *The Fox and the Hound*, *Fun with Mr. Future*, *The Black Cauldron*, *The Great Mouse Detective*, and *Sport Goofy in Soccermania*.

He moved to Walt Disney Imagineering and was responsible for Toontown at Disneyland and Tokyo Disneyland. He retired as senior vice president in charge of WDI projects at Disney Cruise Lines and Hong Kong Disneyland, in the summer of 2016. He continues to work as a consultant on themed entertainment.

Cal Leduc was born in Penetanguishene, north of Toronto near Georgian Bay, and grew up in Mississauga, a city just west of Toronto. He started at Sheridan College in 1981. He graduated in 1984 and got a job at Atkinson on *Raccoons*. While there, he also worked with cartoonist Lynne Johnston on a *For Better or For Worse* Christmas television special (*The Bestest Present*, 1985) and a *Babar* Christmas television special (*Babar and Father Christmas*, 1986). Leduc also spent some time working on the Bagdasarian production, *The Chipmunk Adventure*. Leduc then went to Pascal Blais in Montreal.

Leduc and Nik Ranieri went to Dublin in 1987 to try getting on at Sullivan/Bluth. Instead, they joined the *Roger Rabbit* crew in London. After *Roger Rabbit*, Leduc went to Disney in Glendale and was there until 2003. He also worked for Paramount on *Barnyard*. Leduc has taught at the Vancouver Animation School since 2010.

Richard Leon was twenty years old and had been out of school for two or three years before working as a runner on *Roger Rabbit*. He wrote to Robert Watts before he'd ever heard of *Roger Rabbit*. He was constantly researching opportunities and saw a notice in *Film Log*, a film industry production sheet, about the assembly of a crew for *Roger Rabbit*. He got in touch with Max Howard very early in the staffing process. Howard took Leon on in the spring of 1987, in the very early days of *Roger Rabbit* at the Forum. He was busy with the initial set-up of the studio, but the production hadn't really started to gear up yet and he was let go after the initial flurry of activity. He went off to work on other things but kept in touch with Max Howard.

Meanwhile, as production geared up a team of runners was established: Frazer Diamond, Harry Elvin, and Catherine Stewart. In early 1988, Diamond left the team for other opportunities and Leon came in to replace him for the balance of the production.

Leon operates a publicity firm out of Brighton.

Mery-et Lescher applied after being given a heads-up by Alex Kupershmidt, a friend from college, and started at the Disney Florida studio in April 1989—first, setting up the state-of-the-art Mechanical Concept animation camera. After the Disney Florida studio was closed in 2004, Lescher went to graduate school and is a doctoral candidate at Florida State University in the department of art history.

Fraser MacLean graduated from the Glasgow School of Art in 1983 with a degree in graphic design, although he did little graphic design and got more exposure to film and film editing. The Scottish Film Council administered the Scottish Film Training Trust, which provided grants for successful candidates to get a good grounding in camera, sound, and editing. In 1985 he landed a job as a film editor at Sands Films. Sands is a studio known for the production of costumes for period pieces, but it also had a sound-stage and a fully equipped studio. It was a great experience, and MacLean worked on the six-hour movie adaptation of Charles Dickens's *Little Dorrit*, for which Alec Guinness received an Academy Award nomination as Best Actor in a Supporting Role. There was a lull in the British film industry at the time, so MacLean bought *Screen International* magazine each week in search of new opportunities.

MacLean applied for *Roger Rabbit* after seeing an advertisement in the back of the magazine. Don Hahn told him that they didn't need additional film editing, but asked if MacLean could draw. MacLean dusted off his portfolio and took it in to the Forum in Camden Town. Hahn called Chris Knott, the supervisor of the Effects Department, and MacLean was hired—on the same day, in July 1987, as Jenkins and Graham Burt.

After *Roger Rabbit*, MacLean worked at Passion Pictures for a time, then worked for Warner Bros. in Los Angeles on *Space Jam* and for Disney in Glendale on *Tarzan*. He wrote the book *Setting the Scene: The Art and Evolution of Animation Layout* (Chronicle, 2011).

MacLean teaches art and animation history at Nord University in Steinkjer, Norway. He is one of the co-founders of Animation Centrifuge, an animation education website. He is very active as a judge in international animation festivals.

Greg Manwaring took the foundation program at the Otis-Parsons School of Art and Design. He then got a full class scholarship at CalArts, and was in the class of 1986 with Tony Fucile, Klay Hall, and Ralph Eggleston.

He in-betweened on *Star Chaser: The Legend of Orin* (1985) for Bill Kroyer after his freshman year. After his sophomore year, he got on to the crew of *Sport Goofy in Soccermania* at Disney. After his junior year, he got into the Disney Training Program and worked on *Oliver & Company*. He went on to work on "Family Dog," with Brad Bird, and did not return to CalArts.

He visited Andreas Deja and Phil Nibbelink in London in early July 1987, and bumped into Richard Williams, who asked him to do a Baby Herman animation test. He was hired on the spot and started on *Roger Rabbit*.

Manwaring worked on the *Roger Rabbit* short *Trail Mix-Up* at the Disney Studios in Florida. He worked on *The Iron Giant* at Warner Bros. He started FunToons Animation and relocated back to Germany in 2000. He is an accomplished magician and worked on *The Illusionist*. He directed the *Talking Tom & Friends* television series (2015–16).

Frank Marshall graduated from UCLA in 1968. He played on UCLA's soccer team. He was mentored by Peter Bogdanovich on *The Last Picture Show*
(1971) and was associate producer on the director's *Paper Moon* (1973). He
was the line producer on Martin Scorsese's *The Last Waltz* (1978). Marshall
co-founded Amblin Entertainment in 1981, with Steven Spielberg and
Kathleen Kennedy. His first directorial outing was *Arachnophobia* (1990).
Along with his now wife, Kathleen Kennedy, he formed the Kennedy/
Marshall Company in 1991. Marshall has also directed *Alive* (1993), *Congo*
(1995), and *Eight Below* (2006).

Marshall has a long list of producer and executive producer credits that
include: *Raiders of the Lost Ark* and the rest of the *Indiana Jones* film series,
Poltergeist, the *Back to the Future* film series, *The Color Purple*, *Empire of the
Sun*, *Who Framed Roger Rabbit*, *Hook*, *The Sixth Sense*, the Jason *Bourne* film
series, *Signs*, *Seabiscuit*, *The Curious Case of Benjamin Button*, *Jurassic World*,
The BFG, *Sully*, and *Assassin's Creed*.

Marshall is an accomplished magician, going by the names Dr. Fantasy
and DJ Master Frank.

Barbara McCormack was the Paint and Trace supervisor at Richard Wil-
liams Animation and carried on that function on *Who Framed Roger Rabbit*.
She had an exceptional color sense and did color model development for
The Little Mermaid at Disney. She was the color model supervisor on *The
Thief and the Cobbler*.

Brenda McKie-Chat and Jacques Muller started their own small studio
in Sydney, Australia. McKie was born in Sydney and was educated at East
Sydney Art School and the New York Studio School of Drawing, Painting
and Sculpture. She was an assistant animator on *Tarzoon, la honte de la
jungle* (*Shame of the Jungle*, 1975), the French/Belgian production that was
the first foreign film with an X rating to receive a wide release in the US. She
went back to Australia, working with Muller at Yoram Gross Films and at
Burbank Studio. McKie and Muller were approached by Kennedy-Marshall
for a quote on the film *Babe*, which was ultimately not made until 1995.
They made a four-minute trailer for a feature film that was taken to Cannes,
but wasn't picked up for production. Their friend, Alain Costa, who had
worked with them in Australia, was already working on *Roger Rabbit* and
encouraged them to come to London.

After *Roger Rabbit*, she animated at Amblimation on *An American Tail:
Fievel Goes West*, *We're Back! A Dinosaur Story*, and *Balto*. She went back to

Australia and was the overseas animation director on the *King of the Hill* television series (2007–2009).

Uli Meyer had no formal training in art or animation. He was self-taught, making films as a kid, with a Super 8 camera. He came to know Hans Bacher, a professor in Essen (Germany), and Harald Siepermann, working with them in a co-operative they called MadTParty in Düsseldorf. Bacher had become a professional acquaintance of Richard Williams, a relationship that had been cemented by their mutual love of Milt Kahl's animation and their hobby as animation art collectors. Bacher had been privy to one of the earliest discussions of *Roger Rabbit* in Williams's Soho Square studio and had later extolled the talent of his young colleague. Meyer went to London in late 1986 at Williams's invitation. He was twenty-three years old at the time. He left *Who Framed Roger Rabbit* early and did not receive screen credit.

He helped to set up Amblimation, and in 1991, established his own studio, Ulimation, which eventually became Uli Meyer Animation. The studio was subcontracted for sequences on *FernGully: The Last Rainforest* and *Space Jam*. He did the animation for Disney's *Circle of Life* film at the Land pavilion in EPCOT at Walt Disney World, and he was contracted for sequences in the Mickey Mouse short *Runaway Brain*. Meyer did work on *Lost in Space*.

His studio was well-known for its high-quality commercials. Meyer was a storyboard artist on *King Arthur: Legend of the Sword* (2017).

Ron Miller was Walt Disney's son-in-law. He met Walt's daughter, Diane, while at the University of Southern California and they were married in 1954. He played one season in the NFL with the Los Angeles Rams but was convinced to work at the Disney Studios. He became the president of Walt Disney Productions in 1978 and CEO in 1983. He was ousted after a prolonged episode of corporate raiding.

Ron and Diane Miller developed the Silverado Vineyards winery in Napa Valley and established the Walt Disney Family Museum in The Presidio of San Francisco. They had seven children and thirteen grandchildren. Diane Disney Miller died on November 19, 2013.

Rob Minkoff graduated from CalArts and joined Disney in 1983. He worked on *The Black Caldron* (1985), *The Great Mouse Detective*, and *Sport Goody in Soccermania*. He was an animator on the "Family Dog" episode of

Steven Spielberg's Amazing Stories, the film *The Brave Little Toaster*, and the short *Technological Threat*.

Minkoff came back to Disney and directed two *Roger Rabbit* shorts, *Tummy Trouble* and *Roller Coaster Rabbit*. He directed the short *Mickey's Audition*, which was shown at the Main Street Cinema at the Disney theme parks. He then co-directed *The Lion King* with Roger Allers.

Minkoff left Disney to direct *Stuart Little* and *Stuart Little 2* for Sony. He directed *The Haunted Mansion*, a live-action film, for Disney. He directed *Mr. Peabody & Sherman* at DreamWorks.

Jacques Muller (1956–2018) grew up in France and, after doing his compulsory military service, got a job doing storyboards on the France 3 television series *Il était une fois . . . l'homme (Once Upon a Time . . . Man)* from 1978 to 1981. He worked briefly with Alain Costa at Grimault. He showed his portfolio to another Frenchman and was also enticed to go to Australia. Muller and Costa worked together at Burbank Studio in Sydney on *A Christmas Carol* (1982), *Great Expectations* (1983), and *Sherlock Holmes and the Baskerville Curse* (1983).

Muller stayed on in Sydney, working for Hanna-Barbera Australia and Yoram Gross Films, producers of *Dot and the Kangaroo*, *Blinky Bill*, and other television series. Muller started his own small studio, with Brenda McKie, in Sydney. Muller and McKie were approached by Kennedy-Marshall for a quote on the film *Babe*, which was ultimately not made until 1995. They made a four-minute trailer for a feature film that was taken to Cannes, but wasn't picked up for production. Costa got on the *Roger Rabbit* crew and convinced both Muller and McKie to come to London. On the strength of their work on the film trailer, they were hired at the Forum.

After *Roger Rabbit*, Muller took a position as manager of Character Art for Disney Mechandising in Europe. In January 1989 he flew to Los Angeles to animate on the *Roger Rabbit* short *Tummy Trouble*, *The Little Mermaid*, and *The Rescuers Down Under*. He went back to Europe and animated on *We're Back! A Dinosaurs Story*, *Thumbelina*, *The Pebble and the Penguin*, and *Space Jam*. Back in the US, he animated on *The Magic Sword: Quest for Camelot*, *Small Soldiers*, *Star Wars: Episode I—The Phantom Menace*, and *The Adventures of Rocky & Bullwinkle*. He was an animator on *The Illusionist*.

Muller was a senior lecturer at Nanyang Polytechnic SIDM school in Singapore. He did the cover art for Gary K. Wolf's book, *Who Wacked Roger Rabbit?* He published his autobiography, *40 Years of Animated Cartoons*, in April 2018. Not long afterwards, he moved back to France due to heart issues and died suddenly on November 4, 2018.

Roy Naisbitt's specialty was technical animation. A friend told him about a space film that was being made (in secret) at the MGM-Borehamwood studio, next to Elstree Studio, by Stanley Kubrick. The production was 2001: *A Space Odyssey* (1968), and it needed somebody who could airbrush. Naisbitt was thirty-five at the time and was expecting to work for five months, at double what he had been paid at his previous job. He ended up spending two years on the production, working with Douglas Trumbull on a variety of special effects. Naisbitt played water polo and one of the members of his team was Richard Williams's cameraman. RWA was doing the titles for *The Charge of the Light Brigade* at the time, and a scene required the animation of a paddle-wheel ship engine. Williams contacted Naisbitt after hearing about him being a technical animator and asked whether he could do the job. Naisbitt went to a science museum, found a paddle-wheel engine, and talked the museum staff into showing him how it worked. He animated the engine over the period of a couple of weeks and Williams was delighted with the results. Naisbitt joined RWA in 1968.

Administration and organization wasn't Williams's strong suit, and there was a void in the organization after Williams determined that RWA's first business manager, Omar Ali-Shah, had been stealing from him. Williams wanted somebody to coordinate the administrative aspects of the studio and Naisbitt took on the assignment in a three-month trial. The *Christmas Carol* project was being developed during this time. RWA won the Oscar in 1972 for that project, after which work on *The Thief* began in earnest. Naisbitt spent twelve years working on layout for *The Thief*, during which he worked out all of "the architectural stuff" and the war machine sequence. He was obsessed with the work, and the master "city drawing" was done on his own time at home.

Naisbitt did the layout for the opening Maroon cartoon, but much of his time during the production of *Who Framed Roger Rabbit* was spent at Richard Williams's small nearby studio, working on *The Thief*. Naisbitt was credited as art director on *The Thief and the Cobbler*. He did layout at Amblimation on Balto and also did layout on *Space Jam*. Neil Boyle brought Naisbitt out of retirement for his unique skills at layout on his animated short *The Last Belle*.

Rob Newman had worked for a number of years as an animator on the television series *Danger Mouse*, produced by Cosgrove Hall Films (an ITV company) in Manchester for Thames Television. He felt isolated and believed that the studio was failing. He was told about *Roger Rabbit* by his mate, Simon Turner, who had just been hired on as an in-betweener, and was hired to work on *Roger Rabbit* at the Forum in London.

After *Roger Rabbit*, Newman worked on *DuckTales the Movie: Treasure of the Lost Lamp* and *The Thief and the Cobbler*. He has been a storyboard artist for many television series.

Phil Nibbelink graduated from Western Washington State University and spent a year studying in Italy. He started at Disney in 1978, in the same training class as John Lasseter and Chris Buck. He was made an assisting animator and was assigned to Randy Cartwright's unit. He worked on *The Fox and the Hound* (1981) and *The Black Cauldron* (1985), but was in Story on *Oliver & Company* when Eisner, Wells, and Katzenberg came to Disney. *Oliver & Company* was put on hold when the new management insisted on massive story changes. Nibbelink was disenchanted with the new Disney management at the time that Williams and Zemeckis visited the studio. Nibbelink and Deja were good friends, and Nibbelink let them know of his interest. He had family in England and he was ready for a change, so he jumped at the chance to work on *Who Framed Roger Rabbit* in London. He was always wearing scarves.

After *Roger Rabbit*, he went to Germany as the director on a troubled production, *The Magic Voyage*, but came back to London to be a director at Amblimation on *An American Tail: Fievel Goes West* and *We're Back! A Dinosaur's Story*. He was developing *Cats*, based on the Andrew Lloyd Webber musical, when Amblimation closed. He was the animation director on *Casper* and worked on *The Iron Giant*. He wrote, directed, and single-handedly animated the feature films *Puss in Boots* (1999), *Leif Erickson, Discoverer of North America* (2000), and *Romeo & Juliet: Sealed with a Kiss* (2005). He was a storyboard artist on the *Wolverine and the X-Men* television series (2008) and *Animal Crackers* (2017).

Lori Benson-Noda worked as an in-betweener on *The Great Mouse Detective* and was an assistant animator on *Sport Goofy in Soccermania*. She was a production coordinator and an assistant animator in the *Who Framed Roger Rabbit* Glendale unit. She was an assistant animator on Disney features from *Oliver & Company* through to *Dinosaur*. She was an assistant animator on *Looney Tunes: Back in Action*.

Floyd Norman was hired by Disney in 1956. He was the first black artist to become an animator at the Disney Studios. Following *Sleeping Beauty* he was drafted in to the Army and served in Korea. He returned to Disney on *101 Dalmatians* (1961) and was moved into the Story Department for *The Jungle Book* (1967). He left Disney in 1967, after the death of Walt Disney, to pursue other opportunities and interests. He co-founded Vignette Films with Leo Sullivan. He returned to Disney temporarily in the early '70s to animate on *Bedknobs and Broomsticks* and *Robin Hood*. After spending some time at Hanna-Barbera, Film Roman, and Ruby-Spears, he came back to Disney as part of the comic strip and book illustration department in 1983.

Norman worked on developing a *Roger Rabbit* prequel, *Who Discovered Roger Rabbit*, for producer Jim Pentecost in 1996 and worked on development of a project called the *Wild Life*, based loosely on George Bernard Shaw's *Pygmalion* in 1999. It was canceled in 2000.

Norman worked in Story at Pixar on *Toy Story 2* and *Monsters, Inc.* He was a storyboard artist on *The Tigger Movie*, *Dinosaur*, and the direct-to-video *Cinderella II: Dreams Come True*.

He had always drawn gag cartoons of life at Disney and published several books of his experiences in the animation industry: *Faster! Cheaper!* (Get Animated, 1992), *Son of Faster, Cheaper* (Vignette, 2003), *How the Grinch Stole Disney* (afrokids.com, 2005), *My Animated Life* (blurb.com, 2010), and *Disk Drive* (blurb.com, 2010).

Norman received the Winsor McCay Award in 2002 and he was named a Disney Legend in 2007. Norman is the subject of a documentary, *Floyd Norman: An Animated Life* (2016).

Matt O'Callaghan joined Disney in 1981, working on *Mickey's Christmas Carol* and *The Black Cauldron* as an assistant animator. He was an animator on *The Great Mouse Detective*. He was the animation director on the short *Sport Goofy in Soccermania*. Things were slow during the production of *Oliver & Company*, so he went to the Glendale unit to animate on *Who Framed Roger Rabbit* and then came back to Disney to work on *The Little Mermaid*.

O'Callaghan worked on *Rover Dangerfield*, *Asterix in America*, *The Pagemaster*. He worked with Hyperion Pictures on *The Itsy Bitsy Spider* television series (1994) and the *Life with Louie* television series (1995–98). He worked as a storyboard artist with Pixar on *A Bug's Life*. He worked at Dream Quest Images on visual effects for *Inspector Gadget*, *Mission to Mars*, and *102 Dalmatians*. He directed the CGI video *Mickey's Twice Upon a Christmas* for Disney. He directed *Curious George* and *Open Season 2*. He directed shorts for Warner Bros.: *Coyote Falls*, *Fur of Flying*, *Rabid Rider*, *I Tawt I Taw a Puddy Tat*, and *Daffy's Rhapsody*.

O'Callaghan has been a storyboard artist for *Mr. Peabody & Sherman*, *The Secret Life of Pets*, and the Disney television series *Tangled—The Series* (2017).

Brent Odell started to work at RWA in October 1980. One of the first projects Odell worked on was the *Superman* anti-smoking commercial campaign led by Eric Goldberg. It involved drawing directly onto cels with black crayon. There was always a box of clean-ups for *The Thief* to be worked on whenever things would go quiet with the commercials. He worked on Effects in the *Roger Rabbit* test-of-concept.

After *Roger Rabbit*, Odell worked on *DuckTales the Movie: Treasure of the Lost Lamp*. He freelanced and worked on the Passion Pictures film *Miss Potter* (2006)

Julia Orr worked at Gingerbread Animation and Pizazz Pictures and freelanced in the Soho commercial animation scene in trace and paint. She got into Richard Williams Animation in the Trace and Paint Department, and Barbara McCormack moved her into Checking. She was at RWA the year before *Roger Rabbit*. She became the head of Checking on *Who Framed Roger Rabbit*.

After *Roger Rabbit*, she eventually moved to Los Angeles and worked for a while in the PR department at the Disney Studios in Burbank. She established her own PR firm and is now a social justice activist.

David Pacheco worked for Hanna-Barbera for two years after high school and then brought his portfolio to Disney. He was hired by Disney in 1981. He was an assistant animator on *The Fox and the Hound*, *Mickey's Christmas Carol*, *The Black Cauldron*, and *The Great Mouse Detective*. He was an animator on *Sport Goofy in Soccermania* and *Who Framed Roger Rabbit*. Pacheco was a student of Disney history and used to visit the Disney morgue during lunchtimes; he knew where everything was and became a resource for finding the cameo tidbits that made their way into *Roger Rabbit*. He was an animator on *Oliver & Company* and *The Little Mermaid*.

Pacheco moved into the Consumer Products and Publishing Group, where he became the creative director. He did special projects such as designing the comic characters of the cartoonist (played by Steve Guttenberg) in *3 Men and a Baby* (1987). He did the sketch re-enactments in the documentary film *The Hand Behind the Mouse: The Ub Iwerks Story* (1999). Pacheco also designed all of the Art of Disney stamps for the US Postal Service. He was the associate producer of *Diani & Devine Meet the Apocalypse* (2016).

Shelley Page was working at a movie publicity company and did preproduction visuals for Monty Python's *Meaning of Life* (1983). She then got an assignment to develop promotional materials for Williams's *The Thief and the Cobbler* for fundraising amongst Saudi Arabian princes. During that time, a very young Alex and Claire Williams were her willing assistants ("slaves"). The quick connection to Williams's family and his special charisma soon resulted in Page joining RWA. She was an airbrush artist and painted backgrounds and rendered photorealistic product packaging for the RWA commercials. Williams's early assessment of Page was, "she could be really good, if she could stay at her desk." Page moved on to the *Roger Rabbit* assignment, although she steadfastly refused to sign the Disney contract. She did special rendering, especially on Jessica Rabbit.

After *Roger Rabbit*, Page worked as a background artist at Amblimation on *An American Tail: Fievel Goes West* and *We're Back! A Dinosaur Story*. She was moved to Los Angeles with DreamWorks in 1995 after Amblimation was closed. She became head of artist development and then, as head of International Outreach, created a new DreamWorks team in India.

Mike Peraza went to CalArts, where he met his future wife, Patty Paulick. Both of them were hired by Disney. Peraza was an excellent draughtsman and an innovator. He designed multiplane layout shots on *The Fox and the Hound*. He did concept, design, and layout on *Mickey's Christmas Carol*, *The Black Cauldron*, *The Great Mouse Detective*, the television movie *DuckTales: Treasure of the Golden Suns*. It was during the concept work on *The Great Mouse Detective* that Peraza was loaned to Amblin for half-days to do concept work for Toontown as *Roger Rabbit* was being developed.

Peraza was a concept artist on *Tron*, *Something Wicked This Way Comes*, *Return to Oz*, *Beauty and the Beast*, and *Aladdin*. Peraza was the layout stylist on the *DuckTales* television series (1987–88) and even did some early computer animation on the *TaleSpin* television series and *DuckTales the Movie: Treasure of the Lost Lamp*. He has worked on some non-Disney projects, including Bluth's *Space Ace*, *Dragon's Lair*, and *Thumbelina*, Bagdasarian's *The Chipmunk Adventure*, Phil Roman's *Tom and Jerry: The Movie*, Fox's *Anastasia*, Sony's *Stuart Little*, and Blue Sky's *Ice Age*. He is the production designer on *My Little Pony: The Movie*. He worked at Warner Bros. with Chuck Jones on a Bugs Bunny compilation.

Peraza is very active as a freelance artist and is part of the Disney Fine Art program.

Mike Pfeil went to West Surrey College of Design and joined his mates on the *Roger Rabbit* effects crew at the Forum. After *Roger Rabbit*, he did freelance work in the Soho commercial scene and worked on *Freddie as F.R.o.7*. He later moved to Australia, where he is a scuba-diving guide and photographer.

Silvia Pompei was born in Italy. She met John Halas at a film festival in Bologna when she was sixteen. She moved to London and attended St. Martins Art College, near Covent Garden. She started working at John Halas's studio after graduating and then moved to Eric Goldberg's Pizazz Pictures. She had heard vague rumors about Disney producing a film in London and went to the Chromacolour store in Soho to find out more about it. John Coates, one of the co-founders of TVC, happened to be in the store and overheard her inquiry. He told her about the Forum in Camden Town. She started in September 1987 as an in-betweener in Phil Nibbelink's team. Pompei also assisted Caron Creed and Rob Stevenhagen.

After *Roger Rabbit*, she went with many of the crew to Germany to work on *The Magic Voyage*. She came back to work at Amblimation on *An American Tail: Fievel Goes West* and *We're Back! A Dinosaur's* Story. She went to Los Angeles and worked on *FernGully: The Last Rainforest, Cool World, Mrs. Doubtfire*, and *The Swan Princess*. She did character layout on *Rugrats in Paris: The Movie, The Wild Thornberrys Movie, Rugrats Go Wild*, and *The Simpsons Movie*. Pompei worked as a character layout artist on *The Simpsons* television series starting in 2010.

Dave Pritchard graduated from West Surrey and got on to the *Roger Rabbit* effects crew at the Forum. After *Roger Rabbit*, he worked on *DuckTales the Movie: Treasure of the Lost Lamp, Mickey's Audition, Space Jam*, and *The Magic Sword: Quest for Camelot* in the UK. He moved to the US and worked on *The Iron Giant*. He also worked on *300* and did layout on Disney's *Pixie Hollow Games* direct-to-video release.

Pritchard has worked on pre-visualization on films such as *Captain America: The Winter Soldier, Furious 7, San Andreas, The Angry Birds Movie, Star Trek Beyond, Beauty and the Beas*t, and *The Predator*.

Ken Ralston grew up shooting 8mm effects films with his buddies, as had Zemeckis (and Spielberg before him). At seventeen years old, he was hired for the summer at Cascade Studios, one of the pioneer producers of animated ads for television, to do stop-motion animation. Ralston stayed at Cascade and received a wonderfully complete apprenticeship in most aspects of film production, along with other people, such as Tom St. Amand, who would later become part of the *Roger Rabbit* story. Cascade created the Pillsbury Doughboy and Green Giant interactive animation/live-action commercials. Another coincidence, which made Ralston one of the only direct links to the artist to whom so much homage was directed in the animation of *Who Framed Roger Rabbit*, was that Tex Avery was a freelance director at Cascade Studios at the time, and Ralston got to know him well.

Ken Ralston was the supervisor of visual effects and a key element of the ascendancy of ILM in the special/visual effects field. Ralston had worked with Zemeckis on *Back to the Future*. His credits included *Star Wars: Episove IV—A New Hope, Star Wars: Episode V—The Empire Strikes Back, Dragonslayer, Star Trek II: The Wrath of Khan, Star Wars: Episode VI—Return of the Jedi, Star Trek III: The Search for Spock, Cocoon, Back to the Future, Star Trek IV: The Voyage Home,* and *The Golden Child*. Therefore, one of the first calls Zemeckis made was to Ken Ralston to get him interested in the *Roger Rabbit* project. Ralston brought with him ILM's resources, visual effects wizardry, and twenty-seven ILM wizards who had worked on *Back to the Future* for Zemeckis. Zemeckis knew that one of the major elements in selling the conceit of toons interacting in the real world would be the optical compositing expertise at ILM. They would end up using the same techniques as for compositing models into the *Star Wars* films. Ralston won an Oscar for his work on *Who Framed Roger Rabbit*.

After *Roger Rabbit*, Ralston worked at ILM on films such as *The Rocketeer, Forrest Gump, The Mask,* and *Jumanji*. He moved to Sony Pictures Imageworks in 1996 and worked on films such as *Phenomenon, Contact, Castaway, The Polar Express, Alice in Wonderland,* and *Alice Through the Looking Glass*. He is the senior visual effects supervisor and creative lead at Sony Pictures Imageworks.

Joe Ranft (1960–2005) left CalArts to join Disney in 1980, after his sophomore year. He worked with the Darrell Van Citters team on *Fun with Mr. Future,* the *Roger Rabbit* development, *Sport Goofy in Soccermania,* and with Amblin on Toontown concepts for *Who Framed Roger Rabbit*. He was a puppeteer on Tim Burton's Disney television show *Hansel and Gretel*. He left Disney to work on *The Brave Little Toaster* in Taiwan. He was back at Disney as storyboard artist on *The Little Mermaid* and as story supervisor on *The Rescuers Down Under*. He worked briefly on *The Simpsons* television series (1993) and was storyboard supervisor on *The Nightmare Before Christmas* and *James and the Giant Peach*.

Ranft joined Pixar in 1991 as head of Story and was story supervisor on *Toy Story*, *A Bug's Life*, *Toy Story 2*, *Monsters, Inc.*, and *Cars*. He was killed in a car accident when the vehicle he was a passenger in plunged 130 feet off the Pacific Coast highway. Cars is dedicated to his memory.

Ranft received the Winsor McCay Award posthumously in 2015. He is the subject of John Canemaker's book *Two Guys Named Joe: Master Storytellers Joe Grant and Joe Ranft* (Disney Publishing, 2010).

Nik Ranieri graduated from Sheridan College in 1984. Atkinson had begun production of the television series *Raccoons* and was soaking up a lot of Sheridan graduates. Ranieri moved to Ottawa and worked on *Raccoons* for a couple of years. He moved to Montreal to work at the Pascal Blais commercial studio and then to Toronto to work at the Lightbox studio. Lightbox didn't have a testing machine, so animation was shot on film and sent out for developing. It would come back the next day, but Lightbox would want the footage completed by the next day. At that time in his career, Ranieri had difficulty with rolling and flipping the drawings and seeing whether the animation worked well. He needed to test his drawings against the dialogue—to see that they worked and felt right. He was handicapped by not having access to a test machine and made a case to Lightbox for getting a machine that would enable him to get more, and better, work done and help Lightbox meet its deadlines. There was no test machine forthcoming, and Ranieri was fired.

Ranieri went to Dublin in 1987 to try getting on at Sullivan/Bluth. Instead, he joined the *Roger Rabbit* crew in London. Ranieri was promoted to animator. After *Roger Rabbit*, Ranieri was hired by Disney in Glendale and worked on *The Little Mermaid*.

Ranieri was a supervising animator on *The Rescuers Down Under*, *Beauty and the Beast*, *Aladdin*, *Pocahontas*, *Hercules*, *The Emperor's New Groove*, *Chicken Little*, *Meet the Robinsons*, and *The Princess and the Frog*. He also worked on *Fantasia 2000*, *Treasure Planet*, *Bolt*, *Tangled*, *Winnie the Pooh*, and *Wreck-It Ralph*. During some downtime, he also animated on *Cranium Command*, a filmed attraction at EPCOT in Walt Disney World, *and Mickey's Philharmagic*, a filmed attraction at Fantasyland in most of the Disney theme parks.

Ranieri left Disney in 2013 and was an animation supervisor on *The Prophet*. He worked as the animation lead at Reload Studios, which develops video games such as *World War Toons*.

Ranieri received Annie Awards for Meeko (in *Pocahontas*) and Hades (in *Hercules*). He wrote and illustrated the children's book *The Great Elephant: An Illustrated Allegory* (winepressbooks, 2005).

Jerry Rees worked at the Disney Studios during the summers while a high school student. Disney sent him to CalArts as part of its first character animation class (which also included Brad Bird, John Lasseter, John Musker, and Henry Selick), where Rees served as a teaching assistant to his classmates. He started working at Disney in 1977—before he graduated. He animated on *Small One* and *The Fox and the Hound.* He married Rebecca Lodolo, who was an assistant animator working in Randy Cartwright's group on *The Fox and the Hound* at the time. He asked Tom Wilhite if he could join the *Tron* crew and worked with Bill Kroyer on storyboards. Rees charted the choreography for the CGI-rendered frames of the Recognizer's flights.

Rees was immensely creative. He co-directed fun film projects with Tim Burton—*Doctor of Doom* (1979) and *Luau* (1982). He developed the Computer Oriented Production System (COPS) during his time on *Tron.* Jerry and Rebecca left Disney and joined Brad Bird in San Francisco, where Rees and Bird developed *The Spirit*, a film project based on a character by cartoonist Will Eisner. He directed *The Brave Little Toaster* (1987) and the live-action film *The Marrying Man* (1991), which starred Kim Basinger and Alex Baldwin. Rees was a segment producer on *Space Jam.*

Rees has directed sixteen multimedia Disney themed attractions: *Back to Neverland* (1989), *Tourist from Hell* (1989), *The Editing Story* (1989), *Cranium Command* (1989), *Michael and Mickey* (1991), *Extra Terrorestrial Alien Encounter* (1994), *Countdown to Extinctio,* aka *Dinosaur* (1998), *Sounds Dangerous* (1999), *Rockin' Roller Coaster* (1999), Disney's California Adventure television special (2001), *Cinémagique* (2002), *Disneyland: The First 50 Magical Years* (2005), *O' Canada* (2007), *Animation Magic* (2011), *Mystic Manor* (2013), and *Guardians of the Galaxy—Mission: Breakout!* (2017).

He wrote and directed the film *Susie's Hope* (2013) and was the media director for the touring *Marvel Experience* attraction (2014). Rees worked in association with the Smithsonian Institution to create the first augmented reality US postage stamp. He is also a sculptor and fine artist.

Rees has also written scripts, or been a script doctor, for *Betty Boop, Casper,* a *Roger Rabbit* prequel (sold to Steven Spielberg), *Small Soldiers, Rand Robinson, Robot Repairman, The Kiss, The Brave Little Toaster, Oddyssey, Witchgirl,* and *5 Brothers.*

In the test-of-concept film clips, Eddie Valiant is played by **Peter Renoudet** (also known as Pete Renaday). Renoudet started at Disney in 1959 in the Art Props Department. He made many of the props for *Mary Poppins*. He also often did "stand-ins" during screen tests, and occasionally had bit parts in the Disney comedies of the 1960s (including *The Love Bug* and *The Million Dollar Duck*). He continued his career with Disney and extended it into voice acting. His time on *Roger Rabbit* amounted to "one unremarkable day of filming."

Renoudet has been an active voice actor, with roles as Abraham Lincoln in the Magic Kingdom's Hall of Presidents and Henry and Max in the County Bear Jamboree. He has done voice parts in television series such as *Batman: The Brave and the Bold* (2010–11), *Mad* (2013), and *Archer* (2017).

Renoudet voiced Mickey Mouse on several Disneyland Record albums in the 1980s.

Andrew Ruhemann is one of the many people who became prominent in the European commercial animation industry after having spent time at Richard Williams Animation. He left the *Roger Rabbit* production after it geared up at the Forum and, for a time, managed Richard Williams's new small animation studio located only a couple of blocks from the Forum. In 1987, he founded Passion Pictures, which made a name for itself in commericals and contracted animation and then moved on to include original entertainment and documentary films.

Although mostly assuming the role of producer, Ruhemann co-directed *The Lost Thing* (2010) and won an Oscar for Best Animated Short Subject.

Tom St. Amand worked at ILM and Tippett Studio, specializing in making armatures and performing as a stop-motion animator. He has many visual effects credits, including *The Empire Strikes Back*, *Dragonslayer*, *E.T. the Extra-Terrestrial*, *Return of the Jedi*, *Indiana Jones and the Temple of Doom*, *Howard the Duck*, *RoboCop*, **batteries not included*, *Willow*, *Who Framed Roger Rabbit*, *The Rocketeer*, *Jurassic Park*, *The Nightmare Before Christmas*, *Galaxy Quest*, *The Time Machine*, *Hulk*, and *Spider-Man 3*.

Tim Sanpher graduated from a small film school in Wales in June 1987 at the age of twenty-two. He went to London and spent a couple of months going door-to-door to the Soho commercial studios with his portfolio. He had experience with a rostrum camera and had done a little animation, but his main interest was graphic design such as that done by Saul Bass. He found his way to Stuart Brooks Animation, and it was Jill Brooks, animation art director on *Pink Floyd: The Wall* (1982) and design supervisor on *The Snowman* (1982), who directed Sanpher to the Forum and put him in touch with Chris Knott.

Sanpher has worked steadily as a freelance animator at commercial studios and on several film shorts and television series.

Philip Scarrold trained in graphic design at Bulawayo Art School in Rhodesia (now Zimbabwe) from 1972 until 1974. He then moved to the UK and trained in animation at West Surrey College of Art and Design. After graduation, he got work by making cold calls to various studios in London. It was on a cold call to Richard Williams Animation on Soho Square in May 1987, just as the crew was being moved over to the Forum, where he heard about *Roger Rabbit*. He dropped off his portfolio and showreel at the Forum and started working on *Roger Rabbit* in June 1987.

Scarrold has worked as a freelance illustrator in the UK, Zimbabwe, and Australia.

Arthur Schmidt's father had been a film editor at Paramount. He tried to dissuade his son from entering the film business. Schmidt completed university, with a liberal arts education, and went to find his fortune in Spain—in the film industry. He couldn't get a job in the Spanish film industry and ended up teaching in a private school in Andalusia (southern Spain). He was in Europe for two years, until he got a telegram informing him that his father had died. He returned for the funeral and soon afterwards some of his father's colleagues at Paramount asked whether Schmidt would want to take a film editing apprenticeship at Paramount. After the required eight years as apprentice and assistant editor, Schmidt became a qualified film editor, embarking on a storied career. Much of his work has been in association with Bob Zemeckis. In addition to many other films, Schmidt worked on *Cast Away* (2000) and *Pirates of the Caribbean: The Curse of the Black Pearl* (2003).

Schmidt received an Oscar for Editing on *Who Framed Roger Rabbit* and *Forrest Gump* (1994).

Peter Schneider was the associate director of the 1984 Los Angeles Olympic Arts Festival before being hired by Disney as the first president of Disney Feature Animation. He started at Disney on Monday, October 14, 1985. Schneider was president of WDFA from 1985 to 1999. He arranged Disney's production deal with Pixar. He was named as the head of the Disney Studios in 1999. He left Disney in 2001 to form his own theater production company. He and Don Hahn produced *Waking Sleeping Beauty* (2009).

Schneider is a world champion bridge player and a World Bridge Federation World Life Master.

Peter S. Seaman and **Jeffrey Price** are longtime writing partners. They wrote the screenplay for *Trenchcoat* (1983). It preceded the formation of Touchstone Pictures. It was produced by Disney, but not promoted as a Disney film. Seaman and Price were brought in to Disney's *Roger Rabbit* development unit to write a screenplay for the film. The project didn't get sufficient traction within Disney, but proceeded after Steven Spielberg and Robert Zemeckis were involved. Seaman and Price continued with the screenplay for the Disney/Amblin project.

Since *Who Framed Roger Rabbit*, they have written the screenplays for *Caddy Shack II, Doc Hollywood, Wild Wild West, The Grinch,* and *Shrek the Third*.

Harald Siepermann (1962–2013) was a brilliant sketch artist and character designer. He graduated from the Folkwang University of the Arts in Essen, Germany, and was part of the MadTParty studio in Düsseldorf with Hans Bacher and Uli Meyer. Siepermann and Bacher were involved with early character design and developing Toontown on *Who Framed Roger Rabbit*.

Siepermann was the character designer and storyboard supervisor on the *Alfred J. Kwak* television series (1989–91) and did storyboard work on *Balto*. He did character design and visual development on *Mulan, Tarzan, The Emperor's New Groove, Treasure Planet, Brother Bear,* and *Enchanted*.

He also did character design on *Space Chimps* (2008) and *Little Big Panda* (2011). He wrote the screenplay for *The Seventh Dwarf* (2014) and was directing it when he died suddenly in 2013.

Alan Silvestri was the primary composer for the *CHiPS* television series (1977–83). He met Bob Zemeckis while composing for *Romancing the Stone*, and has since composed the music for all of Zemeckis's subsequent films. He composed the music for *Predator* and *Predator 2*, as well as for John Cameron's *The Abyss*.

He has also composed music for the animated features *Stuart Little, Lilo & Stitch, The Wild,* and *The Croods*. Silvestri wrote the music for *The Avengers* and has written the music for the films in that series set to be released in 2018 and 2019.

Pat Connolly (Sito) and Tom Sito were married in January 1980 and have worked together on many film assignments. Pat has been a blue sketch artist and checker. Her credits include such films and television series as *Rock & Rule*, *Who Framed Roger Rabbit*, *Oliver & Company*, *Tummy Trouble*, *Honey, I Shrunk the Kids*, *The Little Mermaid*, *FernGully: The Last Rainforest*, *Cool World*, *Bébé's Kids*, *The Ren & Stimpy Show* (1992–93), *Pocahontas*, *The Prince of Egypt*, *The Road to El Dorado*, *Spirit: Stallion of the Cimarron*, *Over the Hedge*, *Bee Movie*, *Kung Fu Panda*, and *The SpongeBob Movie*. She was also a stereoscopic artist on *Guardians of the Galaxy*.

Tom Sito attended the High School of Art and Design in Manhattan, as well as the School of Visual Arts, and the Arts Students League. *The Adventures of Raggedy Ann & Andy: A Musical Adventure* was being produced in New York City in 1975, when Sito was in his first year of college. It was the first animated feature film to be produced in New York City since *Gulliver's Travels* had been started there before being moved to Florida. Sito had worked on a couple of small productions, *Journey Through Nutritionland* (Tele-tactics, 1976) and *Isabella and the Magic Brush* (Filmfair, 1976), but on *Raggedy Ann & Andy*, he got to work with people from animation's golden age: Hal Ambro, Art Babbitt, Corny Cole, Emery Hawkins, Irv Spence, and Art Vitello. Sito was nineteen years old and got to work with Grim Natwick, who was eighty-seven at the time. In addition, he formed friendships with people who would later also become involved with *Roger Rabbit*: Bill Frake, Eric Goldberg, and Richard Williams. Sito started in Ink and Paint and finished as an assistant animator. During this New York phase of his career, he also got to work with Shamus Culhane, who ran a small commercial operation out of his apartment.

In 1978, Sito was in Los Angeles, working at Richard Williams's Los Angeles studio. He also spent time at the Lisberger Studio, working on *Animalympics*. He married Pat Connolly and they moved to Toronto to work at Nelvana in 1979. They both worked at Nelvana on productions such as *Easter Fever* (1980), *Take Me Up to the Ball Game* (1980), and *Rock & Rule* (1983). With him at Nelvana were Roger Allers, with whom he had worked at Lisberger Studio, and Chuck Gammage. Tom and Pat Sito were back in Los Angeles in 1982 to work on *Ziggy's Gift* in offices at the historic Crossroads of the World mall, with Richard Williams and Eric Goldberg again. When that production wrapped he joined Ruby-Spears, working on *Saturday Supercade* and *Rubik, the Amazing Cube*, after which he moved to Filmation, working on *He-Man and the Masters of the Universe*, *Challenge of the GoBots*, *Ghostbusters*, and *BraveStarr: The Legend*. Tom and Pat then made a personal short animated film *Propagandance*, which was shown at Annecy, Varna, and Los Angeles Animation Festivals and the Sundance Film Festival in 1987.

Sito worked as an animator on *Who Framed Roger Rabbit* in London. He was hired by Disney in Glendale and worked on *Tummy Trouble*, *The Little Mermaid*, *Beauty and the Beast*, and *Aladdin*. He was one of the writers on *The Lion King* and was the story supervisor on *Pocahontas*. He was a storyboard artist on *Dinosaur*.

Sito moved to DreamWorks in 1995 and worked on *Antz*, *The Prince of Egypt*, and *Spirit: Stallion of the Cimarron*. He was the storyboard director on *Shrek*.

He directed *Osmosis Jones* (2001) at Warner Bros. Sito was president of the Animation Guild IATSE Local 839 from 1992 until 2001. In 1994, he became an instructor at USC School of Cinematic Arts. In 2014, he was named chair of the John Hench Division of Animation and Digital Arts. In 2017, he was elected to the Academy of Motion Picture Arts and Sciences Board of Governors, representing the animation branch.

Sito is the author of the books *Drawing the Line: The Untold Story of the Animation Unions* (University Press of Kentucky, 2006) and *Moving Innovation: History of Computer Animation* (MIT Press, 2013). He is working on a book about the animation renaissance in the 1980s and 1990s. He is writing several other books on animation history, including a collection of favorite cooking recipes from famous animators.

Ric Sluiter graduated from Sheridan College, near Toronto. His early work in the industry was backgrounds for television series at Atkinson in Ottawa. He worked on *The Raccoons* (1985–86), *The Adventures of Teddy Ruxpin* (1987), *Dennis the Menace* (1988) and *C.O.P.S.* (1988–89). Sluiter was hired at the Disney Studios in Florida, where he was a background artist on *Roller Coaster Rabbit*, *The Prince and the Pauper*, *Beauty and the Beast*, *Aladdin*, and *The Lion King*. He was the art director on the shorts *Off His Rockers* and *Trail Mix-Up*, as well as the features *Mulan* and *Lilo & Stitch*.

When the Florida studio was closed, Sluiter went to Disney in Burbank and was part of the preproduction team on *Bolt*, when it was being called "American Dog" under the direction of Chris Sanders. He spent some time with video game producer EA Sports Tiburon, in Florida, and with Laika in Oregon. He joined Blue Sky Studios and worked on *Epic* and *The Peanuts Movie*. He has lent his talents with art direction to Chris Williams's short

The Sketchbook, set during World War I. Sluiter is retired and pursuing his interest as a wildlife artist.

Bruce W. Smith graduated from CalArts and his early animation experience was at Film Roman on *Garfield in the Rough* and *Pinocchio and the Emperor of the Night*. He was in the Glendale unit on *Who Framed Roger Rabbit*. Smith animated on, and even had some screen time in, *Back to Neverland*, a film attraction for the animation tour at the DisneyMGM Studio theme park in Walt Disney World. He was an animator on the Disney shorts, *Tummy Trouble* and *Michael & Mickey*, then moved to Hyperion Pictures, animating on *Rover Dangerfield* and directing *Bébé's Kids*. He worked on *A Goofy Movie* and was a sequence director on *Space Jam*.

Smith created *The Proud Family* and co-founded Jambalaya Studio to produce *The Proud Family* television series (2001–2005) for Walt Disney Television Animation. He moved back to Disney Feature Animation as a supervising animator on films from *Tarzan* to *Winnie the Pooh*. He did visual development on *Wreck-It Ralph* and *Frozen*.

Smith is working on *Hullabaloo—An Animated Steampunk Adventure*, directed by Jamie Lopez.

Len Smith was working on *Pound Puppies* (1987) at Hanna-Barbera when he got the call to assist on layout and design of Toontown on *Who Framed Roger Rabbit* (1998). He then did character design on many Walt Disney Television Animation television series, including *The New Adventures of Winnie the Pooh*, *TaleSpin*, *Raw Toonage*, *The Little Mermaid*, and *Bonkers*. He also worked on the theatrical short that was the pilot of the *Bonkers* series, *Pedal to the Metal* (1992), and a Winnie the Pooh television seasonal special, *Winnie the Pooh and Christmas Too* (1991). Smith also did design work for Disney Consumer Products.

Smith worked with Focus on Family Films on the *Adventures in Odyssey* and the *Kid's Ten Commandments* video series (1993–2003). He continues to work as a freelance illustrator and character designer.

Michael Smith took his formal art training from Central St. Martins in London before spending two-and-a-half years working in the field of medical animation at Medi-Cine. Smith got a call from Andrew Brownlow that people were needed on *Roger Rabbit*. Smith applied for the *Roger Rabbit* crew and was hired into the Matte and Roto Department by Annie Elvins. He was soon transferred to Special Effects. In the first week that MacLean and Jenkins started in Special Effects, they sat at desks facing one another and, having never animated previously, proceeded to start in-betweening in a totally unorthodox, and unworkable, process of their own design. It was Smith who intervened and taught them the basics of flipping drawings and in-betweening.

After *Roger Rabbit*, Smith worked for eighteen months at Hibbert-Ralph, then worked for five years at Amblimation. He later did work on *Space Jam* and *Osmosis Jones*. He teaches at Ravensbourne College of Design and Communication in London.

Dave Spafford grew up in Garden Grove, just down the road from Disneyland. He worked for some time at Disneyland, building sets for Wally Boag at age sixteen and working as a costume character. He started at the Disney Studios in 1975. He worked on *Pete's Dragon* and *The Fox and the Hound*, mostly as an assistant to John Pomeroy. He left Disney along with Bluth, Goldman, and Pomeroy, animating on *Banjo the Woodpile Cat*, *Xanadu*, *The Secret of NIMH*, *Space Ace* and *Dragon's Lair* video games, and *An American Tail* for Don Bluth Studios.

Spafford came back to Disney and was working on *Oliver & Company* when the opportunity came up to go to London on *Who Framed Roger Rabbit*. He came back to the US and was also on the Glendale unit of *Who Framed Roger Rabbit*. He worked on *The Little Mermaid* and then left Disney to work freelance. He did the interactive Woody the Woodpecker animation for presentation of Best Animated Short Film at the Academy Awards in 1991. He animated on *Michael & Mickey* and was a sequence director on *Space Jam*.

Spafford established Spaff Animation and received contracts for segments of *The Jungle Book 2*, *The Lion King 1½*, and *House of D*. He worked on the titles of *The Pink Panther* with Kurtz & Friends. Spafford is a freelance storyboard artist. He also teaches at CalArts. He worked on the documentary *The Officer's Wife* (2010) and was a designer on *Sausage Party* (2016).

In addition to his talent as an animator, he is a magician and an illusion designer. He also is a silhouette artist, appearing regularly at the Magic Castle in Hollywood.

Steven Spielberg directed his first theatrical film by taking the opportunity of getting financing from a first-time producer. Spielberg wrote the screenplay and worked for free. The budget was $15,000 for the twenty-six-minute film. The year was 1968 and Spielberg was twenty-one. The film was called *Amblin'*. Sid Sheinberg (vice president at Universal) saw *Amblin'* and was so impressed that Spielberg became the youngest director to be signed to a long-term deal with a major Hollywood studio. His films have brought in revenues of more than $10 billion. A sampling includes: *Jaws*, *Close Encounters of the Third Kind*, *Raiders of the Lost Ark*, *E.T. the Extra-Terrestrial*, *The Color Purple*, *Empire of the Sun*, *Schindler's List*, *Jurassic Park*, *Amistad*, *Saving Private Ryan*, *War of the Worlds*, *Lincoln*, *Bridge of Spies*, and *The BFG* (for Walt Disney Pictures). He has also been a prolific producer and executive producer.

Spielberg, along with Kathleen Kennedy and Frank Marshall, founded Amblin Entertainment in 1981. Spielberg, along with Jeffrey Katzenberg and David Geffen, founded DreamWorks in 1993.

He won Oscars as Best Director for *Schindler's List* (1993) and *Saving Private Ryan* (1996).

Spielberg received the Winsor McCay Award in 2013.

Robert Spurlock has a long list of credits in special effects, including *Capricorn One*, *Rumble Fish*, *Star Trek IV: The Voyage Home*, *The Witches of Eastwick*, and *Who Framed Roger Rabbit*. He established his own company, Stetson Visual Services, which did a live-action effect on the animated *Roger Rabbit* short *Trail Mix-Up*. It also had credits on *The Abyss*, *Dick Tracy*, *Edward Scissorhands*, *Batman Returns*, and *Honey, I Blew Up the Kid*. Spurlock worked with Dream Quest Images on *Mission to Mars* and with New Deal Studios on *The Aviator*, *Live Free or Die Hard*, and *Inception*. He has been the special effects foreman on *Iron Man 3* and *Captain America: Winter Soldier*.

Steve Starkey is a producer and second-unit director who is closely associated with Bob Zemeckis. He worked on the television series *Steven Spielberg's Amazing Stories* from 1985 to 1987. He worked on the *Back to the Future* film series with Zemeckis, and then continued on *Who Framed Roger Rabbit*, *Forrest Gump*, *Cast Away*, *The Polar Express*, *Monster House*, *Beowolf*, *A Christmas Carol*, *Mars Needs Moms*, *Real Steel*, *Flight*, *The Walk*, and *Allied*.

Animator Dave Spafford said of him on *Roger Rabbit*, "Steve was great . . . such a happy guy. It was infectious."

Dave Stephan was a graduate of Sheridan College near Toronto. He worked on *Animalympics* at Lisberger Studios and came to the Disney Studios with Lisberger on *Tron*. Stephan was hired by Disney and worked as an assistant animator on *The Black Cauldron* and *The Great Mouse Detective*. He was an animator on *Sport Goofy in Soccermania*, *Oliver & Company*, and *The Little Mermaid*. He moved to Florida for the opening of the new Disney studios in 1989, and worked on *Roller Coaster Rabbit* and *The Rescuers Down Under*. He was back in Glendale for *Beauty and the Beast*, *Aladdin*, and *The Lion King*.

Stephan worked on completing *The Thief and the Cobbler*, with Calvert/Cobbler Productions, and animated on *Asterix in America*. He was a storyboard artist on *Mulan 2*, *Curious George*, *Alvin and the Chipmunks*, *Hop*, and *Alvin and the Chipmunks: The Road Chip*. He was storyboard director on the *Axe Cop* television series (2012–13). Stephan is working on *SpongeBob SquarePants 3*, scheduled for release in 2019.

Nick Stern is American, but went to art school in London, England, in the early 1970s. After graduating he went back to California and was eventually accepted into Hanna-Barbera's training program in 1978. He then worked at Filmation for a couple of years on television shows such as *Fat Albert and the Cosby Kids* and *The New Adventures of Mighty Mouse and Heckle and Jeckle*. He moved back San Francisco in 1980 to work on Martin Rosen's *The Plague Dogs*. Stern became the head of the assistant animators and worked with some good English animators and also Retta Scott, the first woman animator hired at Disney in the 1940s.

He started at ILM at the beginning of 1986, when they were staffing up for *Howard the Duck*. He worked on *The Golden Child*, **batteries not included*, *Who Framed Roger Rabbit*, and *Willow*. He worked for Atari on a number of video games in the early 1990s.

Rob Stevenhagen is from the Netherlands. His first job in animation was in Ghent, Belgium, where he met Børge Ring. Stevenhagen went to Paris to work on *Asterix and Caesar* and *Asterix in Britain*. Børge Ring became a mentor to Stevenhagen when they worked together again on *Asterix in Britain*. While there, he worked with at least six other animators with whom he would later work on *Roger Rabbit*. He then went to London to work at Felix Films with Mike Smith, with whom he had worked on *Asterix and Caesar*. While working on commercials at Felix rumors were spreading in the Soho district of Disney and Richard Williams starting a big production in London. It was all very secretive at the time, but Stevenhagen got a call from his friend, Chuck Gammage, who had started working on *Roger Rabbit* while still at RWA in Soho Square. Stevenhagen called on the Disney Studios at the Forum and took the animation test. He started as an animator.

After *Roger Rabbit*, he went went to Germany with many of the other animators from the Forum to work on *The Magic Voyage*. He went back to London to work with Amblimation as a supervising animator on *An*

American Tail: Fievel Goes West, *We're Back! A Dinosaur's Story*, and *Balto*. He worked as a sequence director on *Space Jam*, *The Road to El Dorado*, and *Sinbad: Legend of the Seven Seas* with Dino Athanassiou at Stardust Pictures.

Stevenhagen did storyboards for *The Curse of the Were-Rabbit*. He directed *The Tale of Despereaux* (2008). He was head of Story on *Frankenweenie* (2012) and was a storyboard artist on *The Little Prince* (2015).

Marc Stirdivant graduated from the USC Film School in 1972 and started in the Story Department at Disney in 1976. He became a Disney staff producer and helped develop *The Last Flight of Noah's Ark* (1980). He wrote the screenplay for *Condorman* (1981) and was the producer on *Night Crossing* (1982). He then advocated for Disney to buy the film rights to *Who Censored Roger Rabbit?* and was assigned to the *Roger Rabbit* development unit. He later produced *Without a Clue* (1988) for ITC. Stirdivant was an assistant director on the *Frasier* television series (1996–2004).

Stirdivant left the entertainment industry and became senior administrative analyst of community services and parks for the city of Glendale, California. He has been an activist on land preservation as part of the Santa Monica Mountains Conservancy.

Glenn Sylvester graduated from Sheridan College in 1984, in the same class as Nik Ranieri, Cal Leduc, Ric Sluiter, Dave Nethery, Rej Bourdages, and Howy Parkins. He got a job at Atkinson's Hinton studios in Ottawa in January 1985, working on *Raccoons*. He was hired by a veteran assistant animator, Roger Way, with whom he would later work on *Roger Rabbit* in London.

Glenn Sylvester had planned a trip to Europe for the summer of 1987. He intended to visit some relatives in Germany and friends from Sheridan College who were working with Bluth in Dublin. One of his grandparents had been born in the UK, so he could get a work visa if an opportunity came up. Just before he left, he got a call from Disney UK and an interview was set up for the end of August. He sent his portfolio and then arrived in London at the appointed time for an interview and to take the Baby Herman in-between test. He started at the Forum in September 1987. He would later find out that Cal Leduc had given the studio his phone number.

After *Roger Rabbit*, Sylvester worked at Amblimation. He was a CG animator at ILM on films such as *Men in Black*, *The Mummy*, and *Star Wars: Episode I—The Phantom Menace*. He animated on *The Wild*, a co-production of Disney and Complete Pandemonium-CORE Technologies, in Toronto. He joined Sony and animated on a long list of films, including *Cloudy with a*

Chance of Meatballs, Green Lantern, Oz the Great and Powerful, The Amazing Spiderman 2, The Smurfs 2, Hotel Transylvannia 2, Ghostbusters, Storks, and *Smurfs and the Lost Village*.

Sylvester teaches at Capilano University in Vancouver.

Wes Takahashi was an assistant animator on Ralph Bakshi's *American Pop*. He joined ILM and eventually headed the ILM Animation Department, working on films such as *The Goonies, Back to the Future, Top Gun, *batteries not included, Who Framed Roger Rabbit, Willow, Indiana Jones and the Last Crusade, The Abyss, The Rocketeer*, and *The Mask*. He animated the "boy on the moon" logo for DreamWorks. He was an animator for Hammerhead Productions on *The Core* (2003) and for Helium VFX on Black November (2012).

Takahashi helped Peter Jackson to establish WETA Digital. He teaches at International Technological University in San Jose, California, and since 2011 has been the department chair of digital arts.

Amanda Talbot attended the West Surrey College of Art and Design. The course focus was experimental and avant-garde. After college she got a job as a film editor. She saw ads for *Roger Rabbit* crew in the British Film Union newsletter and submitted her experimental effects student film. Chris Knott called to interview her.

After *Roger Rabbit*, she worked as an effects animator at Amblimation. Talbot was hired by Disney in Burbank and worked on *Hercules, Mulan, Tarzan, Atlantis: The Lost Empire, Treasure Planet*, and *Home on the Range*. She took a break from animation, took acting classes, and went to auditions. She became a magician and is now a member of the Academy of Magical Arts. Talbot returned to animation with Disney on *The Princess and the* Frog, but has trained with Second City and is active in improvisational theater.

Barry Temple joined Disney in 1980. He worked on *Mickey's Christmas Carol* and was an animator on *The Black Cauldron, The Great Mouse Detective, Sport Goofy in Soccermania, Who Framed Roger Rabbit, Oliver & Company*, and *The Little Mermaid*. He moved to Florida in 1989 for the opening of the Disney Studios at Walt Disney World. In Florida, he worked on *Roller Coaster Rabbit, The Rescuers Down Under, Beauty and the Beast, Aladdin, Trail Mix-Up, The Lion King, Pocahontas*, and *Mulan*. He was back in Burbank for *Atlantis: The Lost Empire, Lilo & Stitch*, and *Home on the Range*. He did traditional animation for the CGI test designed to evaluate its potential for animated prop interactions with live action in a *Roger Rabbit* sequel.

Temple animated on *Tugger: The Jeep 4X4 Who Wanted to Fly* (2005). He then worked on commercials and with Electronic Arts on video games. He is teaching animation.

Darrell Van Citters's father was in the military, so there was a lot of moving when Darrell was growing up, but his family lived in Albuquerque when Darrell was in high school. He got a job painting cels for minimum wage at a tiny regional commercial studio and continued doing that during his first year at the University of New Mexico. He was given advanced standing into CalArts the following year. He spent a summer working at Chuck Jones's studio and a summer working at Filmation. His dormitory roommate was John Lasseter and their suite-mates were John Musker and Harry Sabin. Van Citters was the first student to graduate from the CalArts character animation program (excluding Glen Keane), due to his advance standing from the University of New Mexico. He was hired by Disney in 1976, where he became an animator on *The Fox and the Hound*. He worked on some television specials and was then made director with *Fun with Mr. Future*.

Van Citters was the director of the early Disney development unit for *Roger Rabbit* from late 1981 to 1983. He then directed *Sport Goofy in Soccermania*, although the new Disney management appointed in 1984 had issues with it, so the short film was reworked by others and finally released in 1987.

Van Citters moved to Warner Bros. in 1987 to animate on *Daffy Duck's Quackbusters* (1988). He was promoted to creative director and directed *Box Office Bunny*, the first new Bugs Bunny short in twenty-six years.

Van Citters left Warner Bros. in 1992 to found Renegade Animation, with Ashley Postlewaite, in early 1993. It made many classic and successful commercials but was early into internet animation with the *Elmo Aardvark* series (2001). It has also produced the *Hi Hi Puffy AmiYumi* series (2004–2006) for Cartoon Network and *The Tom and Jerry Show* series (2014–16). Renegade Animation celebrated its twenty-fifth anniversary in 2018—successful, growing, and producing original content entertainment.

Van Citters has written two books, *Mister Magoo's Christmas Carol: The Making of the First Animated Christmas Special* (Oxberry Press, 2009) and *Art of Jay Ward Productions* (Oxberry Press, 2013).

Nicolette Van Gendt was born in the Netherlands and went to art school in Utrecht. She moved to England in 1979, at the age of twenty-two. She attended the Norwich School of Art, studying graphic design and illustration. Van Gendt started in the animation industry as a layout artist and background artist for commercials and television specials. She worked at Stuart Brooks Animation and worked on *When the Wind Blows*. She heard about *Roger Rabbit* through the Soho grapevine, applied, and was hired by Don Hahn to assist Phil Nibbelink.

Since *Roger Rabbit*, she has worked as a freelance artist, doing illustration, character design, and storyboards. Van Gendt worked on *The Illusionist* and *Ethel and Ernest*.

Marcelo Vignali worked at DIC Entertainment on *A.L.F.: The Animated Series* (1987–88) and the *C.O.P.S.* television series (1988). He joined Walt Disney Imagineering and was responsible for the Roger Rabbit's Car Toon Spin attraction at Disneyland and Tokyo Disneyland. He moved to Walt Disney Feature Animation and worked on *Mulan*, *Atlantis: The Lost Empire*, *Lilo & Stitch*, and *Brother Bear*. He worked on early visual development on "The Snow Queen," which was eventually released as *Frozen*.

He moved to Sony Pictures Animation, where he was a visual development artist on *Open Season* and *Cloudy with a Chance of Meatballs*. He was production designer on *Hotel Transylvania*, art director on *Surf's Up*, *Smurfs: The Lost Village*, and *Spider-man: Into the Spider-Verse*.

Frans Vischer graduated from CalArts and joined Disney in 1981. He was an in-betweener on *Mickey's Christmas Carol* and *The Black Caluldron*. He was a storyboard artist for DIC Entertainment on the *Kissyfur* television series (1985) and *My Little Pony: The Movie*. Vischer worked on *The Brave Little Toaster* with Jerry Rees. He was animating at Warner Bros. on *Daffy Duck's Quackbusters* and *The Night of the Living Duck*, along with Rebecca Rees, when he heard about the *Roger Rabbit* crew being assembled in Glendale.

After *Roger Rabbit*, Vischer worked on the *Roger Rabbit* short *Tummy Trouble* and then worked with Jerry Rees on the *Back to Neverland* and *Michael & Mickey* filmed theme park attractions. He worked with Hyperion Pictures on *Rover Dangerfield* and *Bébé's Kids*. He was a supervising animator on *Cats Don't Dance*. Vischer moved to DreamWorks in 1996 and animated on *The Prince of Egypt* and *The Road to El Dorado*. He was a storyboard artist on *The Wild Thornberrys Movie* and at Universal on *Curious George*. He did character layout on *The Simpsons Movie*.

Vischer was at Disney to animate on the *Wild About Safety: Timon and Pumbaa Safety Smart* series and then worked on *The Princess and the Frog*, *Winnie the Pooh*, and the short *Paperman*. He was a lead animator on *The SpongeBob Movie: Sponge Out of Water* and a storyboard artist on *Animal Crackers* for Blue Dream Studios. Vischer animated on *Mary Poppins Returns* (2018) and is a supervising animator on the Netflix (Warner Bros.) series, *Green Eggs and Ham*.

Vischer writes and illustrates children's books. His first book, *Jimmy Dabble*, was published by Dutton/Penguin in 2001. He created the character Fuddles, a pampered cat who is the subject of *Fuddles* (2011), *A Very Fuddles Christmas* (2013), and *Fuddles and Puddles* (2016), all published by Aladdin.

Harry Walton did stop-motion animation on *The Gumby Show* television series (1968) and the *Davey and Goliath* television series (1971–72). He did special effects on *Octaman* (1971), *Dark Star* (1974), and *Black Sunday* (1977). He worked at both ILM and Phil Tippett Studio as a stop-and-go motion animator, matte artist, and visual effects photographer on films such as *Young Sherlock Holmes*, *Howard the Duck*, *The Golden Child*, *Innerspace*, *RoboCop*, *Willow*, and *Who Framed Roger Rabbit*.

He has a long list of credits after *Roger Rabbit*, including *Ghostbusters II*, *Hook*, *A Far Off Place* (with Image FX), *RoboCop III* (with Tippett Studio), and *James and the Giant Peach* (with Sony Pictures Imageworks). He was a rotoscope artist on *Death Race 2050* (2017). Throughout the 2000s, he was an animation director on video games with Brain Zoo Studios.

Robert Watts is a British film producer who is best known for his involvement with George Lucas and Steven Spielberg in the *Star Wars* and *Indiana Jones* film series. He had also been a production manager on the James Bond film *You Only Live Twice* (1967), and Stanley Kubrick's *2001: A Space Odyssey* (1968). In 1985, Robert Watts was the vice president of European production for Lucasfilm. He was the producer on *Who Framed Roger Rabbit*.

After *Roger Rabbit*, Watts produced *Indiana Jones and the Last Crusade*, *An American Tail: Fievel Goes West*, and *Alive*. He was the executive producer of *On Deadly Ground* (1994) and several documentary films in recent years.

Roger Way (1940–2016) was born in Ottawa, Canada. He found a job at Crawley Films in Ottawa, working on the *Wizard of Oz* television series in the Paint and Trace Department. He later worked at the National Film

Board in Montreal. In 1964, at the age of twenty-four, he moved to England and found his way to Richard Williams Animation. He worked on titles for the films *Casino Royale* and *The Charge of the Light Brigade*, as well as on many commercials. He left RWA for a while and worked at many of the little studios around Soho. He worked on *Watership Down* at Halas and Batchelor.

Way returned to Canada in the mid-1980s, where he worked at Atkinsons in Ottawa on *The Raccoons* television series (1985) and the television movie *For Better or for Worse: The Bestest Present* (1985). He worked with new Sheridan College graduates Cal Leduc and Glenn Sylvester on those productions. He was back in London for *David MacCauley: Cathedral* (1986) and joined the *Roger Rabbit* crew at the Forum.

After *Roger Rabbit*, Way worked on a number of direct-to-video productions, *Freddie as F.R.O.7.*, *The Thief and the Cobbler*, and *The World of Peter Rabbit and Friends* television series (1993–94). He was interested in philosophy and eastern mysticism and moved to an artist commune near Forres, in northern Scotland, where he lived a simple and unencumbered life.

Simon Wells is the great-grandson of H. G. Wells. He was born in Cambridge and attended the Perse School, a preparatory school founded in 1615. Wells managed to negotiate life at the Perse School well and went on to study audio-visual design at Leicester Polytechnic, now known as De Montfort University. While at Leicester Polytechnic, a tutor sent Wells's portfolio to RWA for consideration. Although Williams was rarely involved in the staffing process, he happened to catch a glimpse of Wells's portfolio and told the studio manager to hire Wells. As a consequence, Wells joined RWA in 1984, immediately upon graduation. He started as an in-betweener, but about a month later, the studio won a small contract and Williams gave the thirty-second commercial to Wells to do on his own. From then on, he was a full-fledged animator—and Williams's budding protégé.

Wells was a supervising animator on *Who Framed Roger Rabbit*. After *Roger Rabbit*, he was with Amblimation, directing *An American Tail: Fievel Goes West*, *We're Back! A Dinosaur's Story*, and *Balto*. When Amblimation was closed, he moved to DreamWorks in Glendale where he directed *The Prince of Egypt*. He later directed the live-action films *The Time Machine* and *Mars Needs Moms*.

Wells has been a storyboard artist on *Antz*, *Chicken Run*, *The Road to El Dorado*, *Spirit: Stallion of the Cimarron*, *Sinbad: Legend of the Seven Seas*, *Shrek 2*, *Shark Tale*, *Madagascar*, *Shrek the Third*, *Flushed Away*, *Kung Fu Panda*, *Kung Fu Panda 2*, *The Croods*, and *Kung Fu Panda 3*. He is directing *Save the Cat*.

Pete Western grew up with animation; his father and mother worked with David Hand at G-B Animation, the studio set up by J. Arthur Rank. Western received his formal art training at Central St. Martins in London. At the time he graduated, in the early 1970s, Richard Williams Animation was well-known to be the best studio in the business. Western worked for a number of small commercial studios throughout his twenties, but went freelance in his thirties. He spent short periods of time at RWA and knew many of the people who had worked there.

After *Roger Rabbit*, Western worked for a while at Oscar Grillo's commercial studio and then went to Amblimation, where he worked on *An American Tail: Fievel Goes West* and *We're Back! A Dinosaur's Story*. He was a supervising painter on *Judge Dredd*. He animated on *All Dogs Go to Heaven 2*, *Space Jam*, *The Broken Jaw*, *The Magic Sword: Quest for Camelot*, and *Jolly Roger*.

Western was a layout artist on the *Angelina Ballerina* television series (2001–2002) and on *Heidi*. He was layout artist, storyboard artist, and lead animator on *The Snowman and the Snowdog*, a television special.

In 2016, Western received the BAFTA Award for exceptional contribution to animation at the BAFTA Children's Award Show.

Colin White worked on commercials in the many small studios in Soho, then got on to *Watership Down* at Halas and Batchelor where he was trained by Harold Whittaker. Following the success of *Watership Down*, another Richard Adams book, *The Plague Dogs*, was to be made into an animated film, only this time it was to be produced in San Francisco. White spent two-and-a-half years in San Francisco on *The Plague Dogs*, eventually being made the animation director. Many on the crew, including Brad Bird, went to work at ILM after the completion of *The Plague Dogs*. Alan Simpson was another British animator working on *The Plague Dogs* who eventually worked on *Roger Rabbit*. White was working at ILM in early 1986 when ILM became involved in the *Roger Rabbit* project and even put in a bid to do all of the animation. White applied to be the animation director, but received a polite "no" from Kathleen Kennedy. White went back to England and got on to *Roger Rabbit* in August of 1987, about six months after *Roger Rabbit* had been in production at the Forum.

White has had an active career as a freelance artist. He was a storyboard artist on *Fantastic Mr. Fox*. He was also a storyboard artist on television series such as *Jungle Junction* (2009–2010), *Nexo Knights* (2017), and *School of Roars* (2017).

Tom Wilhite was born in 1952 in the small town of Keswick, Iowa. He was attending Iowa State University in Ames when he and some dorm mates traveled to a theater in Des Moines that ran revivals of old movies. He saw *Night at the Opera* and *Day at the Races* that night and "discovered" the Marx Brothers. He thought that other students would also like his discovery if it could be made more accessible on the campus. Wilhite made up some stationery in order to make himself look like a big impresario and wrote a letter to Groucho Marx. Sometime later, he was contacted by Groucho's agent, who didn't realize that he was dealing with a nineteen-year-old freshman. The price for Groucho to appear at Ames would be $4,000. Groucho agreed to appear at Ames for a one-man show, with piano accompaniment by Marvin Hamlisch.

Groucho hired the firm of Rogers, Cowan, and Brenner to do his public relations, and the Iowa State appearance was soon followed by other dates, culminating in a show at Carnegie Hall in May 1972. The show was introduced by television talk show personality Dick Cavett, and a live recording was released on an LP as *An Evening With Groucho*. When Wilhite graduated, he was hired as the assistant to Warren Cowan, one of the principals in the PR firm, now called Rogers & Cowan, and helped manage Groucho.

It was as a consequence of his handling the publicity on the film *Rocky*, though, that Wilhite got a call from Walt Disney Productions with an offer of a job as publicity director. Wilhite was hired by Disney in 1976 and spent three years in Publicity before being promoted to head of Live-Action Production.

Wilhite brought *Tron*, *Return to Oz*, and *Who Framed Roger Rabbit* to Disney. He was sympathetic and empathetic with the young talented group of animators, mostly from CalArts, who were frustrated with Disney Animation in the 1980s. He created opportunities for Tim Burton, John Lasseter, and Darrell Van Citters to express their creativity. Eventually, they all left Disney, as did Wilhite. He co-founded Hyperion Pictures in 1984 and produced *The Brave Little Toaster*, *Rover Dangerfield*, the short *The Itsy Bitsy Spider*, and *Bébé's Kids*. Wilhite produced an *Oz Kids* video series, based on the writings of L. Frank Baum. He produced the television series *Life with Louie* (1995–98), *Goosebumps* (1995–98), and *The Proud Family* (2002–2005). He produced *The Brave Little Toaster to the Rescue*, *The Proud Family Movie*, and *Marigold*.

Wilhite and his partner own the world's largest private collection of Oz memorabilia.

Alex Williams was born in 1967. He was the voice of Tiny Tim in his father's (Richard Williams) 1971 production of *A Christmas Carol*. He was in his first year at Oxford when production began on *Roger Rabbit*. He visited the Forum during the school break at Easter 1987, asking Don Hahn whether he could work (for free) as an intern. After a couple of weeks of working without compensation, he asked if he could be paid. It was Patsy de Lord who asked him if he would consider staying on with the *Roger Rabbit* production instead of going back to the University of Oxford. Williams was eager . . . and Oxford agreed to give him a year leave. Alex Williams started working on *Roger Rabbit* in April 1987 as part of the in-betweener pool . . . mostly at the service of Simon Wells. He then went on to be an assistant to Marc Gordon-Bates.

Williams went back to school, graduating in law. He spent his first summer after *Roger Rabbit* working at the new Disney studios in Florida on *Roller Coaster Rabbit*. He became a barrister and also drew the *Queens Counsel* cartoon strip in the *Times*. He left law in 1996 to pursue a career in animation.

Williams worked on *The Thief and the Cobbler* and then went to the US to work on *The Lion King*, *The Magic Sword: Quest for Camelot*, *The Iron Giant*, *The Road to El Dorado*, *Piglet's Big Movie*, *Robots*, and *Open Season*. Back in the UK, Williams worked on visual effects *for Harry Potter and the Half-Blood Prince*.

Williams (and Steve Moore) maintain the *FLiP Animation* blog. He started the online animation school Animation Apprentice in 2012. In 2015, he was able to start offering an online master's in animation through Bucks New University.

Richard "Dick" Williams was born on March 19, 1933, in Toronto, Canada. At fourteen years of age, he traveled on his own to Los Angeles to visit the Disney Studios and was befriended by master animator Milt Kahl. Williams resisted the lure of working for Disney and he emigrated to Ibiza, an island in the Mediterranean Sea off the eastern coast of Spain, in 1953 to develop as a fine artist. He moved to London in 1955 to work on his short subject film, *The Little Island* (1958). He established his own studio, Richard Williams Animation, which did a magnificent variety of commercials and film titles and became the standard-bearer for the British commercial animation industry. He created the title sequences for *What's New Pussycat?* (1965), *A Funny Thing Happened on the Way to the Forum* (1966), *Casino Royale* (1967), *The Charge of the Light Brigade* (1968), *The Return of the Pink Panther* (1975), and *The Pink Panther Strikes Again* (1976). He won an Oscar for his direction of *A Christmas Carol* (1971), a co-production with Chuck Jones. He directed *Raggedy Ann & Andy: A Musical Adventure* in 1977 and *Ziggy's Gift* in 1982. Eric Goldberg worked with Williams on both films, as did another young New York animator, Tom Sito. Williams also did his own projects, often funding them himself out of the proceeds from his successful commercial enterprises. A short animated film, *Love Me, Love Me, Love Me*, was released in 1962.

Then follows the long saga associated with the making of the film *The Thief and the Cobbler*. It is the subject of a number of documentary films, including *Persistence of Vision* (Kevin Schreck, 2012). Williams was the animation director on *Who Framed Roger Rabbit*, partly so that he could attract financing in order to complete *The Thief*, but the project was taken over by the Completion Bond Co. in 1992, when there was only fifteen minutes left to animate. The film was reworked and finished by Fred Calvert in South Korea. Williams kept a low profile after *The Thief* was taken from him. He eventually resurfaced, teaching master animation classes associated with his book *The Animator's Survival Kit* (Faber and Faber, 2001) and a DVD series.

Williams single-handedly animated two magnificent short films, *Circus Drawings* (2010) and *Prologue* (2015). The Richard Williams director's cut, called *A Moment in Time*, was screened at AMPAS on December 10, 2013.

Williams received the Winsor McCay Award in 1984.

Gary K. Wolf was born in 1941 in Earlville, Illinois (pop. 1,406). His father ran a pool hall and his mother was a cook in the school cafeteria. Wolf graduated from high school and went to the University of Illinois at Urbana-Champaign. He majored in advertising. After graduation, he entered the air force and was posted as a public information officer in the Electronic Systems Division at the Air Force Cambridge Research Center located at Hanscom Field, just northwest of Boston. Wolf volunteered for combat duty, considering it to be necessary to advance his career, and had a two-year tour of duty as an air commando in Vietnam. He was awarded the Bronze Star and two air medals. The things that he saw and experienced in Vietnam changed his view of the world and his interest in pursuing a military career. He left the air force as a captain and returned to graduate school, getting a master's degree in communications.

After graduation, Wolf took a job as a copywriter in a San Francisco advertising agency. He later decided to move back to the Boston area and worked at several different ad agencies, eventually becoming vice president and creative director, with clients such as Digital Equipment Corporation (DEC), Wang, and Intel.

He followed his interest in science fiction and had three science fiction novels published by Doubleday Books in the 1970s; *Killerbowl* was published in 1975, *A Generation Removed* was published in 1977, and *The Resurrectionist* was published in 1979. *Who Censored Roger Rabbit?* was Wolf's fourth published novel.

Wolf has written two other *Roger Rabbit* books, *Who P-P-P-Plugged Roger Rabbit?* (Villard Books, 1991) and *Who Wacked Roger Rabbit?* (Musa Publishing, 2013), in addition to several *Roger Rabbit* short stories. *Space Vulture* (TOR-Tom Doherty Associates, 2008) is a science fiction book he co-wrote with his childhood friend, the archbishop of Newark, John Myers.

Julia Woolf graduated from Canterbury Art College in graphic design. She had worked in most of the Soho commercial houses and had been a trace and paint artist for Wicked Witch Animation on *When the Wind Blows* (1986). She got a call to pitch in when Disney realized it needed more assistant animators to get the film completed on time. Woolf worked on *Roger Rabbit* for the last three months of the production. She was an assistant to Phil Nibbelink, along with Nicolette Van Gendt, Silvia Pompei, and Glenn Sylvester.

After *Roger Rabbit*, Woolf worked at Pizazz Pictures and Uli Meyer Animation, and freelanced on television series, commercials, and short films. She went to Germany to work on *The Magic Voyage* and she worked on *FernGully: The Last Rainforest*. She went to Amblimation and was an assistant animator on *We're Back! A Dinosaur's Story* and a lead animator on *Balto*. She moved to the US in 1995 to work for DreamWorks, working as a layout artist on *The Prince of Egypt*, *The Road to El Dorado*, and *Spirit: Stallion of the Cimarron*. She did the illustrated storybook at the opening of both *Shrek* and *Shrek 2*, and she was a visual development artist on *Madagascar*.

Woolf left DreamWorks while on maternity leave and built up her illustration portfolio. She returned to the UK in 2006. She wrote and illustrated the children's book *Giraffe on a Bicycle* (Pan Macmillan, 2016).

Bob Zemeckis attended the USC School of Cinematic Arts, where his student film, *A Field of Honor* (1973), won a student Oscar. It brought him to the attention of Steven Spielberg, who became a mentor. He wrote and directed *I Wanna Hold Your Hand* (1978) and *Used Cars* (1980), but they were box-office flops. He turned it around with *Romancing the Stone* and *Back to the Future*. He directed *Who Framed Roger Rabbit*.

He has directed many films, including *Back to the Future Part II*, *Back to the Future Part III*, *Death Becomes Her*, and *Forrest Gump*, the latter of which won him an Oscar for Best Director. He has also directed *Contact*, *What Lies Beneath*, *Cast Away*, *The Polar Express*, *Beowolf*, *A Christmas Carol*, *Flight*, *The Walk*, and *Allied*.

Zemeckis pioneered motion capture, using it extensively in *The Polar Express*, *Beowolf*, and *A Christmas Carol*. He was part of a joint venture with Disney and ImageMovers Digital starting in 2007.

In 1999, Zemeckis donated $5 million towards the Robert Zemeckis Center for Digital Arts at USC.

NOTES

CHAPTER ONE

1. Gary K. Wolf, interview with author (February 3, 2010); Gary K. Wolf, "Gary K. Wolf, Creator of Roger Rabbit!" (website), accessed October 2, 2013, http://garywolf.com/about. php; Gary K. Wolf, "Two Very Different Career Paths with the Same Destination" (website), accessed October 2, 2013, http://www.spacevulture.com/authors.html.

2. Wolf, http://garywolf.com/about.php.

3. Wolf, interview with author; Wolf, http://garywolf.com/about.php; Wolf, http://www.spacevulture.com/authors.html; Stephen Fiott, "Interview with Gary K. Wolf," *Storyboard/The Art of Laughter*, April/May 1991; Jarrod Canepa, "Exclusive Jessica Rabbit Creator Interview—Gary Wolf," *ImNotBad.com—A Jessica Rabbit Site* (blog), December 6, 2011, http://www.imnotbad.com/2011/12/exclusive-jessica-rabbit-creator.html.

4. Fiott, *Storyboard/The Art of Laughter*.

5. Cory Tibbits and Myles Rourke, "EP 67—with Gary K. Wolf," October 21, 2013, in *End Credits—The Behind the Scenes in Entertainment Podcast*, http://endcredits.podbean.com/.

6. Wolf, interview with author; Fiott, *Storyboard/The Art of Laughter*.

7. Fiott, *Storyboard/The Art of Laughter*; Tibbits and Rourke, *End Credits*, http://end credits.podbean.com/.

8. Wolf, interview with author; Tibbits and Rourke, *End Credits*.

9. Fiott, *Storyboard/The Art of Laughter*.

10. Tee Bosustow, "Interview with Brad Bird," April 22, 2008, in *Toon In! to the World of Animation—with Tee Bosustow* (podcast), http://tooninanimation.net/.

11. Randy Cartwright, interview with author (September 30, 2009); John Musker, interview with author (November 4, 2010); Chris Buck, interview with author (April 5, 2013); Michael Giaimo, interview with author (April 18, 2012).

12. William Kallay, *The Making of Tron: How Tron Changed Visual Effects and Disney Forever* (self-published, 2011), 26.

13. Giaimo, interview with author; Jim Korkis, "The Birth of the Bunny," *Persistence of Vision*, Summer 1993, 27.

14. Darrell Van Citters, interview with author (September 28, 2009).

15. Cartwright, interview with author.

16. Jerry Rees, interview with author (November 1, 2010).

17. Musker, interview with author.

18. Tom Wilhite, interview with author (January 13, 2011).

19. Randy Cartwright, *1983 Disney Studio Tour*, 8mm film, home movie (1983); clips shown in *Waking Sleeping Beauty*, directed by Don Hahn (Los Angeles: Stone Circle Pictures/Walt Disney Studios Motion Pictures, 2009).

20. Ed Catmull with Amy Wallace, *Creativity, Inc.: Overcoming the Unseen Forces That Stand in the Way of True Inspiration* (New York: Random House, 2014), 33.

21. Wilhite, interview with author.

22. Musker, interview with author.

23. Michael Giaimo, interview with author (April 23, 2012); Korkis, *Persistence of Vision*, 27.

24. Van Citters, interview with author.

25. Kallay, *The Making of Tron*, 41.

26. Ron Miller, interview with author (November 11, 2010).

27. Wilhite, interview with author.

28. Ron Grover, *The Disney Touch: How a Daring Management Team Revived an Entertainment Empire* (Homewood, IL: Business One Irwin, 1991), 113.

29. Van Citters, interview with author; Miller, interview with author; Marc Stirdivant, interview with author (November 4, 2010); Darrell Van Citters, "Roger Rabbit's Roots," *Animato!* no. 20 (1990): 20°22.

30. Korkis, *Persistence of Vision*, 27.

31. Cartwright, interview with author; Buck, interview with author.

32. Van Citters, *Animato!* 20.

33. Ibid., 20–21.

34. Cartwright, interview with author.

35. Michael Peraza, interview with author (February 6, 2014).

36. Van Citters, interview with author.

37. Buck, interview with author.

38. Giaimo, interview with author.

39. Van Citters, interview with author.

40. Ibid.

41. Ibid.

42. Jeffrey Price, discussion with author (April 5, 2013).

43. Peter S. Seaman and Jeffrey Price, "Who Framed Roger Rabbit?—Walt Disney Studios Prod. 0237" (screenplay, second draft, Los Angeles, July 26, 1982).

44. Cartwright, interview with author; Stirdivant, interview with author.

45. Van Citters, *Animato!* 22.

46. Stirdivant, interview with author.

47. Cartwright, interview with author.

48. Buck, interview with author; Van Citters, interview with author; Wilhite, interview with author; Miller, interview with author; Stirdivant, interview with author.

49. Korkis, *Persistence of Vision*, 27.

50. Van Citters, interview with author; Wilhite, interview with author; Stirdivant, interview with author.

51. Stirdivant, interview with author.

52. Van Citters, interview with author.

53. "Backstage at Disney," *Walt Disney Studio Showcase*, television, performed by John Culhane (Los Angeles: Disney Channel, April 1983), https://www.youtube.com/watch?v=5qTW6uKjzqI.

54. Peter Renoudet (Renaday), interview with author (April 13, 2012).

55. Cartwright, *1983 Disney Studio Tour*, 8mm home movie.

56. Miller, interview with author.

57. Van Citters, interview with author.

58. Lowell Ganz and Babaloo Mandel, "Who Framed Roger Rabbit?—Walt Disney Studios Prod. 0237" (screenplay, second draft, Los Angeles, December 13, 1984).

59. Van Citters, interview with author.

60. Cartwright, interview with author.

61. Miller, interview with author.

62. Van Citters, interview with author.

63. Miller, interview with author.

64. Buck, interview with author.

65. Giaimo, interview with author.

66. Buck, interview with author.

67. Giaimo, interview with author.

68. Buck, interview with author.

69. Buck, interview with author.

70. Van Citters, interview with author.

71. "Sport Goofy in Soccermania," Wikipedia, https://en.wikipedia.org/wiki/Sport_Goofy_in_Soccermania.

72. https://www.youtube.com/watch?v=ggmVm21jDuw.

73. "Sport Goofy in Soccermania," *IMDb*, https://www.imdb.com/title/tt0278047/.

74. Van Citters, interview with author.

75. Ibid.

76. Michael Eisner with Tony Schwartz, *Work in Progress* (New York: Random House, 1998), 172.

77. Tom Sito, *Moving Innovation: A History of Computer Animation* (Cambridge, MA: MIT Press, 2013), 228.

78. Peter Schneider, interview with author (November 25, 2013).

79. Eisner, *Work in Progress*, 181–82.

80. Schneider, interview with author.

81. Ibid.

82. Giaimo, interview with author.

83. Schneider, interview with author.

84. Ibid.

85. Ibid.

86. Van Citters, interview with author.

87. Musker, interview with author.

88. Ibid.

89. Schneider, interview with author.

90. Ibid.

91. Giaimo, interview with author.

92. Van Citters, interview with author.

93. Giaimo, interview with author; Van Citters, interview with author.

94. Phil Nibbelink, interview with author (August 22, 2013)

CHAPTER TWO

1. Michael Reese, "The Making of Roger Rabbit," *Newsweek*, June 27, 1988, 55.

2. Adam Pirani, "Robert Zemeckis Murder Comes to Toontown," *Starlog*, September 1988, 37; Jeremy Clarke, "Framing Roger," *Films and Filming*, January 1989, 7.

3. John Taylor, *Storming the Magic Kingdom* (New York: Alfred A. Knopf, 1987), 239.

4. Michael Peraza, "Cauldron of Chaos, Part 2" *The Ink and Paint Club: Memories of the Mouse House* (blog), September 7, 2010, http://michaelperaza.blogspot.com/2010/09/cauldron-of-chaos-part-2.html.

5. Nicole LaPorte, *The Men Who Would Be King* (New York: Houghton Mifflin Harcourt, 2010), 47.

6. Ron Grover, *The Disney Touch: How a Daring Management Team Revived an Entertainment Empire* (Homewood, IL: Business One Irwin, 1991), 82.

7. LaPorte, *The Men Who Would Be King*, 37.

8. Bob Thompson, "Looney Toons," *(Totonto) Sunday Sun*, June 19, 1988, S15; David McDonnell, "Who framed Roger Rabbit," *Starlog Yearbook*, vol. 4, 1988, 51.

9. Reese, "The Making of Roger Rabbit," 57.

10. Grover, *The Disney Touch*, 116.

11. LaPorte, *The Men Who Would Be King*, 39.

12. Arthur Schmidt, interview with author (November 11, 2013).

13. Pirani, "Robert Zemeckis Murder Comes to Toontown," 37.

14. Ken Ralston, interview with author (December 4, 2013).

15. Ibid.

16. Ibid.

17. Russell Hall, interview with author (August 30, 2013).

18. Eric Goldberg, interview with author (December 5, 2013).

19. Goldberg; Max Howard, interview with author (September 27, 2013); Silvia Pompei, interview with author (November 29, 2013).

20. Goldberg.

21. John Musker, interview with author (November 4, 2010).

22. Howard.

23. Musker.

24. Robert Watts, interview with author (November 10, 2015).

25. Richard Williams, interview by Luke Menichelli, 1996, unpublished transcript.

26. Watts.

27. Williams.

28. Watts.

29. Pirani, "Robert Zemeckis Murder Comes to Toontown," 38; Kim Masters, "What's Up, Doc?" *Premiere*, July 1988, 35.

30. Masters, 35.

31. Williams, interview by Luke Menichelli.

32. Masters, 35.

33. Goldberg, interview with author.

34. Hans Bacher, interview with author (November 3, 2012).

35. Ibid.

36. Andrew Ruhemann, interview with author (December 2, 2013).

37. Masters, "What's Up, Doc?" 35.

38. Watts, interview with author.

39. Bacher, interview with author.

40. Ibid.

41. Ibid.

42. Ibid.

43. Ruhemann, interview with author.

44. Bacher, interview with author.

45. Ibid.

46. Mike Peraza, interview with author (February 6, 2014).

47. Ibid.

48. John Canemaker, *Two Guys Named Joe: Master Storytellers Joe Grant and Joe Ranft* (New York: Disney Editions, 2010), 49; Mark Kausler, interview with author (August 27, 2013).

49. Kausler.

50. Canemaker, *Two Guys Named Joe*, 49.

51. John Canemaker, "Studio Approaches to Story" (from panel discussion among John Canemaker, Bill Peet, Joe Ranft, Jerry Rees, and Peter Schneider at Second Annual Walter Lantz Conference on Animation—June 11, 1988), in *Storytelling in Animation: The Art of the Animated Image, Vol. 2* (Los Angeles: American Film Institute, 1988), 81.

52. Kausler, interview with author.

53. Ibid.

54. Ibid.

55. Ed Catmull with Amy Wallace, *Creativity, Inc.: Overcoming the Unseen Forces That Stand in the Way of True Inspiration* (New York: Random House, 2014), 90–91.

56. Lou Mongello, "Interview with Don Hahn and Peter Schneider," *WDW Radio* (podcast), show #160, March 7, 2010, http://www.wdwradio.com/2010/03/don-hahn-interview-disney-peter-schneider-show-160-march-7–2010/.

57. Ibid.

58. Ibid.

59. Chris Knott, interview with author (December 18, 2012).

60. Ralston, interview with author.

61. Knott, interview with author.

62. Ibid.

63. Ibid.

64. Shelley Page, interview with author (March 18, 2014).

65. Ibid.

66. Adam Nation, "Who *really* Framed Roger Rabbit?: The Lost Animators," *Starburst*, January 1989, 19.

67. Ruhemann, interview with author.

68. Ibid.

69. Charles Fleischer, interview witth author (December 3, 2013); David McDonnell, "Charles Fleischer's Rabbit Punch," *Starlog*, January 1989, 46.

70. McDonnell, *Starlog*, 46; Scott Huver, "A Re-Tooned 'Who Framed Roger Rabbit?' Celebrates 25 Years," NBC Bay Area Entertainment (blog), March 11, 2013, https://www .nbcbayarea.com/entertainment/entertainment-news/Re-Tooned-for-Blu-Ray-Who -Framed-Roger-Rabbit-celebrates-25-Years-196217071.html.

71. Huver, NBC Bay Area Entertainment; Fleischer, interview with author.

72. McDonnell, *Starlog*, 47.

73. Huver.

74. Reese, *Newsweek*, 58.

75. Masters, *Premiere*, 36.

76. Adam Pirani, "Bob Hoskins, Animated Investigator," *Starlog*, August 1988, 41.

77. Ibid., 41.

78. Joanna Cassidy, interview with author (August 7, 2013); Steve Swires, "Joanna Cassidy: Her Life & Hard (-Boiled) Times," *Starlog*, October 1988, 32.

79. Cassidy, interview with author.

80. Swires, *Starlog*, 30.

81. Cassidy, interview with author.

82. Randall Larson, "Alan Silvestri, Tunes for Toons," *Starlog*, October 1988, 19.

83. Watts, interview with author; Jerry Beck, "A Funny Cartoon for the '80s—A Talk with Robert Zemeckis," *Animation Magazine*, Summer 1988, 29.

84. Watts, interview with author.

85. Schmidt, interview with author.

86. Robert Spurlock, interview with author (February 7, 2014).

87. Cassidy, interview with author.

88. Watts, interview with author.

89. Ibid.

90. Watts; Beck, *Starlog*, 29.

CHAPTER THREE

1. George Gibbs, interview with author (November 9, 2013); Dave Barclay, interview with author (October 17, 2013).

2. Michael Reese, "The Making of Roger Rabbit," *Newsweek*, June 27, 1988, 58.

3. Barclay, interview with author.

4. Adam Eisenberg, "Romancing the Rabbit," *Cinefex*, no. 35 (August 1988), 11.

5. Barclay, interview with author.

6. Ibid.

7. Ross Anderson, "The Secret History of *Who framed Roger Rabbit*," *Cartoon Brew* (blog), April 11, 2013, https://www.cartoonbrew.com/classic/the-secret-history-of-who -framed-roger-rabbit-80963.html.

8. Barclay, interview with author.

9. Ibid.

10. Gibbs, interview with author.

11. Barry Wilkinson, "Painting Rubber Penguins: Making *Who Framed Roger Rabbit*," Elstree Project oral history interviews, October 9, 2012, http://theelstreeproject.org/films/who-framed-roger-rabbit/.

12. Ron Punter, "Painting Rubber Penguins: Making *Who Framed Roger Rabbit*," Elstree Project oral history interviews, October 9, 2012, http://theelstreeproject.org/films/who-framed-roger-rabbit/.

13. Gibbs, interview with author.

14. Ibid.

15. Ibid.

16. Ken Ralston, interview with author (December 4, 2013).

17. Ibid.

18. Barclay, interview with author.

19. Robert Zemeckis, AMPAS Toontown reunion panel discussion (twenty-fifth anniversary screening of *Who Framed Roger Rabbit*, Los Angeles, April 4, 2013)

20. Arthur Schmidt, interview with author (November 11, 2013).

21. Adam Pirani, "Robert Zemeckis, Murder Comes to Toontown," *Starlog*, September 1988, 40.

22. Joanna Cassidy, interview with author (August 7, 2013).

23. Charles Fleischer, interview with author (December 3, 2013).

24. Zemeckis, AMPAS Toontown reunion panel discussion (twenty-fifth anniversary screening of *Who Framed Roger Rabbit*, Los Angeles, April 4, 2013)

25. Warwick Davis, *Size Matters Not: The Extraordinary Life and Career of Warwick Davis* (Hoboken, NJ: Aurum Press, 2010), 87°88; Warwick Davis, interview with author (January 8, 2014).

26. Ralston, interview with author.

27. Gibbs, interview with author.

28. Barclay, interview with author.

29. David McDonnell, "Who Framed Roger Rabbit," *Starlog Yearbook, Vol. 4* (1988), 94.

30. Kim Masters, "What's Up, Doc?" *Premiere* (July 1988), 34.

31. McDonnell, *Starlog Yearbook*, 52.

CHAPTER FOUR

1. Julianna Franchetti, interview with author (September 3, 2014).

2. Andrew Ruhemann, interview with author (December 2, 2013).

3. Simon Wells, interview with author (March 19, 2014).

4. Ibid.

5. Andrew Ruhemann, interview with author.

6. Julianna Franchetti, interview with author.

7. Vincent Woodcock, correspondence with author (March 13, 2014); Vincent Woodcock, correspondence with author (August 3, 2014).

8. Max Howard, interview with author (September 27, 2013).

9. Ibid.

10. Andrew Ruhemann, interview with author.

11. Patsy De Lord, interview with author (January 9, 2013).

12. Annie Elvin, interview with author (March 7, 2014).

13. Martin Elvin, correspondence with author (May 24, 2014).

14. Shelley Page, interview with author (March 26, 2014).

15. Andrew Ruhemann, interview with author.

16. Shelley Page, interview with author.

17. Ibid.

18. Shelley Page, interview with author; Eric Goldberg, interview with author (December 5, 2013).

19. Russell Hall, interview with author (August 30, 2013).

20. Roy Naisbitt, interview with author (December 3, 2013).

21. Shelley Page, interview with author.

22. Julianna Franchetti, interview with author.

23. Tom Sito, *Drawing the Line: The Untold Story of the Animation Unions* (Lexington: University Press of Kentucky, 2006), 262.

24. Chuck Gammage, interview with author (September 19, 2013).

25. Uli Meyer, interview with author (September 11, 2013).

26. Ibid.

27. Ibid.

28. Ibid.

29. Dino Athanassiou, interview with author (November 17, 2013).

30. Roger Chiasson, interview with author (September 18, 2013).

31. Alvaro Gaivoto, interview with author (November 8, 2013).

32. Andy Robin, "The Barber," *Seinfeld*, episode 072, season 5, episode 8, directed by Tom Cherones (Los Angeles: Shapiro/West Productions in association with Castle Rock Entertainment/NBC, November 1, 1993), http://www.seinfeldscripts.com/TheBarber.htm, https://www.dailymotion.com/video/x6i6twr.

33. Didier Ghez, "Interview With Dave Spafford on July 29, 2010," in *Walt's People— Volume 13*, ed. Didier Ghez (Theme Park Press, 2013), 420.

34. Dave Spafford, interview with author (September 28, 2009).

35. Phil Nibbelink, interview with author (August 22, 2013).

36. Alain Costa, interview with author (August 20, 2013).

37. Jacques Muller, interview with author (August 17, 2013).

38. Raul Garcia, interview with author (August 22, 2013).

39. Rob Stevenhagen, interview with author (September 25, 2013).

40. Nicolette Van Gendt, interview with author (September 11, 2013).

41. Marc Gordon-Bates, interview with author March 12, 2014).

42. Philip Scarrold, correspondence with author (March 16, 2014).

43. Nik Ranieri, interview with author (October 1, 2009); Cal Leduc, interview with author (October 19, 2013).

44. Joe Haidar, interview with author (August 10, 2013).

45. Richard Bazley, interview with author (May 14, 2012).

46. Stella-Rose Benson, interview with author (August 21, 2013).

47. Paul Chung, interview with author (September 9, 2013).

48. Elaine Koo, interview with author (October 23, 2013).

49. Robert Newman, correspondence with author (March 9, 2014).

50. Silvia Pompei, interview with author (November 29, 2013).

51. Julia Woolf, interview with author (December 2, 2013).

52. Kevin Jon Davies, interview with author (November 20, 2013).

53. Chris Jenkins, interview with author (October 24, 2013).

54. Fraser MacLean, interview with author (September 17, 2013).

55. Tim Sanpher, interview with author (October 12, 2013).

56. Michael Smith, interview with author (November 22, 2014).

57. Colin Alexander, correspondence with author (June 30, 2017).

58. Stephen Cavalier, correspondence with author (July 19, 2017).

59. Anthony Clark, interview with author (November 26, 2013).

60. Annie Elvin, interview with author; Martin Elvin, correspondence with author.

61. Frazer Diamond, *Frazer Diamond* (blog), homepage, http://www.frazerdiamond.co.uk/bio.html.

62. Richard Leon, interview with author (January 22, 2014).

63. Hans Bacher, interview with author (November 3, 2012).

64. Ibid.

65. Ibid.

66. Ibid.

67. Ibid.

68. Amanda Talbot, interview with author (November 7, 2013).

69. James Baxter, interview with author (October 2, 2013); Neil Boyle, interview with author (September 19, 2013).

70. Boyle.

71. David Bowers, interview with author (October 23, 2013).

72. Amanda Talbot, interview with author.

73. David Pritchard, interview with author (November 17, 2013).

74. Peter Gambier, interview with author (November 8, 2013).

75. Lily Dell, interview with author (November 12, 2013).

76. Roger Way, interview with author (October 1, 2013).

77. Ibid.

78. Peter Western, interview with author (October 12, 2013).

79. Ibid.

80. Alex Williams, interview with author (August 21, 2013).

81. Grag Manwaring, interview with author (November 2, 2013).

82. Tom Sito, interview with author (November 2, 2010).

83. Tom Sito, interview with author (November 2, 2010); Tom Sito and Pat Sito, interview with author (October 14, 2013).

84. Tom Sito, interview with author (November 2, 2010); Tom Sito and Pat Sito, interview with author; Didier Ghez, "Interview With Tom Sito on April 11 and 27, 2007,"

in *Walt's People—Volume 9*, ed. Didier Ghez (Xlibris, 2010), 486; Jason Anders, "#3. A Conversation with Tom Sito," *Fulle Circle Magazine* (blog) (January 9, 2009), http://www .fullecirclemagazine.com/2009/01/conversation-with-tom-sito.html.

85. Tom Sito and Pat Sito, Interview with author; Jason Anders, "#3. A Conversation with Tom Sito," *Fulle Circle Magazine* (blog) (January 9, 2009), http://www.fullecircle magazine.com/2009/01/conversation-with-tom-sito.html; Julia Orr, interview with author (September 13, 2013).

86. Tom Sito and Pat Sito, unterview with author; Didier Ghez, "Interview With Tom Sito on April 11 and 27, 2007," in *Walt's People—Volume 9*, ed. Didier Ghez (Xlibris, 2010), 486.

87. Tom Sito and Pat Sito, interview with author.

88. Dave Bossert, interview with author (May 6, 2011); Dave Bossert, interview with author (May 31, 2011).

89. Bossert, interview with author (May 6, 2011).

90. Tim Sanpher, interview with author; Michael Smith, interview with author; Amanda Talbot, interview with author.

91. Dorse Lanpher, *Flyin' Chunks and Other Things to Duck: Memoirs of a Life Spent Doodling for Dollars* (Bloomington, IN: iUniverse, 2010), 42.

92. Ibid., 59.

93. Ibid., 66–81.

94. Dorse Lanpher, *Flyin' Chunks and Other Things to Duck: Memoirs of a Life Spent Doodling for Dollars*, 104–108; Dorse Lanpher, interview with author (December 10, 2010).

95. Steve Hickner, interview with author (October 2, 2013).

96. Ibid.

97. Alvaro Gaivoto, interview with author; Didier Ghez, "Interview With Dave Spafford on July 29, 2010," in *Walt's People—Volume 13*, ed. Didier Ghez (Theme Park Press, 2013).

98. Rob Stevenhagen, interview with author.

99. Uli Meyer, interview with author; Alain Costa, interview with author.

100. Uli Meyer, interview with author.

101. Ibid.

102. Dino Athanassiou, interview with author.

103. Nik Ranieri, interview with author.

104. Ibid.

105. Ibid.

106. Russell Hall, interview with author.

107. Dave Spafford, interview with author (September 28, 2009).

108. Jacques Muller, interview with author.

109. Dino Athanassiou, interview with author.

110. Patsy De Lord, interview with author.

111. Annie Elvin, interview with author.

112. Tom Sito, interview with author (November 2, 2010).

113. Neil Boyle, interview with author.

114. Dave Spafford, interview with author (September 28, 2009).

115. Peter Western, interview with author.

116. Max Howard, interview with author.

117. Howard; Russell Hall, interview with author.

118. Max Howard, interview with author.

119. Peter Western, interview with author.

120. James Baxter, interview with author.

121. Jacques Muller, interview with author.

122. Shelley Page, interview with author.

123. Ibid.

124. Simon Wells, interview with author.

125. Raul Garcia, interview with author; Robert Newman, interview with author.

126. Elaine Koo, interview with author.

127. Didier Ghez, "Interview With Dave Spafford on July 29, 2010," in *Walt's People—Volume 13*, ed. Didier Ghez (Theme Park Press, 2013), 424; Dave Spafford, interview with author (September 28, 2009).

128. Cal Leduc, interview with author.

129. Stella-Rose Benson, interview with author.

130. Robert Newman, interview with author; James Baxter, interview with author; Glenn Sylvester, interview with author (March 13, 2014).

131. Peter Western, interview with author.

132. Tim Sanpher, interview with author.

133. Kevin Jon Davies, interview with author; Chris Jenkins, interview with author; Fraser MacLean, interview with author; Tim Sanpher, interview with author; Michael Smith, interview with author; Amanda Talbot, interview with author; David Pritchard, interview with author.

134. Amanda Talbot, interview with author.

135. Michael Smith, interview with author.

136. Ibid.

137. Roger Way, interview with author.

138. Al Gaivoto, *Hang Gliding Rabbit Workers*, 12:02, June 12, 2012, https://www.youtube.com/watch?v=_k4TIU9gpQE.

139. Shelley Page, interview with author.

140. Max Howard, interview with author.

141. Dave Spafford, interview with author (September 28, 2009).

142. Colin White, interview with author (August 27, 2013).

143. Anthony Clark, interview with author.

144. Shelley Page, interview with author.

145. Roger Chiasson, interview with author.

146. Ibid.

147. Anthony Clark, interview with author.

148. Kevin Jon Davies, interview with author.

149. Max Howard, interview with author.

150. Greg Manwaring, interview with author.

151. David Pritchard, interview with author.

152. Max Howard, interview with author.

153. Brent Odell, interview with author (September 17, 2013).

154. Ibid.

155. Ibid.

156. Peter Western, interview with author.

157. Kevin Jon Davies, interview with author; Tom Sito, interview with author (November 2, 2010); Andreas Deja, "Roger Rabbit Scenes IV," *Deja View* (blog), June 7, 2016, http://andreasdeja.blogspot.com/2016/06/roger-rabbit-scenes-iv.html.

158. Neil Boyle, interview with author.

159. Roy Naisbitt, interview with author.

160. Neil Boyle, interview with author.

161. Alvaro Gaivoto, interview with author.

162. Ross Anderson, "The Secret History of *Who framed Roger Rabbit*," *Cartoon Brew* (blog), April 11, 2013, https://www.cartoonbrew.com/classic/the-secret-history-of-who -framed-roger-rabbit-80963.html.

163. Max Howard, interview with author.

164. Dave Spafford, interview with author (September 28, 2009).

165. Max Howard, interview with author; Roy Naisbitt, interview with author; Dave Spafford, interview with author.

166. Shelley Page, interview with author.

167. Nik Ranieri, interview with author.

168. Robert Newman, interview with author.

169. Nik Ranieri, interview with author.

170. Richard Leon, interview with author.

171. Ibid.

CHAPTER FIVE

1. Robert Watts, interview with author (November 10, 2015).

2. Don Hahn, "Immersion," in *Brainstorm: Unleashing Your Creative Self* (New York: Disney Editions, 2011): 239–43.

3. Richard Williams, interview by Luke Menichelli, 1996, unpublished transcript.

4. Richard Williams, 1996, unpublished interview; Ken Ralston, interview with author (December 4, 2013).

5. Richard Williams, 1996, unpublished interview.

6. Robert Watts, interview with author; Don Hahn, *Brainstorm*, 243.

7. Shelley Page, interview with author (March 26, 2014).

8. Richard Williams, 1996, unpublished interview.

9. Ibid.

10. Williams; Carl Gover, "Carl Gover, Part 1," *TheThief* (blog), February 5, 2008, http:// thethief1.blogspot.com/2008/02/carl-gover-part-1.html; Carl Gover, "Carl Gover, Part 2," *TheThief* (blog), February 7, 2008, http://thethief1.blogspot.com/2008/02/in-meantime -after-lot-of.html.

11. Richard Williams, 1996, unpublished interview.

12. Shelley Page, interview with author; Carl Gover, "Carl Gover, Part 1," *TheThief* (blog), February 5, 2008, http://thethief1.blogspot.com/2008/02/carl-gover-part-1

.html; Carl Gover, "Carl Gover, Part 2," *TheThief* (blog), February 7, 2008, http://thethief1 .blogspot.com/2008/02/in-meantime-after-lot-of.html; Eric Goldberg, interview with author (December 5, 2013).

13. Eric Goldberg, interview with author.

14. Sheldon Teitelbaum, "Who Drew 'Roger Rabbit'?" *Cinefantastique*, January 1989.

15. Dale Baer, interview with author (September 29, 2009); Jerry Beck, "The Acme Gag Factory—A Talk with Dale and Jane Baer," *Animation Magazine* 2, no. 1 (Summer 1988).

16. Steve Hickner, interview with author (October 2, 2013).

17. Marty Kline, interview with author (February 26, 2014).

18. William H. Frake, interview with author (October 6, 2013).

19. William H. Frake, interview with author (September 22, 2016).

20. Dale Baer, interview with author.

21. Dale Baer, interview with author; William H. Frake, interview with author (September 22, 2016).

22. Frake.

23. Frake; Michael Humphries, interview with author (October 23, 2013).

24. Sheldon Teitelbaum, "Who Drew 'Roger Rabbit'?" *Cinefantastique*, January 1989.

25. Frans Vischer, interview with author (November 5, 2010).

26. William H. Frake, interview with author (October 6, 2013).

27. Jerry Beck, "The Acme Gag Factory—A Talk with Dale and Jane Baer," *Animation Magazine* 2, no. 1 (Summer 1988); William H. Frake, interview with author (October 6, 2013); Adam Eisenberg, "Romancing the Rabbit," *Cinefex*, no. 35, August 1988, 27–28; David Hutchison, "A Special FX Achievement, Part 6," *Starlog*, December 1989; George Turner, "Cartoons Came to Life in *Roger*," *American Cinematographer*, July 1988; Mark Cotta Vaz and Patricia Rose Duignan, "Breakthroughs," in *Industrial Light and Magic: Into the Digital Realm* (New York: Delray/Ballantine Books, 1996), 123–32.

28. William H. Frake, interview with author (October 6, 2013).

29. Ibid.

30. Frake; Frake, interview with author (September 22, 2016).

31. Frake, interview with author (December 31, 2013); Frake, interview with author (January 8, 2015).

32. Randy Fullmer, interview with author (September 18, 2013).

33. Ibid.

34. William H. Frake, interview with author (October 6, 2013); Mark Kausler, interview with author (August 27, 2013); David Pacheco, interview with author (October 17, 2013).

35. Dale Baer, interview with author; Frake, interview with author (September 22, 2016).

36. Frake, interview with author (October 6, 2013).

37. Dale Baer, interview with author; Len Smith, interview with author (September 10, 2013).

38. Dale Baer, interview with author; Mark Kausler, interview with author.

39. Bruce W. Smith, interview with author (November 3, 2010).

40. Steve Hulett, "The Carl Bell Interview—Part 1," *Animation Guild TAG Blog*, November 28, 2011, http://animationguildblog.blogspot.com/2011/11/carl-bell-interview-part-i.html; Steve Hulett, "The Carl Bell Interview—Part 2," *Animation Guild TAG Blog*, November 29, 2011, http://animationguildblog.blogspot.com/2011/11/carl-bell-interview-part-ii.html.

41. Frans Vischer, interview with author.

42. Matthew O'Callaghan, interview with author (April 11, 2011).

43. Matthew O'Callaghan, interview with author (February 23, 2011).

44. Randy Fullmer, interview with author.

CHAPTER SIX

1. Dave Spafford, interview with author (September 28, 2009); Michael Bonifer, "Improvisation, Spaff-Style," *Gamechangers* (blog), October 16, 2007, http://www.gamechangers.com/improvisation-spaff-style/; Steve Kiesel, "Who's Hoo—Dave 'Spaff' Spafford," interview/talk show from the Magic Castle, Los Angeles, February 18, 2013), https://vimeo.com/59926388.

2. Amanda Talbot, interview with author (November 7, 2013); Greg Manwaring, interview with author (November 2, 2013).

3. Chris Knott, correspondence with author (December 18, 2012).

4. Ken Ralston, interview with author (December 4, 2013).

5. Chris Knott, correspondence with author.

6. Adam Eisenberg, "Romancing the Rabbit," *Cinefex*, no. 35, August 1988, 8–9.

7. Shelley Page, interview with author (March 26, 2014).

8. Chris Knott, correspondence with author; Ken Ralston, interview with author; George Turner, "Cartoons Came to Life in *Roger*," *American Cinematographer*, July 1988, 54.

9. Chris Knott, correspondence with author.

10. Adam Eisenberg, "Romancing the Rabbit," *Cinefex*, 9; Mark Cotta Vaz, *Industrial Light and Magic: Into the Digital Realm* (New York: Delray, 1996), 125.

11. Adam Nation, "Who *really* Framed Roger Rabbit?" *Starburst*, no. 125, January 1989, 19.

12. Adam Nation, "Who *really* Framed Roger Rabbit?" 19.

13. George Turner, "Cartoons Came to Life in *Roger*," *American Cinematographer*, 58.

14. Adam Eisenberg, "Romancing the Rabbit," *Cinefex*, 31; George Turner, "Cartoons Came to Life in *Roger*," 58–60; Adam Nation, "Who *really* Framed Roger Rabbit?"19; Mark Cotta Vaz and Patricia Rose Duignan, *Industrial Light and Magic: Into the Digital Realm* (New York: Delray/Ballantine Books, 1996), 130; Nick Stern, interview with author (November 14 and 17, 2013).

15. Wes Takahashi, interview with author (October 22, 2013).

16. Adam Eisenberg, "Romancing the Rabbit," *Cinefex*, 31; Nick Stern, interview with author.

17. Kristian Williams, "Who Framed Roger Rabbit—The 3 Rules of Living Animation," February 24, 2017, in *KaptainKristian Channel*, video essay, 7:23, https://www.youtube.com/watch?v=RWtt3Tmnij4.

18. Fraser MacLean, correspondence with author (September 17, 2013).

19. Nick Stern, interview with author.

20. George Turner, "Cartoons Came to Life in *Roger*," *American Cinematographer*, 60.

21. Wes Takahashi, interview with author.

22. Nick Stern, interview with author.

23. Adam Eisenberg, "Romancing the Rabbit," *Cinefex*, 35; Wes Takahashi, interview with author.

24. Nick Stern, interview with author.

25. Adam Eisenberg, "Romancing the Rabbit," *Cinefex*, 9.

26. Adam Eisenberg, "Romancing the Rabbit," *Cinefex*, 11; George Turner, "Cartoons Came to Life in *Roger*," *American Cinematographer*, 60.

27. Robert Spurlock, interview with author (February 7, 2014).

28. Adam Eisenberg, "Romancing the Rabbit," *Cinefex*, 11.

29. Nick Stern, interview with author.

30. Adam Eisenberg, "Romancing the Rabbit," *Cinefex*, 11.

31. Ibid., 12.

32. George Gibbs, interview with author (November 9, 2013).

33. Kristian Williams, "Who Framed Roger Rabbit—The 3 Rules of Living Animation," February 24, 2017, in *KaptainKristian Channel*; Dave Barclay, interview with author (October 17, 2013).

34. Adam Eisenberg, "Romancing the Rabbit," *Cinefex*, 17–18; George Gibbs, interview with author.

35. Adam Eisenberg, "Romancing the Rabbit," *Cinefex*, 16; David Hutchison, "Who Framed Roger Rabbit—A Special FX Achievement, Part 4," *Starlog*, October 1989, 26.

36. Marielle Wakim, "Here's Why *Who Framed Roger Rabbit?* Is the Most IMPRESSIVE Animated Movie of All Time," *LA Magazine*, February 28, 2017.

37. George Gibbs, interview with author.

38. Adam Eisenberg, "Romancing the Rabbit," *Cinefex*, 28; George Turner, "Cartoons Came to Life in *Roger*," *American Cinematographer*, 58.

39. Adam Eisenberg, "Romancing the Rabbit," *Cinefex*, 28; William H. Frake, interview with author (October 6, 2013).

40. Adam Eisenberg, "Romancing the Rabbit," *Cinefex*, 18–19; George Gibbs, interview with author.

41. Tom St. Amand, interview with author (December 2, 2013); Harry V. Walton, interview with author (December 1, 2013).

42. Adam Eisenberg, "Romancing the Rabbit," *Cinefex*, 12; Mark Cotta Vaz and Patricia Rose Duignan, *Industrial Light and Magic: Into the Digital Realm*, 131.

43. George Turner, "Cartoons Came to Life in *Roger*," *American Cinematographer*, 60.

44. Adam Eisenberg, "Romancing the Rabbit," *Cinefex*, 12.

45. Nick Stern, interview with author.

46. Adam Eisenberg, "Romancing the Rabbit," *Cinefex*, 27; George Turner, "Who Framed Roger Rabbit?" *American Cinematographer*, July 1988, 48; Mark Cotta Vaz and Patricia Rose Duignan, *Industrial Light and Magic: Into the Digital Realm*, 131; William H. Frake, interview with author (September 22, 2016).

47. Adam Eisenberg, "Romancing the Rabbit," *Cinefex*, 28; Mark Cotta Vaz and Patricia Rose Duignan, *Industrial Light and Magic: Into the Digital Realm*, 130; William H. Frake, interview with author (September 22, 2016); William H. Frake, interview with author (October 6, 2013).

48. William H. Frake, interview with author (October 6, 2013).

49. George Turner, "Cartoons Came to Life in *Roger*," *American Cinematographer*, 60.

50. Fraser MacLean, interview with author.

51. Amanda Talbot, interview with author; Fraser MacLean, interview with author; Annie Elvin, interview with author (March 7, 2014); Kevin Jon Davies, interview with author (November 20, 2013); Chris Jenkins, interview with author (October 24, 2013); Tim Sanpher, interview with author (October 12, 2013); Michael Smith, interview with author (November 22, 2014); David Pritchard, interview with author (November 17, 2013); Lily Dell, interview with author (November 12, 2013).

52. Chris Knott, correspondence with author (December 18, 2012).

CHAPTER SEVEN

1. Shelley Page, interview with author (March 26, 2014).

2. Neil Boyle, interview with author (September 19, 2013).

3. Shelley Page, interview with author.

4. Colin White, interview with author (August 27, 2013).

5. Michael Smith, interview with author (November 22, 2014).

6. Adam Nation, "Who *really* Framed Roger Rabbit?" *Starburst*, no. 126, February 1989, 8; Julia Orr, interview with author (September 13, 2013).

7. Jacques Muller, *RR cont Behind the curtain + Barbican singing*, August 12, 2014, videotape recording, 47:39, https://www.youtube.com/watch?v=wJvrqyYEI3w&t=1445s.

8. Shelley Page, interview with author.

9. David Bowers, interview with author (October 23, 2013).

10. Shelley Page, interview with author; Neil Boyle, interview with author; Peter Western, interview with author (October 12, 2013).

11. James Baxter, interview with author (October 2, 2013).

12. Jacques Muller, interview with author (August 17, 2013); Nik Ranieri, interview with author (October 1, 2009); Andreas Deja, interview with author (November 3, 2010).

13. Shelley Page, interview with author.

14. Neil Boyle, interview with author.

15. Anthony Clark, interview with author (November 26, 2013).

16. Max Howard, interview with author (September 27, 2013).

17. Richard Leon, interview with author (January 22, 2014).

18. Glenn Sylvester, interview with author (March 13, 2014).

19. Nik Ranieri, interview with author.

20. James Baxter, interview with author; Cal Leduc, interview with author (October 19, 2013).

21. Michael Smith, interview with author.

22. Smith; Kevin Jon Davies, interview with author (November 20, 2013).

23. Dave Spafford, interview with author (September 28, 2009).

24. Jacques Muller, interview with author.

25. Colin White, interview with author; Michael Smith, interview with author; Julia Orr, interview with author; Peter Western, interview with author.

26. Roger Hurlburt, "'Roger Rabbit' Hops in Sotheby's Auction," *Orlando Sun-Sentinel*, June 10, 1989.

27. Michael Eisner with Tony Schwartz, *Work in Progress* (New York: Random House, 1998), 182.

28. Max Howard, interview with author (April 3, 2014).

29. Alvaro Gaivoto, interview with author (November 8, 2013).

30. Dave Spafford, interview with author (September 28, 2009).

31. Peter Western, interview with author.

32. Ibid.

33. Kathleen Carroll, "Hop Hop Hooray!" *New York EXTRA*, June 22, 1988; Steven Rea, "Making Roger Rabbit a Star—What was Once Seen as a Costly Film Gamble is Now Looking like the Movie Event of the Summer," *Philadelphia Inquirer*, June 26, 1988.

34. Roger Ebert, "Runaway Hit From a Rabbit," *New York Post*, June 22, 1988.

35. Colin White, interview with author.

36. Dave Spafford, interview with author.

37. John Culhane, "For Oscar's Producer, the Key is C," *New York Times*, March 26, 1989.

38. Nik Ranieri, "Nik Ranieri—Animator," *Facebook*, posts throughout April 2013, https://www.facebook.com/NikRanieriAnimator/.

CHAPTER EIGHT

1. Ron Grover, "Hitching a Ride on Hollywood's Hot Streak," *Businessweek*, July 11, 1988, 46.

2. Adam Eisenberg, "Romancing the Rabbit," *Cinefex*, no. 35, August 1988, 26; William H. Frake, interview with author (October 6, 2013).

3. Anthony Clark, interview with author (November 26, 2013).

4. Herbert Schiller, *Culture, Inc.: The Corporate Takeover of Public Expression* (New York: Oxford University Press, 1991).

5. Bernice Kanner, "On Madison Avenue: Frame That Toon," *New York Magazine*, April 17, 1989; Herbert Schiller, *Culture, Inc.: The Corporate Takeover of Public Expression* (New York: Oxford University Press, 1991); Jube Shiver, "Star Struck," *Black Enterprise*, December 1988).

6. Ian Failes, "The Oral History of Space Jam," *Cartoon Brew* (blog), November 15, 2016, https://www.cartoonbrew.com/feature-film/oral-history-space-jam-part-1-launching-movie-144935.html.

7. RaggaR, "Movie References in 'South Park,'" *rateyourmusic.com*, https://rateyourmusic.com/list/RaggaR/movie_references_in_south_park/10/.

8. Max Howard, interview with author (September 27, 2013).

9. Chance Raspberry, "Chance Raspberry presents: The Bill Kopp Extravanganza! Part 2," March 25, 2013, in *Chance Raspberry Newsletter* (podcast), 1:06:02, https://www.youtube.com/watch?v=LyDdZHxgHlM&t=2847s.

10. Chance Raspberry, "Chance Raspberry presents: The Bill Kopp Extravanganza! Part 2," March 25, 2013.

11. Joe Haidar, interview with author (August 10, 2013).

12. Jason Anders, "#38. A Conversation with Tom Bancroft," *Fulle Circle Magazine* (blog), March 2009, http://www.fullecirclemagazine.com/2009/03/conversation-with-tom

-bancroft.html; Chelsea Robson, "Animation Addicts 137: 'Who Framed Roger Rabbit'—I'm Not Bad, I'm Just Drawn That Way—with Tom Bancroft," December 16, 2016, in *Rotoscopers* (podcast), http://www.rotoscopers.com/2016/12/16/animation-addicts-episode-137-who -framed-roger-rabbit-im-not-bad-im-just-drawn-that-way/.

13. Tom Bancroft, interview with author (November 4, 2013).

14. Max Howard, interview with author; Jim Hill, "Disney's Unfinished Featurettes: *Mickey Columbus* and *Mickey's Arabian Adventure*," *Jim Hill Media* (blog), October 10, 2004, http://jimhillmedia.com/editor_in_chief1/b/jim_hill/archive/2004/10/11/477.aspx.

15. Max Howard, interview with author.

16. Max Howard, interview with author (April 3, 2014).

17. Jimmy Jackson, "The Magic of Disney Animation—Animation Tour," *Walt Disney Feature Animation Florida* (blog), http://www.wdfaf.com/misc/tour/index.html.

18. Chance Raspberry, "Chance Raspberry presents: The Bill Kopp Extravanganza! Part 2," March 25, 2013; Mark Kausler, interview with author (August 27, 2013).

19. Barry Temple, electronic message to author (August 21, 2013).

20. Dave Stephan, interview with author (November 13, 2013).

21. Aaron Blaise, interview with author (October 28, 2013).

22. Alex Williams, "Disney MGM Studios, RollerCoaster Rabbit and the Summer of 1989—Part 1," *FLiP Animation* (blog), April 21, 2012, http://flipanimation.blogspot .com/2012/04/disney-mgm-studios-rollercoaster-rabbit.html; Alex Williams, "Disney MGM Studios, RollerCoaster Rabbit and the Summer of 1989—Part 2," *FLiP Animation* (blog), April 24, 2012, http://flipanimation.blogspot.com/2012/04/disney-mgm-studios -summer-of-1989-part.html.

23. Jason Anders, "#38. A Conversation with Tom Bancroft," *Fulle Circle Magazine* (blog), March 2009, http://www.fullecirclemagazine.com/2009/03/conversation-with -tom-bancroft.html.

24. Greg Manwaring, interview with author (November 2, 2013).

25. Tom Bancroft, interview with author (November 4, 2013).

26. Mery-et Lescher, interview with author (October 5, 2016).

27. Rob Bekuhrs, interview with author (November 12, 2013).

28. Mark Kausler, interview with author; Dave Stephan, interview with author; Rob Bekuhrs, interview with author; Steve Hulett, "The Mark Kausler Chat—Part 1," January 24, 2011, in *Animation Guild TAG Blog, with Steve Hulett*, http://animationguildblog.blogspot .com/2011/01/mark-kausler-chat-part-i.html; Ric Sluiter, interview with author (December 4, 2016); Max Howard, correspondence with author (February 8, 2016).

29. Mark Kausler, interview with author; Mark Kausler, interview with author; Dave Stephan, interview with author; Rob Bekuhrs, interview with author; Steve Hulett, "The Mark Kausler Chat—Part 1."

30. Rob Bekuhrs, interview with author.

31. Jim Hill, "The Sad Tail . . . I mean 'Tale' . . . of the Stalled Roger Rabbit Sequel," *Jim Hill Media* (blog), December 21, 2000, http://jimhillmedia.com/editor_in_chief1/b/ jim_hill/archive/2001/01/01/297.aspx.

32. Mark Kausler, interview with author; Aaron Blaise, interview with author; Steve Hulett, "The Mark Kausler Chat—Part 1," *TAG Blog*, January 24, 2011; Ric Sluiter, interview with author.

33. Jason Anders, "#27. A Conversation with Aaron Blaise," *Fulle Circle Magazine* (blog), December 2008, *http://www.fullecirclemagazine.com/2008/12/conversation-with -aaron-blaise.html*.

34. Jason Anders, "#38. A Conversation with Tom Bancroft," *Fulle Circle Magazine*.

35. Steve Hulett, "The Mark Kausler Chat—Part 1," *TAG Blog*, January 24, 2011.

36. Martin Goodman, "Who Screwed Roger Rabbit?" *Animation World Network* (*AWN*) (blog), April 3, 2003, https://www.awn.com/animationworld/who-screwed-roger-rabbit.

37. Barry Cook, interview with author (October 29, 2013).

38. Robert Spurlock, interview with author (February 7, 2014).

39. https://en.wikipedia.org/wiki/Remake.

40. https://www.listchallenges.com/complete-list-movie-series-with-at-least-2-sequels.

41. Martin Goodman, "Who Screwed Roger Rabbit?" *Animation World Network* (*AWN*) (blog), April 3, 2003, https://www.awn.com/animationworld/who-screwed-roger-rabbit; Rich Dees, "Who Delayed Roger Rabbit 2?" *FilmBuffOnline* (blog), August 7, 2005, http:/www .filmbuffonline.com/FBOLNewsreel/wordpress/2005/08/07/who-delayed-roger-rabbit-2/.

42. Simon Brew, "Rob Minkoff on Nearly Making Roger Rabbit 2," *Den of Geek!* (blog), February 7, 2014, http://www.denofgeek.com/movies/who-framed-roger-rabbit/29206/rob -minkoff-on-nearly-making-who-framed-roger-rabbit-2; Floyd Norman, "Fred and Ginger (Almost)," *MrFun* (blog), January 9, 2012, http://mrfun.squarespace.com/blog/2012/1/9/ fred-and-ginger-almost.html.

43. Barry Temple, electronic mail to author (August 21, 2013); Eric Goldberg, interview with author (December 5, 2013).

44. Rich Dees, "Who Delayed Roger Rabbit 2?" *FilmBuffOnline* (blog), August 7, 2005, http:/www.filmbuffonline.com/FBOLNewsreel/wordpress/2005/08/07/who-delayed -roger-rabbit-2/.

45. Barry Temple, electronic mail to author; Eric Goldberg, interview with author; Eric Guaglione, interview with author (December 2, 2013).

46. Eric Goldberg, interview with author.

47. Tom Bancroft, interview with author.

48. Ibid.

49. Martin Goodman, "Who Screwed Roger Rabbit?" *Animation World Network* (*AWN*), April 3, 2003.

50. Martin Goodman; Rich Dees, "Who Delayed Roger Rabbit 2?" *FilmBuffOnline*, August 7, 2005.

51. Eric Goldberg, interview with author.

52. Eric Guaglione, interview with author.

CHAPTER NINE

1. Dale Baer, interview with author (September 29, 2009).

2. Dave Spafford, interview with author (September 28, 2009); Steve Kiesel, "Who's Hoo—Dave 'Spaff' Spafford," interview/talk show from the Magic Castle, Los Angeles, February 18, 2013, https://vimeo.com/59926388.

3. Marcelo Vignali, interview with author (September 15, 2013).

4. Don Carson, interview with author (October 22, 2013).

5. Vignali, interview with author.

6. Ibid.

7. Don Carson, interview with author.

8. Marla Dickerson, "They're Getting a Bit Goofy in Disneyland," *Los Angeles Times*, February 16, 1996; Herbert Muschamp, "Getting Goofy on the Santa Anna Freeway," *New York Times*, November 5, 1995.

9. Don Carson, interview with author.

10. Ibid.

11. Jarrod Canepa, "Exclusive Interview with the Designer of *Roger Rabbit's Cartoon Spin*—Marcelo Vignali," *ImNotBad.com* (blog), April 12, 2012, http://www.imnotbad .com/2012/04/exclusive-roger-rabbit-ride-designer.html.

12. Don Carson, interview with author.

13. Canepa, *ImNotBad.com*.

14. Marcelo Vignali, interview with author; Jarrod Canepa, *ImNotBad.com*.

15. Ricky Brigante, "ITM: Show 309—Interview with Don Carson," March 6, 2011, in *Inside the Magic* (podcast), https://insidethemagic.net/podcasts/309/.

16. Don Carson, interview with author; Ricky Brigante, *Inside the Magic*.

17. Carson.

18. Carson; Marcelo Vignali, interview with author.

19. Marcelo Vignali, interview with author; Jarrod Canepa, *ImNotBad.com*.

20. Vignali; Canepa.

21. Don Carson, interview with author.

22. Marcelo Vignali, interview with author; Jarrod Canepa, *ImNotBad.com*.

23. Jarrod Canepa, *ImNotBad.com*.

24. Gavin Doyle, "Imagineer Don Carson Worked on Splash Mountain and Disneyland Toontown—DD019," November 6, 2014, in *Disney Dose* (podcast), http://disneydose.com/ doncarson/#axzz5KFVU5rGm.

25. Marcelo Vignali, interview with author; Jarrod Canepa, *ImNotBad.com*.

26. Ibid.

27. Jim Hill, "Hare Today, Gone Tomorrow: The Curious Case of the Rapidly Receding Rabbit (Part I)," September 5, 2006, in *Jim Hill Media* (blog), http://jimhillmedia.com/ columnists1/b/jeff_lange/archive/2006/09/06/5591.aspx.

28. Jim Hill, "Hare Today, Gone Tomorrow: The Curious Case of the Rapidly Receding Rabbit (Part II)," September 6, 2006, in *Jim Hill Media* (blog), http://jimhillmedia.com/ columnists1/b/jeff_lange/archive/2006/09/07/5631.aspx.

29. Jarrod Canepa, "Exclusive Jessica Rabbit Artist Interview—Mark Marderosian," *ImNotBad.com* (blog), September 18, 2008, http://www.imnotbad.com/2008/09/mark -marderosian-interview-part-1.html.

CHAPTER TEN

1. Keith Gluck, "Selling Mickey: The Rise of Disney Marketing," *Walt Disney Family Museum* (blog), June 8, 2012, https://waltdisney.org/blog/selling-mickey-rise-disney-marketing.

2. Ron Grover, "Hitching a Ride on Hollywood's Hot Streak," *Businessweek*, July 11, 1988, 46.

3. Jarrod Canepa, "Jessica Rabbit Merchandise Reviews," *ImNotBad.com* (blog), http://www.imnotbad.com/p/jessica-rabbit-merchandise-reviews.html; Thomas Tumbusch, ed., "Who Framed, Molded, Stuffed, Printed or Otherwise Merchandised Roger Rabbit?" *Tomart's Disneyana Update*, no. 21, November/December 1997, 22–26; Thomas Tumbusch, ed., "The Strange Merchandise Tale of 'Who Framed Roger Rabbit,'" *Tomart's Disneyana Update*, no. 69, Winter 2007, 46–51.

4. Jarrod Canepa, "Exclusive Jessica Rabbit Artist Interview—Gary Martin," *ImNotBad.com* (blog), February 25, 2011, http://www.imnotbad.com/2011/02/exclusive-jessica-rabbit-artist.html.

5. Michael Fleming, "Jessica Rabbit Revealed," *Variety*, March 13, 1994, https://variety.com/1994/voices/columns/jessica-rabbit-revealed-119154/.

6. Jarrod Canepa, "Exclusive Jessica Rabbit Artist Interview—Mark Marderosian," *ImNotBad.com* (blog), September 18, 2008, http://www.imnotbad.com/2008/09/mark-marderosian-interview-part-1.html.

7. Jarrod Canepa, "Exclusive Jessica Rabbit Artist Interview—Wendy Gell," *ImNotBad.com* (blog), June 17, 2011, http://www.imnotbad.com/2011/06/exclusive-jessica-rabbit-artist.html.

8. Canepa, "Exclusive Jessica Rabbit Artist Interview—Wendy Gell," *ImNotBad.com*.

9. Jarrod Canepa, "Exclusive Jessica Rabbit Artist Interview—Rachel Sur," *ImNotBad.com* (blog), March 23, 2011, http://www.imnotbad.com/2011/03/exclusive-jessica-rabbit-artist.html.

10. Jarrod Canepa, "Exclusive Jessica Rabbit Artist Interview—Lisa Temming," *ImNotBad.com* (blog), April 20, 2011, http://www.imnotbad.com/2011/04/exclusive-jessica-rabbit-artist.html.

11. Jarrod Canepa, "Exclusive Jessica Rabbit Artist Interview—Tracy M Lee," *ImNotBad.com* (blog), November 16, 2010, http://www.imnotbad.com/2010/11/exclusive-jessica-rabbit-artist.html.

12. Jarrod Canepa, "Jessica Rabbit Merchandise Reviews," *ImNotBad.com* (blog), http://www.imnotbad.com/p/jessica-rabbit-merchandise-reviews.html; Thomas Tumbusch, ed., "Who Framed, Molded, Stuffed, Printed or Otherwise Merchandised Roger Rabbit?" *Tomart's Disneyana Update*, no. 21, November/December 1997, 22–26; Thomas Tumbusch, ed., "The Strange Merchandise Tale of 'Who Framed Roger Rabbit,'" *Tomart's Disneyana Update*, no. 69, Winter 2007, 46–51.

13. Jarrod Canepa, "Exclusive Jessica Rabbit Artist Interview—Tim Rogerson," *ImNotBad.com* (blog), September 2, 2011, http://www.imnotbad.com/2011/09/exclusive-jessica-rabbit-artist.html.

14. Jarrod Canepa, "Jessica Rabbit Merchandise Reviews," *ImNotBad.com* (blog), http://www.imnotbad.com/p/jessica-rabbit-merchandise-reviews.html; Thomas Tumbusch, ed., "Who Framed, Molded, Stuffed, Printed or Otherwise Merchandised Roger Rabbit?" *Tomart's Disneyana Update*, no. 21, November/December 1997, 22–26; Thomas Tumbusch, ed., "The Strange Merchandise Tale of 'Who Framed Roger Rabbit,'" *Tomart's Disneyana Update*, no. 69, Winter 2007, 46–51.

CHAPTER ELEVEN

1. Bruce Moen, "Question and Answer IRC meet with Gary Wolf," *moen@cyberspace* *.com* (blog), August 2, 1995, from http://www.jimdavies.org/roger-rabbit/roger_rabbit_facts .html.

2. Gary K. Wolf, interview with author (February 3, 2010).

3. Gary K. Wolf, "Hare's Lookin' at You, Babs," in *The Fruitful Branch* (Brookline, MA: Brookline Library Foundation, 2002), 111–23.

4. Gary K. Wolf, "Stay Tooned, Folks!" *Amazing Stories* 73, no. 3 (November 2004): 48–53.

5. Gary K. Wolf, "The Warhol of the Worlds: A Radio Drama as performed by the Toontown Theatre On the Air," *Penumbra eMag* 1, no. 10 (July 2012), http://www.magzter .com/preview0/847/5439.

6. Gary K. Wolf, *The Road to Toontown!—Best Short Stories of "Roger Rabbit" Creator Gary K. Wolf*, Smashwords, 2012, https://www.smashwords.com/books/view/209041.

7. Danny Gonzalez, "The 'Wacked' Return of Roger Rabbit," *New York Examiner*, October 20, 2013.

8. Chris Hayden, "Behind the New Roger Rabbit Concept Art," *filmoria.co.uk* (blog), April 25, 2013, https://www.filmoria.co.uk/.

9. Gary K. Wolf, interview with author (February 3, 2010); *Gary K. Wolf*, "Gary K. Wolf, Creator of Roger Rabbit!" (website), accessed October 2, 2013, http://garywolf.com/about .php; Gary K. Wolf, "Two Very Different Career Paths with the Same Destination" (website), accessed October 2, 2013, http://www.spacevulture.com/authors.html.

10. Ross Anderson, "The Secret History of *Who framed Roger Rabbit*," *Cartoon Brew* (blog), April 11, 2013, https://www.cartoonbrew.com/classic/the-secret-history-of-who -framed-roger-rabbit-80963.html; Ross Anderson, "Rabbit Feat," *Disney Twenty-Three* (*D23*) 5, no. 3 (Fall 2013): 25–30.

11. Eric Carter, "1992–93 Theatrical Film Releases, Rev.1.1," January 22, 1992, http:// textfiles.com/media/film92.txt.

12. Simon Brew, "Rob Minkoff on Nearly Making Who Framed Roger Rabbit 2," *Den of Geek!* (blog), February 7, 2014, http://www.denofgeek.com/movies/who-framed-roger -rabbit/29206/rob-minkoff-on-nearly-making-who-framed-roger-rabbit-2.

13. Floyd Norman, "Fred and Ginger (Almost)," *MrFun* (blog), January 9, 2012, http:// mrfun.squarespace.com/blog/2012/1/9/fred-and-ginger-almost.html.

14. Shawn Adler, "*Roger Rabbit* Sequel Still in the Offing? Stay Tooned Says Producer," *MTV News* (blog), December 11, 2007, http://www.mtv.com/news/2429487/ roger-rabbit-sequel-still-in-the-offing-stay-tooned-says-producer/.

15. Peter Sciretta, "Robert Zemeckis Has a New Idea for Roger Rabbit 2," *SlashFilm* (blog), April 29, 2009, http://www.slashfilm.com/robert-zemeckis-has-a-new-idea-for-roger-rabbit-2/.

16. Roger Friedman, "A 'Roger Rabbit' Sequel May Happen After All," *Roger Friedman's ShowBiz • 411: Hollywood to the Hudson* (blog), October 15, 2012, http://www.showbiz411 .com/2012/10/15/a-roger-rabbit-sequel-may-happen-after-all-says-director.

17. Mark Hickson, "Scuttlebut on Roger Rabbit Sequel," (*DbM*) *disneybymark.com* (blog), March 22, 2013, http://www.disneybymark.com/2013/03/22/scuttlebutt-13/.

18. Gregory Wakeman, "Why Who Framed Roger Rabbit 2 Probably Won't Happen, According to Robert Zemeckis," *Cinemablend* (blog), November 2016, https://www

.cinemablend.com/news/1591290/why-who-framed-roger-rabbit-2-probably-wont
-happen-according-to-robert-zemeckis.

19. Doug Walker, "Review of 'Who Framed Roger Rabbit, Disneycember," March 1, 2012, in *Nostalgia Critic, Channel Awesome/YouTube*, http://thatguywiththeglasses.wikia" .com/wiki/Who_Framed_Roger_Rabbit_(Disneycember), https://www.youtube.com/ watch?v=UXQ5v0ZE8-s; Doug Walker, "What You Never Knew About 'Who Framed Roger Rabbit,'" August 11, 2015, in *Nostalgia Critic, Channel Awesome/YouTube*, http://thatguywith theglasses.wikia.com/wiki/What_You_Never_Knew_About_Who_Framed_Roger_Rabbit, https://www.youtube.com/watch?v=1pF7Xvj8i5E&t=29s.

20. Heidi Parker and Jo Tweedy, "Nine Hours, Rubber Eyelids and a Fake Derriere: Heidi Klum Reveals what it REALLY Took to Transform her into Cartoon Siren Jessica Rabbit," *MAILONLINE*, November 2, 2015, http://www.dailymail.co.uk/femail/article-3299910/ Nine-hours-rubber-eyelids-fake-derriere-Heidi-Klum-reveals-REALLY-took-transform -cartoon-siren-Jessica-Rabbit.html.

21. Ross Anderson, "The Secret History of *Who framed Roger Rabbit*," *Cartoon Brew* (blog), April 11, 2013, https://www.cartoonbrew.com/classic/the-secret-history-of-who -framed-roger-rabbit-80963.html; Ross Anderson, "Rabbit Feat," *Disney Twenty-Three* (*D23*) 5, no. 3 (Fall 2013): 25–30.

APPENDIX

1. Jim Korkis, "The Forgotten Brother Who Built a Magic Kingdom," *MousePlanet* (blog), March 16, 2011, https://www.mouseplanet.com/9562/The_Forgotten_Brother_Who _Built_a_Magic_Kingdom.

2. Steve Hulett, interview with author (January 16, 2013).

3. Ed Catmull with Amy Wallace, *Creativity, Inc.: Overcoming the Unseen Forces That Stand in the Way of True Inspiration* (New York: Random House, 2014), 123.

4. David Smith, "Interview With Don Duckwall," in *Walt's People—Volume 13*, ed. Didier Ghez (Theme Park Press, 2013), 273.

5. Dale Baer, interview with author (September 29, 2009).

6. Tom Sito, "Disney's *The Fox and the Hound*: The Coming of the Next Generation," *Animation World Network* (*AWN.com*) (blog), November 1, 1998, https://www.awn.com/ animationworld/disneys-fox-and-hound-coming-next-generation.

7. Clay Kaytis, "Show 021—Dale Baer, Part One," November 4, 2007, in *The Animation Podcast, with Clay Kaytis*, http://animationpodcast.com/archives/2007/11/04/ dale-baer-part-one/.

8. Steve Hulett, "The Randy Cartwright Interview—Part 1," August 29, 2011, in *Animation Guild TAG Blog, with Steve Hulett*, http://animationguildblog.blogspot.com /2011/08/randy-cartwright-interview-part-i.html.

9. Heidi Guedel, *Animatrix—A Female Animator: How Laughter Saved My Life* (Bloomington, IN: 1st Books Library, 2003), 244–50.

10. Ibid., 300–302.

11. Dale Baer, interview with author.

12. Clay Kaytis, "Show 014—Glen Keane, Part One," April 2, 2006, in *The Animation Podcast, with Clay Kaytis*, http://animationpodcast.com/archives/2006/04/02/ glen-keane-part-one/.

13. Tee Bosustow, "Interview with Brad Bird," April 22, 2008, in *Toon In! to the World of Animation—with Tee Bosustow* (podcast), http://tooninanimation.net/.

14. Steve Hulett, interview with author; Steve Hulett, *Mouse in Transition: An Insider's Look at Disney Feature Animation* (Theme Park Press, 2014), 33.

15. Jerry Rees, interview with author (November 1, 2010).

16. Steve Hulett, interview with author; Steve Hulett, *Mouse in Transition: An Insider's Look at Disney Feature Animation* (Theme Park Press, 2014), 31–33.

17. Guedel, *Animatrix—A Female Animator*, 319–20, 328.

18. Rebecca Lodolo-Rees and Jerry Rees, interview with author (September 30, 2009).

19. Ibid.

20. Steve Hulett, "The John Musker Interview—Part 1," March 19, 2012, in *Animation Guild TAG Blog, with Steve Hulett*, http://animationguildblog.blogspot.com/2012/03/john-musker-interview-part-i.html; Steve Hulett, "The John Musker Interview—Part 2," March 20, 2012, in *Animation Guild TAG Blog, with Steve Hulett*, http://animationguildblog.blogspot.com/2012/03/john-musker-interview-part-ii.html; Steve Hulett, "The John Musker Interview—Part 3," March 21, 2012, in *Animation Guild TAG Blog, with Steve Hulett*, http://animationguildblog.blogspot.com/2012/03/john-musker-interview-part-iii.html.

21. Dave Spafford, interview with author (September 28, 2009).

22. John Musker, interview with author (November 4, 2010).

23. Steve Hulett, "The John Musker Interviews—Parts 1, 2, 3," March 19–21, 2012, in *Animation Guild TAG Blog, with Steve Hulett*.

24. Randy Cartwright, interview with author (September 30, 2009).

25. John Cawley, *The Animated Films of Don Bluth* (New York: Image Publishing, 1991), 12–24.

26. Dave Spafford, interview with author (November 3, 2010).

27. Dorse Lanpher, *Flyin' Chunks and Other Things To Duck: Memoirs of a Life Spent Doodling for Dollars* (Bloomington, IN: iUniverse, Inc., 2010), 66–68.

28. John Musker, interview with author (November 4, 2010).

29. William Kallay, *The Making of Tron: How Tron Changed Visual Effects and Disney Forever* (self-published, 2011), 19–20.

30. Ibid., 42.

31. Ibid., 140.

32. Kallay, 145–46; Ed Catmull with Amy Wallace, *Creativity, Inc.: Overcoming the Unseen Forces That Stand in the Way of True Inspiration* (New York: Random House, 2014), 46; Jerry Rees, interview with author.

33. John Cawley, *The Animated Films of Don Bluth* (New York: Image Publishing, 1991), 12–24.

34. William Kallay, *The Making of Tron: How Tron Changed Visual Effects and Disney Forever* (self-published, William Kallay, 2011), 198.

35. Ibid., 195.

36. Kallay, 204; Tom Wilhite, interview with author (January 13, 2011).

37. John Canemaker, *Two Guys Named Joe: Master Storytellers Joe Grant and Joe Ranft* (New York: Disney Editions, 2010), 30–34; Phil Nibbelink, interview with author (August

22, 2013); William H. Frake, interview with author (October 6, 2013); David Pacheco, interview with author (October 17, 2013); Mark Henn, interview with author (April 5, 2013).

38. Barry Cook, interview with author (October 29, 2013).

39. Frans Vischer, interview with author (November 5, 2010); Matthew O'Callaghan, interview with author (February 23, 2011); Walt Disney Productions, "Annual Report 1981 (for Annual Meeting of Stockholders—Thursday, January 28, 1982)," Los Angeles, 1982, 19.

40. Walt Disney Productions, "Annual Report 1981," 19.

41. Randy Cartwright, *1983 Disney Studio Tour*, 8mm film, home movie (1983); clips shown in *Waking Sleeping Beauty*, directed by Don Hahn (Los Angeles: Stone Circle Pictures/Walt Disney Studios Motion Pictures, 2009).

42. John Musker, Randy Cartwright/Darrell Van Citters, "Producers VS Animators Volleyball Game," 6:49, https://www.youtube.com/watch?v=x51NFT0-e70.

43. John Musker, interview with author.

44. Steve Hulett, interview with author.

45. Steve Hulett, "The John Musker Interviews—Parts 1, 2, 3," March 19–21, 2012, in *Animation Guild TAG Blog, with Steve Hulett*.

46. Clay Kaytis, "Show 021—Dale Baer, Part One," November 4, 2007, in *The Animation Podcast, with Clay Kaytis*, http://animationpodcast.com/archives/2007/11/04/dale-baer-part-one/.

47. Clay Kaytis, "Show 002—Andreas Deja, Part Two," May 7, 2005, in *The Animation Podcast, with Clay Kaytis*, http://animationpodcast.com/archives/2005/05/07/andreas-deja-part-two/.

48. Lou Mongello, "Interview with Don Hahn and Peter Schneider," *WDW Radio* (podcast), show #160, March 7, 2010, http://www.wdwradio.com/2010/03/don-hahn-interview-disney-peter-schneider-show-160-march-7-2010/.

49. Steve Hulett, "The John Musker Interviews—Parts 1, 2, 3.

50. Clay Kaytis, "Show 002—Andreas Deja, Part Two," *The Animation Podcast*; Andreas Deja, interview with author (November 10, 2010); Andreas Deja, "Eric Larson," *Deja View* (blog), August 31, 2012, http://andreasdeja.blogspot.com/search?updated-max=2012-09-03T21:33:00-07:00&max-results=20&start=41&by-date=false; Colin Jacobs, "An Interview with Animator Andreas Deja," *DVD MovieGuide* (blog), March 11, 2003, http://www.dvdmg.com/interviewandreasdeja.shtml.

51. John Musker, interview with author.

52. Ibid.

53. Ibid.

54. Tom Wilhite, interview with author.

55. John Musker, interview with author.

56. William Kallay, *The Making of Tron: How Tron Changed Visual Effects and Disney Forever* (self-published, William Kallay, 2011), 48–49.

57. Tom Sito, *Drawing the Line: The Untold Story of the Animation Unions* (Lexington: University Press of Kentucky, 2006), 274–76.

58. Ibid.

59. Ibid.

60. Dave Spafford, interview with author (September 28, 2009).

61. Dave Spafford, interview with author (November 3, 2010).

62. Dave Spafford, interview with author (September 28, 2009); Spafford (November 3, 2010); Tom Sito, *Drawing the Line: The Untold Story of the Animation Unions* (Lexington: University Press of Kentucky, 2006), 268.

63. Spafford (November 3, 2010).

64. Tom Sito, *Drawing the Line: The Untold Story of the Animation Unions* (Lexington: University Press of Kentucky, 2006), 274–76

FILM REFERENCES

AMBLIMATION

An American Tail: Fievel Goes West (1991)
We're Back! A Dinosaur's Story (1993)
Balto (1995)

BLUE SKY

Ice Age (2002)
Robots (2005)
Ice Age: The Meltdown (2006)
Dr. Seuss' Horton Hears a Who (2008)
Ice Age: Dawn of the Dinosaurs (2009)
Rio (2011)
Epic (2013)
Rio 2 (2014)
The Peanuts Movie (2015)
Ice Age: Collision Course (2016)
Ferdinand (2017)
Spies in Disguise (2019)

BLUTH

Banjo the Woodpile Cat (1979)
Xanadu (1980) [animated segment]
The Secret of NIMH (Bluth/Aurora) (1982)
Space Ace (Bluth/Magicom) (1983) [video game]
Dragon's Lair (Bluth/Magicom) (1983) [video game]
An American Tail (Bluth/Sullivan/Universal/U-Drive/Amblin) (1986)
The Land Before Time (Sullivan Bluth/Universal/Amblin/Lucasfilm) (1988)
All Dogs Go to Heaven (Sullivan Bluth/Goldcrest) (1989)
Dragon's Lair II: Time Warp (Sullivan Bluth) (1991) [video game]
Rock-a-Doodle (Sullivan Bluth/Goldcrest) (1991)
Thumbelina (Bluth/Warner) (1994)

A Troll in Central Park (Bluth/Warner) (1994)
The Pebble and the Penguin (Bluth/MGM) (1995)
Anastasia (Bluth/Fox) (1997)
Bartok the Magnificent (Bluth/Fox) (1999) [direct-to-video]
Titan A.E. (Bluth/Fox) (2000)

DISNEY—BURBANK/GLENDALE

Sleeping Beauty (1959)
One Hundred and One Dalmatians (1961)
The Sword in the Stone (1963)
Mary Poppins (1964)
The Jungle Book (1967)
The Aristocats (1970)
Bedknobs and Broomsticks (1971)
Robin Hood (1973)
The Many Adventures of Winnie the Pooh (1977)
The Rescuers (1977)
Pete's Dragon (1977)
The Black Hole (1979) [live action]
The Fox and the Hound (1981)
Tron (1982) [live action]
Fun with Mr. Future (1982) [short]
Mickey's Christmas Carol (1983) [short]
Splash (1984) [live action]
Return to Oz (1985) [live action]
The Black Cauldron (1985)
The Great Mouse Detective (1986)
Oilspot and Lipstick (1986) [short]
Sport Goofy in Soccermania (1987) [TV short movie]
Who Framed Roger Rabbit (Amblin/Touchstone) (1988)
Oliver & Company (1988)
Honey, I Shrunk the Kids (1989) [live action]
Tummy Trouble (1989) [short]
Back to Neverland (1989) [theme park short]
Cranium Command (1989) [theme park short]
The Little Mermaid (1989)
Dick Tracy (1990) [live action]
Arachnophobia (Hollywood Pictures) (1990) [live action]
The Prince and the Pauper (1990) [short]
The Rescuers Down Under (1990)
Beauty and the Beast (1991)
Michael & Mickey (1991) [theme park short]

Aladdin (1992)

Mickey's Audition (1992) [theme park short]

Tim Burton's The Nightmare Before Christmas (Disney/Skellington) (1993)

The Lion King (1994)

Runaway Brain (1995) [short]

Pocahontas (1995)

James and the Giant Peach (Disney/Skellington) (1996)

The Hunchback of Notre Dame (1996)

Hercules (1997)

Mulan (1998)

Tarzan (1999)

Fantasia 2000 (1999)

Dinosaur (2000)

The Emperor's New Groove (2000)

Atlantis: The Lost Empire (2001)

Lilo & Stitch (2002)

Treasure Planet (2002)

Mickey's PhilharMagic (2003) [theme park short]

Destino (Disney France) (2003) [short]

Home On the Range (2004)

The Cat That Looked at a King (2004) [short]

Lorenzo (2004) [short]

One by One (2004) [short]

Chicken Little (2005)

The Little Matchgirl (2006) [short]

Meet the Robinsons (2007)

Gran Fiesta Tour Starring the Three Caballeros (2007) [theme park short]

Enchanted (animation by James Baxter Studio) (2007)

Bolt (2008)

A Christmas Carol (Disney/ImageMovers Digital) (2009)

Tangled (2010)

Mars Needs Moms (Disney/ImageMovers Digital) (2011)

Winnie the Pooh (2011)

The Ballad of Nessie (2011) [short]

Wreck-It Ralph (2012)

Frozen (2013)

Get a Horse! (2013) [short]

Big Hero 6 (Disney/Marvel) (2014)

Zootopia (2016)

Moana (2016)

Ralph Breaks the Internet (2018)

Frozen 2 (2019)

DISNEY—FLORIDA

Roller Coaster Rabbit (1990) [short]
The Rescuers Down Under (1990)
The Prince and the Pauper (1990) [short]
Beauty and the Beast (1991)
Aladdin (1992)
Off His Rockers (1992) [short]
Trail Mix-Up (1993) [short]
The Lion King (1994)
Pocahontas (1995)
The Hunchback of Notre Dame (1996)
Hercules (1997)
Mulan (1998)
John Henry (2000)
Lilo & Stitch (2002)
Brother Bear (2003)
My Peoples/A Few Good Ghosts (canceled due to closure of WDFA-Florida) (2004)

DISNEY UK—LONDON

Who Framed Roger Rabbit (Amblin/Touchstone) (1988)
Frankenweenie (2012)

DISNEYTOONS

DuckTales the Movie: Treasure of the Lost Lamp (Disney UK) (1990)
Bonkers (1993) [TV series]
Aladdin (Disney Australia) (1994) [TV series]
The Return of Jafar (Disney Australia) (1994) [direct-to-video]
A Goofy Movie (Disney Australia) (1995)
The Shnookums and Meat Funny Cartoon Show (Disney Australia) (1995) [TV series]
Timon & Pumbaa (Disney Australia) (1995) [TV series]
Quack Pack (Disney Australia) (1996) [TV series]
Jungle Cubs (Disney Australia) (1996) [TV series]
Aladdin and the King of Thieves (Disney Australia) (1996) [direct-to-video]
101 Dalmatians: The Series (Disney Australia) (1997) [TV series]
Beauty and the Beast: The Enchanted Christmas (Disney Australia) (1997)
    [direct-to-video]
The Lion King II: Simba's Pride (Disney Australia) (1998) [direct-to-video]
Mickey's Once Upon a Christmas (1999) [direct-to-video]
Winnie the Pooh: Seasons of Giving (Disney Australia) (1999) [direct-to-video]
The Tigger Movie (2000)
An Extremely Goofy Movie (Disney Australia) (2000) [direct-to-video]

The Little Mermaid 2: Return to the Sea (Disney Australia) (2000) [direct-to-video]
The Legend of Tarzan (Disney Australia) (2001) [TV series]
Lady and the Tramp 2: Scamp's Adventure (Disney Australia) (2001) [direct-to-video]
Return to Neverland (Disney Australia) (2002)
Jungle Book 2 (Disney Australia) (2003)
Piglet's Big Movie (2003)
Stitch! The Movie (2003) [direct-to-video]
The Lion King 1½ (Disney Australia) (2004) [direct-to-video]
Mickey, Donald and Goofy in The Three Musketeers (2004) [direct-to-video]
Mickey's Twice Upon a Christmas (2004) [direct-to-video]
Pooh's Heffalump Movie (2005)
Tarzan 2 (Disney Australia) (2005) [direct-to-video]
Lilo & Stitch 2: Stitch Has a Glitch (Disney Australia) (2005) [direct-to-video]
Bambi II (Disney Australia) (2006) [direct-to-video]
Brother Bear 2 (Disney Australia) (2006) [direct-to-video]
The Fox and the Hound 2 (Disney Australia) (2006) [direct-to-video]
Cinderella III: A Twist in Time (Disney Australia) (2007) [direct-to-video]
Tinker Bell (Disney/Prana) (2008) [direct-to-video]
Tinker Bell and the Lost Treasure (2009)
Tinker Bell and the Great Fairy Rescue (2010) [direct-to-video]
Planes (Disney/Prana) (2013)
Tinker Bell: A Midsummer Storm (2013) [direct-to-video]
The Pirate Fairy (Disney/Prana) (2014) [direct-to-video]
Planes: Fire & Rescue (Disney/Prana) (2014)
Tinkerbell and the Legend of the NeverBeast (Disney/Prana) (2015) [direct-to-video]

DREAMWORKS

Antz (1998)
The Prince of Egypt (1998)
The Road to El Dorado (2000)
Chicken Run (DreamWorks/Aardman) (2000)
Shrek (2001)
Spirit: Stallion of the Cimarron (2002)
Sinbad: Legend of the Seven Seas (2003)
Shrek 2 (2004)
Shark Tale (2004)
Madagascar (2005)
Over the Hedge (2006)
Shrek the Third (2007)
Bee Movie (2007)
Kung Fu Panda (2008)
How to Train Your Dragon (2010)
Megamind (2010)

Madagascar 3: Europe's Most Wanted (2012)
The Croods (2013)
Mr. Peabody & Sherman (2014)
Home (2015)
Trolls (2016)
The Boss Baby (2017)
Captain Underpants: The First Epic Movie (2017)
How to Train Your Dragon: The Hidden World (2019)
Abominable (2019)

HYPERION PICTURES

The Brave Little Toaster (Hyperion/Disney) (1987)
Rover Dangerfield (1991)
Bébé's Kids (1992)
The Brave Little Toaster Goes to Mars (1998) [direct-to-video]
The Brave Little Toaster to the Rescue (1999) [direct-to-video]
The Adventures of Tom Thumb & Thumbelina (2002) (Hyperion/Miramax)
    [direct-to-video]
The Proud Family Movie (Hyperion/Jambalaya/Disney Television) (2005)
    [direct-to-video]

ILLUMINATION ENTERTAINMENT

Despicable Me (2010)
Hop (2011)
Dr. Seuss' The Lorax (2012)
Despicable Me 2 (2013)
Minions (2015)
The Secret Life of Pets (2016)
Sing (2016)
Despicable Me 3 (2017)
Dr. Seuss' The Grinch (2018)
The Secret Life of Pets 2 (2019)
Minions 2 (2020)

LAIKA

Tim Burton's Corpse Bride (Tim Burton/Laika) (2005)
Coraline (2009)
ParaNorman (2012)
The Boxtrolls (2014)
Kubo and the Two Strings (2016)
Missing Link (2019)

LUCASFILM

Star Wars, aka Star Wars: Episode IV—A New Hope (1977)
The Empire Strikes Back (1980)
Return of the Jedi (1983)
Young Sherlock Holmes (Paramount/Glass Man sequence—ILM/Pixar) (1985)
Star Wars: Episode I—The Phantom Menace (1999)
Star Wars: Clone Wars (2003)
Strange Magic (Lucasfilm/Disney) (2015)
Star Wars: The Force Awakens (Disney/Lucasfilm) (2015)
Rogue One: A Star Wars Story (Disney/Lucasfilm) (2016)
Star Wars: The Last Jedi (2017)
Solo: A Star Wars Story (2018)
Star Wars: Episode IX (2019)

MISC. AMERICAN

Fritz the Cat (Bakshi/Krantz) (1972)
Heavy Traffic (Bakshi/Krantz) (1973)
Coonskin (Bakshi) (1975)
The Plague Dogs (Nepenthe) (1982)
Steven Spielberg's Amazing Stories: "Family Dog" (1987) [TV episode]
The Chipmunk Adventure (Bagdasarian) (1987)
Technological Threat (Kroyer) (1988) [short]
FernGully: The Last Rainforest (Kroyer) (1992)
Cool World (Bakshi/Paramount) (1992)
Cats and Dogs (Village Roadshow/Rhythm and Hues) (2001)
The Pink Panther (titles and credits—Bob Kurtz and Eric Goldberg) (2006)
Hoodwinked! (Weinstein/Prana) (2006)
Gnomeo & Juliet (Rocket/Miramax) (2011)
Saving Santa (Gateway/Prana) (2013)
The Hero of Color City (Exodus) (2014)
Duet (Glen Keane/Google) (2014) [short]
The Prophet (Doha) (2014)
Nephtali (Glen Keane/Opéra National de Paris) (2015) [short]
Lux: Binding Light (Glen Keane/Riot Games) (2017) [short]
Dear Basketball (Glen Keane/Believe) (2017) [short]
Bunyan and Babe (Exodus/Toonz) (2017)
Duck Duck Goose (Original Force) (2018)
Sherlock Gnomes (Rocket) (2018)
Mushka (Andreas Deja) (2019) [short]

MISC. INTERNATIONAL

Little Nemo Adventures in Slumberland (TMD) (1989)—Japan
The Secret of the Magic Gourd (Disney/Centro Digital/China Film Corp.)
    (2007)—China
Roadside Romeo (Disney/Yash Raj) (2008)—India
The Book of Masters (Disney/CIS) (2009)—Russia
Astro Boy (ImagiAnimation) (2009)—Japan
Top Cat: The Movie (Ánima/Illusion) (2011)—Mexico/Argentina
Guardians of Oz (Ánima/Discreet Arts) (2015)—Mexico/India
El Americano: The Movie (Boxel/Animex/Olmos/Phil Roman) (2016)—Mexico
Monster Island (Ánima/Discreet Arts) (2017)—Mexico

MISC. BRITISH

Yellow Submarine (MGM, directed by George Dunning) (1968)
Watership Down (Nepenthe) (1978)
The Snowman (TVC) (1982) [TV short movie]
When the Wind Blows (TVC) (1986)
Freddie as F.R.0.7. (J&M) (1992)
Valiant (Disney/Vanguard) (2005)
The Curse of the Were-Rabbit (Aardman) (2005)
Flushed Away (Aardman) (2006)
Happily N'Ever After (Vanguard) (2007)
Arthur Christmas (Aardman) (2011)
The Last Belle (2011) [short]
The Snowman and the Snowdog (Lupus) (2012) [TV short movie]
The Pirates! Band of Misfits (Aardman/Sony) (2012)
Shaun the Sheep Movie (Aardman) (2015)
Ethel & Ernest (Lupus) (2016)
Early Man (Aardman) (2018)
Farmageddon: A Shaun the Sheep Movie (Aardman) (2019)

MISC. CANADIAN

The Wild (Disney/Complete Pandemonium-CORE Technologies) (2006)

MISC. FRENCH

Asterix and Cleopatra (Dargaud) (1968)
Asterix and Caesar (Dargaud) (1985)
Asterix in Britain (Dargaud) (1986)
Igor (Exodus/MGM/Sparx) (2008)
The Secret of Kells (Cartoon Saloon) (2009)

MISC. GERMAN

The Magic Voyage, aka The Adventures of Pico and Columbus, aka Die Abenteuer von Pico & Columbus (MS Films) (1992)
Asterix Conquers America (Hahn Film) (1994)
Isle of Dogs (Indian Paintbrush/American Empirical) (2018)

PIXAR

Toy Story (Disney/Pixar) (1995)
A Bug's Life (Disney/Pixar) (1998)
Toy Story 2 (Disney/Pixar) (1999)
Monsters, Inc. (Disney/Pixar) (2001)
Finding Nemo (Disney/Pixar) (2003)
The Incredibles (Disney/Pixar) (2004)
Cars (Disney/Pixar) (2006)
Ratatouille (Disney/Pixar) (2007)
Wall·E (Disney/Pixar) (2008)
Up (Disney/Pixar) (2009)
Toy Story 3 (Disney/Pixar) (2010)
Cars 2 (Disney/Pixar) (2011)
Brave (Disney/Pixar (2012)
Monsters University (2013)
The Inside Out (Disney/Pixar) (2015)
The Good Dinosaur (Disney/Pixar) (2015)
Finding Dory (Disney/Pixar) (2016)
Cars 3 (Disney/Pixar) (2017)
Coco (Disney/Pixar) (2017)
Incredibles 2 (Disney/Pixar) (2018)

RICHARD WILLIAMS ANIMATION

What's New Pussycat? (titles and credits) (1965)
A Funny Thing Happened on the Way to the Forum (titles and credits) (1966)
Casino Royale (titles and credits) (1967)
The Charge of the Light Brigade (titles and credits) (1968)
A Christmas Carol (1971) [TV short film with theatrical release]
The Return of the Pink Panther (titles and credits) (1974)
The Pink Panther Strikes Again (titles and credits) (1976)
Raggedy Ann & Andy: A Musical Adventure (1977)
Ziggy's Gift (1982) [TV short movie]
The Thief and the Cobbler (Richard Williams/Allied Filmmaker) (1993)

SONY ANIMATION

Stuart Little (1999)
Open Season (2006)
Surf's Up (2007)
Cloudy with a Chance of Meatballs (2009)
Over the Moon (Glen Keane/Sony/Netflix) (2010)
The Smurfs (Sony/Kerner) (2011)
Hotel Transylvania (2012)
The Smurfs 2 (Sony/Kerner) (2013)
Cloudy with a Chance of Meatballs 2 (2013)
Hotel Transylvania 2 (2015)
Goosebumps (Sony/Moving Picture Co.) (2015)
Smurfs: The Lost Village (Sony/Kerner) (2017)
The Emoji Movie (2017)
The Star (Sony/Jim Henson/Cinesite) (2017)
Peter Rabbit (Sony/Olive Bridge/Animal Logic) (2018)
Hotel Transylvania 3: Summer Vacation (Sony/Media Rights) (2018)
Goosebumps 2: Haunted Halloween (Sony/Original Film Scholastic/Double Negative)
    (2018)
Spider-Man: Into the Spider-Verse (Sony/Marvel) (2018)

20TH CENTURY FOX

Anastasia (1997)
Bartok the Magnificent (1999)
Olive, the Other Reindeer (20th Century Fox/DNA/The Curiosity Co.) (1999)
Titan A.E. (2000)
Monkeybone (2001)
The Simpsons Movie (20th Century Fox/Gracie/Phil Roman) (2007)
Fantastic Mr. Fox (20th Century Fox/Indian Paintbrush/Regency/American Empirical)
    (2009)
Diary of a Wimpy Kid: Rodrick Rules (20th Century Fox) (2011) [live action]
Diary of a Wimpy Kid: Dog Days (20th Century Fox) (2012) [live action]
The Book of Life (20th Century Fox/Reel FX) (2014)
Diary of a Wimpy Kid: The Long Haul (20th Century Fox) (2017) [live action]

WARNER BROS.

The Incredible Mr. Limpet (1964)
The Duxorcist (1987) [short]
Daffy Duck's Quackbusters (1988)
The Night of the Living Duck (1988) [short]
Box Office Bunny (1990) [short]

Batman: Mask of the Phantasm (1993)
A Troll in Central Park (with Don Bluth) (1994)
Chariots of Fur (1994) [short]
Another Froggy Evening (1995) [short]
The Pebble and the Penguin (with Don Bluth) (1995)
From Hare to Eternity (1996) [short]
Space Jam (1996)
Superior Duck (1997) [short]
Pullet Surprise (1997) [short]
The Magic Sword: Quest for Camelot (1998)
The Iron Giant (1999)
Osmosis Jones (2001)
Looney Tunes: Back in Action (2003)
The Karate Guard (2005) [short]
Happy Feet (Animal Logic/Warner Bros.) (2006)
Yogi Bear (Rhythm and Hues/Warner Bros.) (2010)
Coyote Falls (2010) [short]
Fur of Flying (2010) [short]
Rabid Rider (2010) [short]
I Tawt I Taw a Puddy Tat (2011) [short]
Daffy's Rhapsody (2012) [short]
Flash in the Pain (2014) [short]
The Lego Movie (Animal Logic/Warner) (2014)
The Master (2016) [short]
Storks (2016)
The Lego Batman Movie (Animal Logic/Warner) (2017)
The Lego Ninjago Movie (Animal Logic/Warner) (2017)
The Late Batsby (2018) [short]
Teen Titans Go! To the Movies (Slap Happy/Titmouse/Warner) (2018)
Smallfoot (2018)
The Lego Movie 2: The Second Part (Animal Logic/Warner) (2019)

LIST OF INTERVIEWS

Alexander, Colin	June 30, 2017
Athanassiou, Dino	November 17, 2013
Bacher, Hans	November 3, 2012
Baer, Dale	September 29, 2009
	April 5, 2013
Baer, Jane	December 10, 2013
Bancroft, Tom	November 4, 2013
Barclay, Dave	October 17, 2013
Baxter, James	October 2, 2013
Bazley, Richard	May 2, 2012
Bekuhrs, Rob	November 12, 2013
Benson, Stella-Rose	August 21, 2013
Blaise, Aaron	October 28, 2013
Bossert, Dave	May 6, 2011
	May 31, 2011
Bowers, David	October 23, 2013
Boyle, Neil	September 19, 2013
Brown, Maggie	February 17, 2016
Buck, Chris	April 5, 2013
Carson, Don	October 2, 2013
Cartwright, Randy	September 30, 2009
Cassidy, Joanna	August 7, 2013
Cavalier, Stephen	July 19, 2017
Chiasson, Roger	September 18, 2013
Chung, Paul	September 9, 2013
Clark, Tony	November 26, 2013
Cohen, Daniel	September 11, 2013
Cook, Barry	October 29, 2013
Costa, Alain	August 20, 2013
Creed (Painter), Caron	October 11, 2013
Daniels, Eric	September 30, 2013

Davies, Kevin Jon	November 20, 2013
Davis, Warwick	January 8, 2014
Deja, Andreas	November 1, 2010
Dell, Lily	November 12, 2013
de Lord, Patsy	January 9, 2014
Elvin, Annie	March 7, 2014
Elvin, Martin	May 24, 2014
Fleischer, Charles	December 3, 2013
Fletcher, Nick	February 25, 2014
Frake, William H. III	October 6, 2013
	December 31, 2013
	May 13, 2014
	December 11, 2014
	January 8, 2015
	November 30, 2015
	September 22, 2016
Franchetti, Julianna	September 3, 2014
Fullmer, Randy	September 18, 2013
Gabriel, Mike	October 31, 2012
	April 5, 2013
Gaivoto, Al	November 8, 2013
Gambier, Peter	October 12, 2013
	November 3, 2013
Gammage, Chuck	September 19, 2013
Garcia, Raul	August 22, 2013
Giaimo, Michael	April 23, 2012
Gibbs, George	November 9, 2013
Goldberg, Eric	September 20, 2008
	December 5, 2013
Gordon-Bates, Marc	March 12, 2014
	June 30, 2017
Green, Howard	November 2, 2010
Guaglione, Eric	December 2, 2013
Hahn, Don	September 15, 2009
Haidar, Joe	August 10, 2013
Hall, Russell	August 30, 2013
Hamilton, Alyson	December 4, 2013
Healy, Ro	October 29, 2013
Henn, Mark	April 5, 2013
Hickner, Steve	October 2, 2013

Howard, Max	September 27, 2013
	April 3, 2014
	February 8, 2016
Hulett, Steve	February 1, 2013
Humphries, Michael	October 23, 2013
Jenkins, Chris	October 24, 2013
Kausler, Mark	April 30, 2012
	August 27, 2013
Kline, Marty	February 26, 2014
Knott, Chris	December 18, 2012
	November 23, 2013
	October 25, 2014
Koo, Elaine	October 23, 2013
Lanpher, Dorse	December 10, 2010
Leduc, Cal	October 19, 2013
Lee, Tracy	November 18, 2013
Leon, Richard	January 22, 2014
Lescher, Mery-et	October 5, 2016
MacLean, Fraser	November 24, 2010
	September 17, 2013
Manwaring, Greg	November 2, 2013
Meyer, Uli	September 11, 2013
Miller, Ron	November 26, 2010
Muller, Jacques	August 17, 2013
Musker, John	November 3, 2010
Naisbitt, Roy	December 3, 2013
Newman, Rob	March 19, 2014
	October 27, 2015
Nibbelink, Phil	August 22, 2013
Norman, Floyd	September 28, 2009
	October 15, 2013
O'Callaghan, Matt	February 23, 2011
	April 11, 2011
Odell, Brent	September 17, 2013
Oliver, Jennifer	January 27, 2014
Orr, Julia	September 13, 2013
Pacheco, David	October 17, 2013
Page, Shelley	March 26, 2014
Peraza, Michael	February 6, 2014
Pfeil, Mike	May 31, 2017

Pompei, Sylvia	November 29, 2013
Price, Jeffrey	April 4, 2013
Pritchard, Dave	November 17, 2013
Radford, Bonne	December 6, 2013
Ralston, Ken	December 4, 2013
Ranft, Joe	September 15, 2002
Ranieri, Nik	October 1, 2009
	April 5, 2013
Rees, Jerry and Rebecca	September 30, 2009
Rees, Jerry	November 1, 2010
Rees, Rebecca	January 11, 2014
Renoudet (Renaday), Pete	April 13, 2012
Ruhemann, Andrew	December 2, 2013
St. Amand, Tom	December 2, 2013
Sanpher, Tim	October 14, 2013
Scarrold, Philip	March 16, 2014
Schmidt, Arthur	November 11, 2013
Schneider, Peter	November 25, 2013
Siepermann, Harald	February 3, 2009
Sito, Tom	November 2, 2010
	September 22, 2013
Sito, Pat and Tom	October 14, 2013
Sluiter, Ric	December 4, 2016
Smith, Bruce W.	November 3, 2010
Smith, Len	September 10, 2013
Smith, Mike	November 22, 2014
Spafford, Dave	September 28, 2009
	November 3, 2010
Spurlock, Bob	February 7, 2014
Stephan, Dave	November 13, 2013
Stern, Nick	November 14 and 17, 2013
Stevenhagen, Rob	September 25, 2013
Stirdivant, Marc	November 4, 2010
Sylvester, Glenn	March 13, 2014
Takahashi, Wes	October 22, 2013
Talbot, Amanda	November 7, 2013
Temple, Barry	August 21, 2013
Van Citters, Darrell	September 28, 2009
	November 1, 2010
	April 5, 2013

Van Gendt, Nicolette	September 11, 2013
Vignali, Marcelo	September 15, 2013
Vischer, Frans	November 5, 2010
	April 5, 2013
	November 6, 2014
Walton, Harry	December 1, 2013
Watts, Roberts	November 10, 2015
	November 12, 2015
Way, Roger	October 4, 2013
Wells, Simon	March 19, 2014
Western, Pete	October 12, 2013
White, Colin	August 27, 2013
Wilhite, Tom	January 13, 2011
	March 31, 2011
Williams, Alex	August 21, 2013
	September 28, 2015
Williams, Claire	October 9, 2013
Williams, Richard	September 20, 2008
Wolf, Gary K.	February 9, 2009
	September 14, 2009
	July 28, 2010
	July 3, 2011
Woodcock, Vincent	March 13, 2014
	August 3, 2014
Woolf, Julia	December 2, 2013

BIBLIOGRAPHY

Adler, Shawn. "*Roger Rabbit* Sequel Still in the Offing? Stay Tooned Says Producer." *MTV News*. December 11, 2007. Blog. http://www.mtv.com/news/2429487/roger-rabbit-sequel-still-in-the-offing-stay-tooned-says-producer/.

Anders, Jason. "#3. A Conversation with Tom Sito." *Fulle Circle Magazine*. January 9, 2009. Blog. http://www.fullecirclemagazine.com/2009/01/conversation-with-tom-sito.html.

Anders, Jason. "#27. A Conversation with Aaron Blaise." *Fulle Circle Magazine*. December 2008. Blog. http://www.fullecirclemagazine.com/2008/12/conversation-with-aaron-blaise.html.

Anders, Jason. "#38. A Conversation with Tom Bancroft." *Fulle Circle Magazine*. March 2009. Blog. http://www.fullecirclemagazine.com/2009/03/conversation-with-tom-bancroft.html.Anderson, Ross. "Rabbit Feat." *Disney Twenty-Three* (D23) 5, no. 3 (Fall 2013): 25–30.

Anderson, Ross. "The Secret History of *Who Framed Roger Rabbit*." *Cartoon Brew*. April 11, 2013. Blog. https://www.cartoonbrew.com/classic/the-secret-history-of-who-framed-roger-rabbit-80963.html.

"Backstage at Disney." *Walt Disney Studio Showcase*. Performed by Culhane, John. Los Angeles: Disney Channel, 1983. https://www.youtube.com/watch?v=5qTW6uKjzqI.

Beck, Jerry. "The Acme Gag Factory—A Talk with Dale and Jane Baer." *Animation Magazine* 2, no. 1 (Summer 1988).

Beck, Jerry. "A Funny Cartoon for the '80s—A Talk with Robert Zemeckis." *Animation Magazine*. Summer 1988.

Bonifer, Michael. "Improvisation, Spaff-Style." *Gamechangers*. October 16, 2007. Blog. http://www.gamechangers.com/improvisation-spaff-style/.

Bosustow, Tee. "Interview with Brad Bird." *Toon In! to the World of Animation—with Tee Bosustow*. April 22, 2008. Podcast. http://tooninanimation.net/.

Brew, Simon. "Rob Minkoff on Nearly Making Who Framed Roger Rabbit 2." *Den of Geek!* February 7, 2014. Blog. http://www.denofgeek.com/movies/who-framed-roger-rabbit/29206/rob-minkoff-on-nearly-making-who-framed-roger-rabbit-2.

Brigante, Ricky. "ITM: Show 309—Interview with Don Carson." *Inside the Magic*. Podcast. https://insidethemagic.net/podcasts/309/.

Canemaker, John. "Studio Approaches to Story" (from panel discussion among John Canemaker, Bill Peet, Joe Ranft, Jerry Rees, and Peter Schneider at Second Annual Walter Lantz Conference on Animation—June 11, 1988). *Storytelling in Animation: The Art of the Animated Image, Vol. 2*. Los Angeles: American Film Institute, 1988.

Canemaker, John. *Two Guys Named Joe: Master Storytellers Joe Grant and Joe Ranft*. New York: Disney Editions, 2010.

Canepa, Jarrod. "Exclusive Jessica Rabbit Artist Interview—Gary Martin." *ImNotBad .com*. February 25, 2011. Blog. http://www.imnotbad.com/2011/02/exclusive-jessica -rabbit-artist.html.

Canepa, Jarrod. "Exclusive Jessica Rabbit Creator Interview—Gary Wolf." *ImNotBad .com—A Jessica Rabbit Site*. Blog. December 6, 2011. http://www.imnotbad.com/2011 /12/exclusive-jessica-rabbit-creator.html.

Canepa, Jarrod. "Exclusive Jessica Rabbit Artist Interview—Lisa Temming." *ImNotBad .com*. April 20, 2011. Blog. http://www.imnotbad.com/2011/04/exclusive-jessica-rabbit -artist.html.

Canepa, Jarrod. "Exclusive Jessica Rabbit Artist Interview—Mark Marderosian." *ImNotBad.com*. September 18, 2008. Blog. http://www.imnotbad.com/2008/09/ mark-marderosian-interview-part-1.html.

Canepa, Jarrod. "Exclusive Jessica Rabbit Artist Interview—Rachel Sur." *ImNotBad.com* . March 23, 2011. Blog. http://www.imnotbad.com/2011/03/exclusive-jessica-rabbit -artist.html.

Canepa, Jarrod. "Exclusive Jessica Rabbit Artist Interview—Tim Rogerson." *ImNotBad .com*. September 2, 2011. Blog. http://www.imnotbad.com/2011/09/exclusive-jessica -rabbit-artist.html.

Canepa, Jarrod. "Exclusive Jessica Rabbit Artist Interview—Tracy M. Lee." *ImNotBad .com*. November 16, 2010. Blog. http://www.imnotbad.com/2010/11/exclusive-jessica -rabbit-artist.html.

Canepa, Jarrod. "Exclusive Jessica Rabbit Artist Interview—Wendy Gell." *ImNotBad .com*. June 17, 2011. Blog. http://www.imnotbad.com/2011/06/exclusive-jessica-rabbit -artist.html.

Canepa, Jarrod. "Exclusive Interview with the Designer of *Roger Rabbit's Cartoon Spin*—Marcelo Vignali." *ImNotBad.com*. April 12, 2012. Blog. http://www.imnotbad .com/2012/04/exclusive-roger-rabbit-ride-designer.html.

Canepa, Jarrod. "Jessica Rabbit Merchandise Reviews." *ImNotBad.com*. Blog. http:// www.imnotbad.com/p/jessica-rabbit-merchandise-reviews.html.

Carroll, Kathleen. "Hop Hop Hooray!" *New York EXTRA*. June 22, 1988.

Carter, Eric. "1992–93 Theatrical Film Releases, Rev.1.1." January 22, 1992. http://text files.com/media/film92.txt.

Cartwright, Randy. *1983 Disney Studio Tour*. 8mm film home movie. 1983. (clips shown in *Waking Sleeping Beauty*, directed by Don Hahn [Los Angeles: Stone Circle Pictures/ Walt Disney Studios Motion Pictures, 2009].)

Catmull, Ed, with Amy Wallace. *Creativity, Inc.: Overcoming the Unseen Forces That Stand in the Way of True Inspiration*. New York: Random House, 2014.

Cawley, John. *The Animated Films of Don Bluth*. New York: Image Publishing, 1991.

Clarke, Jeremy. "Framing Roger." *Films and Filming*. January 1989.

Culhane, John. "For Oscar's Producer, the Key is C." *New York Times*. March 26, 1989.

Davis, Warwick. *Size Matters Not: The Extraordinary Life and Career of Warwick Davis*. Hoboken, NJ: Aurum Press, 2010.

Dees, Rich. "Who Delayed Roger Rabbit 2?" *FilmBuffOnline*. August 7, 2005. Blog. http:/ www.filmbuffonline.com/FBOLNewsreel/wordpress/2005/08/07/who-delayed -roger-rabbit-2/.

Deja, Andrea. "Eric Larson," *Deja View*. August 31, 2012. Blog. http://andreasdeja.blogspot .com/search?updated-max=2012–09–03T21:33:00–07:00&max-results=20&start =41&by-date=false.

Deja, Andreas. "Roger Rabbit Scenes IV." *Deja View*. June 7, 2016. Blog. http://andreas deja.blogspot.com/2016/06/roger-rabbit-scenes-iv.html.

Diamond, Frazer. *Frazer Diamond*. Blog. http://www.frazerdiamond.co.uk/bio.html.

Dickerson, Marla. "They're Getting a Bit Goofy in Disneyland." *Los Angeles Times*. February 16, 1996.

Doyle, Gavin. "Imagineer Don Carson Worked on Splash Mountain and Disneyland Toontown—DD019." *Disney Dose*. November 6, 2014. Podcast. http://disneydose .com/doncarson/#axzz5KFVU5rGm.

Ebert, Roger. "Runaway Hit From a Rabbit." *Chicago Sun-Times*. June 22, 1988.

Eisenberg, Adam. "Romancing the Rabbit." *Cinefex*. August 1988.

Eisner, Michael, with Tony Schwartz. *Work in Progress*. New York: Random House, 1998.

Failes, Ian. "The Oral History of Space Jam." *Cartoon Brew*. November 15, 2016. Blog. https://www.cartoonbrew.com/feature-film/oral-history-space-jam-part-1-launch ing-movie-144935.html.

Fiott, Stephen. "Interview with Gary K. Wolf." *Storyboard/The Art of Laughter*. April/May 1991.

Fleming, Michael. "Jessica Rabbit Revealed." *Variety*. March 13, 1994. https://variety .com/1994/voices/columns/jessica-rabbit-revealed-119154/.

Friedman, Roger. "A 'Roger Rabbit' Sequel May Happen After All." *Roger Friedman's ShowBiz • 411: Hollywood to the Hudson*. October 15, 2012. Blog. http://www.show biz411.com/2012/10/15/a-roger-rabbit-sequel-may-happen-after-all-says-director.

Gaivoto, Alvaro. *Hang Gliding Rabbit Workers*. June 12, 2012. https://www.youtube.com/ watch?v=_k4TIU9gpQE.

Ganz, Lowell, and Babaloo Mandel. "Who Framed Roger Rabbit?—Walt Disney Studios Prod. 0237." Screenplay, second draft. Los Angeles: December 13, 1984.

Ghez, Didier. "Interview with Dave Spafford on July 29, 2010." *Walt's People—Volume 13*. Edited by Didier Ghez. Theme Park Press, 2013.

Ghez, Didier. "Interview with Tom Sito on April 11 and 27, 2007" *Walt's People—Volume 9*. Edited by Didier Ghez. Xlibris, 2010.

Gluck, Keith. "Selling Mickey: The Rise of Disney Marketing." *Walt Disney Family Museum*. June 8, 2012. Blog. https://waltdisney.org/blog/selling-mickey-rise-disney-marketing.

Gonzalez, Danny. "The 'Wacked' Return of Roger Rabbit." *New York Examiner*. October 20, 2013.

Goodman, Martin. "Who Screwed Roger Rabbit?" *Animation World Network (AWN)*. April 3, 2003. Blog. https://www.awn.com/animationworld/who-screwed-roger-rabbit.

Gover, Carl. "Carl Gover, Part 1." *TheThief*. February 5, 2008. Blog. http://thethief1 .blogspot.com/2008/02/carl-gover-part-1.html.

Gover, Carl. "Carl Gover, Part 2." *The Thief.* February 7, 2008. Blog. http://thethief1 .blogspot.com/2008/02/in-meantime-after-lot-of.html.

Grover, Ron. *The Disney Touch: How a Daring Management Team Revived an Entertainment Empire.* Homewood, IL: Business One Irwin, 1991.

Grover, Ron. "Hitching a Ride on Hollywood's Hot Streak." *Businessweek.* July 11, 1988.

Guedel, Heidi. *Animatrix—A Female Animator: How Laughter Saved My Life.* Bloomington, IN: 1st Books Library, 2003.

Hahn, Don. "Immersion." *Brainstorm: Unleashing Your Creative Self.* New York: Disney Editions, 2011.

Hayden, Chris. "Behind the New Roger Rabbit Concept Art." *filmoria.co.uk.* April 25, 2013 Blog. https://www.filmoria.co.uk/.

Hickson, Mark. "Scuttlebut on Roger Rabbit Sequel." (*DbM*) *disneybymark.com.* March 22, 2013. Blog. http://www.disneybymark.com/2013/03/22/scuttlebutt-13/.

Hill, Jim. "Disney's Unfinished Featurettes: *Mickey Columbus* and *Mickey's Arabian Adventure*" *Jim Hill Media.* October 10, 2004. Blog. http://jimhillmedia.com/editor _in_chief1/b/jim_hill/archive/2004/10/11/477.aspx.

Hill, Jim. "Hare Today, Gone Tomorrow: The Curious Case of the Rapidly Receding Rabbit (Part I)." *Jim Hill Media.* September 5, 2006. Blog. http://jimhillmedia.com/ columnists1/b/jeff_lange/archive/2006/09/06/5591.aspx.

Hill, Jim. "Hare Today, Gone Tomorrow: The Curious Case of the Rapidly Receding Rabbit (Part II)." *Jim Hill Media.* September 6, 2006. Blog. http://jimhillmedia.com/ columnists1/b/jeff_lange/archive/2006/09/07/5631.aspx.

Hill, Jim. "The Sad Tail . . . I mean 'Tale' . . . of the Stalled Roger Rabbit Sequel." *Jim Hill Media.* December 21, 2000. Blog. http://jimhillmedia.com/editor_in_chief1/b/ jim_hill/archive/2001/01/01/297.aspx.

Hulett, Steve. "The Carl Bell Interview—Part 1." *Animation Guild TAG Blog.* November 28, 2011. http://animationguildblog.blogspot.com/2011/11/carl-bell-interview-part -i.html.

Hulett, Steve. "The Carl Bell Interview—Part 2." *Animation Guild TAG Blog.* November 29, 2011. http://animationguildblog.blogspot.com/2011/11/carl-bell-interview-part-ii .html.

Hulett, Steve. "The John Musker Interview—Part 1." *The Animation Guild TAG Blog, with Steve Hulett.* March 19, 2012. http://animationguildblog.blogspot.com/2012/03/john -musker-interview-part-i.html.

Hulett, Steve. "The John Musker Interview—Part 2." *Animation Guild TAG Blog, with Steve Hulett.* March 20, 2012. http://animationguildblog.blogspot.com/2012/03/john -musker-interview-part-ii.html.

Hulett, Steve. "The John Musker Interview—Part 3." *Animation Guild TAG Blog, with Steve Hulett.* March 21, 2012. http://animationguildblog.blogspot.com/2012/03/john -musker-interview-part-iii.html.

Hulett, Steve. "The Mark Kausler Chat—Part 1." *Animation Guild TAG Blog, with Steve Hulett.* January 24, 2011. http://animationguildblog.blogspot.com/2011/01/mark -kausler-chat-part-i.html.

Hulett, Steve. *Mouse in Transition: An Insider's Look at Disney Feature Animation.* Theme Park Press, 2014.

Hulett, Steve. "The Randy Cartwright Interview—Part 1." *Animation Guild TAG Blog, with Steve Hulett.* August 29, 2011. http://animationguildblog.blogspot.com/2011/08/randy-cartwright-interview-part-i.html.

Hurlburt, Roger. "'Roger Rabbit' Hops in Sotheby's Auction." *Orlando Sun-Sentinel.* June 10, 1989.

Hutchison, David. "A Special FX Achievement, Part 6." *Starlog.* December 1989.

Hutchison, David. "Who Framed Roger Rabbit—A Special FX Achievement, Part 4." *Starlog.* October 1989.

Huver, Scott. "A Re-Tooned 'Who Framed Roger Rabbit?' Celebrates 25 Years." NBC Bay Area Entertainment. March 11, 2013. Blog. https://www.nbcbayarea.com/entertainment/entertainment-news/Re-Tooned-for-Blu-Ray-Who-Framed-Roger-Rabbit-celebrates-25-Years-196217071.html.

Jackson, Jimmy. "The Magic of Disney Animation—Animation Tour." *Walt Disney Feature Animation Florida.* Blog. http://www.wdfaf.com/misc/tour/index.html.

Jacobs, Colin. "An Interview with Animator Andreas Deja." *DVD MovieGuide.* March 11, 2003. Blog. http://www.dvdmg.com/interviewandreasdeja.shtml.

Kallay, William. *The Making of Tron: How Tron Changed Visual Effects and Disney Forever.* William Kallay, 2011.

Kanner, Bernice. "On Madison Avenue: Frame That Toon." *New York.* April 17, 1989.

Kaytis, Clay. "Show 002—Andreas Deja, Part Two." *The Animation Podcast, with Clay Kaytis.* May 7, 2005. http://animationpodcast.com/archives/2005/05/07/andreas-deja-part-two/.

Kaytis, Clay. "Show 014—Glen Keane, Part One." *The Animation Podcast, with Clay Kaytis.* April 2, 2006. http://animationpodcast.com/archives/2006/04/02/glen-keane-part-one/.

Kaytis, Clay. "Show 021—Dale Baer, Part One." *The Animation Podcast, with Clay Kaytis.* November 4, 2007. http://animationpodcast.com/archives/2007/11/04/dale-baer-part-one/.

Kiesel, Steve. "Who's Hoo—Dave 'Spaff' Spafford." Interview/talk show from the Magic Castle, Los Angeles, February 18, 2013. https://vimeo.com/59926388.

Korkis, Jim. "The Birth of the Bunny." *Persistence of Vision.* Summer 1993.

Lanpher, Dorse. *Flyin' Chunks and Other Things To Duck: Memoirs of a Life Spent Doodling for Dollars.* Bloomington, IN: iUniverse, Inc., 2010.

LaPorte, Nicole. *The Men Who Would Be King.* New York: Houghton Mifflin Harcourt, 2010.

Larson, Randall. "Alan Silvestri, Tunes for Toons." *Starlog.* October 1988.

Masters, Kim. "What's Up, Doc?" *Premiere.* July 1988.

McDonnell, David. "Charles Fleischer's Rabbit Punch." *Starlog.* January 1989.

McDonnell, David. "Who Framed Roger Rabbit." *Starlog Yearbook* vol. 4, 1988.

Moen, Bruce. "Question and Answer IRC meet with Gary Wolf." *moen@cyberspace.com.* August 2, 1995. Blog. http://www.jimdavies.org/roger-rabbit/roger_rabbit_facts.html.

Mongello, Lou. "Show #160—Interview with Don Hahn and Peter Schneider." *WDW Radio*. March 7, 2010. http://www.wdwradio.com/2010/03/don-hahn-interview-disney-peter-schneider-show-160-march-7-2010/.

Muller, Jacques. *RR cont Behind the curtain + Barbican singing*. August 12, 2014. videotape recording, 47:39. https://www.youtube.com/watch?v=wJvrqyYEI3w&t=1445s.

Musker, John. "Producers VS Animators Volleyball Game." 8mm home movie, 6:49. https://www.youtube.com/watch?v=x51NFT0-e70.

Muschamp, Herbert. "Getting Goofy on the Santa Anna Freeway." *New York Times*. November 5, 1995.

Nation, Adam. "Who *really* Framed Roger Rabbit?: The Lost Animators." *Starburst*. January 1989.

Norman, Floyd. "Fred and Ginger (Almost)," *MrFun*. January 9, 2012. Blog. http://mrfun.squarespace.com/blog/2012/1/9/fred-and-ginger-almost.html.

Parker, Heidi, and Jo Tweedy. "Nine Hours, Rubber Eyelids and a Fake Derriere: Heidi Klum Reveals what it REALLY Took to Transform her into Cartoon Siren Jessica Rabbit." *MAILONLINE*. November 2, 2015. http://www.dailymail.co.uk/femail/article-3299910/Nine-hours-rubber-eyelids-fake-derriere-Heidi-Klum-reveals-REALLY-took-transform-cartoon-siren-Jessica-Rabbit.html.

Peraza, Michael. "Cauldron of Chaos, Part 2." *The Ink and Paint Club: Memories of the Mouse House*. September 7, 2010. Blog. http://michaelperaza.blogspot.com/2010/09/cauldron-of-chaos-part-2.html.

Pirani, Adam. "Bob Hoskins, Animated Investigator." *Starlog*. August 1988.

Pirani, Adam. "Robert Zemeckis, Murder Comes to Toontown." *Starlog*. September 1988.

Punter, Ron. "Painting Rubber Penguins: Making *Who Framed Roger Rabbit*." Elstree Project oral history interviews. October 9, 2012. http://theelstreeproject.org/films/who-framed-roger-rabbit/.

RaggaR. "Movie References in 'South Park.'" *rateyourmusic.com*. https://rateyourmusic.com/list/RaggaR/movie_references_in_south_park/10/.

Ranieri, Nik. "Nik Ranieri—Animator." *Facebook*. Posts throughout April 2013. https://www.facebook.com/NikRanieriAnimator/.

Raspberry, Chance. "Chance Raspberry presents: The Bill Kopp Extravanganza! Part 2." *Chance Raspberry Newsletter*. March 25, 2013. Podcast, 1:06:02. https://www.youtube.com/watch?v=LyDdZHxgHlM&t=2847s.

Rea, Steven. "Making Roger Rabbit a Star—What was Once Seen as a Costly Film Gamble is Now Looking like the Movie Event of the Summer." *Philadelphia Inquirer*. June 26, 1988.

Reese, Michael. "The Making of Roger Rabbit." *Newsweek*. June 27, 1988.

Robin, Andy. "The Barber—*Seinfeld* episode 072." Directed by Tom Cherones. Los Angeles: Shapiro/West Productions in association with Castle Rock Entertainment/NBC, November 11, 1993. http://www.seinfeldscripts.com/TheBarber.htm, https://www.dailymotion.com/video/x6i6twr.

Robson, Chelsea. "Animation Addicts 137: 'Who Framed Roger Rabbit'—I'm Not Bad, I'm Just Drawn That Way—with Tom Bancroft." *Rotoscopers*. December 16, 2016. Podcast. http://www.rotoscopers.com/2016/12/16/animation-addicts-episode-137-who-framed-roger-rabbit-im-not-bad-im-just-drawn-that-way/.

Schiller, Herbert. *Culture, Inc.: The Corporate Takeover of Public Expression*. New York: Oxford University Press, 1991.

Sciretta, Peter. "Robert Zemeckis Has a New Idea for Roger Rabbit 2." *SlashFilm*. April 29, 2009. Blog. http://www.slashfilm.com/robert-zemeckis-has-a-new-idea-for-roger -rabbit-2/.

Seaman, Peter S., and Jeffrey Price. "Who Framed Roger Rabbit?—Walt Disney Studios Prod. 0237." Screenplay, second draft. Los Angeles: July 26, 1982.

Shiver, Jube. "Star Struck" *Black Enterprise*. December 1988.

Sito, Tom. "Disney's *The Fox and the Hound*: The Coming of the Next Generation." *Animation World Network (AWN)*. November 1, 1998. Blog. https://www.awn.com/ animationworld/disneys-fox-and-hound-coming-next-generation.

Sito, Tom. *Drawing the Line: The Untold Story of the Animation Unions*. Lexington: University Press of Kentucky, 2006.

Sito, Tom. *Moving Innovation: A History of Computer Animation*. Cambridge, MA: MIT Press, 2013.

Smith, David. "Interview with Don Duckwall." *Walt's People—Volume 13*. Edited by Didier Ghez. Theme Park Press, 2013.

"Sport Goofy in Soccermania." Wikipedia. https://en.wikipedia.org/wiki/Sport_Goofy _in_Soccermania, https://www.youtube.com/watch?v=ggmVm21jDuw.

"Sport Goofy in Soccermania." *IMDb*. https://www.imdb.com/title/tt0278047/.

Swires, Steve. "Joanna Cassidy: Her Life & Hard (-Boiled) Times." *Starlog*. October 1988.

Taylor, John. *Storming the Magic Kingdom*. New York: Alfred A. Knopf, 1987.

Teitelbaum, Sheldon. "Who Drew 'Roger Rabbit'?" *Cinefantastique*. January 1989.

Thompson, Bob. "Looney Toons." *(Toronto) Sunday Sun*. June 19, 1988.

Tibbits, Cory, and Myles Rourke. "EP 67—with Gary K. Wolf." *End Credits—The Behind the Scenes in Entertainment*. October 21, 2013. http://endcredits.podbean.com/.

Tumbusch, Thomas. "The Strange Merchandise Tale of 'Who Framed Roger Rabbit.'" *Tomart's Disneyana Update*. Edited by Tom Tumbusch. Winter 2007.

Tumbusch, Thomas. "Who Framed, Molded, Stuffed, Printed or Otherwise Merchandised Roger Rabbit?" *Tomart's Disneyana Update*. Edited by Tom Tumbusch. November/ December 1997.

Turner, George. "Cartoons Came to Life in *Roger*." *American Cinematographer*. July 1988.

Turner, George. "Who Framed Roger Rabbit?" *American Cinematographer*. July 1988.

Van Citters, Darrell. "Roger Rabbit's Roots." *Animato!* no. 20. 1990.

Vaz, Mark Cotta, and Patricia Rose Duignan. *Industrial Light and Magic: Into the Digital Realm*. New York: Delray/Ballantine Books, 1996.

Wakim, Marielle. "Here's Why *Who Framed Roger Rabbit?* Is the Most IMPRESSIVE Animated Movie of All Time." *LA Magazine*. February 28, 2017.

Wakeman, Gregory. "Why Who Framed Roger Rabbit 2 Probably Won't Happen, According to Robert Zemeckis." *Cinemablend*. November 2016. https://www.cinema blend.com/news/1591290/why-who-framed-roger-rabbit-2-probably-wont-happen -according-to-robert-zemeckis.

Walker, Doug. "Review of Who Framed Roger Rabbit, Disneycember." *Nostalgia Critic*. March 1, 2012. *Channel Awesome/YouTube*. http://thatguywiththeglasses.wikia.com/wiki/

Who_Framed_Roger_Rabbit_(Disneycember), https://www.youtube.com/watch?v =UXQ5voZE8-s.

Walker, Doug. "What You Never Knew About 'Who Framed Roger Rabbit.'" *Nostalgia Critic*. August 11, 2015. *Channel Awesome/YouTube*. http://thatguywiththeglasses .wikia.com/wiki/What_You_Never_Knew_About_Who_Framed_Roger_Rabbit, https://www.youtube.com/watch?v=1pF7Xvj8i5E&t=29s.

Walt Disney Productions. "Annual Report 1981 (for Annual Meeting of Stockholders— Thursday, January 28, 1982)." Los Angeles, 1982.

Wilkinson, Barry. "Painting Rubber Penguins: Making *Who Framed Roger Rabbit*." Elstree Project oral history interviews. October 9, 2012. http://theelstreeproject.org/films/ who-framed-roger-rabbit/.

Williams, Alex. "Disney MGM Studios, RollerCoaster Rabbit and the Summer of 1989—Part 1." *FLiP Animation*. April 21, 2012. Blog. http://flipanimation.blogspot .com/2012/04/disney-mgm-studios-rollercoaster-rabbit.html.

Williams, Alex. "Disney MGM Studios, RollerCoaster Rabbit and the Summer of 1989—Part 2." *FLiP Animation*. April 24, 2012. Blog. http://flipanimation.blogspot .com/2012/04/disney-mgm-studios-summer-of-1989-part.html.

Williams, Kristian. "Who Framed Roger Rabbit—The 3 Rules of Living Animation." *KaptainKristian Channel*. February 24, 2017. video essay, 7:23. https://www.youtube .com/watch?v=RWtt3Tmnij4.

Williams, Richard. Interview by Luke Menichelli. Unpublished transcript. 1996.

Wolf, Gary K. "Gary K. Wolf, Creator of Roger Rabbit!" Website. http://garywolf.com/ about.php.

Wolf, Gary K. "Hare's Lookin' at You, Babs." In *The Fruitful Branch*. Brookline, MA: Brookline Library Foundation, 2002.

Wolf, Gary K. *The Road to Toontown!—Best Short Stories of "Roger Rabbit" Creator Gary K. Wolf*. Smashwords, 2012. https://www.smashwords.com/books/view/209041.

Wolf, Gary K. "Stay Tooned, Folks!" *Amazing Stories* 73, no. 3 (November 2004): 48–53.

Wolf, Gary K. "The Warhol of the Worlds: A Radio Drama as performed by the Toontown Theatre On the Air." *Penumbra eMag* 1, no. 10 (July 2012). http://www.magzter.com/ previewo/847/5439.

Wolf, Gary K. "Two Very Different Career Paths with the Same Destination." Website. http://www.spacevulture.com/authors.html.

Zemeckis, Robert. AMPAS Toontown reunion panel discussion (twenty-fifth anniversary screening of *Who Framed Roger Rabbit*). Los Angeles: April 4, 2013.

INDEX